Principles of
Web Design

THE ALLYN AND BACON SERIES IN TECHNICAL COMMUNICATION

Series Editor: Sam Dragga, Texas Tech University

Thomas T. Barker
*Writing Software Documentation:
A Task-Oriented Approach*

Carol M. Barnum
Usability Testing and Research

Deborah S. Bosley
*Global Contexts: Case Studies in International
Technical Communication*

Paul Dombrowski
Ethics in Technical Communication

David K. Farkas and Jean B. Farkas
Principles of Web Design

Laura J. Gurak
Oral Presentations for Technical Communication

Sandra W. Harner and Tom G. Zimmerman
Technical Marketing Communications

Richard Johnson-Sheehan
Writing Proposals: Rhetoric for Managing Change

Dan Jones
Technical Writing Style

Charles Kostelnick and David D. Roberts
*Designing Visual Language: Strategies for
Professional Communicators*

Carolyn Rude
Technical Editing, Third Edition

Gerald J. Savage and Dale L. Sullivan
*Writing a Professional Life: Stories of
Technical Communicators On and Off the Job*

Principles of Web Design

David K. Farkas

University of Washington

Jean B. Farkas

Nettraco

Longman

New York San Francisco Boston
London Toronto Sydney Tokyo Singapore Madrid
Mexico City Munich Paris Cape Town Hong Kong Montreal

For three very impressive and much beloved women—
Sally, Ruth, and Eva

Senior Vice President/Publisher: Joseph Opiela
Marketing Manager: Chris Bennem
Production Manager: Denise Phillip
Project Coordination, Text Design, and Electronic Page Makeup: WestWords, Inc.
Cover Design Manager: Nancy Danahy
Cover Designer: Caryl Silvers
Manufacturing Buyer: Lucy Hebard
Printer and Binder: Hamilton Printing
Cover Printer: Coral Graphics

For permission to use copyrighted material, grateful acknowledgment is made to the copyright holders on p. 370, which are hereby made part of this copyright page.

Library of Congress Cataloging-in-Publication Data

Farkas, David (David K.)
    Principles of Web Design/David K. Farkas and Jean B. Farkas.
        p. cm—(Allyn and Bacon series in technical communication)
    Includes bibliographical references and index.
    ISBN 0-205-30291-2 (pbk.)
    1. Websites—Design. I. Farkas, Jean B. II. Title. III. Series.

TK5105.888.F36 2001
005.7'2—dc21   2001038691

Please visit our website at http://www.ablongman.com

ISBN 0-205-30291-2

1 2 3 4 5 6 7 8 9 10—HT—04 03 02 01

BRIEF CONTENTS

DETAILED CONTENTS

━**4**━ Using Content Types Effectively　　　83

9 Designing Effective Links   202

FOREWORD by the Series Editor

The Allyn & Bacon Series in Technical Communication is designed to meet the continuing education needs of professional technical communicators, both those who desire to upgrade or update their own communication abilities as well as those who train or supervise writers, editors, and artists in their organization. This series also serves the growing number of students enrolled in undergraduate and graduate programs in technical communication. Such programs offer a wide variety of courses beyond the introductory technical writing course—advanced courses for which fully satisfactory and appropriately focused textbooks have often been impossible to locate.

The chief characteristic of the books in this series is their consistent effort to integrate theory and practice. The books offer both research-based and experience-based instruction, describing not only what to do and how to do it but explaining why. The instructors who teach advanced courses and the students who enroll in these courses are looking for more than rigid rules and ad hoc guidelines. They want books that demonstrate theoretical sophistication and a solid foundation in the research of the field as well as pragmatic advice and perceptive applications. Instructors and students will also find these books filled with activities and assignments adaptable to the classroom and to the self-guided learning processes of professional technical communicators.

To operate effectively in the field of technical communication, today's technical communicators require extensive training in the creation, analysis, and design of information for both domestic and international audiences, for both paper and electronic environments. The books in the Allyn & Bacon Series address those subjects that are most frequently taught at the undergraduate and graduate levels as a direct response to both the educational needs of students and the practical demands of business and industry. Additional books will be developed for the series in order to satisfy or anticipate changes in writing technologies, academic curricula, and the profession of technical communication.

Sam Dragga
Texas Tech University

PREFACE

A great many books have been written on Web design. This book is different from almost all of them: It is a university-level textbook. We want to explain the implications of this difference.

The difference is not our view of what constitutes a good website. Our opinions are mainstream, much like those you will find in the trade books stocked in bookstores. The biggest difference is that we offer clear, explicit, and—when necessary—detailed explanations of the concepts and principles that underlie our recommendations. Also, we show how these concepts and principles fit together. We believe that those who gain an in-depth, coherent understanding of Web design become the best designers. These people don't just follow advice. Because they truly understand what they are doing and why, they can reason their way through each new design challenge.

Many of the principles in this book pertain to website structure. Thumb through the chapters and you will see many diagrams showing different ways to link the pages of a website. We explain how to devise a structure that fulfills the information needs of your audience and reflects your own goals. We show the many ways in which a website's structure determines the design of the user interface and how it affects writing and graphic design.

Because this is a university-level textbook, we present Web design in a broad cultural context. We include just a bit about postmodernism and Web design and about the history of the Web and hypermedia. There is a whole chapter devoted to ethics and the societal implications of this new medium. Do these topics make this a less practical book? We don't think so. We think a broad understanding of a communications medium contributes to better design.

One area we do not cover is implementation. Because we wanted to focus on design, you will find little here about HTML, XML, JavaScript, CGI, and other Web technologies. We don't, however, ignore Web technology: At many places we point out the best way to implement a design or warn about a potential technical problem. Also, we recommend many good sources of implementation information, including no-cost resources on the Web.

Many of the trade books that focus on design are light reading. You can read them start to finish on a plane flight. This book is intended to enrich a semester or quarter of academic work, and it demands time and concentration. We believe it repays this effort.

The Book's Website

We have created a website to support this book: http://www.ablongman.com/farkas. This website provides supplementary materials (including color versions of many of the book's black-and-white graphics) and will help keep the book up-to-date. The website has a section for each book chapter. We suggest that you visit the appropriate section before reading each chapter. We plan to have something new and interesting to show you.

Acknowledgments

We greatly appreciate the strong support we received from Sam Dragga, the series editor, and Joseph Opiela, Senior Vice President and Publisher, at Longman Publishers. Our thanks to Pat McCutcheon and the staff at WestWords for knowing about and caring about what they do.

These instructors field tested draft versions of this book in their courses: Mark Haselkorn, University of Washington; Alfred Kobsa, University of California, Irvine; Beth Kolko, University of Washington; Claudia Mazzie-Ballheim, Bellevue Community College; and Geoff Sauer, University of Washington. Our thanks to them, to their students, and to our own students, who also used and commented on draft versions of the book.

We wish to thank these academic and industry experts for reading the manuscript in various drafts and for offering helpful suggestions: Michael Albers, University of Memphis; Scott Berkun, Microsoft; Scott Boggan, Aventail Corporation; John Bowes, University of Washington, Terry Brooks, University of Washington; Karen Cheng, University of Washington; George Dillon, University of Washington; Susan Feinberg, Illinois Institute of Technology; Sarah Hart, Rhode Island School of Design; William Hart-Davidson, Rensselaer Polytechnic Institute; Marc Hoffman, Poison Dartfrog Media; Lee-Ann Kastman Breuch, University of Minnesota; Werner Schweibenz, Universität des Saarlandes; Stuart Selber, Penn State University; Clay Spinuzzi, University of Texas; Greg vanHoosier-Carey, Georgia Tech; Joe Welinske, WinWriters; Sean Williams, Clemson University; Tom Williams, University of Washington.

Finally, we wish to acknowledge folks who responded to queries and helped out in a variety of other important ways: Jeff Altman, Alec Appelbaum, Rebecca Armendariz, Beth Chapple, Karen Wetherell Davis, Rick Ells, Greg Frederick, Tom Lenon, Ruth Mosby, Joe Opdahl, and Paul Wolman.

DKF/JBF

Understanding the Web:
A Designer's View

Introduction

In only a decade, starting in the early 1990s, the World Wide Web has emerged as one of the foremost communications media. Designing and developing websites has become an important profession. Furthermore, many people in a very wide range of fields create websites and contribute to websites.

The Web is a complex medium. For example, the Web requires us to organize information in new ways and to employ text and graphics differently than in other media. We now think much more about how people will access the information we are providing and how they interact with information on the screen.

This book provides the concepts and principles that underlie Web design. Through this book you will understand Web design as only the most sophisticated designers do. You will think clearly and confidently about design issues and create high quality websites. You will also be well prepared to discuss, critique, and improve existing websites.

This chapter provides a broad introduction to the Web as a communications medium. You will learn what capabilities distinguish the Web from other media, the general purposes for which websites are built, and key concepts and terms. The chapter also provides historical perspective on the World Wide Web.

The Capabilities of the World Wide Web

What gives the Web its extraordinary appeal and utility? Why has it become so important so quickly? Below we define the Web in terms of the seven key capabilities that it offers. Keep in mind there is no need for all seven capabilities to be implemented in any one website.

1. Global reach
2. Interactivity (choice and responsiveness in experiencing content)
3. Support for multiple content types
4. Support for transactions
5. Online computing functions
6. Support for active social spaces
7. Support for system adaptivity, user customization, and site-wide modification

1. Global Reach

The Internet is a digital communications network that spans the planet and provides the foundation for a variety of communications media. By far the most important of these media are email, instant messaging, and the Web. Because it is built on the Internet, any website (unless gated in some way) can be accessed from almost anywhere on the planet by means of a wide range of computers and computer-like devices.

Global reach doesn't in any way guarantee that people will find out about your website, and it doesn't change the fact that vast numbers of people still do not have access to the Internet and the Web. Even so, never before in human history has there been a means by which almost any individual or group with relative ease and relatively little expense can share their ideas with many millions of people throughout the world.

2. Interactivity (Choice and Responsiveness in Experiencing Content)

Interactivity means that we have many opportunities to act and that our actions get quick responses. With a click we can jump to a new Web page, start an audio sequence, or purchase a product. In contrast, when we go to a movie theater, we do not take actions that affect the movie.

Movies, furthermore, are a linear medium. They are designed to be experienced straight through from beginning to end. Even though DVD lets us jump around within a movie, movies (with rare exceptions) are not designed to make sense this way. That is, they do not support non-linear navigation.

The Web is both interactive and (in most cases) non-linear. Almost all websites invite users to make many choices, to navigate freely through the site. Notice that print encyclopedias and newspapers are non-linear, though we usually don't think of print media in terms of interactivity.

3. Support for Multiple Content Types

The Web supports five fundamental content types:

- Text
- Graphics

- Animation
- Video
- Audio

Text and graphics are static content. They don't move. In contrast, animation, video, and audio are dynamic or "time based." They change with time. It is also convenient to refer to "motion graphics," meaning animation and video. There are, of course, combinations of these five fundamental content types. We can create animated text that moves across the screen. Live Cam (or "Web Cam") consists of photographic images that begin to approach video because the images are continually updated.

These content types create different technological demands. The Web handles text and small graphics (including simple animations) easily. On the other hand, certain graphics and animations, high-quality audio, and especially video do not run well unless users have a capable computer and a reasonably high-speed Internet connection. At the present time, therefore, Web developers must be cautious about incorporating technologically demanding content.

4. Support for Transactions

Transactions include purchasing products and services, moving funds from one bank account to another, selling items at an auction, and even placing a bet. Support for commercial transactions is the basis of e-commerce. More is required in a transaction than communicating information: Transactions entail legal commitments. Therefore, websites that support transactions must be tied into the world's financial system (e.g., accepting credit card payments) and must meet very high standards for reliability and security.

5. Online (Web-Based) Computing Functions

For the most part websites present content. Websites, however, often include capabilities that are much like standard desktop applications. We call these online computing functions. For example, Blox.com offers a full-featured spreadsheet you can use on the Web.

Commercial transactions, such as checkout in an online store, also entail online computing functions: Users type their name, address, and other information into a form, and the data are processed and recorded in a database.

6. Support for Active Social Spaces

When we click links to display Web content, we are on the receiving end of a one-way dialog. The Web, however, also supports active social spaces in the form of two-way or group dialogs. Some websites merely allow you to send a message back to the site owner. Others provide message boards in which you post messages for all site visitors to read and respond to. Many websites also host "real time" chat sessions. These active social spaces are the basis of virtual communities. Virtual communities not only eliminate the barrier of physical distance but potentially make possible forms of human interaction that are not otherwise possible.

Active social spaces are provided by other Internet technologies, such as IRC (Internet Relay Chat), CU-See Me, MOOs, and MUDs, but the Web provides a very rich environment for hosting active social spaces. For example, websites such as Active Worlds and CyberNet Worlds allow users to represent themselves visually in the form of avatars that move and change expression as they communicate with the avatars of other participants. In these virtual communities you can be a human being, a lion, or an angel, and you can move within digital environments that could never exist in the physical world.

7. Support for System Adaptivity, User Customization, and Site-Wide Modification

The Web differs from many traditional media in that a website (using cookies and other means) can recognize and adapt to individual users. An e-commerce website, for example, can welcome you by name, recommend products based on your previous purchases, and display the billing address you usually use.

User customization refers to the user's ability to change part of a website for personal use. For example, EarthLink and other Internet portals (sites that serve as a starting point for the user's Web experience) allow each user to create a customized start page that contains links to favorite websites, news headlines from the user's preferred news sources, and the current stock market price of companies the user has specified.

Site-wide modification refers to changes a user makes that affect other users. For example, a corporation might ask its sales staff to post reports of their visits to customers on the Marketing and Sales section of the corporation's intranet (internal website). The website for the movie *What Dreams May Come* provided graphics tools and invited users to modify images related to the movie. These images were viewable (but not changeable) by subsequent site visitors. Site-wide modification is always a form of social interactivity. This is because users are sharing experiences, participating in an active social space, even though they are not directly addressing each other.

Interactive Multimedia on CDs and DVDs

A communications medium closely related to the Web is interactive multimedia stored on a CD or DVD (and sometimes on floppy disks and other physical media as well). We will use the term CD/DVD multimedia. Individual works of CD/DVD multimedia are usually referred to as "titles," and we will use this term as well.

CD/DVD offers many of the same capabilities as websites, but because CD/DVD titles reside on individual machines, they do not offer global reach, support for transactions, or support for active social spaces. Also, because CD/DVD titles must be distributed on physical media, they entail manufacturing and shipping costs and so cannot be updated with great frequency. Finally, whereas a website can draw upon the massive digital storage and processing power available on servers, CD/DVD titles rely on their own storage capabilities and the processing capabilities of the user's computer.

On the other hand, CD/DVD multimedia does offer some important advantages. Because this medium does not rely on an Internet connection, high-quality video and other technologically demanding content can be displayed more quickly and more reliably than similar content delivered on the Web. Also CD/DVD multimedia does not need to be coded in HTML or displayed using a Web browser. Developers, therefore, have more freedom when they design CD/DVD titles and can use some very powerful authoring tools (such as Macromedia Director and 3D Studio Max) that cannot be fully used on the Web. Finally, while Web content, because it resides on a server, is vulnerable to tampering and corruption of files, CDs and DVDs are more suitable for "archival" content—content that must be retained without any change for a long time. There is also much to be said for hybrid CD/DVD titles that are enhanced by connections to the Internet.

Although this is a book about designing for the Web, much of it applies to interactive multimedia delivered on CD or DVD. When necessary, we explicitly point out differences between the Web and CD/DVD.

The Purposes and Genres of Websites

Websites are created for a vast range of specific purposes. We can better understand the Web by grouping these purposes into a manageable number of broad categories. In Chapter 2, "Planning," you will learn how to define your website's purpose or purposes very specifically. Our eight categories are listed and explained below.

1. Education
2. Entertainment
3. Providing news, public information, and specialized information
4. E-commerce: Promotion/selling/support
5. Web portals
6. Persuasion
7. Building and sustaining community
8. Personal and artistic expression

Naturally many websites will fit more than one category, and a few may not fit comfortably into any of these categories.

Education

Many websites (as well as CD/DVD titles) serve educational purposes. These websites may be designed for students, for employees in corporate training programs, or for individuals pursuing their own interests. At colleges and universities websites often supplement instructor-led courses. But various kinds of online tutorials and training programs are meant to be used with little or no instructor involvement.

The Web can be a very effective technology for education. For example, a university geology course can include rich animations and video sequences of volcanoes and earthquakes. There can also be simulations and mathematical models that users can directly examine and manipulate using online computing functions. Explanations of concepts can be provided at various levels of detail, and there can be links to geology-related resources on the Web.

Online tutorials present content, quiz students, and then adapt the instruction to each student's individual needs. Message boards and real-time chat make possible virtual learning communities that bring together the learners, the instructor, and possibly outside experts.

Entertainment

Much in the world of the Web is entertainment. The Web offers us celebrity news, sports updates, music, and games of all kinds. It is often impossible to draw clear boundaries between entertainment and the other categories presented here. For example, a sophisticated review of a major movie can be thought of as entertainment, educational material, and news or public information. The well-known terms "edutainment" and "infotainment" reflect these fuzzy boundaries.

Providing News, Public Information, and Specialized Information

This very broad category includes news, public information of all kinds, and highly specialized information for scholars and researchers. Traditional newspapers and magazines now publish Web editions in competition with online publications that do not exist in print. Websites have been established to provide information in such categories as health and investments. Cities use the Web to publish such information as city services, directories of city officials, minutes of council meetings, and building codes.

Both individual researchers and research organizations disseminate specialized information on their websites. For example, conference proceedings are often made available online. A great many academic journals now publish Web editions and create digital archives of past volumes. This approach gives subscribers the option of not storing years and years of old issues. Gradually, academic journals are moving toward Web-only publication. Readers still pay for subscriptions, but the benefits and potential benefits of online publication are impressive: Links can be built among the journal articles and to other resources, color graphics can be added without extra expense, dynamic content can be included, and active social spaces can be created for scholars to comment on the articles.

E-Commerce: Promotion/Selling/Support

E-commerce is a broad category with hard-to-define boundaries. The goal of financial gain pervades a great many of the websites in most of these categories.

We consider e-commerce in terms of promotion and marketing, selling, and support.

These days almost all large corporations and a great many small businesses use the Web for promotion. This includes marketing their products, strengthening their brands, and improving their corporate image. Most non-corporate organizations, such as universities and government agencies, also promote themselves on the Web. In fact, more websites exist for promotion than for any other purpose.

No one knows the full potential of directly selling on the Web, but there are now websites that offer consumers almost every kind of product and service. Apart from selling merchandise and services to consumers, corporations procure supplies and conduct other forms of "business to business" e-commerce on an enormous scale.

Along with the marketing and selling of products and services comes customer support—responding to inquiries of all kinds and allowing customers to track their pending orders and shipments. Customer support for companies with technologically complex products includes online help systems, access to tech support technicians, and downloads of product fixes and updates.

Web Portals

Portals are specialized websites that serve as the starting point and home base for Web users. Portals often contain their own news and entertainment content, but their main function is directing users to other websites. Most portals contain very large numbers of links categorized by user interests and Web-wide search engines that let people look for sites using their own specific search criteria.

Persuasion

Many websites exist to promote political, social, cultural, and religious beliefs. Thus, we have identified the category of persuasive websites—a category distinct from the persuasion central to corporate promotion and sales. Persuasive websites often represent major political parties and prominent institutions in our society. But the democratic nature of the Web is such that little-known individuals and groups can publish all kinds of viewpoints (including bigotry and hate-filled ideologies) to their own group members and to anyone who cares to seek out and visit their sites. Even though persuasive sites vary enormously in the reasonableness of their views and arguments, the diversity of viewpoints is one of the great strengths of the Web.

Building and Sustaining Community

In a limited way, every website builds and sustains the community of site visitors. A fan site for a rock star helps to build and sustain a community of people who share this one bond. This community exists, even though the site visitors are barely aware of each other. Website managers, however, know that they can create stronger communities by making site visitors more aware of one another and, especially, by creating active social spaces. A website for asthma sufferers, for example, can employ message boards, real-time chat, and other active social spaces to support a rich dialog of information and encouragement among asthma sufferers as well as their families. Similarly, a virtual learning community greatly enhances online learning.

Personal and Artistic Expression

Personal expression seems inherent to human beings. We express ourselves through our dress and hair styles and through the pictures we hang on our walls. The Web is a natural place for self-expression, and many people have personal websites in which they describe their background, current activities, and interests. Often people combine a personal site with professional information. For example, a college student's personal website is likely to include his or her resumé and portfolio samples.

Closely tied to personal expression is expression for the purpose of creating art. The Web can be the means of publishing traditional prose, poetry, or visual art. But there are newer art forms that include multiple content types and complex forms of interactivity. Often, artistic expression on the Web departs from the principles of efficient communication. For aesthetic and expressive reasons, radical online art projects may overwhelm and confuse the viewer with ever-changing text and images and links to unexpected destinations. You might begin exploring art sites with www.superbad.com, www.futura2000.com, and www.rhizome.org.[1]

Many websites are created with a sense of fun and whimsy or to show off state-of-the-art techniques. These sites do not necessarily claim to be art, but they also do not attempt to be efficient, highly usable sites. Some corporations, especially those that sell consumer goods to the youth market, create websites that are intentionally quirky and whimsical. Finally, professional Web designers often create "showcase" sites that contain both straightforward examples of their professional work and exotic special effects.

Purpose and Genre

Websites that are designed for a specific purpose (or purposes) tend to share various characteristics. They are likely to contain similar kinds of content and employ similar page layouts and styles of writing.

---

[1]URLs do not always stay current. If a URL listed in this book doesn't work for you, please don't give up right away. You may be able to find the page you are seeking elsewhere on that website. Also, try using a Web-wide search engine such as Google.com or Altavista.com. In addition, visit the website that accompanies this book. One purpose of the book's website is to provide updated URLs and new URLs to replace websites that have disappeared.

Over a period of time, these similarities may become stronger as users develop expectations regarding a particular kind of website and as designers borrow ideas from one another. Well-defined Web "genres" have emerged; we see predictable characteristics in Web portals, university websites, the websites of political parties and candidates, and websites intended for many other purposes. This is not unlike the genres we see in print fiction, TV shows, and movies.

Web genres are always evolving. They split, they merge, they are transformed. There are always bold designers eager to depart from an established design idea they find boring. Because genre characteristics significantly affect how people use and respond to a website, we need to stay attuned to Web genres to understand the medium. Designers, moreover, should think about genres as they work.

Important Terms and Concepts

Here we explain some concepts and terms that are important in the world of Web design.

The Web as a Communications Medium

We can distinguish communications media in regard to content types, means of delivery, interactivity, and how they are used and paid for. Television and cinema employ the same content types and are both linear media, but they are delivered differently and function as different media, especially in regard to revenue. Television and radio are both broadcast media, but they employ different content types. Radio and telephone both employ the same content type: audio. The telephone, however, is a highly interactive social space.

Another important distinction pertains to participation. Print and broadcast media are one-to-many media. A few organizations publish books or newspapers or produce broadcasts for a mass audience. The telephone is a one-to-one medium. The Web allows individuals as well as huge corporations to reach a mass audience (one-to-many), but also allows for communication among small groups.

All media compete, trying to adopt the capabilities and steal the audiences of other media—a phenomenon known as "media convergence." Television, for example, is struggling to become interactive, and telephones are blending with computers. The Web is a very strong competitor and has very quickly added new capabilities. Not only has it largely eclipsed CD/DVD multimedia, the Web is competing aggressively with radio, television, telephone, and print publishing. At the same time, media also work in tandem. For example, television shows have their own websites, and TV hosts may solicit email from viewers.

Hypermedia

We clearly need a broad "umbrella" term that encompasses both the Web and CD/DVD multimedia. The term we use is "hypermedia." Hypermedia also includes interactive videodiscs and other technologies that were designed primarily to present dynamic content.

Although hypermedia is not a very familiar term, it works well. The prefix "hyper" suggests interactivity and the idea of navigating from one chunk of information to another. Also, "media" suggests multiple content types.

We are less pleased with other terms that are often used to encompass both the Web and CD/DVD: multimedia, interactive media, New Media, digital media, and hypertext. Multimedia is especially problematical because, in some contexts, it implies dynamic content without interactivity, while in others it refers to hypermedia other than the Web.

Interactive media is a good term, but it's a bit lengthy. New Media is catchy, but it's risky to define concepts on the basis of being new. What will New Media refer to when the Web is 20 years old? Digital media is essentially a technological term. It refers to content—regardless of the communications medium—that is stored and used in digital form, even if there is no interactivity. Cinema, for example, is rapidly becoming a digital medium. Hypertext is an important term with a long history, and so we treat it separately below.

Hypertext

Hypertext is the original term for interactive content. For this reason, we find it in the phrases "hyperlinks," "hypertext jumps," and HTML (Hypertext Markup Language). Because most of the interactive systems of the 1960s, '70s, and early-to-mid '80s displayed only text and static graphics, they were referred to as hyper**text** systems. Following this usage, we use "hypertext" to refer to these pioneering systems and to certain successors to these systems, such as online help, designed primarily to present text and static graphics.

You should know, however, that some people—particularly scholars in the humanities—treat hypertext as the umbrella term for interactive content. Their point of view is that hypertext is the original term and that support for multiple content types and the benefits of the Internet are best seen as new capabilities that enhance hypertext.

Intranets

Intranets are websites used by corporations and other organizations for internal communication. They are not accessible outside the company. Intranets may serve several of the purposes listed above. In particular, they provide specialized information about the organization. This includes policies and procedures and news. Intranets also support various internal transactions, such as applying for a maternity leave or obtaining reimbursements from a travel budget.

In addition to increasing efficiency, a good intranet builds community within the company. Often there are message boards on various topics. Intranets often include educational content, such as tutorials on technologies central to the organization. There may be content for entertainment.

Designing and working on intranets is different from working on public websites. One important difference is that the designer of an intranet can obtain extensive information about the audience—data about education, job functions, equipment being used, etc. Another difference is that the audience is generally required to use the intranet for at least some job-related tasks. This required use does not diminish the need for good design. Without good design, intranet users will make less use of the intranet than they should, will use it less efficiently, and will likely take from it negative experiences and negative feelings about their employer. Although we generally assume public websites in our discussion, almost all of the principles of design presented in this book apply directly to intranets.

Nodes, Links, and Navigation

The concepts of nodes, links, and navigation are central to hypertext theory and to hypermedia and Web design. On the Web, people change what they see and hear by using the mouse or other input devices. These changes in content are often envisioned as navigation in space, as travel from one place to another. The Web, then, is an information environment that users explore.

The chunks of content that we experience are often called "nodes." A node is more or less equivalent to a Web page, and, like a Web page, a node is not restricted to any particular content type. Links are the pathways connecting nodes.

The spot on a Web page we actually click (whether it's a button, a menu item, or something else) is technically a "link origin." Informally, however, people often say, "Click the link," and they think of a spot on a Web page that triggers a link (or causes some other event) as being "hot."

One difference between hypermedia and physical space is that in physical space the time required to reach a destination is tied to the distance traveled so that we expect significant durations for long journeys. In contrast, links "jump" us instantly (or at least quickly) from one node to the next. The science fiction concept of travel in hyperspace, where space ships travel instantly to very distant locations, is close to our experience of travel in hypermedia. (The "hyper" part of the term hypermedia effectively expresses this kind of movement.)

Information Structures and the Hierarchy

The various arrangements of nodes and links are called "information structures." The hierarchy, shown in Figure 1.1, is the most prevalent of the information structures. In a hierarchy, users very often navigate downward from the top node, the home page, to deeper levels (from "parent" node to "child" node). The other information structures are the linear, multipath, matrix, and web. Web designers often represent the structure of their websites in the form of "node-link diagrams."

The Human-Computer Interface

The human-computer interface is the means by which a user interacts with a system. In the case of the Web, the interface consists both of the individual website

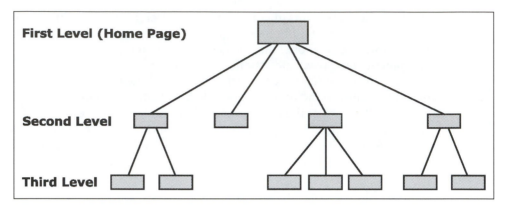

Figure 1.1. Nodes and links arranged in the hierarchical information structure.

and the browser that the site is running in. A website's user interface encompasses all the content on the site; in other words, everything the user reads and sees and listens to in some way affects how the user will interact with the system. But the heart of the user interface consists of the buttons, text links, and other interactive elements on the site as well as the buttons, command menus, and other interactive elements on the browser.

Because most websites are information environments, the primary role of the interface is to support navigation—finding and displaying information. We can refer to this as the navigational aspect of the Web interface.

If a website incorporates a spreadsheet or other software application, if it is a store with a checkout area or an online bank, or if there are other online computing capabilities, you will see command menus, dialog boxes, and other interface elements resembling those in standard software applications. This is the online computing aspect of the Web interface.

A Very Brief History of the World Wide Web

The World Wide Web is the culmination of two separate traditions of thinking and technological development. The first is the hypertext/hypermedia tradition, which gave us new ways to interact with content using computer technology. This tradition is itself composed both of systems intended for small groups of knowledge workers and systems for mass communication and publishing. The second tradition consists of the succession of technological advancements that led to the Internet.

The Hypertext/Hypermedia Tradition

The hypertext/hypermedia tradition encompasses many different systems. Some were popular products, others were developed as research projects, and some were never built at all but embody important ideas. For a good review of these systems, see Jakob Nielsen (1995).

Vannevar Bush—The Conception of Hypertext and a Plan for the Memex

Vannevar Bush was a distinguished professor of electrical engineering at MIT, a co-founder of a high-tech company (Raytheon Corporation), and the director of war-related research for the United States government during World War II. Bush was also the first person to envision hypertext.

Bush's starting point is what we now call "information overload." He recognized, in 1939, that there would soon be more published information, especially research findings, than any person would be able to manage and organize. His solution was to provide knowledge workers with a sophisticated technology for storing and, especially, linking text and graphics. Dynamic content was beyond even Bush's extraordinarily far-reaching intellect and imagination.

In 1945 he offered a detailed description of a non-existent device, the Memex, in a famous article, "As We May Think," published in the magazine *Atlantic Monthly* (Bush 1945). The Memex was not based on computer technology—which barely existed at the time. Rather it assumed that documents would be stored in the form of miniature photographic images (microfiche). The Memex was built into the researcher's desk, and it included both a screen, a keyboard, and something like a scanner. Researchers could access various documents that had been entered into the Memex, add their own annotations, and link the relevant passages of all documents stored in the Memex.

Bush had no thought of hypertext as a mass communications medium. The Memex was a tool for knowledge workers. He envisioned them sharing their documents, links, and annotations, but not through any kind of electronic transmission or network. For more information on the Memex, see Kahn and Nyce (1991).

Doug Engelbart and the Beginning of Modern Computing

Doug Engelbart's contributions to modern computing are enormous. The Augmentation Research Project, which he led at the Stanford Research Institute from 1962 to 1975, resulted in such innovations as multiple-window interfaces, the mouse, word processing, email, the storing of files in a central computer, and sharing files over a local network. His system was called Augment, because Engelbart's underlying idea was the use of technology to augment the native abilities of human beings. The Augment system was used at the McDonnell Douglas Corporation for many years.

One fundamental feature of Augment was that users could build links among documents and could share each other's links—it was a usable hypertext system. Like Bush's imagined Memex, Augment was a means of supporting knowledge workers, a system for office automation, not a mass-communications medium.

Ted Nelson and the Dream of the "Docuverse"

Ted Nelson is a visionary and intellectual rebel who worked for decades trying to build a global hypertext network he called Xanadu. The goal of Xanadu was to make all published information available to everyone and to enable anyone to freely recombine any and all documents and add their own textual content.

Although Nelson never succeeded in creating such a system, the vision of a Xanadu "Docuverse," set forth in his writings and presentations, is a major achievement. It was Nelson who, in 1965, coined the term hypertext. His eccentric homemade book, *Literary Machines* (1992 and 1980), is available today and makes for extremely interesting reading. It is a memoir, a technical description of Xanadu, and an important statement of hypertext theory. His personal website is www.sfc.keio.ac.jp/~ted.

The World Wide Web can be seen as a partial fulfillment of Nelson's vision, but the Web is still far from being a universal publishing system. Xanadu failed for at least two reasons: (1) the daunting technical challenges of implementing such a system, and (2) the complex arrangements necessary before copyright holders would allow their content to be included in Xanadu. Nelson's plan was that small royalty fees would accrue to copyright holders whenever their content was used. Such a system of "micropayments" may ultimately be incorporated into the World Wide Web.

Xerox NoteCards and Other Specialized Systems

Numerous important hypertext and hypermedia systems were developed as academic and industry research projects during the late 1960s and through the '70s and '80s and beyond. These systems incorporated and continue to incorporate the latest advances in computing and interface design and have greatly extended what hypertext and hypermedia systems can do.

Important prototype systems were developed at Brown University, under Andries van Dam, starting in the late 1960s. In the mid-1980s, a sophisticated educational hypertext system, Intermedia, was used in courses at Brown.

One very important system was Xerox NoteCards, developed in 1985 by Frank Halasz and other researchers at Xerox's renowned Palo Alto Research Center (PARC). NoteCards, which ran on Xerox's proprietary computer equipment, made very effective use of multiple windows, could automatically generate a node-link diagram of a hypertext document, and included other features impressive even by today's standards. Furthermore, NoteCards could be extended much further through programming in the LISP computer language.

NoteCards was another tool for knowledge workers. It was originally funded by the U.S. government as a tool that CIA analysts could use to manage and establish links among large numbers of reports, communiques, maps, and other documents relating to the world's political situation.

Some of these early systems, however, were publishing systems. Hyperties, for example, developed by Ben Shneiderman around 1983, offered a well-chosen set of basic features and a highly intuitive user interface. Hyperties was used to create online help systems, museum displays, and hypertext books, including the diskette version of Shneiderman and Greg Kearsley's book *Hypertext Hands-On!* (1989) shown in Figure 1.2.

Aspen Movie Map: The First Hypermedia Project

The Aspen Movie Map, developed by Andrew Lippman and colleagues at MIT in 1978, was the first project that made the transition from hypertext to dynamic content. The heart of the project was an enormous collection of photographs of Aspen, Colorado, carefully taken by cameras mounted on a truck that was driven

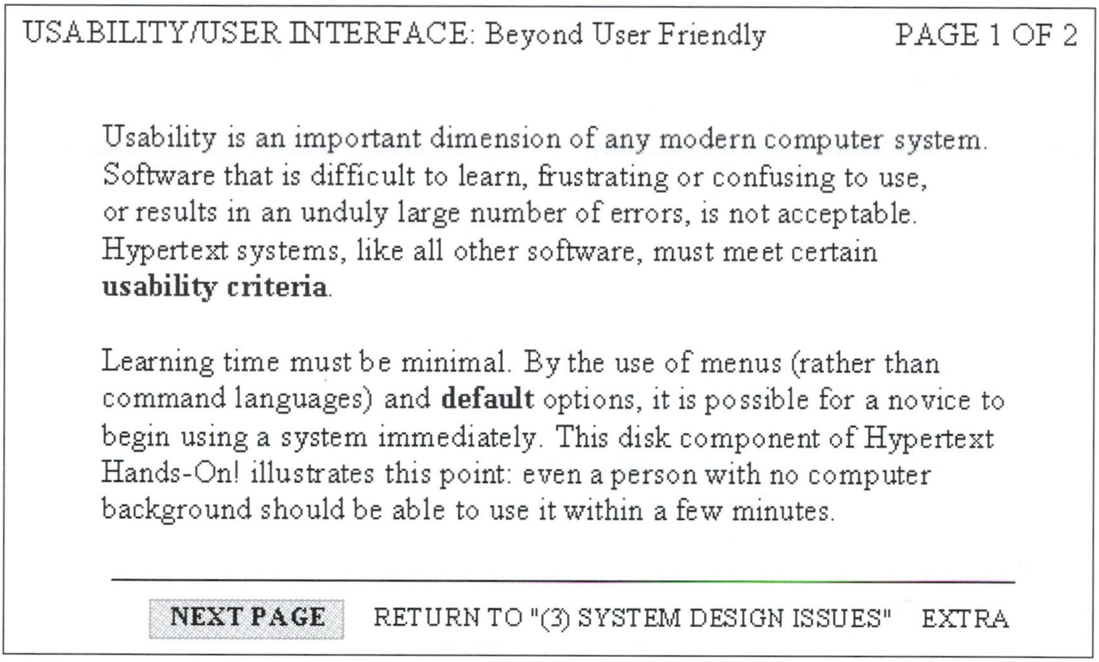

USABILITY/USER INTERFACE: Beyond User Friendly   PAGE 1 OF 2

Usability is an important dimension of any modern computer system.
Software that is difficult to learn, frustrating or confusing to use,
or results in an unduly large number of errors, is not acceptable.
Hypertext systems, like all other software, must meet certain
usability criteria.

Learning time must be minimal. By the use of menus (rather than
command languages) and **default** options, it is possible for a novice to
begin using a system immediately. This disk component of Hypertext
Hands-On! illustrates this point: even a person with no computer
background should be able to use it within a few minutes.

NEXT PAGE   RETURN TO "(3) SYSTEM DESIGN ISSUES"   EXTRA

Figure 1.2. A page from the Hyperties version of Shneiderman and Kearsley's *Hypertext Hands-On!*
There are two links in the body of the text (shown in a darker font) and more links at the
bottom of the screen.

though the city street by street. The photographs were then linked in keeping
with the physical layout of the city.

A user of the Aspen Movie Map could explore Aspen by using a joystick to
navigate through a succession of photographs. Jakob Nielsen (1995, 41) explains:
"The resultant feeling was that of driving through the city and being able to turn
at will at any intersection." The Aspen Movie Map was an academic research project, but it was developed to present a specific body of content in a way that could
engage a general audience.

Guide and HyperCard: Bringing Authoring to the Public

Guide was the first commercially successful hypertext system. Apple Macintosh
and IBM PC versions were released in 1986–87. Guide required no programming
skills and was used to create electronic books, computer manuals, and other kinds
of documents. One innovative feature in Guide was the "stretchtext" link. A user
might, for example, click a one-sentence explanation of an unfamiliar term, and
the sentence would expand into a full-paragraph explanation of that term.

HyperCard was an authoring package for the Macintosh that was introduced
in 1987. HyperCard enabled non-programmers and novice programmers to easily
create a wide variety of visually attractive interactive projects and simple software
applications. HyperCard authors could build links with ready-made buttons and

add scrolling windows and other useful interface elements to their projects. There were built-in drawing tools for adding graphics (generally black and white), and authors could easily incorporate basic sounds and simple animations. HyperCard was initially distributed without cost and finished projects would usually fit on a single floppy disk. A typical hypertext project created in HyperCard is shown in Figure 1.3.

HyperCard created a burst of interest in interactive content. Many thousands of people (especially educators) created tutorials, interactive short stories, and other projects. Greater numbers used them.

HyperCard gradually faded from the scene, due in part to Apple Computer's failure to support it adequately. But a major limitation of HyperCard and all the other pre-Web systems was incompatibility: For example, a project created in HyperCard could not be viewed on an IBM PC or even with SuperCard, a similar authoring tool for the Macintosh. One enormous strength of the World Wide Web is that it is platform independent. Websites look and behave in much the same way and are authored in much the same way regardless of the kind of computer and operating system being used.

Macromedia Director and the CD-ROM

In the ashes, so to speak, of HyperCard and similar products arose a new generation of very sophisticated hypermedia development products. Macromedia Director began life as a product for building animation sequences that would run within HyperCard and SuperCard. Gradually, it developed into a complete authoring

Figure 1.3. A typical HyperCard project. The authoring menu bar is shown at the top.

application with linking capabilities, strong support for all content types (in full color), and its own programming language.

The larger and more elaborate projects that could be authored in Director needed a higher-capacity storage medium than the floppy disk. Fortunately, the CD-ROM drive had arrived, and in the late 1980s and early 1990s Director became the most popular authoring tool for commercial CD titles. Director and similar authoring tools are still used to author many CD/DVD titles.

Online Help

Online help systems are the hypertext equivalent of computer manuals. Throughout the computer era, help has grown in sophistication. A landmark was the appearance, in the early 1990s, of Microsoft's Windows 3.0 and 3.1 help development tools. Windows Help enabled many thousands of help authors to create diverse and sophisticated help systems and other online documents, while the underlying Microsoft help compiler enforced enough consistency that users could switch easily from one product's help system to another.

Much valuable experience and expertise in hypertext design came out of this work. Also online help introduced many millions of computer users to hypertext and to such fundamental hypertext interface elements as underlined text links, pop-up windows, the Back and History features, and the electronic equivalent of print indexes and tables of contents. HyperCard, CD multimedia, and online help were the main ways in which interactive content was known and used prior to the Web.

Mark Bernstein and the Eastgate Circle

Mark Bernstein's Eastgate Systems (www.eastgate.com) has published much hypertext fiction and non-fiction since the mid-1980s. A group of authors associated with Eastgate creates experimental poetry, short stories, and other kinds of literature very often using Eastgate's proprietary authoring environment, Storyspace. Probably the best known of these authors is Michael Joyce, whose radically nonlinear but engrossing short story "Afternoon" is one of the earliest works of hypertext fiction. Another important work is "Patchwork Girl," by Shirley Jackson. Bernstein himself is a major hypertext theorist.

Bernstein and the Eastgate authors do not much concern themselves with dynamic content. Also notable is their strong commitment to "constructive hypertext"—allowing the user to customize the content and structure of a project to a very significant degree. Their ideal is for users to participate as co-authors by adding new nodes and links to the original hypertext. Although Storyspace is built to allow constructive hypertext, one problem with implementing this vision (originally Ted Nelson's) is that Storyspace has limited capabilities on the Web. The idea of constructive hypertext figures prominently in books by George Landow (1997) and Jay Bolter (1991) that explore the connections between hypertext and literacy, education, rhetoric, and postmodern literary theory. To a significant degree these artists and theorists carry forward the theoretical side of Nelson's work (including Nelson's ambivalent attitude toward hierarchical structures). They are helping us understand the full cultural implications of hypermedia.

The Internet Tradition

The Internet tradition consists of a long succession of technological advancements in the area of computer networking and the recognition that computer networking could be the foundation for new communications media. The Internet story is well told by Katie Hafner and Matthew Lyon (1996) and by George Johnson (1999).

J. C. R. Licklider, ARPA, and ARPANET

Throughout the 1960s and early 1970s, groundbreaking research was being conducted in the area of long-distance computer networking. This research led ultimately to the Internet. Much of this work was funded by the U.S. Department of Defense's Advanced Research Project Agency (DARPA), later called ARPA. Unfortunately, this was an era when women and minority groups were largely excluded from engineering research.

A highly influential figure in this research tradition was J. C. R. Licklider. Licklider began his career as a psychologist, became a computer scientist at MIT, and in 1962 moved to ARPA to manage the agency's projects. Licklider recognized that computing would not progress unless data could be shared among physically distributed computers. Also, Licklider foresaw that networked computers could function as a communication system in which human beings could send messages to one another. Though he stayed at ARPA for only two years, Licklider shifted the ARPA research agenda toward the goal of long-distance computer networking.

One of the key advances during this period was the development of "packet switching theory." The underlying idea is that a message can be broken into small packets, transmitted in any order, and then reconstructed as a complete message once all the packets are delivered. A great deal of work needed to be done, much of it funded by ARPA, before packet switching could be implemented on the very primitive computers and telephone systems of the 1960s.

In 1969 the first prototype internet, ARPANET, began service. It connected computers at four universities. The initial goal of ARPANET was to allow researchers at different institutions to share the few computer resources that existed at the time. But the further potential of computer networks was becoming more apparent. In 1968, Licklider, along with Robert W. Taylor, had published a paper entitled "The Computer as a Communication Device." The paper envisioned a network with many of the services we have today—email, online encyclopedias, dictionaries, research materials of all kinds, and even online communities where individuals could share and discuss ideas.

Email, TCP/IP, and Gopher

In 1972 email was introduced on ARPANET and within a year it accounted for 75% of all ARPANET traffic. ARPANET continued to expand, and other networks were established as well.

In 1973 Bob Kahn, Vint Cerf, and other researchers began work that would result in TCP/IP (Transfer Control Protocol and Internet Protocol). TCP/IP remains an essential Internet technology. It is important because it enables clusters of computers at a particular site to be easily linked to the Internet.

The Internet continued to grow through the late 1970s and 1980s. Only universities and research organizations could participate at this point; there was no commercial activity. Important new services were added, such as FTP (file transfer protocol) and listservs (email discussion groups). The Gopher system, a direct precursor of the Web, enabled Internet users to navigate cyberspace and view text-only content posted on Gopher servers. For example, Stanford University used Gopher to allow any Internet user to peruse Stanford's complete library catalog. Often, users would navigate to a Gopher site and then use FTP to move a file (text files, software, etc.) to the mainframe computer where the user had his or her own account.

Tim Berners-Lee and the World Wide Web

In 1991 Tim Berners-Lee, a physicist and computer scientist working for the European research consortium CERN, introduced an innovative hypertext system—the World Wide Web—to allow researchers to share their work using the Internet. If each researcher installed a special software application, a Web browser, on his or her computer and if documents were formatted with a special tagging language, HTML, information could be shared readily both within CERN and elsewhere. Hypertext jumps allowed for flexible linking within and among these documents.

Here the two strands of our history come together. By joining the capabilities of hypertext systems with the global reach of the Internet, Berners-Lee created a new communications medium that within a few years expanded beyond a small research community to the world of mainstream computer users.

In 1993 Marc Andreessen, a student working at a computer laboratory at the University of Illinois, developed a more sophisticated Web browser, Mosaic, with versions for the Macintosh and PC as well as UNIX. In 1994 Mosaic was commercialized as Netscape, and the rapidly growing Web community began to see a steady stream of enhancements to Web technology. In the mid-1990s the business world discovered the Web, and Web design became an exciting new profession. This field attracted many people who had honed their design skills in the pre-Web era of hypermedia and hypertext.

Looking Toward the Future

It is certainly risky to predict the evolution of the Web. Some changes, however, can clearly be anticipated at this time. Already we see increased reliance on wireless, hand-held computing devices that provide email, instant messaging, telephone communication, and software applications along with Web access.

As computers in general become more able to produce and understand spoken language, people will routinely conduct voice dialogs with their browsers. Looking further into the future, it seems likely that the computer monitor will be supplemented or supplanted by some kind of "near-eye" (or "head-mounted") display. Near-eye displays are potentially small and portable and provide a much wider field of view than is possible with a computer monitor.

Also Web agents will perform many tasks on behalf of users, for example, reporting to a user that her automobile is due for maintenance and requesting authorization to schedule an appointment with the mechanic's agent-enabled website.

Amid this narrative of innovation and advancement, it is important to remember that large segments of the world's population do not have Web or Internet access and do not make much use of computers. A change of great importance is the increase in computer and Internet use throughout the world.

Summary

1. We can understand the World Wide Web and its extraordinary success by considering the seven key capabilities that it offers:
   1. Global reach
   2. Interactivity (choice and responsiveness in experiencing content)
   3. Support for multiple content types (text, graphics, animation, video, and audio)
   4. Support for transactions
   5. Online computing functions
   6. Support for active social spaces
   7. Support for system adaptivity, user customization, and site-wide modification
2. CD/DVD titles resemble websites but lack integration with the Internet; CD/DVD, however, does offer advantages: Developers can use more powerful authoring tools and can dispense with a browser, high-quality video can be more reliably displayed, and archiving is more feasible.
3. The Web is used for a vast range of purposes. We can broadly group these into eight categories:
   1. Education
   2. Entertainment
   3. Providing news, public information, and specialized information
   4. E-commerce: Promotion/selling/support
   5. Web portals
   6. Persuasion
   7. Building and sustaining community
   8. Personal and artistic expression

   Websites that are designed for a particular purpose tend to share various characteristics. As users develop expectations regarding these similar characteristics, Web genres develop and evolve.
4. Communications media are distinguished by content types, means of delivery, interactivity, and how they are used and paid for. The Web allows individuals as well as huge corporations to reach a mass audience (one-to-many), but also allows for communication among small groups. In the battle among media—"media convergence"—the Web has largely eclipsed CD/DVD multimedia and competes aggressively with radio, television, and print publishing.

5. We use "hypermedia" as the umbrella term that encompasses both the Web and CD/DVD multimedia. Hypertext, the original term for interactive content, refers to the pioneering systems (and their successors) designed primarily to present text and static graphics.

6. Intranets are websites used and accessed within an organization. Their main purpose is to provide specialized information such as policies and procedures and news, but a good intranet builds community. Intranet designers typically have extensive information about their audience.

7. Nodes, links, and navigation are central concepts in hypertext theory and Web design. A node can be envisioned as a chunk of content, more or less equivalent to a Web "page." A node can be any content type. The pathways that connect one node to another are called links. Web users "navigate" from node to node through information space.

8. The various arrangements of nodes and links are called "information structures." The hierarchy is the most prevalent of the information structures. The other information structures are the linear, multipath, matrix, and web.

9. The human-computer interface is the means by which a user interacts with a system. In the case of the Web, the interface consists both of the individual website and the browser that the site is running in. Because most websites are information environments, the primary role of the interface is to support navigation. E-commerce checkout is an example of the online computing aspect of the Web interface.

10. The World Wide Web is the culmination of two traditions of thinking and technological development. The hypertext/hypermedia tradition gave us new ways to interact with content using computer technology. The Internet tradition first gave us networking technology and a vision of computer networks as a means for human communication. Later it gave us email and the Web.

11. The hypertext/hypermedia tradition includes Vannevar Bush, Doug Engelbart, Ted Nelson, many academic researchers, and the developers of commercial hypermedia products. The Internet tradition includes J. C. R. Licklider, Robert W. Taylor, Bob Kahn, and Vint Cerf. Much of the work on networking and the Internet was funded by the U.S. Department of Defense's Advanced Research Project Agency (DARPA), later called ARPA.

References

Bolter, Jay David. 1991. *Writing Space: The Computer, Hypertext, and the History of Writing*. Hillsdale, NJ: Lawrence Erlbaum Associates.

Bush, Vannevar. 1945. As we may think. *Atlantic Monthly* 176.1 (July): 101–108. This article is available on the Web at www.theatlantic.com/unbound/flashbks/ computer/bushf.htm and a version with valuable commentary was reprinted in the ACM magazine *Interactions* 3.2 (March 1996): 35–46. Sections 6–8 are the key sections in Bush's article.

Hafner, Katie, and Matthew Lyon. 1996. *Where Wizards Stay Up Late: The Origins of the Internet.* New York: Touchstone Books.

Johnson, George. 1999. From two small nodes, a mighty Web has grown. *New York Times,* 12 October, D1–D2.

Kahn, Paul, and James M. Nyce. 1991. *Memex to HyperText: Vannevar Bush and the Mind's Machine.* Boston: Academic Press.

Landow, George P. 1997. *Hypertext 2.0: The Convergence of Critical Theory and Technology.* Baltimore: Johns Hopkins University Press.

Nelson, Theodor. 1992. *Literary Machines.* Sausalito, CA: Mindful Press. Originally published in 1980.

Nielsen, Jakob. 1995. *Multimedia and Hypertext: The Internet and Beyond.* Boston: Academic Press.

Shneiderman, Ben, and Greg Kearsley. 1989. *Hypertext Hands-On!* Reading, MA: Addison-Wesley.

Discussion and Application

Items for Discussion

1. We noted that television is struggling to become interactive and that telephones are blending with computers. Describe specifically what kinds of changes are taking place.

2. Many websites are intended to achieve more than one purpose. This is especially true of large, complex websites in which many separate departments and groups are represented. Examine a university website to see the many purposes it serves, and categorize these purposes according to the list of purposes provided in the chapter. In what ways might these purposes differ among different kinds of universities?

3. Find a website that supports an active social space. How does it do so? How does the active social space help the site owners achieve their goals for the website? In what ways and how successfully does the active social space serve the needs and interests of users?

4. Consider that the term "page" was chosen as the term for a unit of content on the Web. Do you see problems with this choice? What alternative terms, including the possibility of neologisms (newly invented terms), can you think of?

5. How are cities using the Web to provide services to residents and other interested individuals and groups? Examine your home town's website. What purposes does it serve? Do you think it is a high-quality website?

6. Consider the personal home page as a Web genre. (If you wish, focus on the student home page, a subgenre of the personal home page.) What are the characteristics that define this genre? What particular purposes can you discern? What categories of content are typically present? Are these websites typically sedate or are they exuberant in their visual design?

7. What CD/DVD titles are you familiar with? Are they commercial products? Were they made by a school or by individuals without commercial goals? Why do you think the developers chose CD or DVD (or some other physical medium such as a floppy disk) rather than the Web?

8. The movie *Time Code* (directed by Mike Figgis, released April 2000 by Screen Gems) is a drama in which the screen, from start to finish, is divided into four quadrants. Each quadrant shows one of four interconnected strands of a single story. All four strands were filmed simultaneously in real time and were not edited. The sound track was mixed to direct the viewer's attention to one or more of the quadrants, but viewers are always free to focus on the action in any of the quadrants. In what respects is this an interactive or hypertextual movie? Is there some kind of user navigation or "linking"? You can learn more about *Time Code* at www.movieweb.com/movie/time-code/timecode.htm.

9. Compare these passages by two important nineteenth century literary figures, especially as they pertain to the Web and the Internet:

> Passage to India!
> Lo, soul! seest thou not God's purpose from the first?
> The earth to be spann'd, connected by net-work,
> The people to become brothers and sisters,
> The races, neighbors, to marry and be given in marriage,
> The oceans to be cross'd, the distant brought near,
> The lands to be welded together.
> A worship new, I sing;
> You captains, voyagers, explorers . . . !
> You engineers! you architects, machinists . . . !
> You, not for trade or transportation only,
> But in God's name, and for thy sake, O soul.
>
> *Walt Whitman, A Passage to India (3:30–41), 1868*

> Our inventions are wont to be pretty toys, which distract our attention from serious things. They are but improved means to an unimproved end, an end which it was already but too easy to arrive at; as railroads lead to Boston or New York. We are in great haste to construct a magnetic telegraph from Maine to Texas; but Maine and Texas, it may be, have nothing important to communicate.
>
> *Henry David Thoreau, Walden; or, Life in the Woods, 1854, Chapter 1, "Economy"*

10. Identify and gather information about two important changes pertaining to the Web or the Internet that have occurred recently. These may or may not be those we mention at the end of this chapter ("Looking Toward the Future"). How might these changes benefit (and not benefit) peoples' lives?

11. Identify and gather information about two important research projects pertaining to the Web or the Internet. How might these research projects benefit (and not benefit) peoples' lives? A good way to identify important research projects is to visit the websites of pre-eminent media-related research laboratories. These include the MIT Media Lab (www.media.mit.edu) and the Entertainment Technology Center at Carnegie Mellon University (www.etc.cmu.edu).

Application to Your Project

1. State the specific purpose (or purposes) you hope to achieve with your website and the general category that the purpose(s) belongs to.
2. In this chapter you have learned about seven capabilities of the Web. Not every site uses all seven of the capabilities. Which of these will you draw upon when designing your website? Which will be most important for your website?

2

Planning the Project

Introduction

This chapter and Chapter 3 explain the Web development process. By "development" we mean the entire process of creating a website—from early planning through to final launch. As you can imagine, there are a great many tasks that make up this process. These tasks can be divided into three phases: (1) planning, (2) design, and (3) building. This chapter covers planning. Chapter 3 covers design and building. In both chapters we point out some important differences between developing a website and a CD/DVD title.

A summary of the complete Web development process is shown in Figure 2.1. You will very likely perform all or almost all of the tasks you see in this figure. The difference is that in some projects certain of these tasks may require just a few minutes of thinking or checking, while in other projects the same task may require substantial effort. Furthermore, the development process is too complex and variable for there to be a fixed sequence of tasks or for all these tasks to be entirely distinct from one another. For example, there is likely to be mixing of some planning and design tasks and some design and building tasks. Also, as we explain, evaluation tasks should be performed more than once during the planning and design phases.

Formulating Your Purpose

As with almost everything else in this world, Web development will be much more successful if the site is designed for a realistic and clearly formulated purpose. Below we review the broad classification of purposes introduced in Chapter 1.

Planning	Design	Building
Formulating your purpose	Advancing the content list	Setting up the work environment
Analyzing and adapting to your audience	Working out the structure	Developing, revising, and reviewing content
Reviewing other websites	Creating design sketches and sample pages	Coding special features
Choosing a business model	Designing for change and future development	QA (quality assurance) testing
Establishing working relationships with the appropriate people	Building a prototype	Project documentation and reporting: The completion report
Determining and dealing with project constraints	Evaluation—especially user testing	Post-release evaluation
Establishing a theme and style—plus concept sketches	Project documentation and reporting: The design report	
Planning content and content acquisition		
Planning for ample evaluation and performing early evaluations		
Project documentation and reporting: The planning report		

Figure 2.1. A summary of the complete Web development process.

This list can be useful when you begin thinking about the specific purpose of your project or when you try to analyze the purpose or purposes of existing websites.

1. Education
2. Entertainment
3. Providing news, public information, and specialized information
4. E-commerce: Promotion/selling/support
5. Web portals
6. Persuasion
7. Building and sustaining community
8. Personal and artistic expression

As you know, projects are very often designed to achieve a combination of purposes. One special purpose, not mentioned above, is to improve your design and implementation skills (and perhaps to fulfill a school assignment while doing so). This is a totally legitimate and worthwhile purpose. But even a practice exercise should simulate a real-life project with a real-life purpose.

It is an excellent idea to write a purpose statement for your project, to review it regularly, and if necessary to update it as the project progresses. The hypothetical website Asthma Horizons Northwest is intended to provide news and specialized information and to build and sustain community. The design team's statement of the specific purposes of the website appears below:

> Asthma Horizons Northwest will be an important resource for asthma sufferers, their families, and friends. Focusing on the states of Alaska, Idaho, Oregon, and Washington, Asthma Horizons will provide background information about this medical condition, current information on treating and managing asthma, information about regional issues and concerns, and links to further resources. Although there will be references to the medical research literature, the site is not intended for physicians or other medical professionals. The site will include message boards that will provide a social space through which users can share their experiences and gain confidence and inspiration. Asthma Horizons will be an English-language website, but it will be designed to serve non-native as well as native speakers of English.

> The site should project professionalism and objectivity. It should be visually pleasing and informal in style. Because Asthma Horizons is fully supported by foundations, there will be no advertising or other commercial activity on the site.

Often it is desirable, especially in a business setting, to formulate a project's purposes quantitatively. For example, you may specify goals in terms of number of site visitors, average visit time, and anticipated revenue. For an educational project you might specify specific learning outcomes.

The Evolution of Your Purpose

As noted, you may need to revise the original purpose of your website. For example, the officials of the City of Centerville initially assumed that the only purpose of the city's website was to provide information useful to current residents and people working in Centerville. However, after looking at other municipal websites and talking with officials in other cities, the Centerville officials recognized other purposes such as attracting new residents and businesses and advertising the city's job openings. Often establishing the purposes of a project is a long and difficult process. The various stakeholders (people who are concerned about the outcome of the project) may suggest too many or even conflicting purposes for the project and argue about which purposes are most important.

Matching Purpose to Audience Needs and Motivations

In order for your website to succeed, your purposes must be realistic. This means that your website must correspond to real needs and interests. For example, the senior managers of a corporation, recognizing that employees rarely consult the thick volumes of printed procedures, put the procedures on the corporation's intranet so that they will be much easier for employees to access. The employees, however, still prefer their current practice of learning about the procedures from one another. The corporation will certainly save paper and shelf space, and the online procedures will probably stay more current. But the managers will not achieve their main purpose because it does not correspond to the needs of the employees.

Along similar lines, there have been many e-commerce websites that proudly offered services no one wanted. Go ahead, then, create a "Meet My Parakeets" website if you wish, but there may not be many people for whom this website holds any interest.

Analyzing and Adapting to Your Audience

In addition to formulating your purpose, you need to carefully analyze the intended audience of your website. A great many aspects of your design from the most fundamental design decisions down to the choice of individual words and the colors of particular buttons should follow from this analysis. Analyzing and adapting to your audience is, in fact, central to all forms of communication.

Analyzing an audience, however, is as complex as it is important. To give you a useful framework for analyzing website audiences, we distinguish between demographic categories of information and information specific to the subject of the website. Then we address the issues of conducting research, segmenting and prioritizing audiences, and taking full account of international audiences, cultural differences, and accessibility.

Demographic Information

Human beings can be grouped in regard to traits that we all possess. Everyone has an age, a gender, some kind of ethnicity and nationality, some kind of income and financial status. Everyone has an educational background and kinds of knowledge obtained outside of school. Many people adhere to a religious faith or follow a recognized set of philosophical beliefs. By and large, we can classify people as living in particular nations and in urban, suburban, or rural areas.

These categories of demographic information can be very useful in analyzing an audience. Let's say, for example, you are helping to design a website for Secondmarriage.com, a site with information and features for people getting re-married. We know that the audience for this website will be older than people marrying for the first time. We also know that these people, being older, will tend to have higher incomes and more assets. On the other hand, many other categories of demographic information will not be very helpful in analyzing this audience. For example, people who re-marry vary widely in education, ethnicity, and where they live, and so these categories of information will probably not figure significantly in the design.

Similarly, consider the website Centervillestreams.org, a website intended as a resource for Centerville science teachers. These teachers have asked a local hydrologist and others with similar backgrounds to build a website providing general information and specific data (flow rates, water quality, etc.) about local streams. The teachers hope to use this information to devise assignments and plan field trips.

Science teachers all have a high level of education (a college degree and probably further coursework). A designer, then, could confidently use a vocabulary appropriate for college graduates, whereas the editor of Secondmarriage.com might argue against using words such as "gastronomic" and "accoutrements" on the grounds that they may discourage a significant portion of the website's audience from using the site. Other than education, however, science teachers are much like the general population, and in any case such demographic characteristics as age and ethnicity are not highly significant to their use of this website. In both of these examples, then, demography is useful but certainly does not provide adequate information for a designer.

Subject-Specific Information

More directly useful than demographic information is subject-specific information. This consists of your audience's background, beliefs, attitudes, and preferences in regard to the subject matter of your website and how they will use it. For Secondmarriage.com, you would want to learn as much as possible about peoples' beliefs, attitudes, and preferences regarding their second marriages. What are their hopes and concerns? What are the arrangements, financial and otherwise, through which new households and families are formed? What kinds of weddings do they plan? What kinds of assistance are they seeking?

For Centervillestreams.org, the key information is also subject specific. The designers care most about the specific kinds of science training the teachers have and the kinds of assignments and projects they hope to devise.

Conducting Research

Very often, we analyze our audiences by conducting research. The designers of Secondmarriage.com should seek out information regarding marriage, divorce, and remarriage. They want to learn as much as possible about the ages at which people re-marry, the usual durations of the previous marriage (or marriages), how marriages terminate (e.g., divorce, death), how long people remain single after a marriage ends, and the numbers and ages of the children of people who remarry.

Very possibly, designers of Secondmarriage.com will want first-hand contact with members of the potential audience. Why not conduct surveys on issues especially important to the website? Why not interview members of the target audience or conduct focus group meetings that would include soliciting their reactions to preliminary website designs, sample feature stories, and advertising? Gathering, analyzing, and interpreting this kind of information, especially as it pertains to consumer behavior, is a major part of the field of marketing.

Note that in contrast to Secondmarriage.com, the audience of Centervillestreams.org is extremely small and specific. Very likely the entire potential audience for this website could assemble in a single room to explain their backgrounds and needs. Very likely these teachers would share their lesson plans and other teaching materials with the designers. Talking with the teachers, the designers of Centervillestreams.org may well uncover significant issues that would have otherwise escaped their notice. For example, they might learn that the teachers are concerned about the safety of students and the possibility that they might be trespassing along stream banks.

After a website is launched, designers should continue to gather information in order to evaluate the success of the site and guide its future development. It is important to learn who actually uses your website and what they are trying to accomplish.

Segmenting and Prioritizing Audiences

Often when a website is intended for a broad audience, the designers will think of the audience as several subgroups, each with distinctive characteristics. In other words, they "segment" the audience. Sometimes, the segmentation of the audience appears explicitly on the website. For example, the home page of a university website might have separate branches for prospective students, current students, faculty and staff, alumni, and members of the local community. Each branch will provide information especially suited to each audience segment, though in some cases the different branches will converge on content that is relevant to more than one segment. More often, the segmentation is not explicit, but the designers are thinking about different audience segments and expecting each segment to prefer different content. So, for example, the designers of Second-marriage.com might think about the audience in terms of several distinct age groups. They might also distinguish between the newly formed families with and without children living in the household.

It is not always possible or necessary to give equal priority to each segment. So, for example, if one segment does not seem to be making much use of your website, you can make extra efforts to appeal to this segment, but you can also shift your focus away from this segment.

Designing for International Audiences

An important and complex dimension of audience analysis is designing for international audiences. English is to some degree the unofficial language of the Web, and many websites in non-English speaking nations provide complete or partial English-language versions of their site when their intended audience includes users from other nations and cultures. In contrast, many English-language websites, especially in the United States, make little effort to accommodate non-native speakers of English, even when their content is relevant to people in non-English speaking nations. The owners of these sites should think about cross-cultural issues: They should consider adding content in other languages and should accommodate international users by limiting North American cultural references and slang—though in certain cases North American cultural references may be essential to the website.

You should certainly work hard to avoid offending people from other nations and cultures. Consider, for example, an online store in North America that sells decorative objects imported from around the world. The website's graphic designer decides to incorporate Arabic script into the design of the pages advertising merchandise from the Middle East. The designer, however, unwittingly uses passages from the Koran and offends many Muslims in North America and other nations who do not want to see their sacred texts used in a secular context. To learn more about writing English for international audiences and cross cultural communication and marketing, see Nancy Hoft (1995), Lillian Chaney and Jeanette Martin (1995), Elisa del Galdo and Jakob Nielsen (1996), and Jean-Claude Usunier (1996).

Making Websites Accessible

A very important consideration is making your website accessible to people with visual impairments and other disabilities. For example, text-to-voice Web browsers, often used by people with visual impairments, can read HTML, but not graphics files. It is important, therefore, to annotate each graphic with a descriptive ALT tag in your HTML code. Also, designers often supplement graphical buttons and navigation bars with text-only navigation menus at the bottom of each Web page.

The World Wide Web Consortium (W3C), the official standards-setting organization for the Web, publishes complete information on website accessibility. Visit their website (www.w3.org/wai) for the most up-to-date information on the W3C accessibility guidelines, examples and explanations of how to implement them, and links to tools for evaluating the accessibility of web pages. See also Michael Paciello (2000) for good information on accessibility.

Reviewing Other Websites

Most Web designers spend a significant amount of time looking at other websites for design ideas that they can borrow or adapt. For example, someone designing a city website might look at other city sites and get the idea of creating a section on the city's history. You don't want to slavishly copy other websites, but there is no reason to work in a vacuum either. In every field it is inevitable and natural for ideas to ripple through the professional community and for people to adapt these ideas in their own designs.

When reviewing other websites, think in terms of evolving Web genres. Think about what your users may be expecting and how you can fulfill these expectations and, at times, depart from them. Broadly speaking, designers should embrace conventions that help users understand how the website works and that help them achieve their goals, but should look to change accepted practices that are inefficient or irritating through over-use.

In addition, Web developers very often borrow ideas and tricks for implementation. In most cases you can use a Web browser's View Source command to view the HTML code and figure out how some aspect of a website was constructed. Be careful, however, not to use a site's JavaScript, ActiveX, or other custom programming or a lot of a site's specific design ideas, for these are protected by copyright.

Choosing a Business Model

The term "business model" simply means how a website will pay for itself or in some other way justify the work and money that's put into it. Most corporate sites don't generate revenue, but they advertise the company's products, maintain and strengthen relationships with existing customers, and contribute to the company's corporate image. Likewise, although intranets serve vital internal functions, they do not generate revenue. A great many websites, however, are intended to run as profitable businesses.

Finding a workable business model can be very tricky. First, it is often difficult and expensive to draw users to your website. You cannot count on Web-wide search engines to deliver large numbers of site visitors. Submitting your site to the search engines and taking other steps (such as including metatag keywords in the HTML code) do not ensure that the site will appear high on a results list when users type in relevant queries. In many cases, search engines sell the search terms that consumers type when they are shopping on the Web. In other words, if a company buys the search term "shoes," that company shows up high in the Search results list whenever a user types "shoes."

Even if you can draw significant numbers of people to your website, you don't necessarily have a workable business model. Online merchants have experienced difficult times. Many websites support themselves by selling advertising, but potential advertisers want to see proof that their advertisements are producing results. Some advertisers will pay just to have a banner advertisement with a link to the advertiser's site. Other advertisers want to pay only on the basis of the number of users who follow the link back to the advertiser's site. If you maintain, say, a gardening site, recommend a particular gardening book, and provide a link to an online merchant who sells the book, the merchant may pay you a commission for each person who navigates from your site to the merchant's site to buy the book.

Many sites charge for access to their content. These include the online version of the *Wall Street Journal* (www.wsj.com) and various financial investment websites (as well as most pornographic sites). These websites, however, compete with sites whose business model includes free access to similar content.

If you create a website purely for personal expression or to share a hobby or special interest or to make a contribution to society, you don't need a business model—which is perfectly fine. If the website benefits society in some way, you may be able to find an organization that is willing to sponsor the site. For good information about the business side of the Internet, see Internet.com, especially the Ecommerce/Marketing channel.

In most cases, the business model for CD/DVD multimedia is simply the purchase price. In some cases, CD/DVD titles are distributed without charge for corporate promotion, or the cost is figured into the price of an accompanying product, such as a toy or book.

Establishing Working Relationships with the Appropriate People

Unless you are working on a solo project, you will be interacting with people in an organizational setting. Some may be managers, who have a broad understanding of the role of the project within the organization. Some may be subject matter experts, or SMEs (pronounced "smees"). Some may be marketing specialists, who have insights about the impact of the project on the organization's customers. These people can help you greatly with the audience analysis and planning of your project, provide you with content, and check what you've created for accuracy and for its fit with the organization's broad goals and strategies. It is important to start communicating with all of these people early in the project and to maintain communication throughout the project. You don't want to put in a lot of work on something just to find out later that someone has a reason for rejecting what you've done. If you work for a client, you will probably have a single contact person during the proposal stage and access to other people in the organization once you've been hired for the project.

A difficult situation arises when people in the organization disagree strongly about what they want for the website. These people may have different notions about colors and fonts or, more likely, concerns about corporate strategy and the most appropriate content. Sometimes it is necessary to ask the person with ultimate authority to resolve these differences. In the next chapter we will look at the make-up and function of another group of people: your own development team.

Determining and Dealing with Project Constraints

In almost every project you will deal with certain constraints. It is important to recognize these constraints early so you can plan accordingly. The constraints we cover here are money, time, style guides and design policies, and the user's computer technology.

Money

One very common constraint is money. Ample funding means that you can use any content type that seems appropriate to the project, hire any specialists (artists, photographers, videographers, sound technicians, programmers, user testers, etc.) that are needed, and purchase state-of-the-art equipment. Usually, however, there are spending constraints. With limited funds, you will probably need to plan the project around the skills that your own team members bring to the project.

If you don't have a Java programmer, a skilled graphic designer, and first-rate hardware and software, there are certain things you just can't do.

In some cases, you are given a maximum figure at the start of the project. In other instances, you may need to do some planning and design work before you gain approval for a project and negotiate a fee. This is especially true when you are trying to get work from a potential client.

However you are funded, you will very likely be required to prepare a proposed budget and a final budget and to document your expenditures. Even when it is not required, you will need a budget (though perhaps a very simple one) just to manage your funds.

Time and Scheduling

Another constraint is time. This constraint may be a deadline or simply a decision about the total amount of time you or your organization wants to invest in the project. This too may be subject to negotiation. Whether you face a deadline or just a maximum time allocation, you should estimate early on how many person-hours the project will take and when it will be finished.

Unfortunately, accurate time estimates are extremely difficult to calculate in the planning stage. The tendency is to significantly under-estimate the time that will be needed. To come up with your estimate, break the complete project into separate tasks, estimate the time required for each task, and devise a schedule for the project. As the project progresses, you should re-calculate the estimated times for tasks and update the project schedule.

Many project managers create a timeline (or "Gantt chart"), a simple representation of the key tasks that need to be undertaken, along with their starting and ending dates. Managers also need to recognize which tasks cannot begin until other tasks have been completed or have reached certain milestones. The planning report, shown in Appendix C, "Reports," includes a schedule in the form of a timeline.

Unexpected Delays You Should Expect

In almost all projects there are factors that will cost you extra time and could disrupt your schedule. For example, there are often delays getting information from subject matter experts (SMEs) who are not on your team. Your project may not be their highest priority. There are also delays in getting review comments and authorizations from managers and people who are over-seeing your project. If you anticipate and plan for these problems, you will be more likely to stay on schedule. User testing and other forms of evaluation are often very time consuming, and there can be long delays in getting permissions for copyrighted material.

You are also apt to encounter unexpected technical problems, especially if you are using unfamiliar tools and technologies. The best strategy is to prepare a technical demo (or "technical prototype") through which you will be able to uncover and address any technical glitches early in the project.

Managing Scope

For various reasons but especially due to time constraints, don't be overly ambitious in your planning. In your initial enthusiasm, it's very easy to commit to a design you will not be able to complete. One way to limit the project's scope is to narrow your intended audience or the purposes you will fulfill. You can often build links to websites related to yours and thereby reduce the work required to build and maintain your site. The developers of Asthma Horizons chose to link to the medical research literature rather than to assume responsibility for providing and continually updating this content on their website.

You may also want to develop your website in stages. Get the first stage up and running and then begin the next. Your first stage may not have everything you ultimately intend, but at least you will have a functional website without portions that are clearly missing.

For student projects, a reasonable strategy is a demonstration project in which the intent is to build only representative sections of the whole.

Web Style Guides and Design Policies

Many organizations have established design requirements for their intranets and public websites. These requirements often include particular color schemes, specified variations on the use of the organization's logo, and design elements such as a standard navigation bar at the top of each page. These design requirements are usually described in the organization's "Web style guide" along with various communication rules and policies (for example, requirements for non-sexist language). Web style guides are valuable because they lead to consistent design. Also, designers benefit when they can quickly find out what they must do and can't do.

Your Users' Technology

You need to consider the very different computer technologies your users are probably working with. What follows is only a brief, non-technical overview of the three most important issues. For more information, consult up-to-date technical references as well as the websites listed below.

Regarding browsers, you need to recognize that even the most current versions of Netscape, Microsoft's Internet Explorer, and other browsers (Opera, Lynx, HotJava) support various Web technologies (e.g., DHTML) differently or not at all. Also the same browser may behave somewhat differently in its Windows, Macintosh, and Unix implementations. Finally, many users do not upgrade from older versions of a browser, creating still more severe compatibility problems. Therefore, you need to pay close attention to these compatibility issues, avoid non-standard HTML tags and other non-standard authoring technologies, and decide which browsers you will fully or partially support. You can find up-to-date comparisons of browser capabilities on the Web. In the reference list, see WebMonkey, BrowserWars, and BrowserWatch.

Equally important is the speed of the user's connection to the Internet. Although fast connections are becoming much more common, many users are still connected to the Internet through ordinary phone lines with data transfer speeds of 28.8 Kbps (or slower). Slow connections cause delays in displaying large and complex graphics (the key factor is file size) and may cause still greater delays and loss of quality in playing dynamic content such as video files. You should therefore minimize the file size of graphics and avoid burdensome dynamic content, though these constraints are less applicable to most intranet websites or sites specifically geared to high-tech users.

A final issue is the user's monitor and underlying video technology. Monitors vary, of course, in size and overall quality, and the user's video card and other computer capabilities affect image quality and determine what screen resolutions the user can display. Increasingly, designers expect users to display websites at a screen resolution of at least 800 x 600 pixels, but keep in mind that if users can only display at 640 x 480, your Web pages will be wider than their display area, forcing them to scroll horizontally as they view your site.

Here are two key points that emerge from this discussion: First, it is necessary to plan and test for a broad range of user technologies. Second, if you design around high-end technology, you will be excluding or at least discouraging significant numbers of users—many of them less affluent individuals and people living in nations in which the technological infrastructure is less developed. You should work hard not to exclude people from your website.

Finally, we will mention the emergence of hand-held, wireless devices that can display Web content, often in conjunction with email and telephone capabilities. Because they have such very small screens and are, to a large degree, limited to displaying text, these devices require specially designed websites.

Establishing a Theme and Style—
Plus Concept Sketches

Establishing the theme and style are very important planning tasks with far-reaching consequences. Theme and style directly affect the overall appearance of the website, how the text is written, and the selection and design of all the website content.

Theme

Early in the project you need to define your theme. The theme is the core message that connects your website to your audience. It is how the website presents itself and the organization it represents.

Theme is separate from purpose. The websites for automobile manufacturers, for example, have the same basic purposes: promoting and perhaps directly selling automobiles. But the theme that will be expressed for an exotic sports car will be different from the theme for a practical family car. The theme of Asthma Horizons is this:

Asthma can almost always be effectively managed and asthmatics, especially when they take an informed role in managing their condition, can live active, happy lives.

If the purpose of your website is to promote composting, your theme will be something like this:

Composting is easy to do, it benefits the environment, and you will have a supply of rich soil enhancer or mulch for your garden and lawn.

The theme will be expressed in your project's content: the words, images, and overall appearance. So, for example, if you are talking about emptying compost from a compost bin, you would, in keeping with the theme, note: "This will not create a mess." You should formulate your theme early in the project, and keep it clearly in mind right through to launch and as you update the site.

Style

Style is a general term for a wide range of specific decisions that focus and shape content and thereby help to express the theme. As you will learn in Chapter 4, "Content Types," each content type has attributes that can be controlled to produce a particular style. It is convenient to talk about style as something that modifies content or is added to content, but style and content are ultimately inseparable: A change in style is a change in content. The term "mood" is closely related to style but focuses on the overall effect rather than on specific techniques. So, for example, we might speak of the somber or joyful mood of a graphic or animation sequence.

Let's reconsider the theme of Asthma Horizons and examine how it is expressed through various stylistic decisions:

Asthma can almost always be effectively managed and asthmatics, especially when they take an informed role in managing their condition, can live active, happy lives.

The content on this site inherently expresses the idea that asthmatics benefit when they take an informed role in managing their condition. Most of the content provides just this kind of information. In addition, writers can try to evoke the theme as they make highly specific decisions about their style. This includes using a positive tone when describing the prospects of managing asthma successfully—though they cannot unduly downplay the difficulties that severe asthma can cause.

At this point in the project the designers have only talked casually about graphic design. They are thinking about a strong geometric design with bright colors to evoke an upbeat, positive mood.

Concept Sketches

It is perfectly good practice to describe your ideas for a website's visual appearance in words only during the planning stage and to begin sketching (by which we mean any quick rendering whether using a pencil or computer software) in the design phase. On the other hand, human beings tend to think and plan visually, and so it may not be long before someone involved in the project has the urge to go beyond the discussion of theme and style and attempt some rough sketches of the home page and other key pages.

Sketches produced at this stage are only concept sketches. They can help the team visualize the ultimate appearance of the website and think about theme and style. Actual design sketches and sample pages, however, must wait until the design stage when you know more about the content of your pages and what the navigational interface will be like. Figure 2.2 shows a concept sketch someone on the Asthma Horizons design team created for the home page. In keeping with the discussion, the design is geometric and employs bright colors. Thinking about the name of the website, the designer has also added a clever new idea: a bright spot (or "sunburst") on the top diagonal line to suggest the sun coming up over the horizon. Although the home page design will change greatly, this sunburst motif will stay. Note that the creator of this sketch can only guess about the number of links on the home page.

Planning Content and Content Acquisition

Once you understand your purpose, audience, theme, and style, it is time to begin planning the content you will include in your website. This means putting to-

Figure 2.2. A concept sketch of the home page of Asthma Horizons Northwest.

gether a content list and thinking about how you will obtain or create the items on this list.

Putting Together a Content List

A content list is a rough and very tentative roster of the major content elements that you will probably include in your website: text, graphics, animation, video, and audio. The list should be the product of creative thinking, very likely during several brainstorming sessions. A very small team might work around a table with a paper and pencil. Larger teams will want to use a whiteboard or type directly into a spreadsheet or word processing file that is projected on a large screen for everyone to view.

Because the list is just a starting point, there does not need to be any particular sequence to the items. During the design phase, team members will identify new elements, decide to drop elements from the list, and redefine the nature of certain elements on the list. In the process, the content list will be transformed from a rough listing of possibilities to a well-defined and well-organized list of Web pages.

Although you want to be as inclusive as possible when putting together your content list, you should nonetheless take into account the project constraints. So, for example, you should be able to figure out early on if you do not have the funding or time for video sequences or if your audience is not well equipped to display them.

Figure 2.3 shows a three-column content list that the Asthma Horizons team is developing. The Content Element column describes the element very briefly ("New trends in asthma treatment"), the Notes column further explains the content element ("Feature these news items on the home page"), and the Source column records ideas about acquiring the element ("Need to monitor print and online sources").

Acquiring Content Elements

Once you have a tentative content list, you should make plans for acquiring or creating the various content elements. If you are working within or for an organization, there may be quite a bit of existing content that you can use directly or adapt for use on the website. It is often a good idea to enlist members of the organization in the task of sifting through existing content and selecting appropriate material for the website. Not only will this help you to get the best content, but you may well build support and enthusiasm for the project. Much of the time, however, you will face the time-consuming and challenging task of creating your own content.

In the case of text, you can distinguish between content elements that require a significant research effort (e.g., compiling a list of allergens prevalent in the Northwest) and introductions, general descriptions, and other content elements that require writing skill and a general knowledge of the website's subject matter but not extensive research. Regarding graphics, some graphics, of course, will be

Content Element	Notes	Sources
New trends in asthma treatment	Feature these news items on the home page	Need to monitor print and online sources
Animated GIF showing the function of the lungs	Keep it very simple--no need for big graphics files	Can do this in-house
List of support groups in the Northwest		Mike is starting this
School district policies concerning asthma and asthma management	Maybe these are state-wide policies rather than district-level policies	Talk with Karen in WA State Education Office
List of allergens and possible allergens specific to the Northwest		Dr. Jeff Altman can help with this
Map showing the Northwest region	Probably should show up in the NW Focus area	
Air quality statistics by city		Can link to the Nat'l. Air Quality Control Website
Basic information on asthma, testing, and treatments	Needs a consistent writing style	
Graphics showing use of an inhaler	Use line drawings	Can do this in-house
Warning signs of an episode	Each warning sign will need a brief explanation	We may be able to adapt material from the Lung Association--ck with them
Review of current research projects	We don't have the expertise to monitor and summarize the research	Will link to the Journal of the Am. Medical Assoc. (JAMA) site for this
Information on volunteering for clinical drug trials		Will link to the Mothers of Asthmatics site for this
What you can do to manage your environment	We may divide this into ideas for home and school	
Monthly feature	Let's start with a profile of Seattle Seahawk Chad Brown. Could incorporate photos an audi	Assign to a staff writer or use occasional guest writers

Figure 2.3. A content list created with a spreadsheet software application.

much easier to create than others. As discussed in Chapter 4, "Content Types," audio, animation (other than simple animated GIFs), and especially video are the most difficult content elements to create.

Another set of considerations relates to quality level. In many cases you will have the option of capturing content at different levels of quality. For example, you can digitize sound at different sampling rates (44 KHz, 22 KHz, or 11 KHz) and sample sizes (16 bits vs. 8 bits). High-quality content requires more storage capacity and may be more difficult to work with, but—if it is feasible—you should capture and store at the highest level of quality that you might possibly want to use. Once you've dropped from high-quality to lower-quality content, you can't go backwards.

One special problem with video is that you often need to "over shoot" to make sure that you have all the raw footage you need. There are two reasons for this. First, it is often time consuming and expensive (rental costs, etc.) to gear up for a video shoot, and you don't want to have to do it more than once. Second, it is often impossible to re-create the situation of your initial shoot. The street fair is over, the summer landscape is now covered with snow, and so forth.

One crucial issue regarding content acquisition is copyright. Most content created after 1922 is protected by copyright and cannot be used legally or even adapted without permission of the copyright holder. You can't legally appropriate graphics, motion graphics, or sound you find on the Web or on a CD or DVD. The problem of copyright is sufficiently important and complex that we treat it separately in Appendix B.

You can, however, license photographs and dynamic content from "stock" media companies. Companies such as Eyewire (www.eyewire.com), Corbis (www.corbis.com), PhotoDisc (www.photodisc.com), The Music Bakery (www.musicbakery.com), Artbeats Digital Film Library (www.artbeats.com), and Stock Video (http://members.aol.com/stockvideo/main.html) have large, easily searchable collections and generally moderate fees.

There are also a great many images (including Web icons, buttons, and backgrounds) that, with certain restrictions, you can copy or download from websites free of charge. To find many of these sources, type "free clip art" into a Web-wide search engine, such as Google.com or Altavista.com. Also, Microsoft offers a collection of images, animation sequences, and sound sequences without charge to registered owners of various Microsoft products at http://dgl.microsoft.com.

If you are intent on using a well-known piece of recorded music, you can set about obtaining the license to do so. Very likely, however, this will be an expensive and time-consuming effort. A good starting point is the website of the National Music Publishers' Association, at www.nmpa.org.

Planning for Ample Evaluation and Performing Early Evaluations

In Web design (as in many other kinds of projects) we need to periodically stop and evaluate our work to be sure that the project is headed toward success. A general principle is that we want to perform evaluations as early as possible. The sooner we know that we are off-course, the less effort is wasted. One part of the planning phase, therefore, is to schedule evaluation tasks at appropriate milestones during the project. Another part of the planning phase is to perform evaluations that pertain specifically to the planning tasks.

Profile: Points West Kayak Tours

Annie Sokolow and Peter Hayes own Points West Kayak Tours, one of several small guide services that take visitors on day-long and longer excursions around Homer, Alaska. Most of their customers are tourists, and most are not experienced kayakers. During their three years in business, Annie and Peter have marketed their company through a storefront (open during the tourist season), a full-color brochure (available in local restaurants and motels), and advertisements in the *Homer Visitor's Guide.* Now they are building a website. Let's take a close look at how they plan their site.

Purpose

Annie and Peter quickly decide that the main purpose of the website is to advertise their company to tourists. More specifically, they hope that potential clients will visit the site, email or phone for more information, and book a trip. Another purpose is that potential clients who do not contact Points West before arriving in Homer will still visit the Points West storefront (rather than that of a competitor) and book a kayak trip. A possible future purpose is to enable customers to book trips right on the website and complete the financial transaction online.

Audience

Annie and Peter know a lot about their audience and do not need to conduct further research. Still, they spend some time reviewing their knowledge and taking notes. The key points of their analysis appear below.

The people who take kayak tours in Homer like nature and the outdoors and often take part in outdoor activities at home. For the most part, they are not the same folks who come to Homer to fish for halibut on the charter boats. Most have little or no experience with kayaks. They range in age from twenty-year-olds to people in their fifties

and beyond. Some bring teenage children. They usually have the following questions on their minds:

- Will I see special scenery and get really close to wildlife?
- Do I need to have experience with kayaks, and do I need to be in top physical shape?
- What is the cost?
- What about rainy weather?
- Is this a safe activity, even for my kids?

Annie and Peter currently address these issues in their brochure and plan to address them on their website as well.

Review of Similar Projects

Annie and Peter look at other websites offering kayak excursions in Alaska and other parts of the United States and Canada. They immediately see interesting possibilities. The website can provide the same basic information that the brochure does, but now potential clients can choose to learn much more about Points West and the trips they offer.

Theme and Style

Annie and Peter derive the theme from their audience analysis and their purpose. Stated briefly, the theme is this:

We provide safe, relaxed kayak outings. No experience is necessary. You will have an active day of adventure and get a really close-up view of the wildlife and some of the finest scenery in Kachemak Bay.

Their ideas regarding style include writing in a personal style, conveying their deep appreciation for the natural beauty of Alaska, and expressing their commitment to providing a memorable experience for every guest. They expect to use vivid color photographs and make extensive use of blue and green in their design.

Project Constraints

Annie and Peter have talked to friends and have done a little reading about HTML and Web development, and they recognize that one project constraint is that most of their clients will be visiting the Points West website from home, where their Internet connection may be slow. Both Annie and Peter agree that color photographs really sell people on kayak trips. But they will have to pay some attention to the file sizes of the photos that will appear on the website.

Content Acquisition

Annie and Peter do some brainstorming about content elements they may want to use. Their content list is divided into a text section and a graphics section.

Text Elements

- A welcome paragraph that briefly describes Kachemak Bay and their tours
- A two-paragraph personal statement that talks about their backgrounds and philosophies as tour guides. This includes comments about safety and protecting the environment.
- A paragraph describing Homer's generally sunny summer weather with a comment that rain does not spoil a good kayak trip
- Descriptions of each of the four trips they usually offer, with prices
- A list of what to bring on a trip and what's provided
- A page describing the wildlife their guests usually see on trips plus a list of local birds

Graphics Elements

- A road map of Homer, with a close-up of the famous Homer Spit, where their storefront is located

- A map of Kachemak Bay showing the many islands and inlets
- A scenic photograph of kayakers paddling across Kachemak Bay with snow-covered mountains in the background (from the brochure)
- A close-up photo of kayakers paddling close to an island (from the brochure)
- A photograph of Seal Rock, where thousands of seabirds nest each year
- A photo of kayakers enjoying lunch on a sandy beach
- A close-up of a female otter swimming on her back with a baby sleeping on her belly

Annie and Peter don't have to worry about obtaining these content elements. The text elements can be easily written or adapted from their brochure. Three graphics can be taken from their brochure. Also, Peter is an accomplished photographer with a good collection of photographs for them to draw upon, and the Homer Chamber of Commerce provides maps and other graphics to local businesses.

Annie suggests adding a whole section for birders. They decide to put this idea on hold until the site is up and running. For now, they will provide a single page listing local species.

Evaluation

Because their brochure has been well received, Annie and Peter feel confident about the effectiveness of their overall theme and their ideas regarding style. Therefore, they do not include evaluation tasks in the planning phase, but they begin thinking about how to get evaluations from knowledgeable peers and potential users during the design phase. We will revisit Peter and Annie in later chapters.

There are many forms of evaluation. One of the simplest is to ask for reactions from knowledgeable peers and whatever experts may be available. Another form of evaluation is to systematically review your design against a good set of design guidelines or existing websites that you admire. In many respects, however, the most revealing and reliable form of evaluation is getting feedback from the kinds of people who will actually be using your website.

In the planning phase you can ask potential users whether your website meets a real need. You can explain the theme you have in mind and get their response. You may even be able to get reactions to your ideas regarding style, though this may need to wait for the design phase. It is very important to determine the usefulness of the major content elements and to find out what useful content elements you may have omitted. If your business model entails generating revenue, you need to know how many users will potentially subscribe to the site, buy merchandise on the site, or take whatever actions you are counting on for revenue.

User testing is a form of evaluation in which potential users actually work with a paper or clickable prototype of a website. As the users work, testers observe and take notes on the problems that arise and often collect quantitative data. User testing is performed primarily on the prototype during the design phase, and so we discuss user testing in the next chapter.

Project Documentation and Reporting

Web developers document projects to keep track of the decisions that have been made and the current plans and design ideas. Even the smallest projects require some documentation. At a minimum, the team should keep a project notebook (which can be maintained as computer files rather than on paper) that will serve as a record of decisions regarding purpose, audience, theme, and style and will include the concept sketches, content list, schedule, and budget. Most projects require more extensive documentation in the form of memos, progress reports, and other reporting documents. If plans change, which is very likely, the project documentation should reflect these changes. Resist the temptation to let project documentation get out of date.

Why is documentation so important? It fights "drift," the slow, unnoticed deviation from the project goals. In other words, it helps all members of the team stay focused on the audience, purpose, schedule, and other considerations. Finally, documentation is an important way to communicate beyond the project team, in particular with managers or clients who must approve the project at various stages.

It is very likely that the team will be required to prepare a report at the end of the planning phase. There are many ways to organize and write a planning report. Figure 2.4 shows a list of sections that are frequently included. A sample planning report with a timeline and budget appears in Appendix C, "Reports."

```
┌────────────────────────────────────────────────┐
│                                                  │
│  Planning Report                                 │
│                                                  │
│  Statement of Purpose                            │
│  Audience Analysis                               │
│  The Business Model                              │
│  Comparison with Similar Websites                │
│  The Design                                      │
│        Theme and style                           │
│        Early concept sketches                    │
│        Early design reviews                      │
│  Plans for Content Acquisition                   │
│  Plans for Project Evaluation                    │
│  Requirements: Staffing, Equipment, Schedule,    │
│  and Budget                                      │
│                                                  │
└────────────────────────────────────────────────┘
```

Figure 2.4. Possible section headings for a planning report.

Summary

1. The many tasks that comprise the Web development process can be divided into three phases: planning, design, and building. These tasks are performed very differently depending on the project.
2. Begin by determining your purpose(s) and writing a clear and specific purpose statement.
3. Carefully analyze your audience, possibly by conducting research. Your knowledge of the audience will guide a great many design decisions. Demographic information is important. Still more important is subject-specific information. Often you will design for specific audience segments.
4. Whenever possible, accommodate international audiences. Also, English-language websites should accommodate non-native speakers of English. Be careful to avoid offending people from other nations and cultures.
5. Make your website accessible to people with visual impairments and other disabilities. In particular, design for text-to-voice Web browsers. Follow the accessibility guidelines of the W3C.
6. Without copying, review other websites looking for ideas about design and implementation. Stay attuned to evolving Web genres and the expectations they create.
7. Many websites are intended to generate revenue or otherwise pay for themselves. However, finding a workable business model is tricky. In particular, it is often difficult and expensive to draw users to your website.
8. It is very important to establish good communication with key people—subject matter experts, marketers, managers—in the organization for whom the website is being developed.

9. Important project constraints are time (either a deadline or a maximum time allocation), money, style guides and design policies you must adhere to, and limitations in the user's technology. There are many unexpected delays in a project; therefore, schedule carefully and avoid overly ambitious plans. You may also want to develop your website in stages.

10. Early in the project you need to define your theme. The theme is the core message that connects your website to your audience. Also, begin thinking about style and mood.

11. You can begin making concept sketches of key pages, but these sketches are very tentative until you know much more about the website's content and navigational interface.

12. Put together a content list. This is a preliminary roster of the content elements that you think will find a place in your website. This will later be transformed into a well-defined and well-organized list of Web pages.

13. Once you have a content list, make plans for acquiring or creating the various content elements. If you are working within or for an organization, there may be existing content you can use directly or adapt. If you obtain content, avoid violating copyright. You can license content from stock media companies and use free stock content.

14. Evaluation tasks must be undertaken periodically throughout the development process to ensure the project is on track. In the planning phase you can ask potential users whether your website meets a real need, whether the theme generates a positive response, and whether specific content elements will be useful to them. You should also plan the evaluation tasks for the design and building phases.

15. Every Web development project requires documentation. Documentation fights "drift," the slow, unnoticed deviation from the project goals, and is an important way to communicate beyond the project team. Minimally, the team should keep a project notebook. Very often memos and reports are required.

References

Artbeats Digital Film Library. www.artbeats.com

BrowserWars.com. www.zdnet.com/products/browserwars/index.html

BrowserWatch. http://browserwatch.internet.com

Chaney, Lillian H., and Jeanette S. Martin. 1995. *Intercultural Business Communication.* Englewood Cliffs, NJ: Prentice Hall.

Corbis. www.corbis.com

Eyewire. www.eyewire.com

Galdo, Elisa del, and Jakob Nielsen, eds. 1996. *International User Interfaces.* New York: John Wiley & Sons.

Hoft, Nancy. 1995. *International Technical Communication: How to Export Information about High Technology.* New York: John Wiley & Sons.

Internet.com. www.internet.com

Microsoft Design Gallery Live. http://dgl.microsoft.com

Paciello, Michael, G. 2000. *Web Accessibility for People with Disabilities.* San Francisco: CMP Books.

Stock Video. http://members.aol.com/stockvideo/main.html

The Music Bakery. www.musicbakery.com

Usunier, Jean-Claude. 1996. *Marketing Across Cultures,* 2d ed. Englewood Cliffs, NJ: Prentice Hall.

WebMonkey. Browser Chart. http://hotwired.lycos.com/webmonkey/reference/browser_chart/index.html

World Wide Web Consortium. Accessibility Guidelines. www.w3.org/wai

Discussion and Application

Items for Discussion

1. Look at a website for a utility company (electricity, water, etc.). How many audiences does the site seem to address? What are the information needs of these audiences?

2. Make a list of business models that websites employ to justify the money and effort required to create and maintain them.

3. What effect does selling advertising space on websites have on the user's experience? What are the better and worse ways to present advertising on a website?

4. Look at three websites for food products. What theme is expressed in each of the sites? How are the themes expressed through stylistic choices? Three possible websites to examine are: pepsi.com, benandjerrys.com, and hickoryfarms.com.

5. An online, for-profit business university was using the name Unnexus University until they were forced to choose a new name due to a trademark dispute with another online learning company, UNext.com. The new name is Lansbridge University. The university's administrators are fully aware that this is a very different kind of name. They know that it will change the way the university is presenting itself to the public and affect the theme of their website. Describe this difference. Which name do you prefer?

6. What colors might you consider for a website that promotes composting? What colors might you consider for the website of a radio station that plays rock music? Why?

7. What might be the benefits of transforming a traditional print magazine into a CD magazine that would be mailed to subscribers and sold in stores along with conventional print magazines? Can you envision individuals who would prefer CD magazines to either print magazines or "Webzines," magazines that exist only on the World Wide Web?

8. Visit the websites of various stock media companies. What differences can you find in regard to the kinds of content available, the ways in which you search their collections, the ways in which the content is licensed or sold, and the restrictions on the use of the stock content?

Application to Your Project

1. Write a purpose statement for your project.
2. Define your audience. What do you know about your audience? What information do you need to gather about the audience? What design decisions or issues are immediately apparent now that you have determined your purpose and analyzed your audience?
3. Write a statement of your website's theme.
4. What are your plans for making the site accessible to people with disabilities?
5. Are you hoping to draw international audiences? If so, is your website designed for their use?
6. Write a planning report summarizing the early plans you have made for your website.

3

Designing and Building the Project

Introduction

In Chapter 2 we looked at the initial phase of development: planning. Now in Chapter 3 we consider the rest of the development process: the design and building phases. At the end of the chapter, we turn from the process to the people and the skills needed to design a website. Figure 3.1 (repeated from Chapter 2) summarizes the complete development process.

Broadly speaking, the development process proceeds from planning to design to building as shown in Figure 3.2. The figure also shows that the progression is not a simple straight line from start to finish, but rather a fluid process with significant blending among the phases. We can see that there is building in the design phase and design still to be done in the building phase. The Planning bar at the top of the figure shows the continuation of planning tasks throughout the project. For example, you need to monitor the schedule on a regular basis and deal with any unexpected problems such as someone leaving the project. The Evaluation bar at the bottom of the figure shows that evaluation tasks are performed throughout the project and that poor results may force you to loop back (the dotted lines) to an earlier phase of the project. Some projects include large and complex components, such as a video sequence, that are best regarded as partially independent sub-projects with their own planning, design, and building phases.

Let's turn now to the design phase. Note that while the development process presented in this book applies to all information structures, our explanation generally assumes a hierarchical website. We do this because, without a doubt, the great majority of all the websites on the World Wide Web are fundamentally hierarchical.

Planning	Design	Building
Formulating your purpose	Advancing the content list	Setting up the work environment
Analyzing and adapting to your audience	Working out the structure	Developing, revising, and reviewing content
Reviewing other websites	Creating design sketches and sample pages	Coding special features
Choosing a business model	Designing for change and future development	QA (quality assurance) testing
Establishing working relationships with the appropriate people	Building a prototype	Project documentation and reporting: The completion report
Determining and dealing with project constraints	Evaluation—especially user testing	Post-release evaluation
Establishing a theme and style—plus concept sketches	Project documentation and reporting: The design report	
Planning content and content acquisition		
Planning for ample evaluation and performing early evaluations		
Project documentation and reporting: The planning report		

Figure 3.1. A summary of the complete Web development process.

The Design Phase

In the design phase you draw upon all the thinking you did in the planning phase. But now you are thinking in concrete terms about the particular pages that will make up your website. You need to make considerable progress along several fronts:

- *Content.* You will need a much fuller understanding of the eventual content of the website than what your content list shows you. You don't create many of the graphics or write most of the pages, but you need a fairly good idea of what topics the website will cover, the level of detail, and what content types you will be using.

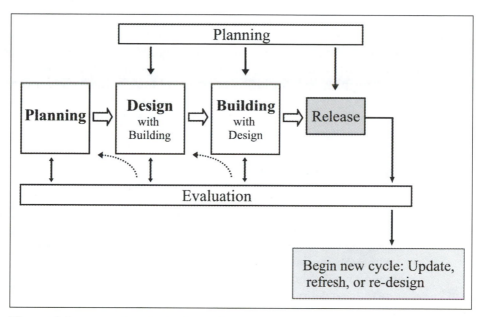

Figure 3.2. A model of the Web development process.

- *Structure.* You need to know how the pages fit together into a well-organized structure. You don't need to know how every page will be linked, but you do need to know the main branches of your hierarchy and the other major links. Without this broad understanding of the linking, you can't move from concept sketches to true design sketches. Why? Because the buttons and other links are a major part of the page design.
- *Appearance.* You need a good idea of what the pages will look like, starting with the home page but including "interior" pages as well. You should think through color schemes and the different page layouts, including the general appearance and placement of the links.

A very important part of the design phase is creating sample pages and eventually a prototype—a test version of your website. With the prototype you can perform realistic tests of your design. When the prototype proves itself through evaluation, you are ready to build the website, and the design phase ends in success.

Advancing the Content List

You will want to review, expand, and refine your content list, transforming it into a list of Web pages. Are there elements that still need to be added to the list? Are there elements that no longer seem appropriate for the website?

Some of the elements on the list will need to be specified more fully. For example, the designers of the City of Centerville website listed city council information on their early content list. In the design phase, they realize that this one item is very broad and should be the basis for several Web pages—a page describing the make-up of the council and council procedures, a page for each member of the council, a page listing the agenda of the next meeting, and so forth.

If your plans call for hiring an artist, photographer, or other content creator, this is a good time to make the arrangements. You will probably want to talk with several candidates, examine their work samples, and negotiate the schedule, cost, and other matters.

Working Out the Structure

Now you must organize the items on your expanded content list. You need to think about your users, their information needs, and the pathways you need to provide to enable them to navigate the website efficiently. Often entirely new ideas for the website come to mind as you work out the structure.

Although the design for the website's structure can conceivably reside in someone's head, this is a bad plan. Even in small projects it is very desirable to devise a representation of the evolving structure. This representation provides a record of the design work that has taken place, and it's something you can study and share with others. We will consider three kinds of representations here: (1) a node-link diagram, (2) a set of note cards, and (3) an outline. We will also consider the related issue of top-down and bottom-up design.

Web development projects differ greatly in size, purpose, design, and the nature of the development effort. These differences, plus the personal preferences of individual designers, will determine which of these representations are employed and how much effort is put into each of them. As you will see, all three are valuable. They can be used very productively in combination, and there is no sequence in which they need to be employed.

One difference among Web development projects is worth noting here. Sometimes the design team has a fairly complete understanding of the overall structure at the beginning of the design phase. Perhaps this website is being added to a family of similar sites. Perhaps the content just lends itself strongly to a particular structure. For example, Annie and Peter's Points West website promises to have a relatively simple, easy-to-anticipate structure. In other projects, the structure is not well understood in advance, but must be painstakingly worked out throughout the design phase. Many projects are combinations in which certain portions are easy to organize while others are more difficult.

The Node-Link Diagram

Node-link diagrams go by a variety of names, including "structure diagram" and "navigation flowchart." You can simply sketch a node-link diagram on a sheet of paper or you can create them with drawing and flowcharting software applications, among them Inspiration (from Inspiration Software) and Visio (from Microsoft). Certain Web authoring tools generate a node-link diagram as the designer builds the pages of a website. A node-link diagram of an early version of Asthma Horizons appears as Figure 3.3.

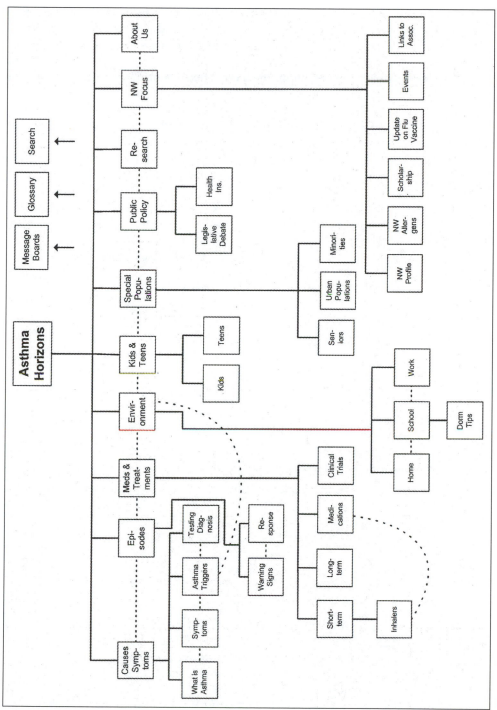

Figure 3.3. A node-link diagram, prepared using Visio, of Asthma Horizons Northwest. Not every page and link is shown, and the page names are abbreviated.

Node-link diagrams, however you create them, are a flexible, highly intuitive means of representing a website's structure. To encode different kinds of information about your design, you can show nodes as different shapes and in different sizes. Link lines can be thick, thin, curved, dotted, and so forth. We explain more about node-link diagrams in Chapter 6, "Hypertext Theory."

Node-link diagrams do have drawbacks. First, it takes some effort to prepare and update them. If the website is really large, it may be difficult or impossible to do more than represent a portion of the website—perhaps just the first three or four levels of the hierarchy or perhaps just a portion that is presenting special navigation problems. Also, if the website is heavily linked, it is difficult or impossible to show all the linking without making the diagram look like a plate of spaghetti and meatballs. These problems can be partly alleviated by abbreviating page names and by excluding certain categories of links.

Note Cards

Note cards take the form of 3 x 5 index cards, yellow "sticky notes," or something similar. Cards, representing potential Web pages, are named or briefly described and sorted into piles representing categories. The cards are then laid out on a table or taped or pinned to a wall. It is easy to add, remove, modify, and move cards. If the cards are affixed to a large sheet of blank paper, lines representing links can be drawn between the cards. An excellent technique for organizing a website is to ask potential users to sort your cards into a hierarchy that makes sense to them. Invite them to add, discard, and re-phrase the cards.

As with node-link diagrams, it is difficult to represent more than a portion of a large website. You may find yourself looking for a very large table or wall. Another problem is retaining a permanent record of the design work that has been done. Sometimes a wall or table of note cards can be photographed.

Using the Outline Feature of a Word Processor

Very likely your word processing program includes an outline feature. When you work in outline view, you enter text using different heading levels, and the outliner formats what you've typed as indented entries in an outline. Outline entries, therefore, can represent individual Web pages. An outline view of an early version of the Asthma Horizons hierarchy is shown in Figure 3.4. (Note that "Medications and Treatments" is a second-level entry; "Short-term relief" is a third; and "Inhalers" is one of the few at the fourth level.)

The outliner offers some major advantages:

- You can represent a website consisting of hundreds of pages extending down to five or more levels.
- You can quickly add, delete, change, and move entries.
- Your keystrokes can be copied or imported into your Web authoring tool.
- You can add notes (in the form of body text) directly beneath any outline entry. For example, notice the notes under the entries "Long-term help" and "Northwest Focus." You can even include draft versions of text that will appear on a Web page.

- # Asthma Horizons
  - ## Causes and Symptoms
    - *What is asthma?*
    - *Symptoms*
    - *Asthma triggers*
    - *Testing and diagnosis*
  - ## Dealing with an Episode
    - *Early warning signs*
    - ### *Responding to an episode*
      - Discuss mild, moderate, and severe episodes
  - ## Medications and Treatments
    - ### *Short-term relief*
      - **Inhalers**
    - ### *Long-term help*
      - Check on long-term treatment with inhalers
    - *List of medications*
    - *Participating in drug studies*
  - ## Controlling Your Environment
    - ### *At home*
      - Discuss dust mites, cleansers, second-hand smoke
    - ### *At school*
      - **Tips for dorm life**
    - *At work*
  - ## Children and Teens
    - *Childhood asthma*
    - *Asthma and teens*
  - ## Special Populations
    - *Asthma and seniors*
    - *Urban populations and asthma*
    - *Minorities and asthma*
  - ## Public Policy
    - *Legislature debates administering medications at school*
    - *Health insurance issues*
  - ## Research
    - *Links to research studies and summaries*
  - ## Northwest Focus
    - Provide external link to stats on daily pollen count and air quality
      - *Profile: Chad Brown, Seattle Seahawk*
      - *Allergens prevalent in the Northwest*
      - *Scholarship established in honor of Dr. Jeff Altman*
      - *Update on flu vaccine availability*
      - ### *Regional events*
        - Summer camps, walkathons, etc.
      - *Links to associations and support groups in the Northwest*
- # About Us

Figure 3.4. The initial outline of Asthma Horizons Northwest.

The outliner, however, has two major drawbacks. First, it is not feasible to represent anything but a hierarchical website. Second, links cannot be explicitly represented. The levels of indentation clearly imply that there are links from one level to the next, downward links pointing from parent to child nodes. But there is no way to show the many other kinds of links (such as links across branches of the hierarchy). These are the links represented with dotted lines on the Asthma Horizons node-link diagram.

It takes several hours to learn and become comfortable with the outline feature. The outliner, however, despite its drawbacks, is an effective tool for organizing websites (as well as print documents), and so this time will prove to be an excellent investment.

Top-Down and Bottom-Up Design

Designing the structure of a website requires both top-down and bottom-up thinking. Top-down design starts with broad categories that are divided into more specific categories. In other words, a designer will come up with an idea for content, such as how to deal with an asthma episode, and will say, "What ideas might fit under here?" Then, several ideas come to mind (such as knowing the early warning signs) and the designer must decide whether these ideas will become separate pages or just sections of the Dealing with an Episode page.

Bottom-up design starts with individual Web pages, which are then grouped. For example, a designer might be looking at a note card labeled "Improving Your Environment at Home" and a card labeled "Improving Your Environment at School." She might decide to create a new card "Improving Your Environment at Work" and to group all three cards under a new general card, "Improving Your Environment at Home, School, and Work."

All three kinds of representations allow for top-down and bottom-up design, but node-link diagrams tend to favor top-down design, and note cards tend to favor bottom-up design. Outliners favor top-down or bottom-up design depending on how they are used. Given the strengths and drawbacks of these three means of representing website structure, you can see the benefit of using more than one in a project.

Creating Design Sketches and Sample Pages

Once you have worked out the structure of your website, you can begin to create design sketches and sample pages. Keep in mind that we use "sketch" to mean either a paper-and-pencil sketch or a computer rendering. Design sketches and, especially, sample pages should not be far from the final design.

In many ways this is the climax of the creative process. If you are going to get really good design ideas, this is when you want to get them. Team members should spend time working alone to see what they come up with, but there should also be extensive sharing of ideas. Teams may assign two people to work independently on a key task so the team will have two designs to look at. Often, you can make something brilliant from the best aspects of two flawed designs.

Certain implementation decisions should be made at this point. For example, you can't work out your page layout in detail without deciding what screen resolution (e.g., 800 x 600 pixels) you are designing for. If the development team is committed to avoiding certain Web techniques (such as framesets), these decisions must now be figured into the design. It is also necessary to establish a maximum acceptable file size for your Web pages, and determine how you will restrict the number, dimensions, and other characteristics of graphics (and dynamic content) to stay below that limit.

You should certainly get feedback from potential users when you create design sketches and sample pages. You can ask questions about the appeal of the overall design, how well the graphic elements fit the design, how informative the writing is, and so forth. If this feedback reveals any design flaws, you'll need to re-think the design and create new sketches and sample pages.

Let's see what the Asthma Horizons team has done, starting with the home page.

Asthma Horizons: The Home Page

Looking at the sample page shown in Figure 3.5, you immediately see that the geometric design, created as a concept sketch in the planning stage, is gone. Two

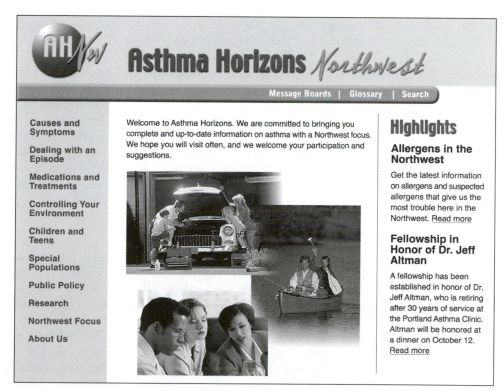

Figure 3.5. A sample page of the Asthma Horizons Northwest home page.

experienced graphic designers told the design team that the geometric design seemed somewhat cold and impersonal, hardly the look they wanted for Asthma Horizons. Nor did the various asthma patients who looked at the concept sketch respond with great enthusiasm. Furthermore, the design team decided that they wanted space for featured content on the home page.

In the new design, the name of the website, large and prominent, appears in a banner across the top of the page. At the upper left is a blue circle with the abbreviated form of "Asthma Horizons Northwest" and (at the circle's left edge) a sunburst, the only aspect of the concept sketch that has been retained. The blue circle and sunburst suggest bright skies and a hopeful future and will become the logo of the Asthma Horizons website. The background of the banner and navigation column is a sunny yellow; the bar below the banner (with the Message Boards, Glossary, and Search links at the right) is a tawny yellow.

The new design features photographs of people engaging in work and recreational activities. The photographs, licensed from stock vendors, will help express a key part of the Asthma Horizons theme: Asthma sufferers can live active, happy lives.

Asthma Horizons: The Interior Pages

After some careful thinking and discussion, the design team has reached agreement on the design of the interior pages, and they have made a combination of design sketches and sample pages at the second, third, and fourth levels of the hierarchy. One of these design sketches appears below as Figure 3.6.

Notice that the name of the website appears in the banner but in a smaller font that signals an interior page. The blue circle will appear on every page and will consistently serve as a link to the home page. The name of this page (Controlling Your Environment) appears in bright red at the top of the main content area. Below are three links to the child nodes.

The team has also worked together on the text of all of these design sketches and sample pages and has agreed upon the vocabulary level, style, and other characteristics. The design team believes that these design sketches and sample pages are highly informative and engaging and that they fit the overall design. The evaluation tasks performed so far confirm this judgment.

Working from a Grid

Grid systems are sets of horizontal and vertical lines that are almost always used in the design of print publications and have now become a key technique in Web design. The role of a grid system is to specify what variations in the basic design are permissible. Grid systems, therefore, enable designers to maintain consistency in page layout, especially when several people are designing Web pages. Once the grid has been established, any variation from the grid should be discussed. No one should informally create a new page layout for any portion of the website. Figure 3.7 shows the use of a grid system in Asthma Horizons. You can see how the various pages are variations on the same basic dimensions established by the master page.

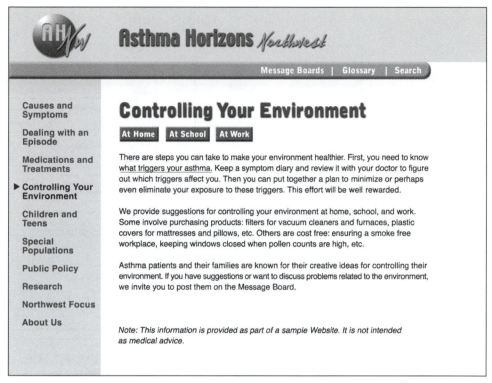

Figure 3.6. The sample second-level page Controlling Your Environment.

Closely related to grid systems are templates. A template is a computer file that incorporates grid lines and a variety of other recurring page elements such as the logo and navigation bar. Templates both enforce consistency and save time.

Designing for Change and Future Development

As you design, you need to think ahead to the long-term future of the website. CD/DVD titles are somewhat like books. Once completed, they do not change, at least not until a new version is created and distributed. On the other hand, most websites continue to change, perhaps every few months and perhaps much more often. Designers need to anticipate the various kinds of change.

When fundamental changes are likely, avoid design ideas that cannot readily accommodate such changes. Consider, for instance, a home page with links to seven main branches of a website's hierarchy. The designer has come up with a rainbow motif, with seven large links each representing one of the seven colors of the rainbow. If it proves necessary to add or drop a branch, the rainbow motif will need to be discarded.

In many other cases, the basic structure of the website is stable, but there is regular updating of content elements. For example, the website of a nightclub

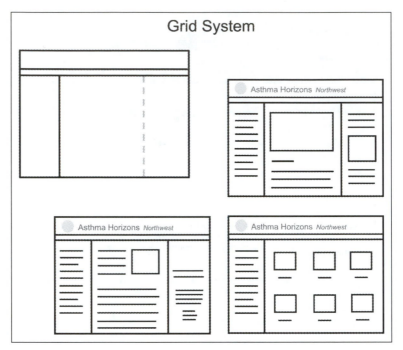

Figure 3.7. A grid system for Asthma Horizons. All pages in the website are variations on the master page.

must announce—and prominently—what band is currently playing and what band will be playing next week. Therefore, the home page must have areas set aside specifically for this frequently updated information.

Some websites, including some of the most visited websites, update their content daily or even more often. These include news sites, portals, and some online stores. There are limits to the attention that designers can give to Web pages that will disappear in 24 hours. Continual updating, therefore, requires special content-management software and a semi-automatic database-driven development process. Each day's content is "poured" into a stable template following sophisticated rules for the placement of text and graphics. Because no one will be hand-crafting the design of each day's pages, it is necessary to create an overall design that can accommodate, in a functional and attractive manner, different amounts of text and different numbers and sizes of graphics. Working out the design principles for continually updated websites is a new and intriguing aspect of Web design. For more information on content management, see www.arbortext.com, www.meta-torial.com, and www.hablador.com.

At times a different kind of problem arises: Site designers create a design that commits the site owners to more updating than they are prepared for. Don't create a category entitled "Special Monthly Feature" unless you are sure that the owners are prepared to carry out this kind of change. There are many websites whose special monthly feature is many months out of date.

As websites change, there are likely to be certain kinds of older content that remain important and should be retained and moved to an archive. For example, many corporations provide archives of past press releases, and many online magazines provide archives of past issues. Designers need to consider the ways in which visitors will be able to access the archived content. For example, will the archive be organized chronologically or by topic as well? If the website utilizes a Search feature, the archive should be part of the website's searchable content.

Another kind of change is a "refresh." A refresh changes the look of the website, possibly by changing the graphics on the home page or the color scheme. A refresh rewards regular visitors and prevents the site from seeming stale. One risk of periodic refreshes is that you need to find new design ideas that are as good as the earlier ones.

Eventually almost every website requires a complete re-design. Your purpose and intended audience may change over time. New categories of information often necessitate a completely new look for the home page and perhaps the rest of the website. New Web technologies may make certain design approaches feasible for the first time. A complete re-design requires a lot of effort, but it is a highly creative and rewarding task that most Web designers look forward to.

Building the Prototype

Once you are confident in the design of your sketches and sample pages, you can build the prototype. Achieving this milestone often gives design teams a morale boost, for this is when they really see the project coming together. The prototype is also the basis for the most extensive evaluation tasks you will perform. This is because the prototype is complete enough to provide really meaningful feedback and because you are still not too far along in the project to make the changes indicated by the evaluation.

The prototype is built by linking your sample pages and, usually, by creating new pages as well. You want to be really sure that you have a truly representative sampling of the different kinds of pages that will appear in the finished website. Be sure to include any pages you have special doubts about. Prototypes are also often used as technology demos in which you test your JavaScripts, integration of video content, and other technologies that might give you trouble. If the website is small, you may choose to make a clickable prototype of the entire website. You can also prototype pages reflecting two competing design ideas so that you can make an informed choice between the alternatives. Note that prototyping is one task in which the building phase blends with the design phase.

Some design teams regard a collection of paper sketches as a prototype. And, yes, various kinds of useful evaluations can be performed with a paper mock-up. But there are also significant limitations to what you can learn with only a paper prototype. In particular, paper prototypes do not give users the full experience of navigating a complex website.

Evaluations—Especially User Testing

As we've noted, it's very desirable to perform evaluations "early and often." Evaluation tasks begin in the planning phase and continue through the design and building phases. Useful forms of evaluation performed in the design phase include soliciting feedback from knowledgeable peers and experts and from potential users. You can also check your design against well-established guidelines and successful, well-respected websites. Good guidelines include the IBM Ease of Use Guidelines (www-3.ibm.com/ibm/easy/eou_ext.nsf/publish/561) and the Microsoft Web Design Guidelines (http://msdn.microsoft.com/workshop/management/planning/improvingsiteusa.asp). See also the special issue of *Technical Communication*, "Heuristics for Web Communication" (2000) for guidelines that include numerous citations of the research literature.

No form of evaluation, however, substitutes for user testing. Observing users as they work with your prototype provides you with the most revealing and reliable information about the success of your various design decisions.

User testing and evaluation comprise an entire field. In many well-funded projects, usability specialists are brought in to design and perform user tests and analyze the results. You do not need to be an expert in user testing, however, to perform valuable tests. For more information on user testing, see Joseph Dumas and Janice Redish (1993) and Jeffrey Rubin (1994). Below, we outline some of the major issues and provide an overview of the process.

Choosing and Working with Subjects

Recruit test subjects who are as similar as possible to the eventual users of the website. Don't use team members or anyone else who is close to the project: They are almost always "contaminated" by their understanding of the design and how things are supposed to work. Also avoid people who, for whatever reason, will not be sufficiently candid. Always encourage subjects to be tough on your design.

Be sure to make the test experience comfortable for your subjects. When you first solicit your subjects, you should tell them how long the test will take and you should stick to the time you specify. When you solicit your subjects and again at the beginning of the test, you should make clear that it is the design, rather than the subjects themselves, that is being tested. When subjects are nervous about looking stupid, they provide less useful information.

You must observe ethical standards in your testing. Causing discomfort and distress not only reduces the effectiveness of your test, it is unethical. Another important ethical requirement is not compromising your subjects' privacy in any way—for example, by gossiping about a subject's performance. You do not have to fully inform subjects about what you are trying to learn or about the design of the test, but you cannot perpetrate significant deceptions. In university settings you may need to follow standard procedures for working with human subjects.

User testing is not formal research and doesn't have to meet the rigorous demands of the experimental method. Your goal is to gather enough information to feel confident about the design decisions you need to make. Very often four or five subjects are sufficient for a particular test, although some test designs require more subjects. It can be difficult to find appropriate subjects, and testing subjects, tabulating their responses, and analyzing the data are time-consuming tasks.

Designing Your Test

The design of your test depends largely on the kinds of information you are look-ing for. You can simply ask subjects to explore your prototype. In this way you can observe and record what parts attract them and hold their attention and what navigation problems they encounter. Also, you can ask various questions about their reactions to what they've looked at. Often, however, there is more value in structured kinds of tests in which you ask your subjects to perform specific tasks. For example, the designers of a city website might ask test subjects to find the lo-cation of Harold Blank Park or determine whether it is necessary to obtain a per-mit to hold a neighborhood block party.

As the subjects proceed through the tasks, you may wish to record data re-garding the frequency and types of errors and the time required to complete tasks. A different and often better approach (which invalidates data about perfor-mance time) is to ask your subjects to vocalize their thoughts as they work through the tasks. Their ongoing commentary provides very rich information, particularly about the difficulties they are having.

You can also learn a great deal by asking subjects to make predictions: "What kind of information do you think you will get if you follow this link?" "What do you think will happen if you click the Back button?"

If a subject gets stuck, you usually want to help the person get going again; however, if you've given a subject a lot of help, you need to be very cautious bas-ing design decisions on the performance of that subject. It is often useful to video-tape the test sessions, though you will need your subjects' permission.

If you test several subjects in a relatively short period of time, you may want to conduct a "focus group" meeting in which the subjects share their reactions with each other. Often subjects reveal more when they bounce their reactions off each other, and you can often get a meaningful consensus on various questions. "OK, how many people agree with Ivana that the background was too busy for you to read the text easily?" To a large degree the success of a focus group de-pends on the objectivity and skill of the focus group leader. In large, well-funded projects, professionals are often brought in to moderate focus groups.

Often clients or managers will ask you to write a report or give a presentation summarizing the tests you performed, your findings, your interpretations and ex-planations of these findings, and the design decisions (if any) you think should be made.

Tracing User Scenarios

Tracing user scenarios is not really user testing at all. But there are important sim-ilarities. At times, we can gain valuable design information by putting ourselves in the role of users and clicking through the prototype. In other words, once the prototype makes the design concrete, some unquestionably bad aspects of the de-sign can be readily identified if we simply trace the actions that a user would al-most inevitably take in a particular situation. For example, we might discover pages that require too much scrolling, that load too slowly, that contain too many links, and that contain links that do not clearly indicate their destinations.

Following Up on the Evaluation

The purpose of performing evaluations is to correct any design flaws before investing in the building phase of the project. Unfortunately, this does not always happen. Sometimes, designers or their managers persuade themselves that the design is "basically OK" in the face of strong evidence that it is not. In other instances, schedules simply do not permit re-designs—at least not until after the initial release of the website. If your project has been well planned, however, there should be time to assess the feedback from your evaluation tasks and incorporate necessary changes into the design you take into the building phase.

If you determine that your prototype is severely flawed, the scope of the re-design effort may be large enough that you need to re-visit the broad design decisions you made at the beginning of the design phase or even in the planning phase—this is the dotted arrow in Figure 3.2 extending from the Evaluation box back to planning. For example, your subjects may tell you forcefully that the structure of the hierarchy, from the home page on down, confuses them or that the theme of the website does not appeal to them. Bad news indeed! After you revise your plans (including the schedule), create a new design, and build a new prototype, you should perform another round of evaluation. How else will you know for sure that your new design has addressed the problems you uncovered and that it hasn't introduced new ones? Contemplating these potential problems should persuade you to follow a good development process with lots of evaluation built in from the beginning.

Design Reports

Here we discuss both task reports and the comprehensive design report.

Task Teams and Task Reports

During the design phase and in the planning and building phases as well, project teams often divide into various small groups to tackle particular parts of the project. We will call these groups "task teams." For example, two members of the Asthma Horizons design team might be assigned to the task team responsible for the animation showing the function of the lung. They will design this animation, and they may later build the animation. Another task team might focus on the monthly profile feature that is planned for the site. They will create guidelines for creating each month's profile. Another task team may take responsibility for user testing and other forms of evaluation. Very likely, one individual will take part in more than one team, especially because many teams will complete their tasks in a few weeks and disband.

These task teams are likely to report orally to the entire project team during meetings. Also, they should produce one or more reports that explain how they are progressing on their task. These reports should be incorporated into the project notebook, which should be available to everyone on the project. So, for instance, the task team working on the text of the "Causes and Symptoms" section will consult the project notebook because they need to know exactly what the lung animation is going to show. The report of the Monthly Profile Task Team is shown in Appendix C, "Reports."

The Comprehensive Design Report

Often, especially in the case of larger projects, a comprehensive design report is compiled toward the end of the design phase. This report updates the planning report and provides a more detailed account of the current state of the project, in particular the design. Like the planning report, the comprehensive design report helps the members of the project team maintain a common image of the website they are working on. Also, it will prove valuable to anyone who needs to understand the project. But the most important audience of this report consists of the managers or clients who must approve the design and the project as a whole before the building phase starts. Very possibly, these individuals will expect the report to be submitted in conjunction with a face-to-face meeting and presentation.

This report is drawn in large part from the project notebook. As you can see in Figure 3.8, this report resembles the planning report and has many of the same sections. Naturally, a key component of the report is the prototype, whether in the form of screen captures or just a URL. Equally important are the findings of the user tests and other evaluation tasks. The report should also include the most current representations of the structure of the website. A selection of older diagrams,

Design Report

Statement of Purpose
Audience Analysis
Website Theme and Style
Site Design
    Analysis of key design issues
    Examples from prototype
    Content list
    Node-link diagram
    Summary of user test results
Plans for Content Review and QA Testing
Schedule and Budget
Appendixes
    User test data
    Early design sketches

Figure 3.8. Possible section headings for a design report.

design sketches, and other documents that explain the evolution of the design may also be included, probably in an appendix.

The Building Phase

Building is the third and final phase of the Web development process. The word "building" refers to creating and completing all aspects of the website. Whatever hasn't been built for the prototype needs to be built now.

The building phase naturally varies enormously with the nature of the project. Building an online resumé requires much less content and a lot less coding than building a large commercial website. However much work is required, the key point regarding the building phase is that you want it to proceed in a steady, predictable manner.

As we noted, design and planning tasks will continue into the building phase. In particular, as you create graphics, write text, and create other content elements and as you lay out the pages that contain these content elements, you will be making a large number of design decisions. These decisions, however, should be extensions or more specific instances of more general design decisions you made and evaluated during the design phase.

Setting Up the Work Environment

Beginning with your prototype, you will start accumulating a large number of files: HTML files, graphics files, etc. You will accumulate far more once you've started your "Web page factory" in the building phase. To avoid complete chaos, you will need to work out a logical and efficient scheme for naming and storing your files and for naming and organizing the folders (directories) in which the files are contained.

Some teams maintain separate folders for various content types (a folder for HTML files, a folder for graphics files, etc.). Others create a folder for each part (or branch) of the website (a folder for Medications and Treatments, a folder for Northwest Focus, etc.). Still others use a combination of strategies—separate folders for graphics, audio, and video files and a folder for HTML files with subfolders for each branch of the website. It can be very disruptive to make changes in filenames or the organization of the folders. In fact, changing folder names may result in broken links between Web pages. So plan carefully before you start naming and saving files.

Unless you are working alone, you will need to establish policies for who is authorized to change various parts of the project and under what circumstances. The larger the team, the more important it is to devise and communicate these policies.

Most important, you need to back up your work frequently and store at least one of your back-ups off-site. Files become corrupted; hard drives crash; machines are vandalized or stolen; and other mishaps occur that will make you very thankful if you've backed up your files recently.

Developing, Revising, and Reviewing Content

Developing quality content is hard work. Even though you are carrying through design ideas that have been previously worked out, both text and graphic elements must be designed, created, carefully reviewed, and very likely revised at least once. Furthermore, even if you've created and updated a node-link diagram and other representations of website structure, more linking will probably be necessary. Only as paragraphs of text are actually written and added to pages will certain opportunities for useful links, especially secondary links, become apparent to the writer and to editors and reviewers.

One challenge in the content development process is achieving consistency among content elements. If there is more than one writer, the writing must be coordinated to prevent unwanted differences in level of technicality, level of detail, style, and so forth. Consistency must also be maintained for other content types. For example, if two people are creating graphs and illustrations, they must adopt the same overall approach. Consistency can be difficult to achieve even on a solo project.

To help achieve a high level of consistency, you should keep a record (often called a "project style sheet") of the team's decisions regarding consistency. So, for example, the Asthma Horizons style sheet might specify "non-smoker" rather than "nonsmoker" and asthma "episode" rather than "attack." Many organizations compile and distribute an organizational style guide, which records how the organization wishes to handle various issues. Finally, it is very wise to draw upon a comprehensive, widely used style manual such as the *Chicago Manual of Style, The Style Manual of the American Psychological Association,* or the *MLA Style Manual and Guide to Scholarly Publishing.*

Once the content is prepared, it should be subjected to a careful review. Table 3.1 describes the standard reviews for text and graphics.

Dynamic content (animation, video, and audio) goes through a similar process, but there are additional considerations. How clear is the sound? How smooth is the animation? How sharp is the video, and is it sufficiently free from visual flaws? Lapses in quality do not necessarily require obtaining new content; there are sophisticated editing tools that can improve the quality of audio and video sequences.

Coding Special Features

Often there are scripts, applets, and online computing functions built into a website. To help keep your project on schedule, you will usually want to make progress on these aspects of the website even before all the content is complete. For example, someone can begin to work out the details of implementing a calendar page before anyone knows the first month's calendar items. Similarly, you can code a text-entry form that collects user-supplied information and generates an automatic email response before all the content is in place. Regardless of the timing of the work, you will want to establish check points to ensure that the technical side of the project is on track.

Table 3.1 **Standard Reviews for Text and Graphics**

Review	Purpose	Reviewers
Editorial review for text elements	• Is the topic covered adequately? Are the information needs of the audience being met? • Is the theme of the website expressed? • Is the writing clear, fluent, and well organized? • Is the text properly divided by headings and subheadings? • Is the writing correct in regard to spelling, punctuation, usage, and grammar? • Do links clearly indicate their destinations?	Writers other than the author; editors
Editorial review for graphics	• Does the graphic accurately and meaningfully represent something in the physical world, convey a concept, or express quantitative relationships? • Is the level of detail appropriate for the intended purpose? (Watch especially for unnecessary detail and clutter.) • Does the styling of the graphic express the website's theme? • Is the styling of the graphic consistent with other graphics and visual content? • Is the graphic well positioned with adequate spacing?	Other graphic artists; editors
Accuracy review for text and graphics	• Is the content—both scientific and technical content and general content—accurate and fair-minded?	Subject matter experts (SMEs); editors
Policy and legal reviews for text and graphics	• Does the content represent the organization appropriately, adhere to legal requirements, and uphold ethical standards?	Managers, attorneys, etc.

Quality Assurance Testing

Websites are susceptible to a wide range of bugs and malfunctions. These include broken links, links that go to the wrong place, video and audio sequences that don't play properly, and scripts that do not run (sometimes generating error messages and sometimes just not producing the expected behavior). Also, there is the very considerable problem, discussed earlier, of browser compatibility: A project may run perfectly on one browser but not display properly on another or on a different version of the original browser.

You need to conduct a comprehensive set of quality assurance (QA) tests. Many tests need to be repeated more than once and some do not. A button may work one week but fail the next because the page to which the button linked was cut from the project. You are especially apt to find bugs and malfunctions if your website is moved from a development server to the server on which it will be launched. The specific tests you will need to conduct depend, of course, on your particular project. Table 3.2 lists some tests that are necessary for most projects.

Similarly, CD/DVD titles may work differently or not work at all on different computers. If you are developing a CD/DVD title, you will want to make a limited number of preliminary copies and test them extensively.

The Completion Report

Very often a completion report or perhaps just a cover letter or memo is prepared at the end of the project. This report is the formal presentation of the project to managers or clients. It will explain changes in design and parts of the project that may have been scaled back or left undone. It will specify or suggest future development plans.

Post-Release Evaluation

Once the website is released, you can get certain types of feedback that were previously impossible. Websites (and CD/DVD titles) are frequently reviewed in both newspapers and specialized periodicals. Web servers can collect (in server "logs") valuable information about site visitors, including the number of visitors, when they visit, the pages they visit, and how long they stay (Rosenstein 2000). In the case of e-commerce websites, there are revenue figures. You can also ask visitors to

Table 3.2 **List of Tests**

Links	Check that all links function correctly. There are programs that automate much of the link testing.
Code	Check that all scripts and code function properly. Create tests that check for basic functionality. (Does the system display a confirmation message when a user submits a form?) Test also for atypical situations. (What does the system do if a user types a name that will not fit in a text box?)
Platforms, browsers, and screen resolution	Check that the pages display properly and function correctly on all the platforms (PC, MAC, Unix) and versions of browsers you have targeted. Check that the design works with different screen resolutions (no horizontal scrolling).
Speed	Check that the pages and elements on pages load quickly at the Internet connection speeds you have designed for.
Accessibility	Check to ensure that your project meets the accessibility requirements you established. You can use the software tool, Bobby (www.w3.org/wai/), to check accessibility.

fill out feedback forms. The information you gather through post-release evaluation will be extremely valuable as you plan for the next update, refresh, or redesign of your website.

People and Their Roles

Now that we have seen the complete development process, we can look more closely at the people who do the work and the roles they perform. Because projects and the size of project teams differ greatly, we will describe a large number of relatively specific roles. Very often, however, one person performs several roles—"wears multiple hats." The smaller the team, the more hats team members are likely to wear. The roles we cover are summarized in Table 3.3.

Producer

The head person on a project is often called the producer. Producers have experience and expertise in staffing, scheduling, and budgeting. They know how to manage the members of the project team and how to solve personnel problems. They know how to work with people outside the project team, in particular, clients or other people who authorize and approve the work. Often, producers write progress reports and give presentations to these people. All the skills mentioned thus far can be summed up in the phrase "project management."

In addition to project management skills, producers need a broad background in Web development, both design and implementation. The producer doesn't need to be an expert HTML coder, a talented artist, a polished writer, or have any other specific area of expertise. But the producer does need to create a

---

Table 3.3 **Roles in a Web Development Project**

Producer
Marketer
Information designer (or information architect)
Core content creators: Writers, artists, photographers, animators,
    videographers, and audio specialists
Graphic designer
Editor
Interface designer
Information retrieval specialist
Usability specialist
Instructional designer
Quality assurance specialist
HTML coder, programmer, documentation specialist, and tech
    support technician

---

vision of the final website, make sure this vision is attainable, communicate the vision to others, devise a set of appropriate and coherent project objectives, and make sure they are met. Usually, the people who become producers have extensive experience in the field of Web design and other media. Very often, they are experts in several areas of Web development.

Marketer

In the case of corporate websites intended for promotion or commerce, there is likely to be at least one marketing specialist involved. The marketing specialist contributes to the design—often from the beginning of the project. Marketers research the audience, usually with a special interest in their behavior as consumers. Marketers also help strategize the business model. For example, if the marketer's company operates a website featuring research reports for investors, the marketer will determine whether it is best to sell yearly subscriptions or let people purchase individual reports.

Marketers use various techniques to increase the number of visitors to a website. For example, they will arrange deals, such as reciprocal linking with another (non-competing) website and set up other kinds of partnerships. They are also the people who make sure that the site's URL is included in the organization's non-Internet advertising. In the case of CD/DVD titles, marketers figure out how to advertise, distribute, and sell the product, much like book publishers market and sell books.

Information Designer (or Information Architect)

The information designer, also referred to as an "information architect," takes broad responsibility for the design of the website. The information designer will work closely with the producer and marketer on strategy and goals, which includes defining the theme. Also, the information designer takes primary responsibility for the design of the navigational interface.

Information designers come from numerous fields, notably user interface design, graphic design, and professional and technical communication. The job, however, requires a complete understanding of Web design and development, including Web technologies. The job also requires creative vision and the ability to work well in teams. Information designers must also be willing to quickly become familiar with the subject area (e.g., asthma) of the websites they work on.

Core Content Creators

Writers, artists, photographers, animators, videographers, and audio specialists create the core content elements. Core content creators must, of course, be highly skilled in the medium in which they specialize, but they must also have a broad understanding of Web design. Core content creators must fully understand the goals of the project for their content to fit the overall design. For example, both the writer and the videographer must express the same theme, even though they are working in different media. The writer's choice of words and syntax and the videographer's decisions regarding camera angle, lighting, and lens focus will both reflect their understanding of the theme.

Graphic Designer

Graphic design encompasses a broad range of decisions about the visual appearance of a website. Designing page layouts, devising color schemes, and choosing fonts are all tasks associated with graphic design. The graphic designer makes sure that all the pieces of the visual design fit together. If a graphic or photograph needs to be modified in some way, graphic designers will do this. Often graphics designers choose pre-existing photographs and drawings from an organization's library of corporate art or from a stock media collection. Finally, graphic designers often serve as graphic artists and create graphics and simple (GIF) animations.

Although there are many self-trained graphic designers, the ideal background includes a bachelor's or master's degree in graphic design. Graphic designers now work primarily on the computer, and so must be highly proficient with an illustration software application such as Corel Draw or Adobe Illustrator and an image editing package such as Adobe Photoshop or JASC's Paint Shop Pro.

Editor

Editors improve the quality of text. They look for specific problems in grammar, punctuation, spelling, usage, and consistency, but they also consider the overall effectiveness of text elements. Also, just as in the world of print, editors do not restrict themselves to text. Editors will flag a graphic that is too small, too dark, or doesn't capture the subject appropriately. They will note problems in a video or audio sequence. Often editors check for broken links and other coding errors.

Interface Designer

Interface designers specialize in designing systems of all kinds so that they are easy to understand and use. Interface design is often taught at universities in departments of psychology, computer science, industrial engineering, and technical communication.

Interface designers are well prepared to design the navigational interface and may serve as a project's information designer. Interface designers are especially important in websites such as online stores and banks in which there are important online computing functions.

Information Retrieval Specialist

Information scientists study how people search for information. Consequently, they are the real experts in choosing and implementing the website's Search feature and ensuring that the site's content is as searchable as possible.

Because it is usually crucial for a website to draw as many visitors as possible, information retrieval specialists take steps to get their websites noticed by the various Web-wide search engines.

Usability Specialist

Usability specialists determine how successful users will be in working with a website. Usability specialists design and perform studies, then analyze, interpret, and present their findings. Usability specialists have a background in such fields as user interface design, psychology, and technical communication.

Instructional Designer

An instructional designer focuses on designing the content so that it is easy to learn and remember. Not surprisingly, instructional designers are usually brought into projects for which education and learning are primary objectives. This includes projects intended for corporate training, those that combine entertainment and education, and projects specifically intended for use in schools. Instructional designers should have backgrounds in instructional design, cognitive psychology, or a similar field. Because many information designers have instructional design backgrounds, they can often assume this role.

Quality Assurance Specialist

Quality assurance specialists make sure the website has been correctly implemented. They devise systematic and comprehensive tests that will uncover coding errors and similar problems. QA specialists often automate tests using special tools that have the same effect as someone manually clicking a button or entering data in a form. QA specialists usually have a background in computer programming or software engineering.

HTML Coder, Programmer, Documentation Specialist, and Tech Support Technician

While writers and other team members can usually code HTML or work with authoring tools that create HTML code, there are coding specialists and programmers who usually handle the more complex aspects of implementing a website. This is especially true in the case of database-driven websites.

Some websites, especially those with extensive online computing functions, will require a significant amount of on-screen help. This documentation should be created by a documentation specialist, and so there should either be a documentation specialist on the development team or one should be called in to assist with this aspect of the project.

With either a website or a CD/DVD title, it is possible that users will encounter technical problems. This may require a tech support person to answer telephone, email, and message board queries and to participate in real-time dialogs with users. Often tech support is handled by a website's webmaster.

Profile: Points West Kayak Tours

Let's sit in on another work session with Annie and Peter as they tackle the design of their website.

Advancing the Content List and Working Out the Structure

Annie has her laptop out and, looking closely at the content list, she begins to work out a tentative hierarchy using her word processor's outline feature. The first-draft outline is shown in Figure 3.9. The first, second, and third levels of the outline (formatted in boldface) all represent pages. Annie also adds various notes under the headings using body text.[1]

Peter and Annie then examine the outline closely and make many changes. In particular, as you can see in Figure 3.10, they simplify the first-draft outline, consolidating several branches. For example, they realize that the branch Kamechak Bay and Surrounding Areas overlaps the branch Scenery, Wildlife, and Local History, and so they remove the Kamechak Bay page from the outline. Also, they decide that they do not need the four third-level pages Experience, Fitness, Age, and Safety. The content of these pages will fit easily on the single parent page Experience, Fitness, Age, and Safety—which, in response to a friend's comment, is given a shorter and more positive name, No Experience Necessary! When they have finished with the outline, they have planned out a website consisting of 10 pages.

Peter draws a node-link diagram, shown in Figure 3.11, that corresponds to the revised outline. Note that the node-link diagram shows what the outline did not: links between branches of the hierarchy.

Drawing Design Sketches and Creating Pages

Soon Peter begins sketching the home page for their website (see Figure 3.12). The sketch is not final; Peter will improve upon the design considerably before it goes public.

The photos on the home page echo the theme of the website. One shows a group of kayakers paddling near a rocky island with glacier-covered mountains visible in the background against a brilliant blue sky. The other photograph shows a group of kayakers eating lunch on a sandy beach. Not only is the subject matter appropriate, but the rich greens and blues are vibrant and cheerful and suggest the enjoyment of nature. Annie and Peter rejected some moody, fog-enshrouded photos, even though they personally like them.

Annie and Peter then create design sketches for the remaining 9 Web pages. Because this is a small, straightforward website and because much of the content has been "tested" in the form of their brochure, these design sketches will serve as a paper prototype for evaluation purposes.

Evaluation

As a first step in evaluating their website, Annie and Peter review their design sketches against a set of design guidelines they find in a book. What they read prompts a discussion.

---

[1]Here is a useful trick that Annie and Peter have figured out. It seems logical to format the outline entry for the home page as a Heading 1 and to format the outline entries for second-level pages as Heading 2 (and so on). However, especially if your outline will extend to three or more levels, it's best not to "waste" a level with the home page entry. Use Heading 1 for your second-level entries as well as for the home page entry and simply increase the font size of the home page entry so that it is distinguishable from the second-level entries. Then, use Heading 2 for your third-level entries, and so forth.

✢ **Points West Kayak Tours**
- Include welcome paragraph with quick information for busy folks.

✢ **Where we go**
- Describe full- and half-day trips.
  - ✢ *Special trips*
    - Mention charters, group rentals.

▢ **Kamechak Bay and surrounding areas**

✢ **Schedule, pricing, reservations**
- Include cancellation policy. Mention that we run trips in light rain.

✢ **What to bring**
- Include lunches and snacks as items we provide.

✢ **Experience, fitness, age, and safety**
- General stuff about experience, fitness, age, and safety.
  - ✢ *Experience*
    - No experience necessary at all.
  - ✢ *Fitness*
    - Expect a reasonable level of health and fitness— especially for full-day trips. But pacing is slow, with breaks.
  - ✢ *Age*
    - Trips suitable for seniors. Trips, especially full-day trips, are not suitable for children.
  - ✢ *Safety*
    - Usual stuff

✢ **Homer area weather**
- Mention that summer weather is generally clear and sunny.
- Add external link for local weather websites.

▢ **Lunches and snacks**

✢ **Finding us**
- Map of Homer. Map of Homer Spit.

✢ **Who we are. What we do**
- Brief bio sketches of Annie, Peter, and Kim.

✢ **Scenery, wildlife, and local history**
- Describe scenery, wildlife, and local history.
  - ▢ *Homer area bird list*

✢ **What to do in Homer**
- External links (maybe just to Chamber of Commerce page).

Figure 3.9. Annie and Peter's first-draft outline.

⟡ **Points West Kayak Tours**
   ▫ Include welcome paragraph with quick information for busy folks.

⟡ **Where we go**
   ▫ Describe full- and half-day trips.
      ⟡ *Special trips*
         ▫ Mention charters, group rentals.

⟡ **What to bring**
   ▫ Mention that we provide lunches and snacks.

⟡ **No experience necessary!**
   ▫ Cover fitness and safety here.

⟡ **Making reservations**
   ▫ Include cancellation policy. Mention that we run trips in light rain.
   ▫ Provide external links to Chamber of Commerce, Bed and Breakfast Association, restaurant listings, weather information, etc.

⟡ **Finding us**
   ▫ Map of Homer. Map of Homer Spit.

⟡ **Local scenery, wildlife, and a bit of history**
   ▫ Describe scenery, wildlife, and local history.
      ▫ *Homer area bird list*

⟡ **Who we are**
   ▫ Brief bio sketches of Annie, Peter, and Kim.

Figure 3.10. Annie and Peter's revised outline.

Peter: Listen to this:

Make sure none of your pages scroll. Some people don't know how to scroll, some people know how but won't notice that the page scrolls, and some people will refuse to scroll. One way or another, no one will ever see what's below the scroll line.

Annie: I don't buy it, Peter. I scroll. Not always, but when I'm interested.

Peter: Yes, I'm not sure we should follow every piece of advice we come across.

Next Annie reviews the design sketches trying to imagine how their clients might respond to the content and overall design. Peter makes a few changes and then asks for feedback on the revised design sketches from some friends, including a professional graphic designer. Peter asks his evaluators to be candid about anything they don't like.

Building

Because Annie and Peter only used design sketches rather than sample pages as their prototype, they need to do a lot of writing and layout work as they build. They work carefully, reviewing and editing each other's work. Once the pages are built, they test their links and experiment with viewing the site at different screen resolutions. Finally, Annie moves the files to the server of their ISP (Internet Service

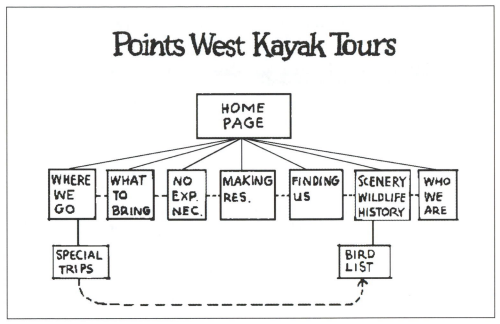

Figure 3.11. Peter's node-link diagram that corresponds to the revised outline.

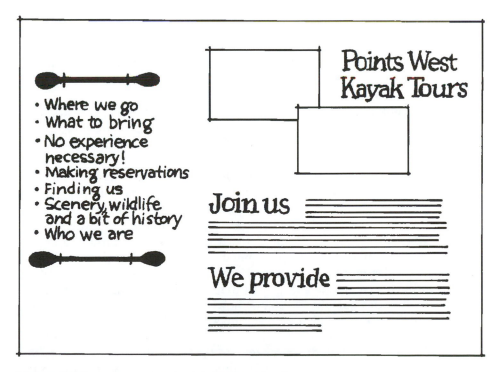

Figure 3.12. A design sketch of the Points West home page.

Provider), and they've "gone live." They add the URL to their magazine advertising and business cards. The next time they reprint their brochure, it will feature the URL.

A website is never really finished, and Annie and Peter continue soliciting feedback and thinking about enhancing the site. When they get their first emails asking for trip information, Annie's response includes a few questions asking these people about their use of the Points West website.

Summary

Chapter 2 covered the first phase of Web development: planning. This chapter focuses on the design and building phases and completes our discussion of the development process.

1. The progression from planning to design to building is not a simple straight line. There is significant blending among the phases.
2. In the design phase you draw upon the work you did in the planning phase. You must now gain a much fuller understanding of (1) the eventual content of the website, (2) how the pages fit together into a well-organized structure, and (3) what the eventual pages will look like.
3. You need to review, expand, and refine your content list, transforming it into a list of Web pages. You need to think about your users and their information needs in order to create an understandable, easy-to-navigate structure.
4. Even in small projects it is very desirable to represent the structure using at least one of the following: a node-link diagram, a set of note cards, and an outline. Each has its own advantages and drawbacks.
5. Node-link diagrams can be sketched or created by a software application. Although flexible and intuitive, they take effort to prepare and update. If the website is really large, it may be difficult or impossible to do more than represent a portion of the website.
6. Note cards take the form of 3 x 5 index cards or something similar. Cards, representing Web pages, are laid out on a table or taped or pinned to a wall. Lines representing links can be drawn among the cards. Cards can be easily added, removed, or changed, and you can ask potential users to help you sort the cards into a meaningful hierarchy. It is difficult to represent a large website with cards and to retain a permanent record of the design work.
7. The entries of a word processor's outline feature can represent Web pages. Outlines accommodate large hierarchies and let you add, delete, change, and move entries quickly. Outliners, however, can only represent the basic hierarchical structure. Other kinds of links cannot be shown.
8. Designing the structure of a website requires both top-down and bottom-up thinking. Node-link diagrams tend to favor top-down design, note cards tend to favor bottom-up design, and outliners favor top-down or bottom-up design depending on how they are used.

9. Once you have worked out the structure of your website, you can begin to create design sketches and sample pages. In many ways this is the climax of the creative process. Certain implementation choices should be made at this point such as deciding on the screen resolutions you will design for.

10. Grid systems are sets of horizontal and vertical lines that enable designers to maintain consistency by specifying the permissible variations in page layout. A template is a computer file that incorporates grid lines and various other recurring design elements and so serves as a starting point for designing and building Web pages.

11. As you design, think ahead to the long-term future of the website. When fundamental changes are likely, avoid design ideas that cannot readily accommodate such changes. When there will be regular updating of content, carefully plan how this will be done. Don't, however, commit the site owners to more updating than they are prepared for. Often it is important to retain older content in an archive.

12. Websites that are continually updated usually employ special content-management software and a semi-automatic database-driven development process. Each day's content is "poured" into a stable template following sophisticated rules for the placement of text and graphics.

13. Once you are confident in the design of your sketches and sample pages, you can build a prototype. This is a test version of the website, and it is the basis for the most extensive evaluation tasks you will perform.

14. Perform evaluations early and often. The many useful forms of evaluation include soliciting opinions from knowledgeable peers and experts and from potential users. You can also check your design against well-established guidelines and successful, well-respected websites. User testing provides the most revealing and reliable information.

15. Recruit user test subjects who are as similar as possible to the eventual users of the website. Make your subjects comfortable and make clear that it is the design that is being tested. Observe ethical standards in your testing. Keep in mind that user testing is not formal research; the goal is simply to gather enough information to make design decisions with confidence.

16. Often individual task teams prepare brief reports on a particular part of the project to which they have been assigned. In the case of larger projects, a comprehensive design report is often compiled toward the end of the design phase. Very often a completion report is prepared at the end of the project. Oral presentations may also be necessary.

17. Building is the third and final phase of the Web development process. Although the building phase varies enormously with the nature of the project, the key idea regarding the building phase is that you want it to proceed in a steady, predictable manner.

18. In the building phase content (often large amounts of content) must be designed, prepared, carefully reviewed, and very likely revised at least once for quality and consistency. Get an early start coding scripts, applets, and online computing functions. Bugs, malfunctions, and compatibility problems can only be caught by systematic and repeated quality assurance testing.

19. In a Web development effort, team members play many roles: (1) producer, (2) marketer, (3) information designer (information architect), (4) core content creators, (5) graphic designer, (6) editor, (7) interface designer, (8) information retrieval specialist, (9) usability specialist, (10) instructional designer, (11) quality assurance specialist, and (12) HTML coder, programmer, documentation specialist, and tech support technician. Websites can be created with a small, versatile team or may involve a large group of people each of whom undertakes just one or two roles.

References

Arbortext. www.arbortext.com

Dumas, Joseph S., and Janice Redish. 1993. *A Practical Guide to Usability Testing.* Norwood, NJ: Ablex Publishing.

Hablador. www.hablador.com

IBM Ease of Use Guidelines. www-3.ibm.com/ibm/easy/eou_ext.nsf/publish/561

Metatorial Services, Inc. www.metatorial.com

Microsoft Web Design Guidelines: Improving Web Site Usability and Appeal, Guidelines compiled by MSN Usability Research (Kevin Keeker). 1997. http://msdn.microsoft.com/workshop/management/planning/improvingsiteusa.asp

Rosenstein, Mark. 2000. What is actually taking place on Web sites: E-commerce lessons from Web server logs. *Proceedings of the 2nd ACM Conference on Electronic Commerce* 38–43. www.apparent-wind.com/mbr/papers/ec2000.pdf

Rubin, Jeffrey. 1994. *Handbook of Usability Testing: How to Plan, Design, and Conduct Effective Tests.* New York: Wiley.

Technical Communication Special Issue. 2000. Heuristics for Web communication. *Technical Communication* 47.3: 301–410.

Discussion and Application

Items for Discussion

1. The model of the development process shown in this chapter borrows from two traditions: software engineering and print publishing. Putting aside the obvious differences between paper and the Web, compare the development process for a website with the development process for a print publication. What similarities do you see between the two? What are the differences? What similarities and differences can you find between Web development and the development of software applications?

2. A well-known adage in the world of engineering is that your biggest mistakes are made on the first day. Discuss this adage in the context of Web design.

3. When the first units of the Saturn automobile rolled off the assembly line, the inside of the glove compartment door had round recessed areas intended to serve as cup holders. The door, however, was hinged so that it would not lie flat enough to support a cup. How might such an engineering design glitch occur? What would be an analogous problem in a Web development project?

4. Imagine that you are working for a company that publishes a monthly employee newsletter. Your manager has decided to publish the newsletter both in the traditional print format and on the company's intranet. What are the main design issues that you will need to deal with in preparing the online version? Should the online version look like the print version or have its own look?

5. Identify a website that exhibits good page design and, in particular, an appropriate degree of consistency among the pages. Try to reconstruct the grid system that was used by the designers. How much and what kinds of variation did the designers allow themselves? Which aspects of the page design were especially successful? Are there flaws?

6. The figure below shows the first design sketch for the home page of Community Composting, a non-profit organization that promotes composting as a sound environmental practice. The theme for the website is this: "Composting is easy to do, it benefits the environment, and you will have a supply of rich soil for your garden and lawn." Do you think the design team is making a good start on the design of the home page? What do you like or dislike?

Figure 3.13. An early design sketch for the Community Composting home page.

7. Examine two sets of Web design guidelines such as those cited in this chapter. How do they differ? Which do you find most useful?
8. Interview a Web designer to learn what strategies he or she uses in planning, designing, and evaluating projects. Try to find out how planning and design differ from one project to the next and what factors cause these differences.

Application to Your Project

1. The three ways of representing the structure of a website are a node-link diagram, a set of note cards, and an outline created with the outline feature of a word processing program. Which of these representations will you employ in designing your website?
2. If you are working on a team project, how will you assign the project roles to the team members?
3. What kinds of evolution (if any) do you foresee for your website? Are you designing your website to accommodate the changes you envision?
4. If you are building your website on a server that will not permanently host your site, have you considered the change-over? What issues and problems do you foresee, and what steps can you take to minimize the potential problems?
5. Make a plan for user testing your prototype. Decide whether it is feasible to conduct a focus group in conjunction with the testing.
6. Create a quality assurance test plan for your project. Identify any tools you will use in the testing process.

4

Using Content Types Effectively

Introduction

Designers of print documents work exclusively with static content: text and graphics. Filmmakers work primarily with dynamic content: video, animation, and sound. Web designers face a greater challenge: They work with all of these content types, and they work in an interactive environment.

This chapter explains how to employ the five content types in Web and CD/DVD design. It will prepare you to make decisions such as these:

- Should I explain a concept entirely with text, or should I incorporate graphics into the explanation? Should the graphic be a photograph or a drawing?
- What kind of animation will best suit my needs?
- Should I add background music?
- Should my video sequence employ an on-screen or a voice-over narrator?

To make these kinds of decisions, you need to consider the information needs and preferences of your audience.

You also need to consider implementation issues and how various content types will fit (or not fit) into the overall development process that you learned about in Chapters 2 and 3. For example, do you have the technical skills, time, and budget to add a video sequence to your website? Will your users be able to display this video without undue delays? Often, you cannot implement everything you really want to. Note that website implementation is beyond the scope of this book, and so this chapter offers just the briefest introduction to the implementation issues surrounding each content type. Useful resources on implementation are listed in the appropriate sections below and in Appendix D, "Implementation Resources."

Text

Discourse means communicating through language—both text and speech. Most complex ideas cannot be expressed without discourse. For example, no purely pictorial form of communication (whether static or dynamic) can explain when to prefer one asthma drug over another or the reasons behind the formation of NATO (the North Atlantic Treaty Organization) after World War II.

In the print media, of course, only text discourse is possible. On the Web, however, a designer can choose between text and audio discourse. Text proves to be far more prevalent; in fact, text along with static graphics predominates on the vast majority of websites. There are several reasons for favoring text over audio discourse:

1. *Text is instant and scannable.* We see text the moment a Web page displays. Also, we can scan text for the specific information we are interested in—at least if the text has been formatted for easy scanning. In contrast, there is no easy way to access just a portion of an audio sequence or to quickly find out if the desired information is present.
2. *Text can be readily studied.* We can pause over and study text and compare portions of a text (or different texts if they are juxtaposed). In contrast, we can re-play and pause an audio clip, but we can never hold audio still in order to examine it. The ability to scan and study text is essential for a vast number of tasks.
3. *You can place links on text.* We can easily add links to text. No one can place a link directly on a sound.
4. *Text is easy to employ.* Educated people can write, and most use a word processor with some facility. Once written, Web text can be modified quickly and easily. Text displays quickly and reliably even for users with slow Internet connections. In contrast, there are technological barriers to recording audio, modifications are difficult or impossible, and audio may cause difficulties for some Web users.

Audio discourse offers different benefits:

1. *Audio offers the expressiveness of the human voice.* Punctuation, boldface and italics, fonts, and so forth do not begin to approach the remarkable expressiveness of the human voice. Audio (especially in conjunction with video or animation) is ideal for making a personal statement.
2. *Audio, at times, is preferred over text.* When the subject matter is not difficult, listening is often less taxing than reading. Also, listening leaves the eyes free to look at a graphic or some other visual element.

Using Text Effectively on the Web

To write successfully for the Web, writers need to understand the differences between the Web and print media. These issues are fully covered in Chapter 10,

"Writing." Here we focus on a few key issues. Most important: Avoid a long, unbroken wall of extended text, especially on the home page.

Very often Web users have only a casual interest in a website when they arrive at the home page for the first time. Limiting the amount of text, adding blank space, making key points scannable, and creating an attractive format will engage users. Furthermore, limiting the amount of text minimizes the need for scrolling, which is also especially desirable on the home page. Just how big is the difference between a wall of text and sparser page design? Compare the pages in Figure 4.1.

You certainly can present extended text on a website and allow pages to scroll. Extended text will be read if readers find it important. But even extended Web text should be formatted in a functional and attractive manner.

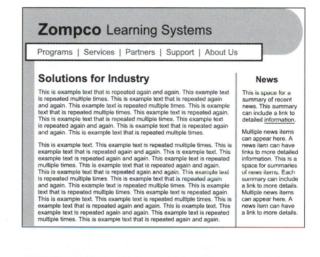

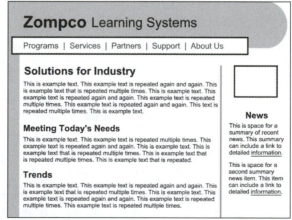

Figure 4.1. A home page with too much text and a more appealing home page with sparser text.

Layering

Layering is a valuable technique that makes it possible to limit the amount of text on a page. Layering consists of initially presenting users with relatively brief information and letting them access another layer of more detailed information if they want it. We often use this technique in print—for example, when we include one paragraph about legal issues in the body of a report along with a cross reference to an entire appendix about these issues. Because Web pages are linked, layering is especially effective on the Web, not only for text but for other content types.

Let's consider resumés on the Web. In the world of print, job seekers provide different amounts of information in their resumés. Indeed, there is much disagreement about how much information to include and whether a resumé should be more than a single page. On the Web, this problem can be eliminated: You can present brief information at the top level—much like a one-page print resumé—and then build links to much more complete information that the potential employer can choose to read. For example, under the heading "Professional Experience," you might describe each of your work experiences in a sentence or two and then provide a link to a more complete explanation. (You might also provide a link to a version of your resumé that is designed to be printed.)

Style

Style is a general term for a wide range of specific decisions that focus and shape content and thereby help to express the theme. Each content type has attributes that can be controlled to produce a particular style. Writers control style through their choice of words and sentence structure. For example, the following passage employs action verbs and a direct sentence structure (subject + verb + direct object) to evoke a mood of drama and excitement:

> As the Monterrey fans held their breaths, Mendoza took aim and blasted a desperate shot from 25 meters out. But the Nuevo Leon keeper leapt high and lifted the ball over the crossbar.

With little change in content however, this passage can be shifted into a less direct, more noun-oriented style, resulting in a more subdued, even mournful mood:

> Mendoza's desperate blast from 25 meters out did nothing for Monterrey as the Nuevo Leon keeper leapt high to lift the ball over the crossbar.

Similarly, while the underlying ideas are similar, there are great differences in style and mood between these two passages promoting pianos by Steinway & Sons, a very traditional, prestigious, and expensive brand:

> For real quality, the top of the line, you want a Steinway piano. Yes, they cost more. But a Steinway is worth the difference. Don't settle for less than the very best!

A Steinway piano is a fine investment that grows in value through the years. Furthermore, a Steinway is a treasured possession that is handed down with pride from one generation to the next.

For this product, the excited, "hard-sell" approach of the first passage is far less appropriate than the more dignified style of the second passage.

We all write in different styles, much as we instinctively speak differently on different occasions. Skillful writers, however, have a sure control of vocabulary and syntax and can succeed in a wide range of styles. Similarly, skillful graphic designers, videographers, animators, and sound recording specialists can control the stylistic attributes of the content type they work with.

Graphics

The graphic image is the oldest content type in human culture. As far back as 30,000 years ago, long before writing, our early ancestors drew figures of animals on cave walls. The basic purpose of a graphic is to show something's appearance or to represent abstract relationships concretely. To convey the appearance of a llama to someone unfamiliar with llamas, you will do much better with a graphic than with text. What about abstract relationships? We use organizational charts to show the management structure of an organization, a flow chart to represent a process, and a graph to show the relationships among variables. For an excellent guide to using graphics in print and online documents, see Charles Kostelnick and David Roberts (1998).

If you want to explain not just the appearance of a llama but the typical personality traits of llamas, the personality quirks of your pet llama, or how much you loved the llama you grew up with, you will need to supplement graphics with discourse, very likely text. Text with graphics is the single most flexible and most broadly useful combination of content types.

Photographs vs. Drawings

Graphics take the form of photographs and drawings. Photographs are captured images. They start with a technology that captures the light reflected off an actual object. Drawings start with a human being turning a mental image of something into lines and shapes rendered on canvas, paper, or the computer screen. In general, photographs give us a close approximation of the true appearance of something at a particular moment in time. That is, a photograph is likely to provide a lot of detail—including shadows and scratches and incidental objects you don't want in the picture.

Drawings are less faithful to actual appearances; they give the artist (at least a skilled artist) more control over the content. For example, an artist may choose to employ a line drawing to eliminate unnecessary detail and focus the user's attention on the essential information. If the goal is to show a piston in a cylinder, there is no need for anything but outlines of the metal parts and just enough shadowing to suggest depth. A drawing can also show various views of an object—such as cutaway views—that we rarely encounter in the physical world.

In the digital era the distinction between a photograph and a drawing is not crisp. A photograph can be captured digitally (or scanned) and then altered enormously with an image editing software package such as Photoshop or Paint Shop Pro.

Integration of Graphics with Text

An important consideration in the planning of a graphic is how closely the graphic will be integrated with text. Tight integration means that the specific elements of the graphic are referred to in the text. For example, Mad River, a manufacturer of canoes, provides an online product catalog in which the text description of each canoe is illustrated with a top-view and side-view photograph. Sharply focused and set against a white background, these diagram-like photographs are intended to clearly reveal the dimensions, contours, and product features explained in the accompanying paragraph. On the other hand, the product overview page for Mad River's line of whitewater canoes includes an action photograph of a paddler in heavy rapids. This photograph is meant to establish a mood, and it shows few details. It is loosely integrated with the accompanying text that talks about Mad River's heritage in whitewater competition.

Style

Artists, graphic designers, and photographers express visual styles through choice of color, shape, line (thick, thin, soft, etc.), and many other stylistic attributes. Some visual styles derive from and are named for particular historical periods, artistic movements, and cultures. For example, the Bauhaus movement of the mid-twentieth century gave us an unadorned, industrially inspired visual style that remains influential today. Other styles are not tied to history or culture, but are designed to express and evoke moods. The connection between style and mood is looser and less predictable than the connection to history and culture, but we all have some notion of what a person means by a graphic that is dark and somber, bright and cheerful, etc. Often styles are difficult to articulate in words, and even expert designers will make conflicting judgments regarding style. Still, there is always a style, even if it is confused, contradictory, or so familiar and routine that we barely notice it.

Backgrounds

From a designer's standpoint, the category of graphics also includes the backgrounds of Web pages. A background is the visual environment for other, more prominent content elements such as blocks of text, graphics, and interface elements such as buttons (which themselves consist of text and graphics). Backgrounds can be solid colors, abstract patterns, gradients (a color that gradually changes its tint), or something else. Backgrounds are a major factor in establishing the overall style of a website. A general design principle is that backgrounds should not distract from the foreground content elements.

Graphics as Links

Web graphics can be link origins. The most obvious examples are buttons. Any kind of graphic, however, can be "hot," and there are many uses for hot graphics. For example, an online art gallery or museum display can show relatively small (thumbnail) photographs of the paintings. By clicking a thumbnail, the user can display a larger photograph of the painting. Note that this is a form of layering.

You can also invisibly divide a single graphic into multiple hot areas (or make one area of a graphic hot). This is called an "image map." So, for example, in the image map graphic of the State of Oregon, shown in Figure 4.2, users can click any region of the state to display a list of links for tourist information about that region.

Surrogate Travel

Surrogate travel is a technique in which designers try to simulate the experience of navigating through physical space. In one form of surrogate travel, users click their way through a group of carefully coordinated photographs. The designer may establish a single path through the physical space or may allow users to choose a route. The Aspen Movie Map, described in Chapter 1, "Understanding the Web," is the earliest instance of surrogate travel in hypermedia.

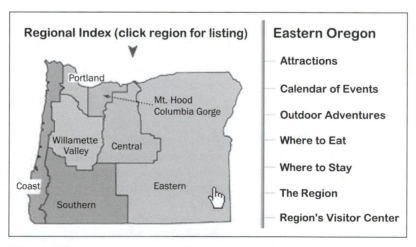

Figure 4.2. An image map graphic in which each region of Oregon is a separate "hot" area. (www.traveloregon.com/sitemap.cfm)

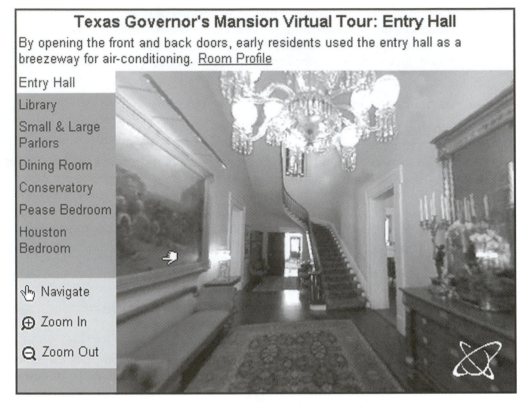

Figure 4.3. A panoramic IPIX graphic that invites users to explore a physical environment. (www.ipix.com/gallery/index.html)

Another kind of surrogate travel, shown in Figure 4.3, is achieved using technologies such as QuickTime VR and IPIX. Multiple graphics are digitally "stitched together" into a panoramic graphic that the user can explore with the mouse. By clicking and dragging within the graphic, the user can digitally "pan" in any direction or zoom in for a close-up. The persuasiveness of the illusion approaches virtual reality.

Implementation Issues

A significant issue is the speed at which graphics will display on the user's computer—especially users with less capable computers and slow connections to the Internet. The larger the file size of the graphic, the slower it will display. The more graphics, the longer the user must wait before the complete page can be viewed. There are many techniques for controlling the file size of a graphic, in particular limiting the dimensions and visual complexity of the graphic and choosing the optimum file format.

Many authorities recommend keeping each Web page below 40 or even 30 KB (Nielsen 2000). A 30 KB page will require about ten seconds to fully display for users with a 28.8 Kbps Internet connection. Because even simple graphics routinely require 5 KB, it's easy to see how total page size can grow quickly. When designing for an environment in which all users have fast Internet connections (often the case with corporate intranets), designers can allow the file size of pages to become larger. For more information on these issues, see Lynda Weinman (1999). There are similar though more severe file size considerations for animation, video, and audio files.

Animation

Animation is complex. There is all the complexity of drawn graphics, plus motion. Animation is suited for many uses; the most important are discussed below and summarized in Table 4.1.

One use of animation is simply to draw the user's eye. If a corporate logo (or almost anything else) is moving or rotating, people will be more apt to notice it. Most often, this use of animation is merely an annoying gimmick, but at times such animations can be used meaningfully. For example, a flashing arrow might be used to draw the user's attention to a particularly important location on a map. Because our world is a world of motion, another use of animation is to add realism to a Web page. An animated flag waving in the breeze is more realistic than a static graphic.

Animation is very valuable for explaining processes and concepts, especially concepts that involve motion. Either a brief or an extended animation showing the moving parts of an internal combustion engine or the division of cells is far better than several static graphics. Animation is often better than video (just as drawings may be better than photographs), because the animator has more control over what the user sees. For example, shadows, reflections, and irrelevant detail are excluded from animations.

Another useful kind of animation is an animated gallery of brief news items or similar content elements that appear successively in the same physical space.

Table 4.1 **Uses of Animation**

Uses of Animation	Example
Drawing the eye	A rotating corporate logo; a blinking arrow
Adding realism	A flag waving in the breeze
Explaining a process or concept	An animation of the moving parts of an internal combustion engine
Animated galleries	Displaying a succession of messages, such as news items, in the same space
Splash animations	An extended animated sequence that runs when a website first opens

Usually, the user can click each item to display more detailed information. Animated galleries draw the eye and conserve screen real estate. In a sense, time is being turned into space.

Some websites open with an extended and often very elaborate "splash" animation. The goal, which is not always achieved, is to establish the theme of the website in a vivid and compelling manner. Users may see large geometric shapes moving across the screen and turning into other shapes. Letters and words fly around and fall into place. There may be audio and cinematic transitions (such as wipes and fades). Buttons and other hotspots appear so that the user can stop the animation and access the rest of the website.

User control is a key issue regarding both animation and other types of dynamic (time-based) content. Designers must decide whether a dynamic content element will start automatically ("system initiated") or be started by the user ("user initiated"). Certainly the user should be able to immediately stop any extended animation, audio, or video sequence. For the maximum amount of user control, dynamic content is made to run in a "player," a special kind of window with controls for starting, stopping, pausing, and re-starting the action and changing the volume of the audio. The Web players are these: Apple's QuickTime Player, Microsoft's Windows Media Player, and RealNetworks RealPlayer.

Stylistic Choices in Animation

Designers should recognize that animation offers an extremely broad range of stylistic possibilities. Almost all the stylistic possibilities of drawn and painted graphics are possible, and then there are all the extra stylistic choices that derive from motion. Animations can present a scene in a flat, two-dimensional manner, or they can convey depth. Animations can be cartoon-like or realistic. We tend to think of animations as cheerful and playful, but any kind of viewpoint and mood is possible. Indeed, it takes real creativity to envision all the possible ways in which to share ideas and experiences through animation and then to make the right design decisions.

Implementation Issues

Animations are created in very different ways, and so the implementation issues differ. Brief animations are often animated GIFs. These are essentially a sequence of static graphics that the user's browser can swap in a specified manner. So, for example, the flag waving in the breeze might consist of three slightly different flag images being displayed in succession. Animated galleries are similar. Animated GIFs are created easily, much like conventional GIF graphics. The file size of the animated GIF depends on the number and complexity of the separate images that comprise the animated GIF.

Extended animations are very often produced with Macromedia Flash. Flash animations can be quite compact, but they may still cause delays for users with slow Internet connections. For more information on creating animations, see Lynda Weinman (1999) and Hillman Curtis (2000).

Video

Video is photography with the addition of motion and, very often, an audio track. Like photography, video is best for showing what something really looks like. If you really want people to appreciate the friendly, frisky qualities of your pet llama, you probably want to use video. The audio track will be an ideal way to supplement the video with llama sounds and your narrative.

Stylistic Choices in Video

There are a great many stylistic attributes in video. Videographers control lighting, camera movement, lens focus, transitions between scenes, and more. They give directions to actors. Something as simple as a conversation between two people sitting at a table can be filmed in many different ways, and well-known styles of videography have evolved in the motion picture and television industries.

A very basic video style is the steady, unobtrusive use of the camera to follow a conversation or record an event. Soaring, sweeping camera shots can show off a city or other scene in a majestic manner and then move in for close-ups. Quick, jumpy camera shots taken from surprising angles, perhaps with discordant rock music, convey energy and freedom from tradition. In a corporate video, for example, the camera might zoom in on the huge manufacturing facility, steadily track the CEO as she walks down an outdoor pathway explaining the corporation's vision for the future, and then take quick jumpy camera shots to show activity on the factory floor. For a good introduction to the technologies and techniques of digital filmmaking, see Ben Long and Sonja Schenk (2000). For a good general guide to the art of cinema, see Jon Boorstin (1995).

Live Cam

Although we tend to think of video as "canned" video sequences that are created, stored, and then displayed, there is also live video, where the designer simply sets up the camera. The Web offers Live Cam technology (also called Web Cam), which is a hybrid of static graphics and video. The user sees a succession of real-time static video images. Live Cam content includes traffic on highways and surfing conditions on a beach. The immediate, authentic nature of Live Cam engages many people, and so we see Live Cam cameras placed in restaurants, offices, and homes. In some instances controls are provided so that individual users can pan and zoom the Live Cam camera.

Implementation Issues

Video presents challenges both in creation and delivery to the user.

The Challenge of Creating Quality Video

Anyone can make a video—video cameras are relatively cheap and easy to operate—but high-quality video is surprisingly difficult to achieve. You will find that lighting is difficult to control, make-up makes a real difference, and dialog and even simple sounds, such as footsteps, are hard to record properly. Amateur camera work tends to look like amateur camera work, although your camera work will look more professional if you stick to basic techniques. Time and skill are also required in the post-production phase when the digitized video is edited using tools such as Adobe Premiere and After Effects. Video also requires developers to have highly capable computers, often with special video hardware.

Quality can be improved by hiring a professional videographer—although doing so will impact your budget. Hiring trained actors, of course, costs still more. Professional videographers distinguish between "Hollywood quality" vs. "corporate" or "industrial" quality, and for many purposes corporate or industrial quality is fully adequate. Often it is best to initially shoot prototype or proof-of-concept video that is intended only to represent the higher quality video that would be produced for a final, commercial version of the website. This strategy makes good sense because you can focus less on specific techniques such as positioning microphones and lights and more on the broader design issues: What should be shot and what is the message you are trying to convey.

Do not overlook the possibility of stock video. If stock video meets your needs, you will have high quality at a relatively low cost.

Challenges in Delivery

More than any other content type, video presents potential problems for your users. Each second you must deliver a lot of bits to the user's screen and probably to the user's speakers as well. At the present time, CD-ROM and DVD are better choices than the Web for projects in which video is central.

For all but brief video sequences, websites usually employ "streaming" technologies—which means that the data is sent continuously. Otherwise users must wait for huge files to be downloaded to their machine. Streaming video, however, is not ideal in regard to reliability or quality. For users with slower Internet connections you must provide low-bandwidth versions of your video files in which quality is compromised. You may need to limit the dimensions of the video window, the image quality and smoothness, and the quality of the sound. You should consider these limitations in the planning stage. If the dimensions will be small, avoid distance shots of small objects. If the frame rate will be low, try to limit the amount of motion in the scene.

Audio

Sound can be broadly categorized as background sound and core content. Music can fall into either category. Such sounds as crickets chirping and the wind blowing are usually background sound. Almost all human discourse (whether spoken or sung) is core content.

Background Sound

Music is used as background sound to create an appropriate mood and help establish the theme of a website. Other kinds of sounds can also fulfill this role. For example, the section of a petroleum company's website devoted to demonstrating its commitment to the environment might include chirping crickets and bird song. Very often, however, background sound simply annoys users, especially when they visit a website to get some work done. Also, users may well be listening to their own music. Therefore, employ background sound very cautiously.

Audio for Core Content

Discourse and music often make up some of the core content of a website. For example, in a website for teaching elementary school students about music, the student might click a graphic of a musical instrument to trigger an audio sequence of that instrument. Core-content audio can also be used effectively in conjunction with static graphics. For example, a rock band's website might include a photograph of each band member with a button that plays a brief audio greeting. A city's website might include a self-running sequence of photographs of city landmarks along with a narrator's brief comments.

Voice Quality and Voice Styles

There are great differences in voice quality. Be careful, therefore, about casually asking a friend to be your narrator. Your friend may have a perfectly nice voice for everyday conversation, but this does not translate into being an effective narrator in an electronic medium. Trained narrators (or at least drama students) really do speak more clearly and more expressively than untrained people, and the difference is usually quite noticeable.

Furthermore, there are many styles of narration. Voices can project informality or dignified reserve. Voices can be business-like or alluring. Speakers possess (or can affect) various regional and national accents. There are also many ways to use pauses, changes in pitch, and other vocal intonations.

In some cases, the project requires an audio sequence from someone, such as the CEO, who is not a particularly good speaker. In this case, you should work with the person to optimize his or her voice and narrative style.

On-Screen vs. Voice-Over Narrators

Many video sequences employ narration. When you plan video sequences with narration, you must decide whether the narrator will be visible in the video or whether the narration should come from an unseen, "voice-over" narrator. In general, on-screen narrators should be used when the individual is personally a part of the subject matter—like the CEO or an elderly citizen recounting an important historical event. Otherwise, voice-over narrators are usually preferable.

Videographers sometimes combine on-screen and off-screen narration. For example, in a video sequence introducing people to an exotic animal such as a koala, you might show the koala and its handler appearing together in many shots but you might also include extended koala close-ups in which the handler is heard but not seen. Similarly, if an instructor is explaining how to assemble a mechanical device, you might briefly introduce a full-body shot of the instructor and then use mostly close-up shots showing the instructor's hands doing the assembly.

Implementation Issues

It is difficult to achieve high-quality Web audio. You need good recording equipment, including a room free of ambient noise and echoes. When recording conditions are challenging, for instance, an outdoor location, multiple speakers, or ensemble music, an audio specialist may be needed. Large-size audio files load slowly, especially for users with slow Internet connections. Files, of course, are smaller when you keep audio sequences brief. You can also reduce file size by reducing the sampling rate and bit depth and by recording monaural rather than stereo—though these techniques degrade sound quality. Streaming media provides an increasingly effective means of delivering audio over the Web, even for users with a relatively slow Internet connection. Apart from the user's technology, your streaming media may degrade in quality if your website's server is unable to meet the demands placed on it. For a complete reference on audio, see Josh Beggs and Dylan Thede (2001). For useful online resources, see Marc Hoffman's Poison Dart Frog Media and Jay Rose's Digital Playroom.

Complex Combinations of Content Types

In the preceding discussion of audio, we saw instances of audio being used in conjunction with video. It is also possible to create complex combinations of dynamic and static content and to give users significant control over what they see and hear. Authoring tools such as Macromedia Director make this feasible in CD/DVD multimedia. This capability is more difficult to achieve on the Web, although it is happening with the adoption of new standards and technologies (SMIL and MPEG-4).

To investigate the design issues surrounding complex combinations of content types, we will envision the opening sequence of a CD title that teaches elementary school students about four species of freshwater fish. This title will teach students basic facts about each species, the species' reproductive behavior, and how the viability of the species in a stream is affected by the water quality and other environmental factors.

The opening screen, shown in Figure 4.4, consists of four small, fixed-sized windows. Each window displays a static image of a particular species of fish and is set to run a brief video sequence showing that species. There is also a larger display area that initially shows a static image of children on a field trip at a stream. There is an audio sequence of background guitar music. Playing over this background is narration that introduces the CD title and the topic of freshwater fish and then explains that clicking on a particular window will lead to information about that species. This opening sequence is represented in Figure 4.5.

Three seconds into the narration, Window A plays a 2-second video of the fish in motion and ends, returning to the static image. One-half second later (with the narration continuing) a similar video sequence plays in Window B for 2 seconds and ends—and so on until all four videos have played. When the last video has played (Window D) and one more half-second has elapsed, the large display

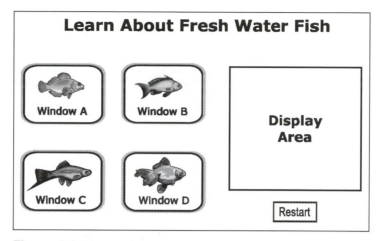

Figure 4.4. The opening screen of a CD title that displays dynamic and static content.

area changes from the image of the children at a stream to a text message inviting the user to click one of the four windows to display more information on that species. The sequence has taken 13 seconds (3 + 2 + 0.5 + 2 + 0.5 + 2 + 0.5 + 2 + 0.5). The purpose of the half-second pauses is to guide the user in switching attention from one window to another. When this sequence ends, the guitar music continues for another few seconds and then stops; otherwise, the music might annoy users who simply choose to let the CD sit for awhile.

The designer knows that some users will not want to sit through the complete 13-second sequence before clicking one of the four windows. In fact, the user can click any window at any time. The stars at both ends of the lines representing the four video windows indicate that these windows are hot, both when they are playing their video sequence and when they are showing a static image of a fish. If the user clicks one of the four windows before the opening sequence finishes, the sequence will stop so that the user is now viewing a static image in each of the four video windows. The selected window will also show a highlight in response to the user's click. More important, the display area (at the right of the screen) changes to a menu of choices for further information about the particular species of fish shown in the selected window. Figure 4.6 represents a situation in which a user clicks Window C while it is playing.

The kind of complex interactivity described above poses both design and technical challenges. As you have seen, the designer must give the user considerable freedom but must also direct the user's attention. Technical challenges include synchronizing narration, background music, and video. In particular, as this technology moves to the Web, how will these files remain synchronized if there are momentary slow-downs in the user's Internet connection? For a look at some older but very interesting projects incorporating complex combinations of content types, see Matthew Hodges and Russell Sasnett (1993).

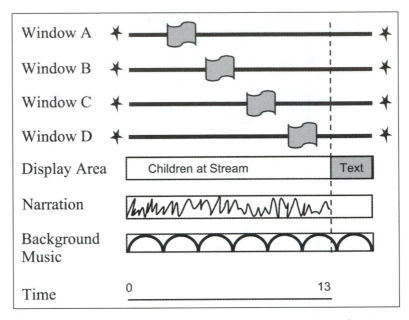

Figure 4.5. A diagram representing complex combinations of content with no user action.

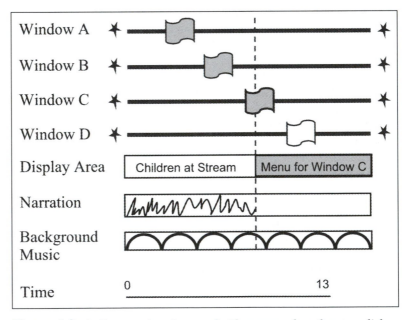

Figure 4.6. A diagram that shows what happens when the user clicks Window C. The video in Window C stops running, and the display area changes from a graphic to a menu.

Profile: Points West Kayak Tours

"Your website really sucks!" says Hank, the resident Web expert at the Red Dog Tavern.

"Thanks," answers Peter. "We aim to please."

"Just what don't you like?" asks Annie.

"Well, what you guys don't understand," says Hank, "is that a website needs to really grab people's attention. This is the age of multimedia. I have three suggestions for you.

"First, it would be easy to put an animated GIF of a paddling kayaker with bobbing waves right on top of each page. Second, you need video footage. Maybe a momma otter floating on her back with a baby on her tummy. The tourists love that. I bet you could get great footage for free from the Marine Nature Center. My third idea is an audio sequence. It would mostly be seabirds, but maybe the sound of waves lapping against the shore. This would play automatically as soon as the site loads—sort of to set the mood."

"We'll think about it," says Peter.

Question

What do you think of Hank's three suggestions?

Summary

1. There are five content types: text, graphics, animation, video, and audio. When you design a website, you must decide which content types to employ and how to use them. Your decisions depend largely on your audience and their needs. There are also implementation considerations and challenges.

2. Discourse means communicating through language—both text and speech. One issue designers face is when to use text discourse and when to use audio discourse.

3. The key advantages of text over audio discourse are these: (1) Text is instant and scannable, (2) text can be readily studied, (3) you can easily place links on text, and (4) text is easy to employ. Audio, however, offers the expressiveness of the human voice and, at times, is preferred over reading.

4. Avoid a long, unbroken wall of extended text, especially on the home page. Limit the amount of text, add blank space, make key points scannable, and create an attractive format. People will read extended text if it is important to them and if it is formatted functionally and attractively.

5. Layering is a technique that enables you to limit the amount of text on a page. Layering consists of initially presenting users with brief information and letting them access another layer of more detailed information if they want it. Layering works well on the Web, both for text and other content types.

6. Style is a general term for a wide range of specific decisions that focus and shape content and thereby help to express the theme. Each content type has attributes that can be controlled to produce a particular style and evoke appropriate moods. For example, writers control the vocabulary and sentence structure of text.

7. Graphics take the form of photographs and drawings. The basic purpose of a graphic is to show something's appearance or to represent abstract relationships concretely. A photograph catches something's overall appearance, but is likely to include unnecessary and perhaps unwanted detail. Drawings are less faithful to actual appearances but give the artist more control over what is shown. The single most flexible and most broadly useful combination of content types is text with graphics. Graphics can be loosely or tightly integrated with text.

8. The category of graphics also includes the backgrounds of Web pages. Graphics can be hot and can be invisibly divided into multiple hot areas, an "image map." Surrogate travel, another use of graphics, attempts to simulate the experience of navigating through physical space.

9. Animation is suited for many uses: drawing the eye, adding realism, explaining a process or concept, animated galleries, and splash animations. Brief animations are often animated GIFs. Extended animations are often created with Macromedia Flash. A key issue in regard to animation as well as the other dynamic (time-based) content types is user control.

10. Video adds the element of motion to photography and, like photography, is best for showing what something really looks like. It is difficult to create high-quality video, and video often makes significant demands on the user's computer equipment and Internet connection.

11. The "almost live" snapshots of Live Cams can be used to provide practical information, such as current traffic conditions, as well as a strong sense of immediacy and authenticity.

12. Functioning as background sound, music can create an appropriate mood and help establish the theme of a website. Music and audio discourse often make up some of the core content of a website.

13. In creating video sequences, designers often must choose between on-screen and voice-over narration. You will find that trained narrators speak more clearly and more expressively than untrained people. It is difficult to create high-quality Web audio and video as well.

14. CD/DVD multimedia and, to a lesser degree, the Web, allow for complex combinations of dynamic and static content that give users significant control over what they see and hear. This capability raises challenging technical and design issues.

References

Beggs, Josh, and Dylan Thede. 2001. *Designing Web Audio.* Sebastopol, CA: O'Reilly & Associates.

Boorstin, Jon. 1995. *Making Movies Work: Thinking Like A Filmmaker.* Los Angeles: Silman-James Press.

Curtis, Hillman. 2000. *Flash Web Design.* Indianapolis, IN: New Riders Publishing.

Hodges, Matthew, and Russell Sasnett. 1993. *Multimedia Computing: Case Studies from the MIT Athena Project.* Reading, MA: Addison Wesley.

Hoffman, Marc. Poison Dart Frog Media. www.dartfrogmedia.com

Kostelnick, Charles, and David Roberts. 1998. *Designing Visual Language: Strategies for Professional Communicators.* Boston: Allyn & Bacon.

Long, Ben, and Sonja Schenk. 2000. *The Digital Filmmaking Handbook* (with CD-ROM). Hingham, MA: Charles River Media.

Nielsen, Jakob. 2000. *The Practice of Simplicity.* Indianapolis, IN: New Riders Publishing.

Rose, Jay. Digital Playroom. www.dplay.com

Weinman, Lynda. 1999. *Designing Web Graphics 3: How to Prepare Images and Media for the Web.* 3d ed. Indianapolis, IN: New Riders Publishing.

Discussion and Application

Items for Discussion

1. Examine two or more Web resumés to see how layering is employed. Which layering techniques seem most effective? You can find many Web resumés as well as good information on resumé design at http://www.eresumes.com.

2. Revisit the design sketch of the Asthma Horizons home page, Figure 3.5 (Chapter 3, "Design and Building"). How closely are the photographs integrated with the text? Try to imagine a graphic on this website in which the degree of integration with text would be very different.

3. Examine a book or books containing graphics in the form of scientific or technical graphs (line graphs, bar graphs, etc.) and diagrams. Can you identify one or more of these graphics that would be more effective if it were an animation rather than a static graphic? Explain.

4. Animation can be used effectively to demonstrate or teach a process. Casey Reas has created a project in which origami (the Japanese art of paper-folding) is demonstrated using Flash animation. Examine the animation (http://acg.media.mit.edu/people/creas/eat/iogami.html). What are some of the techniques that help people understand how the paper should be folded? Would video have been better than animation? If this site had been created to actually teach origami (as opposed to demonstrating the possibilities of Web animation), what other elements might have been added?

5. Find two websites not devoted to music in which sound is used effectively. Explain.

6. Do these uses of background music make sense: (1) rock music for an online clothing store and (2) Greek folk music for a website that promotes a Greek heritage festival?

7. Consider virtual reality as a form of hypermedia. What content types may it employ? What is the nature of interactivity and active social space in a virtual world? Is VR possible in a Web browser?

8. A manufacturer of watersports equipment has developed a very new and highly efficient design for the fins used by scuba divers. These fins push the water in a radial direction and require a special flutter kick. What content types would you use to tell this story?

Application to Your Project

1. What content types, in addition to text, do you intend to use in your project?
2. If you have chosen to use dynamic content, explain the benefits of doing so.

5

Societal Implications
and Ethical Choices

Introduction

Technological change brings with it societal change, and societal change always has ethical implications: The world is made better and worse in various ways, and some people benefit while others fall behind. For example, the all-pervasive technological advancements of the Industrial Revolution also changed patterns of living in harsh ways. People began working in large factories rather than in their homes or small shops. Cities grew rapidly as people moved from villages and farms to urban centers in search of work. For many this was a time of poverty and dislocation.

In the last few decades, computer technologies and the people who develop and work with these technologies have transformed our world. One computer technology in particular—the Internet—has vastly changed the way we communicate and access information. It has led to new kinds of education and entertainment, new kinds of commerce, new kinds of communities, and new kinds of artistic and personal expression.

The Internet has profound societal and ethical implications. It affects the relationships of power and influence among nations, corporations, and other institutions. For certain, but not all, segments of society it brings greater wealth, knowledge, and political influence. The kinds of websites that are built, the standards for truthfulness and reliability of content that evolve, and the kinds of business practices that are accepted will affect our world in important ways. The Internet is already affecting education, and over the long term it may well affect literacy—how we read, write, and even think.

Technological change, however, is not an inevitable trajectory into the future. As with other technologies, the Internet may evolve in many different directions and have very different kinds of impact on our world. These directions are largely determined by enormous numbers of groups and institutions that are advancing their own viewpoints and agendas. Each of us, both through our individual actions and the organizations we are part of, is also involved in determining the future of the Internet.

There is a special role and responsibility for those who design and work on websites. As Internet professionals, we often make significant ethical choices—whether we choose to think about them or not. When a designer plans a website that will be utterly useless to someone who is blind, an ethical choice has been made. Similarly, if a designer finds a way to trick people into coming to her employer's website, she is helping to make the Web a less trustworthy communications medium. We also make important ethical choices away from the workplace in our interactions with friends and colleagues, in the products we choose (or refuse) to buy, and when we vote.

In this chapter we discuss 12 especially important societal issues and the ethical choices they present. Furthermore, we suggest actions you can take regarding these issues. These issues appear below, organized into three groups:

Power and Control

- Insufficient access to computers and the Internet
- Domination of the Web by powerful corporations
- Erosion of privacy at home
- Erosion of privacy in the workplace
- Health and safety concerns—especially in the workplace

The Web as a Communications Medium

- Unethical promotional tactics
- Unreliable, deceptive, and offensive content
- Hiding information
- Violations of intellectual property rights

Long-Term Societal Implications

- Education and hypermedia
- Participation in virtual communities
- Changes in literacy and human consciousness

We do not ask or expect you to agree with our positions on all of these issues. Our goal is that you will enlarge your awareness, stay alert to new issues and events, reach thoughtful conclusions, and act responsibly on the basis of your convictions.

Power and Control

The economies of most nations and the global economy are dominated by a relatively small number of large corporations. These corporations greatly affect the economic conditions in our communities and influence the political process in the nations in which they operate. They establish to a large degree the conditions and rules of the workplace. They not only develop the products and services we use, but they work hard to create or at least focus our desires and perceptions of good living.

These corporations have been the engines of tremendous wealth and opportunity; however, they are overwhelmingly concentrated in a relatively few nations, and so many nations are largely excluded from the wealth and opportunity created by the global economy. Much of their workforce struggles at the lowest levels of the economic ladder, often assembling manufactured goods for very low wages rather than participating in the more profitable activities of designing and selling. In 1999, the "G-7" group of nations (Canada, France, Germany, Great Britain, Italy, Japan, and the United States) accounted for approximately 65% of the world's economic activity (measured as gross domestic product).

In this section we consider the societal implications and ethical issues that arise from the enormous influence of corporations in our lives. We focus particularly on the role of computers and computer use. Also, because the Web is a communications medium, we look closely at corporations that are involved in the communications media and the Web.

Insufficient Access to Computers and the Internet

Perhaps the single most important ethical issue is that many groups of people worldwide have limited or no access to computers and to the Internet. They do not get to use and learn about technologies that lead to economic and professional advancement, they do not participate in one of the most dynamic segments of world commerce, they do not enjoy the many benefits of participating in virtual communities, and they do not have ready access to essential information of all kinds, including political information that might lead to social change. Often we speak of a "digital divide" that separates those who have access to and can benefit from these technologies and those who do not. In most cases, the underlying cause of the digital divide is the lack of money and education.

The digital divide separates wealthy from poor nations. In many parts of the world, computers are scarce and often old. Internet access—and especially Web access—is limited, slow, unreliable, and expensive. Another factor limiting access to the Internet is the language barrier. Much of the content of the Web is in English. Thus, many people must know a second language before they can make full use of the Web.

There is also a digital divide between the rich and poor within nations. In the United States, for example, there are large communities in both rural and urban areas in which poverty and lack of educational opportunities prevent or limit participation in the world of computers and the Internet.

Political repression also contributes to the digital divide. Some governments limit Internet access and censor Internet activity to squash dissent and maintain political control. For example, in the People's Republic of China, government agencies often shut down message boards and websites on which anti-government or other unacceptable ideas are expressed (AP Wire, Dec. 5, 2000; Jan. 29, 1999).

Also, people with various disabilities—especially visual and motor impairments—have great difficulty using computers unless special hardware is made available and accessibility features are built into the operating systems and software programs. The Web is especially problematical because it is a highly visual medium.

The problem of unequal access is extremely serious and demands our attention. There are, however, many reasons for optimism: With decreasing costs and other factors, Internet use is growing rapidly, even in less wealthy parts of the world. Significantly, some large employers, recognizing the need for a technologically sophisticated workforce, are taking steps to lessen the digital divide. For example, the Ford Motor Company recently offered to provide its worldwide workforce with a well-equipped computer and Internet access for the equivalent of $5/month (Bradsher 2000).

Taking Action

What steps can socially responsible individuals and, in particular, Internet professionals take to address the problem of insufficient access? In many communities there are opportunities to teach computer skills. See, for example, the activities of Voluntech.org, a volunteer organization serving the New York City area. In addition, Web designers can ensure that their websites adhere to accessibility guidelines. Finally, as voting citizens we can support policies, especially in regard to international trade, that enable poor nations to more fully and more equitably participate in the global economy, and we can support efforts by our own government and non-governmental organizations for progressive political change within nations that oppress their citizens.

Domination of the Web by Powerful Corporations

Although the Web began as a means for scientists to communicate, it is now very much a vehicle for global capitalism. A variety of powerful corporations, some born on the Web, are striving to dominate one or more aspects of this new medium. Amazon is by far the world's largest and most visible online merchant. Ebay created and dominates the auction form of e-commerce. Microsoft owns a major Web portal, MSN (and other Web businesses), and through Internet Explorer (the most widely used Web browser) and in many other ways is seeking to extend its dominance of operating systems and software applications to the Web. AT&T, once the largest telephone company in the United States, has added newer services and is now a leading provider of cable-based and wireless Internet access. Partnerships among these and many other important Internet corporations are commonplace.

Media companies have undergone tremendous consolidation. The Disney Corporation, in addition to theme parks, owns some of the world's largest broadcast and cable TV networks, major film studios, a large recorded music business, and major websites (Go.com, ESPN.com, ABC.com, etc.). Bertelsmann is a giant in print publishing, recorded music, film and television, and the Web

(CDNow, Lycos, etc.). In 2001 AOL, the largest ISP and Web portal[1] and the owner of other major Web holdings, merged with Time Warner to create the world's largest Internet and media corporation. The Time Warner holdings include Time Magazine, dominant cable TV networks offering both entertainment and news (HBO, Turner, and CNN), CNN.com, film studios, four sports teams, and major recorded music companies.

There are compelling arguments that highly concentrated corporate power, even when that power is not abused, is inherently detrimental. Furthermore, there is much potential for abuse, and abusive acts perpetrated by media companies are especially serious because media companies so directly affect what we know and think. For example, a corporation's news businesses—print, broadcast, and Web—might be told to manage the news to benefit the corporation's newest entertainment project or a political figure whose support it seeks.

Amid these ominous prospects, several observations are appropriate. First, the people who staff these corporations are not villains, but have about the same commitment to ethical conduct as the rest of the population. Also, there is intense competition among these corporations, which provides a corrective force against the misdeeds of any one corporation. Furthermore, there are government regulations that curb monopolies and various forms of misbehavior.

Finally, despite the many ways in which these powerful corporations exercise great influence on contemporary life, the Internet remains egalitarian to a significant degree. Individuals and groups with modest means can publicize their views by building a website or establishing an email list (or both). If people are interested in the message, these individuals and groups can communicate very widely. Similarly, small niche businesses thrive on the Internet, in the face of much larger competition.

Taking Action

We can and should view the concentration of corporate power, especially in regard to communications media, with concern and demand that corporations commit to and then uphold acceptable standards of behavior. We can do this as citizens, consumers, stockholders, articulate members of our professional and personal communities, and employees of these corporations. As consumers, we can value diversity in the marketplace and go to the trouble of looking beyond heavy advertising to find businesses whose values and products most deserve our respect.

Erosion of Privacy at Home

The erosion of privacy is a widespread and disturbing phenomenon that has become far more significant as the world has become increasingly computerized over the last several decades. All kinds of information about individuals are collected,

---

[1]The AOL holdings consisted of AOL.com, Netscape.com, and CompuServe.com. Together these are the most visited Web portals. We should note, however, that there are various ways of compiling these kinds of statistics and that patterns of Web use and the business activities of media and Internet companies are always changing.

stored, and shared electronically—often without notification or permission—by corporations (large and small), government agencies, health care organizations, and other institutions.

Those who erode our privacy often do so with good intent. Indeed, collecting and exchanging information about people provides important benefits. It makes sense for a government agency in California to gain access to the employment and bank records of an absentee parent who has moved to Minnesota to avoid paying child support and alimony. Many people welcome print and email advertising keyed to their interests and therefore do not object when merchants share mailing lists and email addresses. The issues, therefore, are subtle. We must look closely at what kinds of information are collected and by whom, for what purposes, and with what permissions, notifications, and safeguards.

The newest threat to privacy is the Internet. Many websites collect extensive information about site visitors, often requiring visitors to complete forms in order to use portions of the site. The site may also place a "cookie" (a small piece of computer code) on that user's hard drive so that the website can identify the user each time he or she visits the website. In this way, an online merchant can use the information that has been collected, including records of previous purchases, to adaptively generate pages that can best meet each user's needs.

There are many ways in which a website can abuse an individual's right to privacy. A notable instance, uncovered in November 1999, involved RealNetworks' RealJukebox software and its related website. RealJukebox is a music management system that enables users to play music CDs, record CD tracks onto their hard drives, and download music from the Internet. It also can be used to organize digital music collections and create playlists of the user's favorite artists.

According to a *New York Times* article appearing November 1, 1999 (Robinson 1999), each time RealJukebox was used, it connected to the Internet and told RealNetworks the number of songs stored on the user's hard drive, the file formats of the songs, the musical genre, and further information as well. In addition, if its default settings were used, RealJukebox gave RealNetworks the title of any CD the user played in the computer's CD-ROM drive. Users were not informed of these violations of privacy. RealNetworks discontinued this practice and offered a public apology immediately after this invasion of privacy became known to the public (*Seattle Times*, 1999).

In response to the threat to privacy, many nations, among them Canada, are passing strong legislation to protect people's privacy rights (Pritchard 2000). It is also noteworthy that in November 2000 IBM appointed Harriet P. Pearson as the company's first chief privacy officer. Pearson's mandate is to lead numerous initiatives across IBM that will strengthen consumer privacy protection.

Taking Action

As Internet users, we need to make thoughtful decisions regarding what kinds of personal information to reveal. Users can reject or purge cookies, and many people regularly do so to maintain their privacy. On the other hand, many others value the convenience of a personalized website and have a higher tolerance for the loss of privacy. At the very least, users should carefully read and assess the privacy policies of websites they visit, especially when these sites ask for personal information.

As Internet professionals, we should dissuade employers from implementing objectionable practices. Often we will succeed by pointing out the possibility of legal penalties and bad publicity. If necessary, Internet professionals should be prepared to quit their jobs or expose these practices. As citizens, we must be alert and sensitive to the privacy issue and support appropriate legislation.

Erosion of Privacy in the Workplace

Another set of privacy issues pertains to email and Web use in the workplace. Most people will agree that employers have significant rights to know what employees are doing on company time. First and most obviously, employees may be goofing off when they should be working. But, there are other considerations as well. Employees, for example, could circulate pornographic images and sexist jokes that would make the work environment inhospitable for others and leave the company open to sexual harassment lawsuits. Employees could compromise trade secrets via email.

The question, then, is just how far should an employer's rights extend. In the United States, Federal law allows employers to eavesdrop on people's email in the workplace and to monitor Web use. Employers are increasingly turning to internet-surveillance software that can analyze company-wide Internet usage and produce profile reports on any and all employees (McCarthy 1999). On the other hand, in many other nations, such as Germany, employers do not have such rights (McCarthy 1999). Some argue that employers should only be permitted to monitor email and Web use when there is prior reason to suspect an employee of inappropriate behavior. The issue of eavesdropping on email and Web use extends readily to eavesdropping on all computer use. For example, a company might install software that would record what users are typing into their word processors and how long people seem to be pausing from their keyboarding.

Closely related to privacy issues is the question of employee use of the Internet for non-work purposes. Many companies allow limited non-work use, in the same way that employees have traditionally been permitted to make a limited number of personal phone calls while at work. Other companies take a harder line prohibiting all forms of personal Internet use and all personal use of company computers (McCarthy 1999).

Taking Action

As before, Internet professionals should address this problem on many fronts: as voters and articulate members of professional and other communities and as employers and supervisors. Internet professionals should think twice about working for companies whose policies, even if legal, are ethically unacceptable or simply too burdensome.

Health and Safety Concerns—Especially in the Workplace

Computers pose significant health and safety problems, notably repetitive stress injuries from excessive keyboarding and eyestrain from staring at the screen for long periods of time. There are also concerns about the effects of electromagnetic radiation from computer monitors. These problems pertain to Internet use along with all uses of computers.

Health and safety issues are of special concern in regard to workplace computing, for here the individual does not choose the amount and kind of computer use (including break time) and the nature of the equipment. Indeed, it is in the workplace that we often see long hours of data entry and other highly repetitive keyboard work. What limits should be placed on employers in regard to unhealthy computer use?

Taking Action

We should all welcome the development of healthier computer and office technologies such as ergonomic keyboards and desk chairs and easier-to-view monitors. Furthermore, as employers, supervisors, and influential employees and as community members and voters, we should support the widespread implementation of healthy computer technologies and workplace practices along with other workplace rights.

The Web as a Communications Medium

Because the Internet and the Web are emerging communications media, the rules and the culture surrounding them are still new and shifting. Responsible people want to see the Internet and the Web become communications media characterized by safety, honesty, and freedom from annoyances and intrusions.

Issues considered in this section include how online businesses promote themselves, the kinds of information presented via email and on websites, and how information may be hidden unethically on a website. We also consider the unethical behavior of Web users, in particular the theft of intellectual property.

A key point is that the Internet and Web will never be free of people who behave in irresponsible and destructive ways, and so both as profesionals and as consumers of information we must be on guard against people who behave unethically. We especially need to protect children.

Unethical Promotional Tactics

There are many unethical ways to promote a product or service on the Internet. Some practices are unethical because they mislead users into displaying advertising; some are unethical because promoters are forcing advertising messages on people.

Spamming

Spamming is one of the oldest unethical practices. The most prevalent form of spamming is sending unwanted email messages to many thousands of people. These messages are certainly annoying, and many people are particularly offended by spam email messages that promote pornography sites.

Re-Routing

Re-routing refers to various ways of bringing people to a website they did not intend to visit. One technique is to purchase URLs that are likely misspellings of frequently visited sites.

Another technique is to trick Web-wide search engines (such as Altavista and Excite) into including a website's URL in a search results list when the website is not relevant to the search. For example, an unscrupulous Web merchant can trick a search engine into displaying the merchant's URL whenever a user types the name of a competitor's site. This is often done by putting the competitor's name in the website's keyword metatag—although search engines are becoming better able to foil this and similar tricks.

Deceptively Drawing Users to Advertising

There are various unscrupulous ways to motivate a user to read an advertisement the user would typically ignore. One technique is to create what seems like a system message (usually a bogus system warning) to grab the user's attention. For example, many websites allow advertisers to use the kind of deceptive banner advertisement shown in Figure 5.1.

Trapping

Trapping refers to practices intended to prevent users from leaving a website. One technique is to write code to disable the Back button on the user's browser. A variation is to force the user's browser to open a new instance of the browser that displays the same website the user is trying to leave.

Another form of trapping is to keep the user within a website's frameset. In other words, the user can navigate to new websites, but these websites always appear within the frameset of the original site. There are just a few situations in which this technique is appropriate; for example, a website that lists the sites that help users select a law firm might display each law firm's site within the website's own frameset so that users can quickly and easily compare law firms and keep the list of firms in view at all times.

Figure 5.1. A deceptive advertising banner.

Taking Action

As these unscrupulous practices vary considerably, so do the solutions. There are various defenses against spamming, including laws against spamming and steps taken by ISPs to shield their customers from spammers.

In the United States, the Federal Trade Commission (www.ftc.gov) can pursue legal action against websites engaging in certain kinds of unscrupulous practices. *Playboy Magazine* successfully sued a competing website that put the name Playboy in the site's keyword metatag, charging that this practice is an abuse of the Playboy trademark (Playboy Enter., Inc. v. Asiafocus Int'l, Inc., 1998 WL 724000 (E.D. Va. 1998)).

Internet professionals should refuse if their employers or clients ask them to engage in these and many other kinds of unscrupulous practices. Also, as members of their professional communities, Internet professionals can express their disapproval of these practices and website managers who engage in them. Finally, in our role as consumers, we should all avoid companies that engage in these practices—not only for ethical reasons but because these companies are likely to be sleazy in all their business dealings.

Unreliable, Deceptive, and Offensive Content

We noted above that the Internet is an egalitarian medium insofar as almost anyone can communicate widely. In other words, the gatekeeping function performed to both good and bad effect by book and magazine publishers, broadcasters, and other traditional media is largely absent. One consequence of the unrestricted nature of Internet communication is the vast number of hoaxes and groundless rumors that spread unchecked throughout the world, especially via email. Some have to do with non-existent computer viruses or exaggerated claims about the capabilities of actual computer viruses. But there are hoaxes of all kinds. One example is the totally false story, circulated widely via email during the year 2000, that anyone could email the Coca-Cola Corporation and receive a free case of their product (http://hoaxbusters.ciac.org).

People who participate in investor chat sessions and who maintain investment-oriented websites regularly offer strong opinions about the prospects of publicly traded corporations. Who is the savvy investor generously offering valuable advice? Who is an uninformed kook? Who is committing the fraudulent practice of spreading very good news (or very bad news) about a corporation in order to make a quick profit by selling (or buying) the stock after the phony information has influenced its price?

There are many other forms of misrepresentation. A website that offers parents, apparently as a public service, tips and product reviews to help them choose educational toys reveals only subtly its ties to a toy manufacturer. A legal dictionary, available on an individual's website, looks superficially like a respectable reference work, but there are falsehoods and ideologically weighted comments running through many of the definitions.

These practices are harmful in varying degrees. But there may be consequences more serious than anything mentioned above. For example, Web users looking for information on cancer treatments might stumble upon the website of a highly respected medical center or the website of a highly questionable clinic that make claims and offers treatments that lie well beyond mainstream medical science. Furthermore, in contrast to "brick and mortar" buildings, the website of a tiny, unknown clinic may look similar to and suggest a similar degree of trustworthiness as the website of a highly respected medical center. Perhaps the unknown clinic really has found a medical breakthrough. More likely, cancer patients who rely on such clinics will deny themselves the most appropriate treatment.

Offensive content includes the very prevalent category of pornography as well as the sites of hate organizations (which usually offer unreliable and deceptive information as well). Pornography raises complex issues, such as the right to free expression and distinguishing between pornographic expression and erotic expression (possibly with artistic value). Both pornographic and hate sites may be legal, even when we judge their activities immoral and harmful to society.

Young People as Web Users

The unrestricted nature of Web communication raises special issues in regard to children and young adults, both at home and at school. Given the prevalence of pornography, hate sites, and general craziness, it is reasonable for parents and educators to want to limit young people's Web use. A further concern is the possibility that young people will become targets of sexual predators who can cause psychological damage through nothing more than online conversations but who might attempt to arrange direct personal contact.

Taking Action

We ourselves, of course, should abstain from dishonest and irresponsible behavior, and we should strive to prevent others from engaging in this behavior. But how far can and should we go? Beyond support for laws to curb sexual predation, fraud, and other highly destructive practices, should we support censoring the Web, presumably by government agencies? Few people want this. Surely there are enormous drawbacks and risks to censoring content (or trying to censor content) on the Internet, just as there are to large-scale censoring of print.

Short of censorship, what can be done? If we want the Internet to be a rich, complex communication environment full of diverse opinions, some of the opinions and people expressing them will be untrustworthy and worse. One focus for action, then, is personal responsibility; we must know how to evaluate Web content, and we must be alert for unreliable and deceptive information. There are a variety of resources that can assist us in assessing the reliability of online content and in identifying hoaxes. These include the following:

- Widener University's Evaluating Web Resources Home Page (www2. widener.edu/Wolfgram-Memorial-Library/webevaluation/webeval.htm)
- Internet Scambusters (www.scambusters.org)
- U.S. Department of Energy CIAC (http://hoaxbusters.ciac.org)

In regard to children and young adults, one solution is to employ software that blocks access to websites (and in some cases email, news groups, and live chat sessions) that contain specified words and phrases. Some of these products are designed for home use, others for schools. (See for example Pearl Software's Cyber Snoop and Symantec's I-Gear.) Although blocking access at the user's end is much better than censoring the Web, this solution is far from perfect. For example, unless the blocking software is expertly configured, it can block websites of legitimate interest to young people (Hartocollis, Nov. 11, 1999; Nov. 10, 1999). Many young people could not get Web access to information about the 2001 North American Super Bowl professional football championship because the Xs in the phrase "Super Bowl XXXV" were interpreted as a pornography website. In many ways, a better solution than blocking access is for adults to pay attention to young people's Internet use and to educate them about threats to their safety and well being, both on the Internet and elsewhere in their lives.

Hiding Information

In the world of paper documents we often speak of hiding important information "in the fine print." The equivalent on the Web to this unethical practice is placing information behind obscure links—links that are hard to spot on a Web page or that are buried deep in the interior of a website. For example, if a university's athletic department is required to reveal the percentage of athletes in each sport who do not graduate within five years and if the university's statistics are unfavorable, the athletic department might decide to place these statistics behind a link that no prospective student athlete will be likely to notice. More broadly, we need to recognize that on any website some items of information are given more prominence than others and that there are very often ethical implications to these choices.

Taking Action

Responsible writers and designers should not intentionally hide information from users and should—along with all Web users—condemn this practice.

Violations of Intellectual Property Rights

In Appendix B, we explain the most fundamental issues of copyright from the perspective of what is and is not legal. Here we consider intellectual property from an ethical perspective. Most people accept the idea that there can be intellectual property as well as physical property; that intellectual property, like physical property, can be stolen (or reduced in value); and that the creators of intellectual property should have legal protection. The underlying rationale for these ideas is that without legal protection there will be less incentive to invest the effort and money necessary to produce quality movies, books, fine art, and so forth and to develop inventions and technical innovations (which are protected primarily by patent rather than copyright laws). There are, on the other hand, those who philosophically oppose the idea of intellectual property or question whether intellectual property laws can and should apply to the Internet (Goldhaber 2000; Barlow 2000, 1994).

Intellectual property violations are very common, even among people who consider themselves honest and ethical. One reason is that some violations, such as appropriating a cool graphic or poem from someone's website, do not appear to harm the creator/owner. Indeed, this person may have no interest in charging for the use of this content and no concern about who uses it and for what purpose. We would argue, however, that Web users have no right to make that decision for the creator of the content. Along similar lines, many otherwise ethical people cheerfully appropriate digitized popular music and other intellectual property that is clearly intended to be sold, because the owners are large corporations or rich celebrities. We would argue that this is not adequate justification.

One can, however, accept the idea of intellectual property and still quarrel with how the laws are written and interpreted. For example, there is considerable controversy over the patent granted to Amazon.com by the U.S. Patent Office (now being appealed) for "one-click checkout." Should such a broad concept be anyone's intellectual property? Also controversial is the recent law enacted by the United States Congress extending copyright protection by 20 years.[2] On one hand, this law benefits copyright owners, who may be individual authors and artists but who are very likely to be large corporations. On the other hand, it harms society as a whole by restricting the flow of copyrighted content and harms authors and artists in particular by limiting their use of existing works of literature and art in their creative activities.

Taking Action

Internet professionals should try to keep informed on the complex (but very interesting) area of intellectual property and should develop thoughtful positions on intellectual property issues. At work, we should abide by copyright laws both for ethical reasons and to protect our employers from expensive lawsuits and embarrassment. Finally, we should avoid violating copyright in our private lives.

Long-Term Societal Implications

No one can say for sure how the nine issues discussed so far will play out over time. Now we consider three issues whose long-term consequences, while certainly profound, are especially hard to predict. These are the use of the Internet and hypermedia for education, the increasing importance of virtual communities, and the impact of the Internet on literacy and our thought processes.

Education and Hypermedia

During the past 10 or so years, hypermedia has had a definite impact in the world of education. There are well-designed CD/DVD titles for teaching a variety of topics in grades K–12. College textbooks often come packaged with a CD containing examples and supplemental resources. More recently, the Web has become an

---

[2]For works created on or after January 1, 1978, copyright duration is now the life of the author plus 70 years and for works created for hire and owned by corporations copyright duration is now 95 years.

important part of educational technology. Hypermedia will certainly lead to profound changes in education, but the long-term implications of these changes are hard to see and not entirely positive. We will first consider very briefly how hypermedia can contribute to education and then what new forms education may take as it incorporates hypermedia and, especially, the Internet and Web.

The Web and CD/DVD titles provide dynamic content that print resources cannot. Also, they provide forms of interactivity impossible with video and film. For example, a physics student can interact with an animated model and change the load on a truss until it deforms. With another click or two, the student can display and, if desired, solve an equation representing the deformation of the truss. For teaching difficult concepts in math and science, even the very best instructor using traditional methods will be hard pressed to compete with these capabilities. Looking beyond current technologies, virtual reality will enable students to participate in and construct complete alternative worlds designed to help them learn new concepts.

Websites can adaptively employ numerous instructional strategies, for example, pacing instruction in response to the student's performance on quizzes, and can support virtual learning communities through message boards, real-time chat, and even video conferencing. Students from across a city or across the planet can work closely on group projects, with the active involvement of the instructor. These advanced capabilities have invigorated distance learning, which once relied on the mailing of assignments between instructor and student.

With the promise of Internet-based education dangers arise. In particular, the Internet might become a means to provide cut-rate, low-quality education. At least in some communities, privileged students may enjoy the best combinations of face-to-face and online learning while others are consigned to schools that rely excessively on less expensive digital solutions in which instructors play little part. Inferior online education might then prove to be a cruel reversal of the digital divide.

Taking Action

We all benefit from the emergence of high-quality online instruction. Some of us will work on commercial Internet products intended for use in schools. Others can assist their local schools and individual teachers in creating better websites and selecting the most appropriate commercial products. In some communities, computer professionals have volunteered for such hands-on tasks as stringing fiber-optic cable through public schools.

As Internet professionals, we can help explain that high-quality instruction built around the Internet and CD/DVD hypermedia is not cheap and that saving money is rarely a good reason to employ technology in education. As enlightened citizens, we should support quality education for all students with and without the extensive use of technology.

Participation in Virtual Communities

Virtual communities consist of people who interact over a period of time and form human bonds through such digital technologies as email discussion groups, message boards, real-time chat, and MUDs and MOOs.

Clearly virtual communities hold great potential to enrich our lives. For example, gay teenagers in isolated, gay-hostile communities look to online communities for friendship and understanding. Groups of professionals, such as women who work in the computer industry, exchange opinions on various work-related issues. People with unusual hobbies, fans of obscure film stars, and many others have good reason to seek out virtual communities.

On the other hand, there are many unanswered questions about participation in virtual communities. In a major research study called HomeNet (Kraut et al. 1998) the Internet use of research subjects was observed over a two-year period. The subjects' activities included social interactions (email, chat rooms, and discussion groups) as well as time spent simply visiting websites. The investigators found that some subjects experienced a moderate increase in loneliness and depression. There was a tendency to substitute weak Internet ties for closer, face-to-face ties with friends and family members.

Participation in virtual communities, however, may bring about more severe consequences. Some people seriously neglect family relationships, work responsibilities, and other aspects of normal life. People experience rejection and other painful psychological experiences within virtual communities, much as in physical communities. Some virtual communities built around hatred and bigotry attract susceptible people and lead them toward more extreme views and behavior. It seems fair to say that the impact of virtual communities on society will be varied but that the total impact will be significant.

Taking Action

We should monitor the effects of our participation in virtual communities and not forget the value of a picnic on a sunny day. When we see people being harmed by their participation, we should offer our assistance—as we would in other situations. As members of virtual communities, we should promote good values and establish practices that will make virtual communities more satisfying places to spend time.

Changes in Literacy and Consciousness

We have now considered some of the ways in which the Internet is changing how we work, shop, entertain ourselves, become educated, and share our lives with one another. But there is another dimension of change: Slowly, and in ways we cannot predict, the Internet is changing literacy—how we read, write, and in some ways, how we think.

This should not be a surprise. Major advances in information technology have had similar consequences in the past. Literacy and even human consciousness changed with the advent of alphabets, the invention of printing, and the emergence of film and television. Because the long-term consequences of the Internet are so hard to predict, we cannot suggest what ethical choices will arise or what steps we might take.

Optimists such as Douglas Rushkoff (1999), a well-known commentator on media and culture, suggest that those raised on the Web, on computer games, and on TV may achieve higher forms of literacy and consciousness. Rushkoff looks to future generations who are better able to synthesize knowledge from many sources and who are more successful in dealing with complexity and change.

But less optimistic scenarios are also possible. Because the non-linear nature of the Web accustoms us to navigate freely among short chunks of information, the Web may further the erosion of essential literacies. Already we are a restless culture that is increasingly pervaded by the summary and sound bite. If large numbers of people become unwilling to read or even listen to lengthy explanations and arguments, how will society as a whole carry out complex affairs, including the requirements of citizenship? Do you think we can begin to discern, even faintly, which vision of the future is more accurate?

Summary

This chapter discusses 12 important societal issues related to the Internet, the World Wide Web, and communications. Each issue presents various ethical choices. We do not conceal our viewpoints, but we don't ask you to adopt them either. We seek to extend your awareness of ethical issues and to encourage you to reach thoughtful conclusions, stay alert to new issues and events, and act responsibly on what you come to believe.

References

AP Wire. 2000. China to tighten Web regulation. 5 December.

AP Wire. 1999. China to hunt sedition on Internet. 29 January.

Barlow, John Perry. 2000. The next economy of ideas. *Wired,* October.
    www.wired.com/wired/archive/8.10/download.html

Barlow, John Perry. 1994. The economy of ideas. *Wired,* March.
    www.wired.com/wired/archive/2.03/economy.ideas.html

Bradsher, Keith. 2000. Ford offers its workers PC's and Internet for $5 a month. *New York Times,* 4 February, Business/Financial Desk.

Cotton, Bob, and Richard Oliver. 1993. *Understanding Hypermedia.* London: Phaidon Press.

Goldhaber, Michael H. 2000. The Napster revolution and the law. 29 June.
    www.heise.de/tp/english/kolumnen/gol/default.html

Hartocollis, Anemona. 1999. School officials defend filtering of web sites. *New York Times,* 11 November, C29.

Hartocollis, Anemona. 1999. Board blocks student access at school computers to some web sites. *New York Times,* 10 November, A22.

Kaminer, Wendy. 1999. *Sleeping with Extra-Terrestrials: The Rise of Irrationalism and Perils of Piety.* NY: Pantheon Books.

Kraut, Robert E., Vicki Lundmark, Michael Patterson, Sara Kiesler, Tridas Mukopadhyay, and William Scherlis. 1998. Internet paradox: A social technology that reduces social involvement and psychological well-being? *American Psychologist,* 53.9: 1017–1031.

McCarthy, Michael J. 1999. Now the boss knows where you're clicking. The boss sees your every click. Virtual morality: A new workplace quandary. *Wall Street Journal*, 21 October, B1, B4.

Pritchard, Timothy. 2000. Canada strengthens Internet privacy. *New York Times*, 23 December, B2.

Robinson, Sara. 1999. CD software said to gather data on users. *New York Times*, 1 November, C1 and C10.

Rushkoff, Douglas. 1999. *Playing the Future: What We Can Learn from Digital Kids.* New York: Berkley Publishing Group.

Seattle Times. 1999. RealNetworks has apologies, plus a patch for Jukebox. 3 November, C2.

Discussion and Application

Items for Discussion

1. A senior citizens' residence has recently acquired a computer with Internet access so that residents can use email (especially to communicate with their children and grandchildren) and surf the Web. The computer is located on a table in the main lounge and is quite popular. Several residents, however, have observed other residents viewing pornographic websites and want this practice stopped. This issue is on the agenda for the next management meeting.

   You are the assistant manager of the facility. You are also the facility's system administrator and the designer of the facility's own website. Because of your expertise and professional responsibilities, you will be expected to take a leadership role at the meeting. What information will you gather to prepare yourself for the meeting? What is your overall viewpoint on this issue?

2. The managers of Asthma Horizons Northwest are contacted by a new company, Northwest Asthma Consultants, that plans to assist asthma patients in modifying their homes to alleviate their condition. The principals of this new company have good medical credentials, and so Asthma Horizons tentatively agrees to build an external link to this company's website when it is launched.

   When the company contacts Asthma Horizons with the URL for their new site, the Asthma Horizons managers notice at once that the color scheme and several of the key page elements of the Northwest Asthma Consultants website bear a strong resemblance to the Asthma Horizons website. What are the ethical and legal implications of this situation? If you were a manager of the Asthma Horizons website, what steps would you consider?

3. What are some of the ways in which you determine whether the websites you visit are trustworthy? Identify two websites that you do not regard as trustworthy and explain why you think so.

4. Consider the possibility that the interactive and adaptive capabilities of the Web could be utilized as a very powerful means of persuasion. For example, let's envision a public policy advocacy group opposed to capital punishment in the United States. One branch of the website makes this offer to site visitors:

> If you favor capital punishment but have an open mind or if you are undecided on this important issue, we invite you to participate in an informative and challenging dialog with us.

The website then asks the user a series of questions such as these:

> Please tell us if your support for capital punishment comes partly from the conviction that it deters crime.
>
> ☐ Yes
> ☐ No
> ☐ Unsure

> Please tell us if you support capital punishment because you believe society owes this to the victim's relatives.
>
> ☐ Yes
> ☐ No
> ☐ Unsure

> Please tell us if you support capital punishment because you believe society owes this to the victim's relatives.
>
> ☐ Yes
> ☐ No
> ☐ Unsure

Based on these responses, sophisticated software on the website's server devises a persuasive strategy custom tailored to this user. The software selects the arguments and makes choices in phrasing. Periodically, the software asks further questions and continues to adapt the persuasive strategy.

Do you think an adaptive dialog of this kind might be more persuasive than a conventional argument presented either in print or online? Are adaptive techniques unethical?

5. Peruse the website of Computer Professionals for Social Responsibility (www.cpsr.org). Describe the nature, activities, and goals of this organization and your assessment of the group and its activities.

6. Research ways in which people with Web and Internet skills can serve as volunteers in your community. Look into volunteerism in schools, libraries, and community organizations. What types of computer projects are being staffed by volunteers?

7. Identify a societal issue pertaining to the Web, the Internet, or computing not covered in this chapter. What ethical choices does the issue present to us both as citizens and Internet professionals?

8. Few people would agree to read books from only one publisher or view movies from only one studio. Do you support the traditional idea that students should enroll at a particular university and take all (or most) of their courses there? Do you see promise in a "pick and choose" system of higher education? For example, if Lockwood University has a poor chemistry department, many Lockwood students might take their chemistry courses over the Internet from other universities, perhaps motivating Lockwood to take strong steps to improve its own chemistry courses. What are the risks of a pick and choose system?

9. Social commentator Wendy Kaminer (1999) explains in the preface to her book that she has changed her way of writing:

> I have changed the way I conceive of my books. I digress. I imagine each chapter as an autonomous essay, because I know that people no longer read books about ideas sequentially.

Respond to Kaminer's claim about changes in literacy and the decisions she has made as a writer.

10. The digital media theorists and designers Bob Cotton and Richard Oliver, in their 1993 book *Understanding Hypermedia* (a book written without reference to the World Wide Web), offer a statement about a possible future in which humankind moves away from text-based literacy. What assumptions underlie their argument? Do you agree with them?

> For centuries the written word has had a central authority in society. Indeed, it could be strongly argued that our notions of rationality and valid argument are all bound up with modes of thought that are derived from writing as a medium. The only real challenge to the primacy of the written word has come from its more esoteric cousin, the mathematical expression. Both these media are extremely abstract and their mastery takes many years of education and training. While most people in modern society can read, write and handle simple mathematics, the greatest concentration of mastery in these media is found in the elite professions, and is the source of some of their power and much of their authority.
>
> The development of hypermedia represents a return to richer, pre-print modalities of expression, as if we are "coming to our senses" after the anesthetic of monochrome words. The opportunity it offers to reason, to think, to speculate, to debate and to learn in more concrete, multi-sensory terms may have a deep significance in terms of what we are able to think about. Indeed, a move away from a reliance on the peculiar abstraction of written or mathematical expression may be the only way we can tackle the complexities of the modern world.
>
> But the use of hypermedia for learning traditional subjects may well be seen by many as trivializing or debasing. Those who owe their position and status to the mastery of the written word are those who may have the greatest difficulty in "writing" and "reading" in this new medium, and will resist most strongly this threat to the primacy of the written word. (p. 88)

Application to Your Project

1. Review your planned or existing website for possible intellectual property violations. If you encounter any potential violations, how will you deal with them?
2. Consider carefully the societal and ethical implications of your planned or existing website. Does the website engage in any questionable business practices? If so, what are the most appropriate steps you can take?

6

Hypertext Theory and Node-Link Diagrams

Introduction

There are many perspectives that help us understand the World Wide Web and design effective websites. For example, "media richness theory" explains how various content types affect the user's experience (Steuer 1992; Lombard and Ditton 1997). Also, there are theories that explain the relationships between older media and the Web (Bolter 1991; Bolter and Grusin 1999), and theories that focus on the potential of hypermedia for education (Duffy and Jonassen 1992; Jones and Spiro 1995). There are also highly significant political perspectives (Greco 1996; Johnson-Eilola 1997).

From an information-science perspective, a website is a kind of unstructured database, and the central problems have to do with information retrieval. Contemporary rhetoricians often view texts as dialogs, even though the audience is not directly exchanging information with the author (Bakhtin 1989; MacOvski 1997). The idea of text as dialog applies especially well, as you shall see, to the Web.

This book reflects these and other ways of understanding and studying the Web and hypermedia. But we also draw heavily on a set of ideas known as hypertext theory. The core of hypertext theory is already familiar to you. It is the idea that hypermedia can be usefully described in terms of nodes and links. Hypertext theory considers how various arrangements of nodes and links express meaning and how these arrangements are reflected on the user interface. Hypertext theory classifies these arrangements of nodes and links into various kinds of hierarchical and non-hierarchical structures, often called "information structures."

Hypertext concepts pervade Vannevar Bush's groundbreaking acticle of 1945, a description of a world in which experts could better surmount intellectual challenges by interweaving disparate documents. Hypertext theory has evolved since then through the work of Ted Nelson (1992), Jeff Conklin (1987), Frank Halasz (1988), Jay Bolter (1991), William Horton (1994), Cliff McKnight, Andrew Dillon, and John Richardson (1993, 1991), Diane Greco (1996), Catherine Marshall (1998; Golovchinsky and Marshall 2000), Mark Bernstein (1998, 1991), George Landow (1997), and others. Many of these theorists derived their ideas in large part from hypertext systems they designed and built. The importance of hypertext theory is such that most people who study the Web draw upon hypertext theory in one way or another.

Hypertext theory is especially valuable to designers. Something like an X-ray machine, hypertext theory gets us below surface appearances and lets us see how websites are held together and how they support user navigation. The most concrete benefit that hypertext theory provides for designers is the node-link diagram. Even designers who choose not to draw node-link diagrams, *think* them much of the time. This chapter, therefore, demonstrates a variety of techniques for drawing node-link diagrams.

There are two broad traditions into which most hypertext theorists can be placed. The first tradition is grounded in cognitive science and human-computer interaction (HCI). These theorists (e.g., Conklin, Halasz, Horton) focus on creating usable systems for managing and presenting content. The second tradition is grounded in rhetoric and, at times, postmodern thought. These theorists (e.g., Bolter, Greco, Landow) focus on hypermedia as a new form of authorship and literacy and seek to enlarge our understanding of how we communicate in this new environment. This book draws upon both traditions. Furthermore, we have in certain respects extended familiar hypertext concepts to accommodate capabilities that have emerged with the World Wide Web. Our goal is to offer a perspective on the Web and hypermedia that is intellectually fulfilling, inspires further thought, and serves as a springboard for good design.

The Navigation Paradigm

Closely tied to the concepts of nodes and links is the navigation paradigm. The navigation paradigm consists of envisioning Web use in spatial terms, as navigating from one node to the next, and it includes the claim that navigation in information space is part of the user's experience. The navigation paradigm does not insist that everything that happens on the Web should be envisioned as navigation or even that navigation is foremost in users' minds. But it does hold that living in the world of physical space and, especially, finding our way in the physical world significantly influences how we use and experience the Web.

There are various reasons why navigation is part of the user's experience. The Web, first of all, in contrast to cinema and certain other media, is discontinuous. We experience the Web primarily as a succession of discrete Web pages. With each click one page is replaced by another. Users can and do remember the pages they've seen, and they create a coherent experience out of this succession of pages by understanding them as visits to locations. Users, for instance, know when they have followed a path and then backtracked. In fact, users employ many of the same strategies we all employ when navigating unfamiliar environments in the physical world (what psychologists call "wayfinding"). Both on the Web and in wayfinding, we choose among likely pathways, we keep track of where we've been, and we use certain locations as landmarks. If we get lost we are apt to backtrack to familiar locations, including our entry point, in order to get our bearings. Just as in the physical world, Web users will gradually develop a good mental model if they repeatedly visit a "terrain" of nodes and links.

These activities, furthermore, take place in a cultural context that is pervaded by the navigation paradigm. The terminology of the Web is largely spatial: We speak of "cyberspace," "surfing," and "home pages." We "browse," often with Internet "Explorer." We are often invited to "enter" or "visit" a website.

There is also a strong semantic aspect to Web use that encourages spatial thinking and the navigation paradigm. "Semantics" refers to meaning, and every Web page has meaning—it "says something." As we view a succession of Web pages, we are aware of the "distance" between ideas. That is, we understand different degrees of relatedness as semantic distance. So, for example, we sense a closer connection between the 10 Web pages describing 10 products in an online catalog than the connection between one of the product pages and a page describing the history of the company or the new facility it is opening in Rotterdam.

Especially in the case of hierarchical structures, we have a spatial understanding of the semantic relationships of general and specific information that we call subordination ("sub" meaning under) and super-ordination ("super" meaning above). As we navigate a website, we are aware when we are moving "downward" through the hierarchy to more specific information, when we are moving "across" the hierarchy to information at the same level of specificity, and when we move "upward" toward more general information. For example, we move downward from the Women's Clothing branch of an online store to Sportswear and then to sweaters. We move across from one sweater to another. We may move back up to Sportswear or all the way up to the home page to descend the Men's Clothing branch of the hierarchy.

All these semantic relationships are reinforced visually because we carefully design interfaces to reveal the underlying hierarchical structures along with the other information structures that may be employed. Also users may choose to consult a site map, which, like a node-link diagram, is an explicit spatial representation of the structure of the website.

These semantic relationships of subordination correspond to the way in which we navigate the physical world. As travelers we understand the hierarchical aspect of routes and physical environments. We note when we begin on a broad thoroughfare, then choose a smaller road, and finally enter a narrow lane. We understand the hierarchical aspect of driving to the Zompco Corporate Campus, parking by the Engineering Building, finding the Microelectronics Laboratory, and sitting down in Dr. Nganga's office. Note, by the way, that kinship relationships—parent, child, sibling, and so forth—are a natural non-spatial way for designers to understand information organized in hierarchical structures.

We do not wish to overstate how often or how strongly people experience Web use as navigation. First of all, the competing spatial metaphor of picking things out and summoning them to us is strong and corresponds to the actual technology of the Internet—we do, in fact, summon files from remote servers. Furthermore, the main focus of the user's attention is not on navigation, summoning, or any other metaphor for Web use. Users are busy finding out about tomorrow's weather, buying products, and playing games.

The spatial dimension of Web use, therefore, varies with the circumstances and very likely varies among users as well. Here are some circumstances that bring forth strongly the experience of navigating information space:

- Users are planning an information-seeking strategy. They want to reach a particular destination in a website.
- Users are having trouble finding information or are "lost" in hyperspace.
- Users consciously seek to remember the structure of a website and the route to certain information they have visited.

A spatial understanding of the Web is essential for designers. Whatever other metaphors and perspectives contribute to their experience of websites and to their design efforts, they need to envision Web structure as configurations of nodes and links in information space and, very often, to draw node-link diagrams that explicitly represent the structure of the websites they are designing.

Finally, there is a deep-seated cultural association between new experience and travel. At least when we learn something really new, we feel that we have "gone somewhere." One eloquent formulation of this idea are the opening lines of this poem by the nineteenth century American poet Emily Dickinson. She writes: "There is no frigate like a book to take us lands away." (A frigate is a sailing vessel known for its speed.) Our hypertext jumps enable us to explore new and vast worlds of experience. Designers will intentionally evoke the navigation metaphor, for example, when the pages of a website depict the controls of a space ship with destination nodes represented as bodies in galactic space. Similarly, the antique book graphic for a martial arts club shown in Chapter 11, "Graphic Design," evokes the navigation paradigm by suggesting visually that learning Gongfu is a life-changing journey.

Nodes

We can make good use of this simple and general definition of a node: A node is a substantial chunk of digital content. By "chunk" we mean that a node is perceived by users as internally coherent and as having some kind of boundaries. These boundaries are in part semantic; in a very general sense, a node is "about one thing." Nodes are also bounded semantically by their relationships to other nodes; a node is a "child" of another node, providing further detail, or it's the next stage in a narrative, and so forth.

Very often a node is a physical Web page, and certainly being bounded within a physical page contributes strongly to the user's perception of a node. In fact, we can say that under typical conditions the user's default perception is that a Web page is a node. It is also true, however, that multiple nodes can occupy a single physical page when they are semantically and visually distinct and, especially, when each of these distinct regions of the page is the destination of different links. (Look ahead if you wish to Figure 8.22.) Also, in some circumstances a cluster of closely related pages can best be regarded as a single node. Although our definition of a node comfortably fits a great deal of what we find on the Web, various capabilities of the Web complicate the concept of a node. These include multiple windows, small-size page elements, audio, and pages consisting of independent sections, in particular, framesets.

Let's look first at multiple windows. Though in most cases one Web page replaces another, the user's click sometimes displays a new Web page (in a new instance of the browser) while the first page persists, partly or fully visible. What are we to make of this? Do we want to say that the user is in two places at the same time? It seems more reasonable to say that if the user's attention switches from one window to another, the user has effectively left the old node for the new one.

The Web and many other hypermedia systems allow for small and typically minor screen elements such as pop-up messages and small supplementary windows. Might they be nodes? We argue, no. These are not substantial chunks of content, just behaviors on a page. Even so, we must recognize that some behaviors, notably video and animation sequences, often occupy a small portion of a Web page and yet strongly draw the user's attention. In fact, it may make sense to think of certain behaviors as nodes within nodes, but for the purpose of this book we avoid this and related complexities.

What about audio? Audio sequences that play automatically as background sound are behaviors of a node. But what if the user clicks a link and starts an extended audio sequence? Perhaps we should say that the user has moved into a separate "world" of sound. This idea seems especially plausible when the Web page is essentially a menu (or jukebox) that exists simply to trigger sequences of music. Without a doubt, all the dynamic content types complicate to some degree the concept of a node.

And what do we say when the user clicks a link and a significant portion of the page changes while another significant portion stays the same, as is often the case with framesets? Do we regard this as navigation to a new node or a change within the existing node? The answer depends largely on how much of the page changes: The more that changes, the more the experience resembles changing location. But the specifics of the design can also influence our perception of navigation. For example, if the part of the page that stays the same is a space ship's large control panel and the part that changes is a small "porthole view" of the galaxy, we will still interpret the change as navigation.

Clearly, hypertext theory (and especially the basic version of it presented here) leaves some uncertain and borderline cases in deciding what is and what is not a node. But this does not prevent the concept of a node from serving as a fundamental concept in our efforts to understand the Web and design effective websites.

Graph Theory and a Preview of Hypermedia Information Structures

Much of the value of hypertext theory comes from classifying the various arrangements of nodes and links. These are the hypermedia information structures. The most widely used classification is shown and briefly explained in Figure 6.1.

These structures can be used in combination and blended in various ways. In fact, because the hierarchy is by far the most prevalent information structure, the other structures are often included within hierarchical structures, as shown in Figure 6.2. For example, a tour or demo may appear as a linear sequence within a fundamentally hierarchical website.

A branch of mathematics known as graph theory is devoted to rigorously analyzing and classifying configurations of node and links (Wilson and Watkins 1990; Bollobas 1998). Graph theory is employed in various fields. For example, airlines use graph theory to determine the best ways to schedule flights among a network of cities. Computer scientists model software algorithms as networks of nodes and links and use graph theory to understand and improve performance. Graph theory also tells us much about hypermedia information structures, although these structures do not always conform closely to the classifications used in graph theory. The reason for the divergence is that the hypermedia information structures are not primarily mathematical; rather, they are rhetorical in nature. They describe how people express meaning in non-linear information environments.

Understanding the hypermedia information structures is essential for designers because each structure constitutes a different experience for the user: Each structure expresses different logical relationships, significantly influences writing, makes possible different kinds of navigation, and calls for different interfaces. For example, the same Web pages that we choose to link as a matrix could be strung together as a linear sequence. Doing so, however, would largely dissolve the relationships that the matrix is able to express and would defeat attempts at a workable interface for exploring those relationships. In particular, the matrix allows for comparisons in a way that the linear structure does not. Because the hierarchy is so prevalent on the Web, hierarchies are the main focus in most of the chapters of this book. We focus on the alternatives to the hierarchy in Chapter 13, "Non-Hierarchical Structures."

Links and Linking

Here we explain some important ideas regarding links. You will learn much more about links and linking in later chapters.

Primary and Secondary Links

The distinction between primary and secondary links is traditional in hypertext theory and is very important to Web designers. Primary links establish the basic

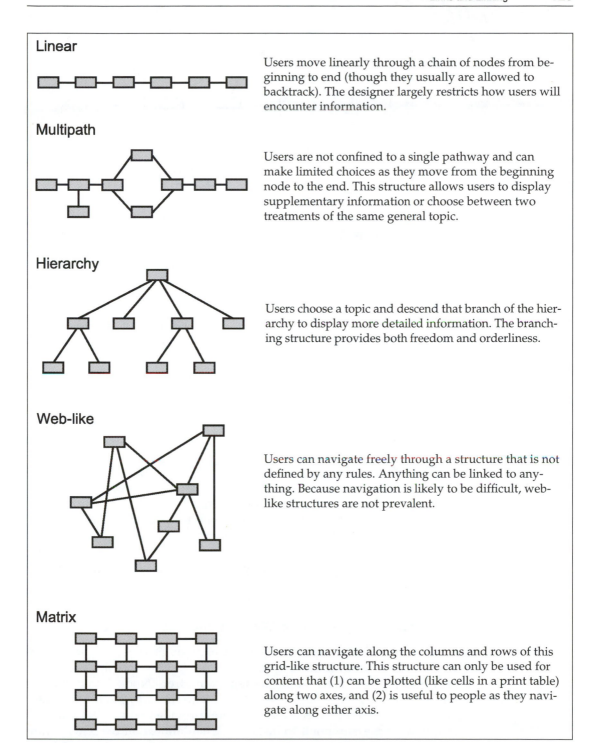

Figure 6.1. The major hypermedia information structures.

Linear

Users move linearly through a chain of nodes from beginning to end (though they usually are allowed to backtrack). The designer largely restricts how users will encounter information.

Multipath

Users are not confined to a single pathway and can make limited choices as they move from the beginning node to the end. This structure allows users to display supplementary information or choose between two treatments of the same general topic.

Hierarchy

Users choose a topic and descend that branch of the hierarchy to display more detailed information. The branching structure provides both freedom and orderliness.

Web-like

Users can navigate freely through a structure that is not defined by any rules. Anything can be linked to anything. Because navigation is likely to be difficult, web-like structures are not prevalent.

Matrix

Users can navigate along the columns and rows of this grid-like structure. This structure can only be used for content that (1) can be plotted (like cells in a print table) along two axes, and (2) is useful to people as they navigate along either axis.

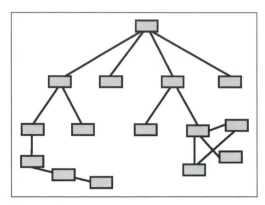

Figure 6.2. A hierarchical website with a linear portion (on the first branch) and a web-like portion (on the third branch).

information structure. In the case of a hierarchical website, all the downward links that make up the branching structure are primary links. In the case of a matrix structure, all the horizontal and vertical links are the primary links. Primary links are very often heavily traveled, but this is not necessarily the case.

Secondary links are additional links that provide greater navigational freedom. They are built when primary links do not suffice for effective navigation. Designers imaginatively locate themselves on the pages of their website and try to anticipate what other pages users will want to visit (or what pages they want to call to the user's attention). If there is no direct route to these pages via primary links, secondary links become desirable. For example, the Asthma Horizons design team might create a secondary link from a page explaining a particular form of asthma to a page on another branch explaining a particularly relevant treatment. Very likely, the designers will also build a reciprocal link from the treatment page to the asthma page. Figure 6.3 shows how secondary links, represented as dotted lines, supplement the primary links in the hierarchy and matrix structures. Just as with primary links, secondary links may or may not be heavily traveled.

Directionality: One-Way and Two-Way Linking

A link is a one-way pathway from, say, Node A to Node B. These one-way pathways, however, allow for backtracking (under most circumstances) via the Back button. Very often, if there is reason for users to jump from Node A to B, there is also reason for users who are on Node B to want to jump to Node A. Consequently, designers often build a reciprocal link and provide two-way linking.

We can, however, easily point to instances when almost all users will want only a one-way pathway. For example, on the Zompco Corporation's website,

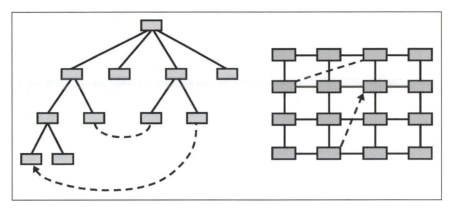

Figure 6.3. A hierarchy and a matrix in which the primary links are supplemented by secondary links. Arrowheads are used to show one-way linking.

there is a page containing the President's welcome address at the yearly stockholders' meeting and another page recounting the history of Zompco. Because the president remarked in the address that she finds the history of the corporation very inspiring, a designer has built a link from this remark to the history page. But few people who decide to learn about Zompco's history would care about the president's remark, and so the designer will not build a link from the history page to the president's address. Similarly, in Asthma Horizons, the page What Is Asthma? mentions that asthma is especially prevalent in urban populations and includes a link to the Urban Populations page. Few people, however, who explore the relatively specialized topic of asthma in urban populations would need a link to a basic explanation of asthma.

As shown in Figure 6.3, the directionality of a link can be represented on node-link diagrams by means of an arrowhead. Although it is logical to represent a two-way link with a double-headed arrow, designers often let plain lines (lines without arrowheads) represent two-way linking for convenience and to avoid visual clutter. In some cases, directionality isn't even decided until relatively late in the development process while text is being written, and so plain links may indicate only that directionality hasn't yet been determined.

In this book we make the default assumption of two-way linking, and our practice is to draw plain lines. We use arrowheads to indicate both one-way linking (the user can only return with the Back button) and situations in which two-way linking is present but traffic is headed almost entirely in a single direction.

Internal and External Links

Another important distinction is between internal and external links. Internal links are the ones you build within your website. External links are the ones that you build to other websites and that other websites build to yours.

To achieve its full potential as a communications medium, the Web should function as a global communications network. From this point of view, providing users with relevant (and frequently updated) links to other websites accords with the spirit of the Internet. Well-chosen external links also make a website more useful and keep people coming back. One of the key aspects of the Asthma Horizons website is its rich collection of external links. Designers should, however, make clear which links are external. Users are disconcerted when they are unexpectedly ejected from the website they chose to visit.

Nodes and Links as Dialog

Contemporary rhetoricians often view texts as a dialog. Readers do not just passively receive information; rather, they interact with the text. By contributing their own thoughts and experiences, readers work with authors to create a unique reading experience. Texts are also dialogic in another sense: To better succeed with their audience, authors instinctively incorporate some of the thinking and attitudes of the audience within their writing.

At the same time, this text dialog is significantly limited because the communication has been fixed, frozen in time, and because the communication moves in only one direction, from the author to the reader. Hypertext theorists with an interest in rhetoric generally assert that the two-way character of textual dialog is greater on the Web than in print. This is because Web users navigate freely within a website (and to other websites) and thereby exercise a kind of control over the dialog by actively choosing what part of the Web "conversation" to listen to. This theoretical perspective can be used to further explain the connection between meaning and navigation in hypermedia information structures.

We can think of a website as a lecturer and the user as the sole member of the audience. (Actually, numerous separate lectures to one-person audiences are taking place simultaneously.) Perhaps the lecturer is an expert in African Studies. Links are akin to moments when the lecturer pauses and asks the audience what aspects of the topic he or she wants to hear about next. The lecturer, however, entertains choices only within the parameters of the lecturer's conception of the subject matter and how the lecturer plans to explain it.

A hierarchical website is roughly akin to the lecturer offering to speak on Kenya, Tanzania, Ghana, and other nations. You choose Tanzania, you learn interesting things, and the lecturer suggests more specific topics about Tanzania. The lecturer is going from general to specific and expects to follow this same structure when explaining the other nations as well. A multipath structure is akin to the lecturer who pursues a single topic, say drought in North Africa, but pauses at times to ask if you would like a point explained in greater depth and, at other times, to ask which of two ways you would like a point explained (e.g., a focus on individual nations or a focus on the region as a whole).

In a matrix structure, the lecturer says: "In regard to any nation in Africa, I am prepared to speak on any of these topics: politics, economics, education, women's issues, family life, music, and visual art. Call out the nation and topic." Note, however, that while the subject area of African Studies can be divided up in this tabular manner, a great many subject areas cannot. The web-like structure is akin to the lecturer taking a very unsystematic approach. The lecturer starts by listing five or six interesting points and says, "Which of these points would you like to hear me speak about?" There is no overall logic or pattern to these points. After you have chosen and heard some interesting material, you are invited to choose among a new set of interesting points.

If the lecturer does not ask for any input from the audience, the lecture is adhering to a linear sequence. In contrast to the lecture, a chat session is a true back-and-forth conversation among the audience members and perhaps the lecturer as well.

Secondary links represent a further set of invitations on the part of the lecturer. These invitations depart from the general plan of the lecturer. For example, the lecturer who normally follows a hierarchical approach says: "There is an interesting connection between what I've been telling you about family life in Tanzania and family life in Ghana. Would you like me to pursue this?" Or, the linear lecturer might say, "You may already be familiar with the introductory portions of my talk. Shall I jump ahead to the more advanced material?"

If the lecturer's initial intentions seemed inflexible and restrictive, you can appreciate the importance of providing secondary links to add flexibility (navigational freedom) to the five hypermedia information structures.

The Navigational Interface and Situation Awareness

Because most websites are first and foremost information environments rather than environments for online computing, the primary role of the interface is to support the navigation of Web content. In other words, the website interface is fundamentally a navigational interface. Navigation implies a destination and some knowledge of the environment. An effective navigational interface, therefore, should do the following:

1. Reveal the underlying information structure—or at least significant portions
2. Reveal the means to reach other parts of the structure
3. Reveal the user's location in this structure

We can summarize these three requirements by stating that the interface should enable users to attain "situation awareness." Without a reasonable level of situation awareness, users cannot navigate effectively (Whitaker 1998). Similarly, in the physical world, if a vessel is sailing through a cluster of islands, the captain should know the positions of all the islands as a group (the overall structure), the vessel's current position, and the open channels of water through which particular islands can be reached. Simply looking for familiar contours of the shoreline and for other landmarks is not as efficient or reliable.

Designing for Situation Awareness

Leaving out the Search feature and index, the navigational interface consists of various kinds of links that properly chosen, grouped, positioned, and labeled enable users to attain situation awareness. Among the most prevalent kinds of links are buttons and underlined text. Important kinds of link groups are navigation bars and navigation columns. Navigation ("nav") bars and columns are orderly arrays of buttons or text links that extend across the top of the page (nav bars) or down the left or right side (nav columns). Other link groups appear not at the top or side but in the main content area (MCA), often in a vertical list.

Figures 6.4 and 6.5 show how the navigational interface reveals the user's location in information space. Figure 6.4 shows a Web page in which the nav bar, nav column, and MCA links collectively reveal a small hierarchy with four levels (shown in Figure 6.5) and reveal the user's location: on the first branch, at the third level, on the third of four sibling nodes. How is this so? The highlight on the nav bar reveals that the user has descended the first branch of the hierarchy. The heading Product 3, in conjunction with the highlight on the nav column, reveals that the user has moved to the third level of the website and is on the third (of four) product pages. The three MCA links to the features of Product 3 reveal that this branch has a fourth level with three children. The semantic relationships (Zompco Corporation→product line→individual products→features) in conjunction with the visual hierarchy of dominant and subordinate page elements enable the user to comprehend what is shown in Figure 6.5.

Keep in mind that you are viewing a single page, a kind of limited snapshot of a user's actual experience. In actual Web use, greater situation awareness is attained in several stages as the user navigates through the site, usually starting

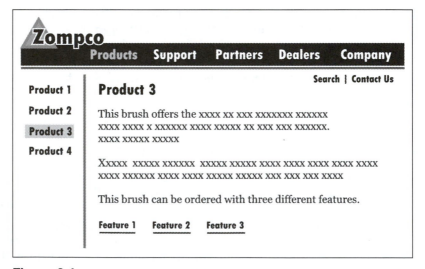

Figure 6.4. A Web page in which the interface reveals the location of the page in the website hierarchy.

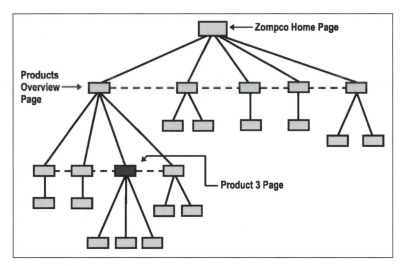

Figure 6.5. A website hierarchy showing the location of the
Product 3 page.

from the home page. In much the same way, it is much easier to grasp the structure of a physical environment by moving around within it. If a user returns regularly to this site, he or she may well build up a detailed and very firm understanding of the site structure.

Readers of a printed book also gain situation awareness. Not only do they understand the progress they are making through a book, but they understand that they are moving through a hierarchy of chapters, sections, and subsections. When a reader finishes the last subsection of Chapter 2 and begins reading the initial paragraphs of Chapter 3, the reader knows she has ascended to the top of the next branch and therefore expects a general discussion on a new topic.

Limits to Situation Awareness

Figure 6.4, to be sure, shows an ideal case. This is because the website is unrealistically small and for other reasons as well. There are, in fact, many circumstances in which users will have much more difficulty attaining situation awareness. Many websites are very large, with thousands of pages and a great many links to those pages. Even when users navigate successfully, they are unlikely to know the specific level and branch they are on. Worse yet, websites of all sizes are often badly designed. Users are confronted by links that are poorly chosen and grouped, confusingly labeled, and overshadowed by competing design elements. Finally, users may be unfamiliar with the subject matter; they may have little semantic understanding of the hierarchical relationships.

Situation awareness, however, is useful, even when approximate. Without knowing their exact location, users can attain situation information that will support effective navigation. In much the same way, a visitor to an unfamiliar city might say to a companion, "As long as we keep following the boulevard, we will eventually come to the street our hotel is on." Even with a complex website, the interface should make clear which of the main branches of the hierarchy the user is on, whether the user is deep or shallow in the hierarchy, and which links will take the user up, down, and across the hierarchy.

There are also differences in how much situation awareness users seek. Deliberate navigation results in greater situation awareness. On the other hand, all of us navigate casually much of the time, focusing on what seems to be the pathway to the content we want, paying little attention to anything else. The most casual form of navigation we term "opportunistic." When engaged in opportunistic navigation, users don't have fixed goals, but attend to what's close at hand if it piques their interest. For example, if a user sees a link for special discounts, he will click, setting aside whatever first brought him to this online store.

We can usefully compare the different degrees of situation awareness in the digital and in the physical worlds. Let's consider how people visit a zoo. This zoo, like many, is laid out hierarchically. From the main gate (equivalent to the top node) there are signs for main categories of zoo animals: reptiles, primates, big cats, etc. In each of these areas, there are signs to more specific zoo "content" deeper in the hierarchy. Thus, the visitor who is intent on seeing snow leopards will surely follow the Big Cats sign rather than the signs for the other main categories. This visitor will then choose the Leopards branch of the big cats exhibit and finally (at the fourth level) will find the snow leopards.

If this person navigates the zoo in a deliberate manner, he or she will notice that the pathway to the big cats starts next to the pathway to the primates and will notice where the lion exhibit is located in relation to the leopards. Soon this person will understand the layout of the zoo. Someone who expects to return to the zoo is especially likely to seek situation awareness. A more casual zoo visitor follows signs to the snow leopards but gains significantly less situation awareness. Finding the snow leopards will not much help this person find other animals in the zoo. Still more casual about navigation is the opportunistic visitor. This person navigates without goals or shifts goals readily. Part way along the route to the snow leopards, this person might notice a sign for the tigers or the reptile house and head that way. This person might navigate all day in an undirected manner and will attain little situation awareness.

Designers should support deliberate, casual, and even opportunistic behavior, and a well-designed interface—like good zoo signage—can serve these different modes of navigation. These issues are discussed further in Chapter 7, "Hierarchies," and Chapter 8, "The Navigational Interface."

Following the Scent of a Link

The concept of "scent," based on animal foraging theory, is a relatively new way to think about Web navigation (Pirolli and Card 1999). The idea is that users follow an information scent to the page with the content they are looking for. As they get closer to their destination, the scent gets stronger.

Users can follow scents without a great deal of situation awareness, but the user does need to distinguish between promising and unpromising pathways and recognize when he or she is moving toward the destination node. From the designer's point of view, the goal is to create links that provide distinct scents that can be recognized and followed.

Scent also helps us understand how persistent users will be when following a series of links to a destination. With a weak scent, a user perceives that he is not close to the destination and that several clicks will be required. With an indistinct scent, the user has little confidence in reaching the destination at all. Web users (somewhat like foraging animals) perform an informal and largely unconscious cost-benefit analysis. They weigh the value of reaching the destination (the reward promised by the scent) against the time and effort required, and they factor in the prospect of failing to reach the destination and thereby wasting their effort. Furthermore, the user may also be picking up at least a faint scent from competing websites. Designers, therefore, must ensure that the user's cost-benefit analysis consistently favors following scents to their pages.

Node-Link Diagrams

Hypertext theory and the navigation paradigm are the theoretical basis for representing the node-link structure of a website using a node-link diagram, a set of note cards, and an outliner. Of the three representations, the node-link diagram is best able to visually convey information about structure. Now you will learn to make node-link diagrams that will serve you well in designing websites.

Representing Nodes and Links Effectively

Designers need to consider what kind of node-link diagram will best meet their needs. Issues to consider are whether to create a complete representation of a website's nodes and links, how much information to encode in the diagram, and (especially in hierarchical diagrams) what format to use.

Partial Diagrams and Visual Shorthand

Although designers certainly benefit from a visual overview of an entire website, this may not be feasible, especially when websites consist of hundreds or thousands of pages and the great many links that connect these pages. (Recall the crowded node-link diagram of Asthma Horizons shown in Figure 3.3.) It is often better, therefore, to diagram just the main parts of the project or the parts you are currently working on and to rely on an outline (or spreadsheet or database) for a listing of all the pages in the website.

There are, however, techniques for saving time and conserving space. These techniques let you create more comprehensive diagrams. In Figure 6.6 a designer is planning the center branch of a hierarchical website. The designer knows that the left branch of the hierarchy has 11 nodes at the third level, but she doesn't

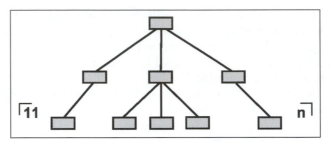

Figure 6.6. A technique for saving time and representing more nodes than can fit on a diagram.

want to invest the time or space drawing these nodes. So, she uses a bracket and number to indicate that the one pictured node stands for all 11 nodes. The designer has barely begun to think about the third branch. But the bracket and letter "n" (the mathematical notation for "any quantity") indicates that the one pictured node stands for whatever number may ultimately appear on the third branch. Another common sense idea is to simply write text notations to explain parts of the diagram that you don't want to or can't draw. So, for example, the designer of a large online store might note, "We expect 400 to 450 nodes on this branch, each representing a product description."

Encoding Extra Information

In many node-link diagrams only basic information is represented. A rectangle (or other shape) tells us nothing about the node except that it is a node. Much the same for link lines, except that dotted lines often indicate secondary links and arrowheads may be used to indicate directionality.

Designers, however, can encode extra information in these diagrams. So, for example, in the node-link diagram for the multipath tutorial shown in Figure 6.7,

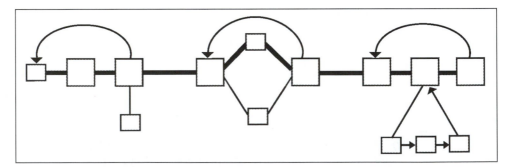

Figure 6.7. A node-link diagram of a multipath tutorial in which a significant amount of extra information has been encoded. The backward-pointing, curved arrows represent the student's opportunity to repeat each of the three lessons.

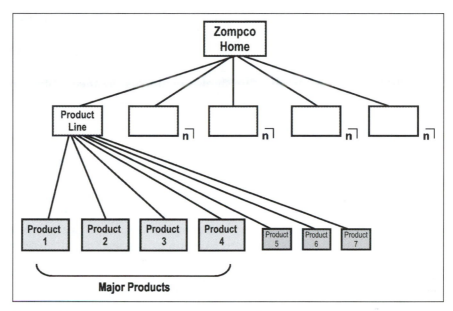

Figure 6.8. Encoding distinctions about the Zompco Corporation's product line.

the thickness of the lines indicates which pathways the designers expect to be most used, the size of the boxes indicates very roughly the amount of content on the pages, and the distance between the nodes, indicating semantic distance, reminds the design team that the tutorial consists of three lessons.

Very often the child nodes of a parent node belong to different logical groups—for example, the node introducing the Zompco Corporation's product line might have four child nodes representing major products and three child nodes representing minor products. These distinctions can be encoded as shown in Figure 6.8. This diagram will remind the design team that when the product overview page is designed, the four links to major products should be more prominent (perhaps larger, but perhaps just placed higher in a list) than the three links to minor products.

Node-link diagrams resemble various kinds of process flowcharts, and so various flowchart conventions, such as using a particular shape to represent decision points or user input, can be employed in node-link diagrams. For a good treatment of node-link diagrams that incorporate various flowcharting concepts and conventions, see Jesse James Garrett's "A Visual Vocabulary for Describing Information Architecture and Interaction Design" at www.jjg.net/ia/visvocab.

Different Formats for Node-Link Diagrams

Thus far in this book we have drawn node-link diagrams using the very familiar and intuitive "inverted tree" format. There are, however, two other important formats: the "indented" format and the "radial" format. In Figures 6.9–6.11, we show the same hierarchical structure represented in the three formats and explain each format's benefits and drawbacks.

The *inverted tree* format has become very prevalent because it communicates the idea of branches and levels very clearly and because secondary links can easily be added to the diagram. It also reinforces the idea that we navigate downward in a hierarchical structure. One drawback is that the inverted tree format consumes a lot of space, especially horizontal space, on the page or screen. Note that (at least for readers of languages that are written left-to-right) there is an implied left-to-right sequence among any group of sibling nodes. For example, the left-most child of Node C seems to have some kind of precedence over the middle and right nodes.

The *indented* format is visually more complex than the inverted tree, but it is easy to draw and it is compact. Better yet, it uses more vertical space than horizontal space, which is very advantageous because printed pages are usually longer than wide and because computer displays scroll. Note that there is a strongly implied top-to-bottom sequence among the child nodes.

The *radial* format gives the designer a very different feeling about the hierarchy because the nodes emanate (like the spokes of a wheel) from a central point. You do not navigate downward but rather outward. Also, there is only a faint (clockwise) sense of precedence among sibling nodes. One drawback of the radial format is that diagrams are more difficult to draw and label. Also, the lines representing secondary links extend all over the diagram and are visually distracting.

The key idea behind all kinds of node-link diagrams is to do what works best for you and your design team. Different projects will call for different formats, different ways of encoding information, and different degrees of completeness. There are no rules except that everyone involved in the project must know what conventions are being followed.

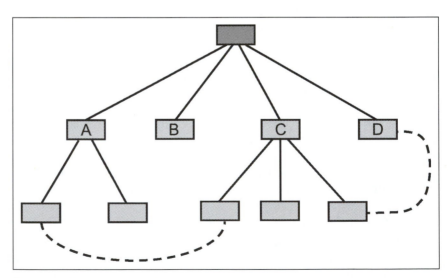

Figure 6.9. The inverted tree format.

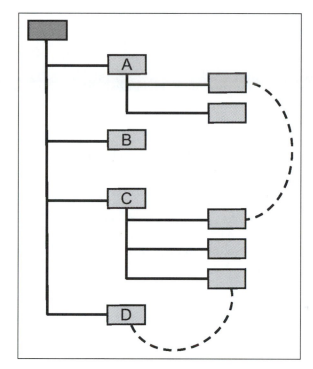

Figure 6.10. The indented format.

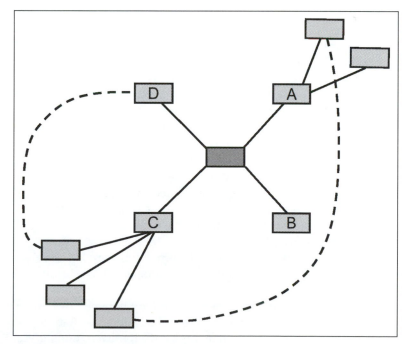

Figure 6.11. The radial format.

Summary

1. Hypertext theory is fundamental for understanding the Web and hypermedia. Because it is akin to taking an X-ray of a website, hypertext theory is especially important for designers. Hypertext theory is grounded in both rhetoric and cognitive science/human-computer interaction (HCI).

2. Hypertext theory considers how various arrangements of nodes and links express meaning and how these arrangements are reflected on the user interface. Hypertext theory classifies these arrangements of nodes and links into various kinds of hierarchical and non-hierarchical structures, often called "information structures."

3. The navigation paradigm, an aspect of hypertext theory, envisions Web use in spatial terms as navigating from one node to the next and includes the claim that navigation is a part of the user's experience. The spatial dimension of Web use varies with the circumstances and among users.

4. A node is a substantial chunk of digital content. By "chunk" we mean that a node is perceived as internally coherent and as having some kind of boundaries. Nodes often correspond to physical Web pages, but multiple nodes may reside on a single page and a node can encompass several pages.

5. Various Web capabilities complicate the concept of a node. These include multiple windows, small-size page elements, audio, and pages consisting of independent sections (in particular, framesets). Even so, the node remains a fundamental concept in our efforts to understand the Web and design effective websites.

6. Hypertext theory defines five information structures: the linear, multipath, hierarchical, matrix, and web-like structures. Each structure expresses different logical relationships, significantly influences writing, makes possible different kinds of navigation, and calls for different interfaces. The hierarchy is the most prevalent, and very often the others are included within a hierarchical website.

7. We can distinguish between primary and secondary links. Primary links establish the basic information structure. Secondary links supplement the primary links and provide greater navigational freedom. Secondary links are often represented in node-link diagrams with dotted lines.

8. Links are inherently one-directional, although users can backtrack using the Back button. Very often, however, designers provide two-way linking. In this book, two-way linking, represented by plain lines, is assumed. Link lines with arrowheads represent both one-way links and situations in which traffic is headed almost entirely in a single direction.

9. We can also distinguish external links, those pointing to other websites, from internal links. Well-chosen external links make a website more useful and keep people coming back. Designers should indicate clearly which links are external.

10. Web use can be understood as a dialog between designers and users. Each information structure can be viewed as a lecturer with a particular plan for presenting the subject matter. Links are the invitations given to the audience to

re-direct the lecturer. Secondary links are invitations to direct the discourse in a manner that departs from the overall plan of the lecturer.

11. The primary role of the interface is to support navigation of Web content and to allow the user to attain situation awareness. The interface, therefore, should do the following:

    1. Reveal the underlying information structure—or at least significant portions
    2. Reveal the means to reach other parts of the structure
    3. Reveal the user's location in this structure

12. The links that make up the navigational interface must be chosen, grouped, positioned, and labeled to enable users to attain situation awareness. Even so, because of the complexity of many websites, because of poor design, and because users may not be familiar with the subject matter, only partial situation awareness may be attained.

13. There are also differences in how much situation awareness users seek. Deliberate navigation results in greater situation awareness. Often, however, users navigate casually or opportunistically and gain less situation awareness.

14. Web navigation can be understood in terms of "scents" that users follow to reach their destination. The closer the user gets, the stronger the scent. The designer's goal is to create links with distinct scents that can be distinguished and followed.

15. Hypertext theory and the navigation paradigm are the theoretical basis for representing the node-link structure of a website using an outline, a set of note cards, or a node-link diagram. There are various techniques through which node-link diagrams become especially rich and useful representations of structure.

16. A complete node-link diagram is usually not feasible. Various techniques, however, save time and conserve space.

17. Node-link diagrams may encode only basic information about structure. But designers can also encode information about the amount of content on each page, the semantic distance among pages, the amount of traffic that is expected, and how prominent a link should be on the interface.

18. Node-link diagrams are very often drawn using the highly intuitive inverted tree format. The indented format and radial format are also useful. The indented tree format is easy to draw and conserves horizontal space. The radial format gives the designer a very different feeling about the hierarchy because the nodes emanate from a central point.

References

Bakhtin, Mikhail M. 1989. *The Dialogic Imagination: Four Essays.* Caryl Emerson, trans. Michael Holquist, ed. Austin, TX: University of Texas Press.

Bernstein, Mark. 1998. Patterns of hypertext, *Proceedings of ACM Hypertext '98* (Pittsburgh, PA), 21–29.

Bernstein, Mark. 1991. Deeply intertwingled hypertext: The navigation problem reconsidered. *Technical Communication* 38.1: 41–47.

Bollobas, Bela. 1998. *Modern Graph Theory*. New York: Springer Verlag.

Bolter, Jay David. 1991. *Writing Space: The Computer, Hypertext, and the History of Writing*. Hillsdale, NJ: Lawrence Erlbaum Associates.

Bolter, Jay David, and Richard Grusin. 1999. *Remediation: Understanding New Media*. Cambridge, MA: MIT Press.

Bush, Vannevar. 1945. As we may think. *Atlantic Monthly* 176.1: (July) 101–108. This article is available on the Web at www.theatlantic.com/unbound/flash-bks/computer/bushf.htm and a version with valuable commentary was reprinted in the ACM magazine *Interactions* 3.2: (March 1996) 35–46. Sections 6–8 are the key sections in Bush's article.

Conklin, Jeff. 1987. Hypertext: An introduction and survey. *IEEE-CS Computer* 20.9: (September) 17–41.

Duffy, Thomas M., and David H. Jonassen, eds. 1992. *Constructivism and the Technology of Instruction*. Hillsdale, NJ: Lawrence Erlbaum Associates.

Garrett, Jesse James. A visual vocabulary for describing information architecture and interaction design. www.jjg.net/ia/visvocab

Golovchinsky, Gene, and Catherine Marshall. 2000. Hypertext interaction revisited. *Proceedings of ACM Hypertext '00.* (San Antonio, TX) 171–179.

Greco, Diane. 1996. Hypertext with consequences: Recovering a politics of hypertext. *Proceedings of ACM Hypertext '96.* (Bethesda, MD), 85–92.

Halasz, Frank G. 1988. Reflections on NoteCards: Seven issues for the next generation of hypermedia systems. *Communications of the ACM* 31.7: (July) 836–852.

Horton, William K. 1994. *Designing and Writing Online Documentation: Hypermedia for Self-Supporting Products*. 2d ed. New York: Wiley.

Johnson-Eilola, Johndan. 1997. *Nostalgic Angels: Rearticulating Hypertext Writing*. Norwood, NJ: Ablex Publishing.

Jones, Robert A., and Rand Spiro. 1995. Contextualisation, cognitive flexibility, and hypertext: The convergence of interpretive theory, cognitive psychology, and advanced information technology. In *The Cultures of Computing*. S. L. Star, ed. Cambridge, MA: Blackwell, 146–57.

Landow, George P. 1997. *Hypertext 2.0: The Convergence of Critical Theory and Technology*. Baltimore: Johns Hopkins University Press.

Lombard, Matthew, and Theresa Ditton. 1997. At the heart of it all: The concept of presence. *Journal of Computer Mediated Communication*. 3.2 (September). www.ascusc.org/jcmc/vol3/issue2/lombard.html

MacOvski, Michael, ed. 1997. *Dialogue and Critical Discourse: Language, Culture, Critical Theory*. Oxford: Oxford University Press.

Marshall, Catherine, C. 1998. Toward an ecology of hypertext annotation. *Proceedings of ACM Hypertext '98.* (Pittsburgh, PA) 40–49.

McKnight, Cliff, Andrew Dillon, and John Richardson. 1993. *HyperText: A Psychological Perspective*. Chichester: Ellis Horwood.

McKnight, Cliff, Andrew Dillon, and John Richardson. 1991. *Hypertext in Context*. Cambridge: Cambridge University Press.

Nelson, Theodor. 1992. *Literary Machines*. Sausalito, CA: Mindful Press. Originally published in 1980.

Pirolli, Peter, and Stuart Card. 1999. Information foraging. *Psychological Review* 106.4: 643–75.

Steuer, Jonathan. 1992. Defining virtual reality: Dimensions determining telepresence. *Journal of Communication* 42.4: (Autumn) 73–93 .

Wilson, Robin J., and John J. Watkins. 1990. *Graphs: An Introductory Approach.* New York: John Wiley & Sons, Inc.

Whitaker, Leslie A. 1998. Human navigation. In *Human Factors and Web Development.* Chris Forsythe, Eric Grose, and Julie Ratner, eds. Mahwah, NJ: Lawrence Erlbaum Associations, 63–71.

Discussion and Application

Items for Discussion

1. There are many ways to study and understand the Web and Web design. Identify courses you have taken (or knowledge you have gained outside of courses) that pertain in some way to the Web and Web design. What disciplines do these courses represent? What perspective do they offer?

2. Find a website that explicitly evokes some form of the travel/navigation metaphor. How is this accomplished. Find an example other than a website that welcomes users with "Enter."

3. When movies are distributed on DVDs, they usually are divided into separate "chapters" that users can access individually. Discuss these chapters. Do you regard them as distinct nodes making up a linear sequence? Is it useful to think of a movie as a set of nodes?

4. Find two websites, one a commercial website and one non-profit, that provide external links. What kinds of benefits do these external links offer users? What cues are provided that these are external links?

5. Think about an occasion when you were lost in physical space. Why did you get lost? What kinds of information or cues about your environment were lacking? How did you reach your destination (e.g., finding a landmark, asking for directions, stumbling upon your destination)? Did you gain significantly greater situation awareness in the process of reaching your destination? Compare this experience with problems you have had getting lost in a website.

6. Think about the ways in which designers and planners in various fields create representations of what they hope to accomplish. What do these representations show, what do they look like, and how are they used?

7. Attempt to extend standard hypertext theory. For example, we have seen that various capabilities of the Web complicate the concept of a node. Might it be possible to modify the concept of a node to better accommodate these capabilities? Consider also how designers might usefully represent behavior taking place within a node? Do you have any other ideas?

8. Examine the home page of a (hierarchical) website you know well. Using both your existing knowledge of the site and what you can infer from the

home page, describe the content under each main branch of the hierarchy. What else can you remember or infer about the content and structure of the site?

9. Create a node-link diagram for a website. Draw a complete node-link diagram only if the website is small. Choose a format and decide what kinds of information you will encode in the diagram.

10. This chapter shows how various kinds of information about a website can be encoded in a node-link diagram. Can you think of other kinds of information that, under certain circumstances, can be usefully encoded?

11. Concept maps are a well-known way to diagram ideas using nodes and links. What are the similarities and differences between node-link diagrams and concept maps? For information about concept maps see the concept map section of the website of the University of West Florida's Institute for Human and Machine Cognition, http://cmap.coginst.uwf.edu/info/faq.html.

12. You are attending a meeting of Web designers and find yourself discussing hypertext theory with a Web designer from another company. The other designer refers to two information structures with which you are unfamiliar. These are the "open web" and the "closed web." The designer sketches them for you. Analyze the two sketches (shown below) using the concepts presented in this chapter. Would you say that these sketches represent a web-like structure? Characterize the information structures shown in the sketches.

13. A fourth format for representing hierarchical structures in node-link diagrams is the nested box format. In this format the top node is represented by a large rectangle. The second-level nodes are rectangles placed within the top-node rectangle, and all lower-level nodes are boxes placed within their parent node. Link lines are drawn among the boxes. Draw a nested box version of the same hierarchy that appears in Figure 6.9. Why is this format less prevalent than the others?

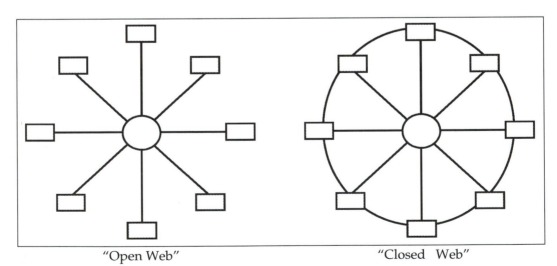

"Open Web"   "Closed Web"

Figure 6.12. Two information structures that a designer has referred to as an "open web" and a "closed web."

Application to Your Project

1. Create several node-link diagrams for the project you are developing. Experiment with the different formats, with different levels of detail, and with the kinds of information you choose to encode in your diagram. Explain what worked best and why.

2. What plans do you have for external links? How will these external links add value to your website?

7

Hierarchies and Organizing Content

Introduction

In this chapter, we focus specifically on the hierarchical information structure, which, as you know, is by far the most prevalent information structure on the Web. In this chapter you will learn the following:

- The three kinds of hierarchies and when each should be used
- More about the use of links in hierarchical structures. You will learn about the different kinds of primary and secondary links and about other kinds of links as well.
- The specific tasks necessary to organize content into an understandable, navigable hierarchical structure

In the next chapter you will learn how to design Web pages to reveal the underlying structure of a website to the user.

The Prevalence and Usefulness of Hierarchies

How prevalent is the hierarchical information structure? We judge that at least 95% of all websites are fundamentally hierarchical. This is not a result of a fashion or trend. It is because we as human beings naturally build coherence and order into our world by establishing categories and subcategories. We divide our planet into continents, nations, and smaller divisions such as provinces and states. We divide the animals and plants around us according to the categories of kingdom, phylum, class, order, family, genus, and species. When we design traditional print books, we typically divide them into chapters, sections, and subsections. The world doesn't always divide neatly and cleanly into hierarchies:

There are many hierarchies in which entities fit into two (or more) locations in the hierarchy—for example, food items in a supermarket may fit two categories. But the basis of the classification is still hierarchical.

The central role of hierarchies both in Web design and human culture in general is affirmed in a sophisticated book on Web design written by the information retrieval experts Louis Rosenfeld and Peter Morville (1998):

> The foundation of almost all good information architectures is a well-designed hierarchy. In this hypertext world of nets and webs such a statement may seem blasphemous, but it's true.... Hierarchy is ubiquitous in our lives and informs our understanding of the world in a profound and meaningful way. (p. 37)

Another way to explain the prevalence and usefulness of hierarchies is that the hierarchy is the ideal combination of freedom and orderliness. The freedom comes, first of all, from the branching structure that defines the hierarchy. There may be few or many branches, but the primary links that make up the branches consistently offer users choices as they descend deeper into the hierarchy. This navigational freedom is greatly supplemented by the possibility of secondary links. The orderliness comes from the logic of branches and levels. Broadly speaking, every node in a hierarchy exists on a particular branch and at a particular level—almost like a street address. Often users remember the path they have taken and are aware of their exact or approximate location within the hierarchy. Often they don't. But in either case, the orderly arrangement of nodes and links makes navigation easier and lends a sense of structure to the user's experience.

Three Kinds of Hierarchies

One strength of the hierarchical structure is that it allows for much diversity in design. The starting point for this diversity is that there are three different kinds of hierarchies: the strict hierarchy, the hierarchy with secondary links, and the hierarchy with converging links. Each variation provides a different experience for users, and each requires different design strategies.

The three kinds of hierarchies differ on the basis of the kinds of links they employ. Therefore, we will be looking carefully at linking. You have already learned about the standard primary links that define the branching structure of a typical hierarchy; in this section you will learn the function of special "converging" primary links. You have already learned about secondary links; in this section you will learn the distinctive uses of associative and systematic secondary links. You will also learn about the function of some special kinds of links that are used in all kinds of hierarchical websites.

The Strict Hierarchy

The strict hierarchy, shown in Figure 7.1, is defined by its reliance on standard primary links. Originating on the home page (the first level of the hierarchy), they

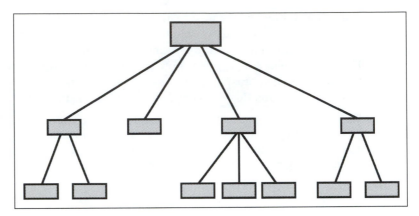

Figure 7.1. A strict hierarchy. The structure is defined by standard primary links.

link to the second-level pages and thereby define the branches of the hierarchy. More standard primary links extend down from the second-level pages and continue to divide at each level until the bottom of the hierarchy is reached.

The strict hierarchy is very orderly. A user who descends one main branch in a strict hierarchy must return to the home page before descending another main branch. Because users are always starting new journeys from the home page, they are more apt to learn how the website is organized and to know their current location in the hierarchy.

On the other hand, the strict hierarchy is restrictive and unrevealing (recall the analogy of the inflexible lecturer in the previous chapter). For example, the State of West Virginia might create a website for tourism that contains four main branches—one for the north, south, east and west regions of the state. The third level on each branch promotes the tourist attractions in a particular region, and so there might well be a node promoting whitewater rafting at the third level on both the Northern West Virginia branch and the Eastern West Virginia branch. Very likely a tourist interested in one rafting opportunity would be interested in another, but in the strict hierarchy there is no direct route between the rafting nodes. Not only does this mean more clicks, but the user who explores the Northern West Virginia branch may never even learn about the rafting opportunities in Eastern West Virginia. This problem and others are solved by the hierarchy with secondary links.

Hierarchies with Secondary Links

Secondary links supplement the navigation pathways provided by the standard primary links. Because of this additional navigational freedom, the hierarchy with secondary links is far more prevalent than the strict hierarchy. With a rich network of secondary links, the user is like a squirrel jumping freely among the branches of the hierarchy rather than a caterpillar crawling up and down along

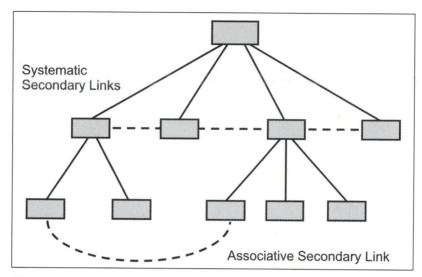

Figure 7.2. A hierarchy with systematic and associative secondary links.

the branches. There are two kinds of secondary links: associative and systematic. As shown in Figure 7.2, systematic secondary links connect a group of nodes in a systematic pattern whereas associative secondary links simply connect two nodes. Both kinds of secondary links are explained in the following sections.

Associative Secondary Links

Associative secondary links are built when a designer sees a relevant association or connection between two Web pages, very often pages on different branches of the hierarchy. These links, then, are similar to the cross references in traditional books. Well-chosen associative links add considerable value to a website. For example, two-way associative secondary linking certainly solves the whitewater rafting problem, as you can see in Figure 7.3. Similarly, the Asthma Horizons website might provide a two-way associative secondary link between a page explaining a particular form of childhood asthma and a page explaining a particularly relevant treatment.

To help users grasp the structure of the hierarchy, associative secondary links should be visually distinct from primary links. As shown in Figure 7.4, associative secondary links often appear in a brief list strategically placed alongside a column of text. The list is frequently introduced by a heading such as "Related Links" or "See also." As the figure also shows, it is good practice to list external links in a similar way.

Both associative secondary links and external links may be embedded in a paragraph of text as shown in Figure 7.5. Embed links with discretion, however, for numerous embedded links make a paragraph difficult to read. Also,

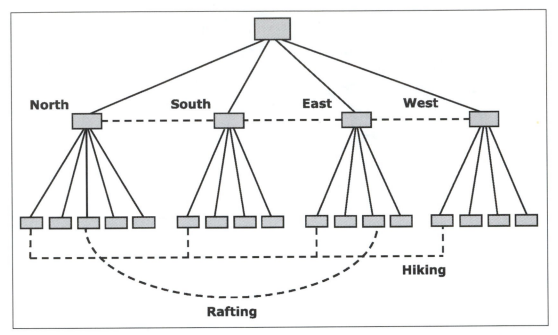

Figure 7.3. A West Virginia tourism website with systematic secondary links connecting the regions (second-level siblings) and the hiking pages (cousins) across all regions. Associative secondary links connect two whitewater rafting pages.

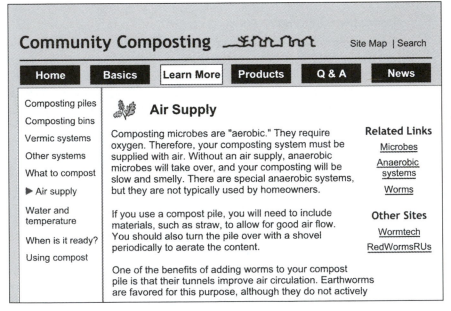

Figure 7.4. A third-level Web page with both associative secondary links and external links listed to the right of the text column.

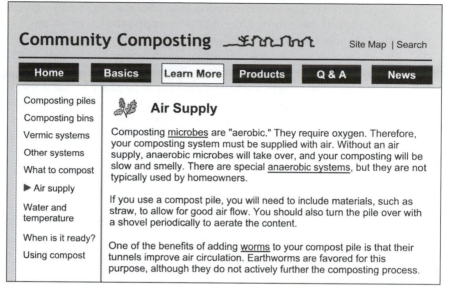

Figure 7.5. A third-level Web page with associative secondary links embedded in paragraphs of text in the main content area. There is also a nav bar with systematic secondary links to each of the five main branches of the hierarchy plus a link to the home page. The nav column contains systematic secondary links connecting the third-level pages.

embedded links frequently reveal less about the destination of the links. Will users be able to determine whether the embedded link "worms" is an internal or external link?

Systematic Secondary Links

As stated, systematic secondary links connect a group of nodes in some kind of systematic pattern. Very often systematic secondary links are used to connect a group of sibling nodes (all the children of one parent). For example, as shown in Figure 7.3, it makes sense to build a set of systematic secondary links across the four second-level pages representing the regions of West Virginia. It might also make sense to build systematic secondary links connecting the hiking pages on the third level of each branch—a linking of four cousins. At times it's a judgment call whether a group of links is systematic or associative. This is ok. The distinction remains useful for designers.

Systematic secondary links can be implemented as Next and Previous buttons. Much more often they are implemented as a navigation bar that extends across the top of the page or as a navigation column that extends down the left (or right) side of the page. Nav bars and columns are excellent interface elements for several reasons. First, in contrast to Next and Previous buttons, nav bars and nav columns link all-to-all and thereby provide accelerated navigation: The user can jump from one sibling directly to any of the other siblings. Second, nav bars and columns contribute to a consistent appearance from page to page and remind the user what the available navigation options are. Finally, as Figure 7.5 shows, they often feature highlights and markers (often wedge-shaped) that help reveal the user's current location in the hierarchy.

Figure 7.6a depicts a set of systematic secondary links connecting the second-level siblings of a hierarchy. To be precise, this representation corresponds to an interface with Next and Previous buttons rather than a nav bar or a nav column. This is because the diagram shows the user moving "one step at a time" across the

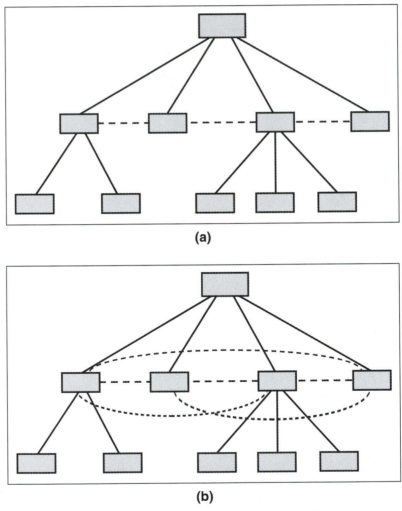

(a)

(b)

Figure 7.6. Figure 7.6a is the standard representation of systematic secondary links. Figure 7.6b more accurately represents this idea but is overly cluttered.

sibling nodes. The all-to-all linking of a nav bar or column is represented precisely in Figure 7.6b. Designers, however, avoid this cluttered representation; they prefer the less complicated diagram shown in Figure 7.6a.

Hierarchies with Converging Primary Links

The third kind of hierarchy is distinctive because it employs converging primary links, links that converge on a single child node so that the child has two (or more) parent nodes. This child node may or may not have its own children. Two converging primary links and their child node are shown in Figure 7.7. In the case of standard primary links, a node can only have one true parent, even though it may be the destination of one or more secondary links. As we will show, converging primary links are valuable whenever a Web page seems to fit more than one logical category so that users may want to reach it by means of more than one branch. Also, we will explain the difference between converging branches on a small scale and on a large scale.

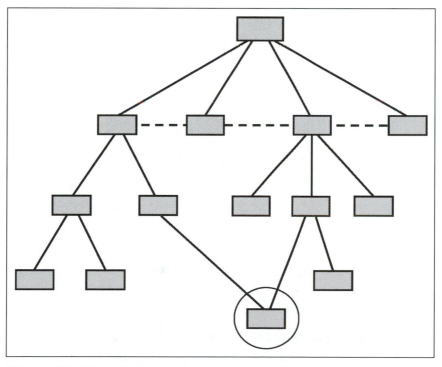

Figure 7.7. A hierarchy with converging primary links. The circled node has two parent nodes.

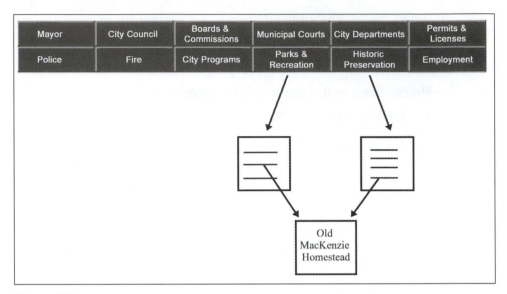

Figure 7.8. A node that can be accessed by two converging branches.

Converging Primary Links on a Small Scale

This technique is employed when just one page or a few pages fit two or more logical categories. For example, in the City of Centerville website depicted in Figure 7.8, some users are apt to look for information about the Old MacKenzie Homestead (which is located in a small park) on the Parks & Recreation branch and others on the Historic Preservation branch. Rather than frustrate half the users, the designer places the page under both branches.

Although converging primary links solve a major navigation problem, they pose certain difficulties. First, the Old MacKenzie Homestead page must be written to make sense in the context of either branch. For example, if the writer describes the homestead entirely as a park facility, the text may well confuse users who reach this page from the Historical Preservation branch. Second, if the website employs highlights (or markers) to show the user's location in the hierarchy, the highlighting should reflect each user's particular path. In other words, if a user reaches the Old Mackenzie Homestead page via the Historical Preservation page, the nav bar on the Old Mackenzie Homestead page should show a highlight on the Historical Preservation button rather than the Parks & Recreation button.

Converging Primary Links on a Large Scale

On many websites, branches converge in an extensive and systematic manner with many nodes appearing at the bottom of multiple overlapping hierarchies. The reason is to give users multiple views of and pathways to the same content in order to

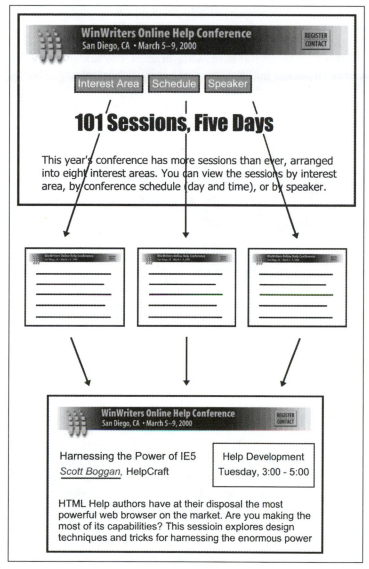

Figure 7.9. Converging primary links on a large scale. Each page describing a conference presentation exists on three branches. A user, for example, can navigate from the Interest Area link to a list of conference topics and then to Scott Boggan's presentation. (www.winwriters.com)

support different ways of thinking about the content and different tasks. For example, in the WinWriters website, shown in Figure 7.9, potential conference attendees can peruse the presentations by interest area, conference schedule, or speaker.

Online stores, eager not to miss any selling opportunities, often make extensive use of converging primary links. For example, an online computer store might provide three routes to the page describing the Palm M–505 PDA (personal digital assistant): the Hardware branch, the Lifestyle branch, and the Brands We Carry branch. Finally, note that we can characterize a website as being both a hierarchy with secondary links and a hierarchy with converging primary links. Indeed, a great many websites belong to both categories. But the strict hierarchy excludes the other two categories.

Special Purpose Links: Upward Links, Links to Utility Pages, and Links for Spotlighting Key Content

A key objective of this book is to provide you with a design vocabulary that is complete enough to help you understand the great diversity of designs that you encounter when you explore the Web and to serve as a springboard for your own creative efforts. To do so, we need to introduce a few more kinds of links: upward links, utility links, shortcut links, and duplicate links. These links may also meet the definitions of primary and secondary links, but we are mainly interested in the functions they serve as special purpose links. These special purpose links can be used with all three kinds of hierarchies. Finally, external links are also a kind of special purpose link.

Upward Links

Users spend most of their time moving down and across hierarchies. But they most certainly ascend hierarchies as well. Very often users return all the way to the home page to begin a new information-seeking task on another branch. Also, when users have become disoriented in a website, they may jump to the home page to make a new start. Finally, although designers tend to assume that users will enter their website at the home page, anyone can build a link into the interior of another website, and Web-wide search engines often send users directly to interior pages. These users are especially apt to want to jump directly to the home page in order to learn the website's purpose and gain other orientation information. To accommodate these needs, websites normally provide a link to the home page on every page. An emerging convention is to use an organization's logo as a link to the home page.

Users also are likely to want to ascend one level, and so designers very often provide a link to each page's parent node (and perhaps to the aunts as well). Other upward links may be provided. It is not always feasible, however, to provide unlimited upward linking. For example, if a website has a fifth level, there will probably not be direct links to pages at the third level. The user may need to ascend to the second level and then click down.

Links to Utility Pages

Just as we routinely link almost every page of a website to the home page, there are often other pages (or clusters of pages) that are linked to from almost every page on the site. These include the help system, the site map, the Search feature, and the checkout area of an e-commerce site. These pages can be referred to as "utility pages." This name is meant to suggest that they do not contain regular content, but serve other important functions.

Figure 7.10 shows how a website's utility pages might be shown on a node-link diagram. Their special status is suggested by their location to the upper right of the home page. The upward arrows indicate that these pages can be accessed throughout the website. Note that the help system is represented as being composed of a cluster of pages.

As shown in Figure 7.11, utility links often appear together at the top right of the page. Quite often they appear on a special utility bar (or "function bar") located just below the banner or nav bar. Normally it is bad practice to include links for regular content among utility links.

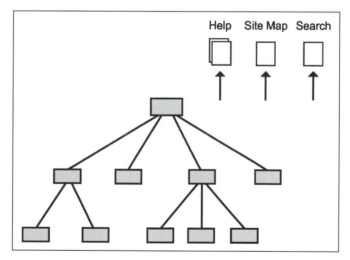

Figure 7.10. Utility pages shown on a node-link diagram.

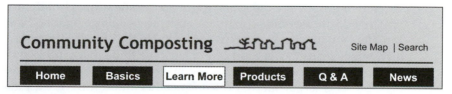

Figure 7.11. Utility links (Site Map and Search) located at the top right of the page.

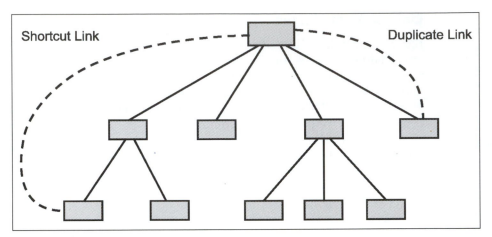

Figure 7.12. A node-link diagram showing a shortcut spotlight link and a duplicate spotlight link.

Spotlighting with Shortcut Links

A shortcut link, represented in Figure 7.12, is a downward link that skips one or more levels. Shortcut links are usually used in a strategy we call spotlighting. This is the attempt to entice the user to a page that the designer considers important without relying on the user to follow a link on the nav bar or another standard interface element. For example, on the Tully's Coffee Website, the page devoted to recruiting is located on the Company branch of the hierarchy at the third level. Potential employees visiting the Tully's home page, Figure 7.13, should be able to determine that Company is the most likely choice on the navigation bar for finding information on jobs. But the shortcut link Now Hiring is a more specific and direct invitation: "Are you passionate about coffee? Join the Tully's team!" Furthermore, the shortcut link occupies a relatively large amount of space in the home page's main content area. Along the same lines, if an online store's newest products appear on the fourth level of the hierarchy (Home→ Fashions for Women→New fall line-up→Madras blouses), there will be a compelling reason to build a "New for fall! Madras blouses" shortcut link on the home page.

Spotlighting with Duplicate Links

Often two links share the same origin and destination. Usually one is a spotlight link that duplicates the primary link on a website's navigation bar or column. On the Tully's home page, the nav bar includes the standard primary link Community, which leads to a second-level page. The link Giving Back to the Community is a spotlight duplicate link. It doesn't provide a shorter path than the primary link, but it is larger and more conspicuous and allows for a more specific and inviting statement: "Discover how Tully's lends a helping hand to communities across the nation."

Figure 7.13. A home page with a shortcut spotlight link (Now Hiring) and a duplicate spotlight link (Giving Back to the Community). (www.tullys.com)

Duplicate spotlight links do not have to originate on the home page. For example, a website's second-level pages A, B, C, D, and E are linked by a shared nav bar (systematic secondary links). The designer, however, considers it important to draw users from page B to E. Rather than relying on users to make use of the nav bar, the designer builds a conspicuous, inviting associative secondary link—a spotlight duplicate link—from page B to page E.

The spotlighting strategy is the flipside of opportunistic navigation, discussed in the previous chapter. Because users often shift their goals (or barely have goals), they can be enticed by a link to an item on sale, a news bulletin, and so forth. Because these are shortcut or duplicate links, they offer a very strong scent that often overpowers the weaker scents emanating from the links on the nav bar, nav column, or other standard interface elements.

Spotlighting is an effective and sensible strategy, especially in highly competitive business environments. It only becomes a problem when extreme spotlighting re-

Table 7.1   A Web Designer's Classification of Links

Primary links	Standard primary links: Establish the branching structure of a hierarchy. Converging primary links: Converge on a single node. This node has two (or more) parents.
Secondary links	Associative secondary links: Connect two nodes based on the designer's judgment that there is a meaningful relationship between them. Systematic secondary links: Connect a group of nodes in a systematic pattern. For example, all the second-level siblings may be linked.
Special links	Upward links: Connect to the home page or another higher-level node. Links to utility nodes: Connect to pages that serve special functions, for example the Search page, site map, and help system. Shortcut links: Skip a level in the hierarchy. They are often used to spotlight an important Web page. Duplicate links: Share the same origin and destination as a primary or systematic secondary link. Duplicate links very often serve a spotlighting function. External links: Connect to a page of a different website.

places or visually overwhelms the logical hierarchy. Very often people do not want to navigate opportunistically. Instead they want the branches of the hierarchy set forth clearly before them so they can make their own choices about what parts of the site to visit. Fortunately, as the Tully's home page demonstrates, there is no inherent conflict between spotlighting and clearly revealing the hierarchy.

In Table 7.1, we provide a brief review of the nine types of links treated in this book. In the next chapter you will see how this classification of links is put to work in explaining much more about the interface of websites.

Organizing Content into a Hierarchy

In Chapter 3, "Designing and Building," we saw how working out the structure of the website fits into the development process. In particular, we considered the role of three different ways of representing a hierarchy: a node-link diagram, note cards, and an outline. Now we focus on how to organize your Web pages into an effective hierarchy. No part of the design process is more important than this.

The procedure of organizing a hierarchy should be familiar from your experience writing reports and other print documents. In a print document both the table of contents and the system of headings and subheadings delineate the document's hierarchical structure. Although there are differences between print and Web hierarchies, your experience and skill with print will certainly prove valuable in Web design. For Web hierarchies there are four main tasks:

1. Devising meaningful groups
2. Sequencing pages within groups
3. Shaping the hierarchy for breadth and depth
4. Accommodating the page design

Devising Meaningful Groups

The fundamental activity in organizing a hierarchy is creating groups. The links on the home page that establish the main branches correspond to the broadest groups. At each level down in the hierarchy the groups become more specific. Creating groups is both a bottom-up process in which pages or ideas for pages are placed into broader groups and a top-down process in which general categories are subdivided into more specific ones.

In navigating the hierarchy, the user makes a succession of choices, choosing one group after another until he or she finds the sought for content. For the user to succeed, to make the correct choices, the groups must correspond to how the audience thinks about the subject matter. We can say, then, that the website's hierarchy attempts to approximate the user's mental model of the subject matter.

Asthma Horizons does not assume an audience with a medical background, but users must understand a great many common sense distinctions, not all of them obvious, in order to make the correct choices and navigate successfully. For example, the user must understand how Medications and Treatments differs from Controlling Your Environment. Both links suggest ways to achieve better health, but controlling the environment is an attempt to eliminate or lessen causes of asthma whereas medications and treatments combat the condition.

An Earlier Design for Asthma Horizons That Failed

It is very, very easy to misjudge the navigation choices that users will make. For example, an earlier design of the main branches of Asthma Horizons was not successful. It consisted of these six home page links:

- Understanding Asthma
- Taking Steps for a Healthier Life
- Northwest Focus
- Research and Readings
- Message Boards
- About Us

Can you guess the problem? It concerns the first two categories. Information that provides a better understanding of asthma tends to be intertwined with information asthmatics can act on to lead a healthier life. For example, understanding the problem of stress implies limiting the stress in your life. This flaw became painfully clear because user test subjects often chose the wrong category when asked to find information on topics such as stress and asthma. The designers came up with a new set of more specific categories that provide more distinct scents. In other situations, the problem may be groups that are too specific for users to discriminate among them.

Working with Standard Categories

As the Web has evolved, various Web genres have emerged. Familiar genres include portals, online stores, personal websites, news websites, and corporate websites. Each genre tends to employ standard links, especially on the home page. So, for example, if you find yourself developing a corporate website, standard categories such as Products, About Us, Careers, and Investor Relations will come to mind. There is nothing wrong with using such standard categories; indeed they are probably what your users expect.

Devising a Functional Sequence of Pages Within a Group

Organizing a website's content into a hierarchy also entails sequencing the pages (nodes) in each group. This is similar to sequencing the sections that make up a book chapter and the sub-sections that make up each section. The sequence of the pages is reflected in the order in which the links to those pages appear in navigation columns, navigation bars, and elsewhere. Consequently, sequencing the nodes and sequencing the links are essentially the same thing.

The goal is to devise a sequence that best suits the user's needs. A very widely used sequencing principle is order of importance. But what is most important, of course, is a matter of interpretation. When sequencing by importance, make sure that you consider what is important to your users as well as to your organization. For example, the link for technical support should not be lost near the bottom of a long list of links just because technical support doesn't generate revenue.

Sometimes the best sequencing principle is chronological or inverse chronological order—depending on the user's task. In the case of city council minutes, inverse chronological order (most recent to oldest) would be best. Note that while importance is subject to interpretation, chronological and inverse chronological order are fixed principles. When the sequencing is flexible, the designer can sequence links on the basis of visual appearance. For example, a designer might sequence links to fit neatly around an irregular graphic or might sequence the links in a navigation bar so as to alternate the longer and shorter buttons.

At times, two links must be sequenced only in regard to each other. Consider an automaker whose home page navigation bar includes two links leading to the events the company takes part in: Motorsports and Other Events. Clearly users would be confused encountering Other Events before Motorsports.

While designers sometimes adhere to a single sequencing principle, they more often devise a "holistic" sequence that embodies various principles. For example, though it seems intuitively "right," there is no quick and easy way to articulate the logic behind the main categories on the Tully's site: Coffee, Shopping, Community, Wholesale, Company. Similarly, the 10 links on the Asthma Horizons home page are sequenced holistically, and though the sequence seems to work well, different designers might well come up with different sequences for these links.

An interesting design choice regarding sequencing is shown in Figure 7.14. The figure shows two competing designs for a navigation column listing the destinations served by an Amtrak passenger train. Each of the Destinations Served links will display tourism information for that city. In the first design, the Destinations Served links are sequenced geographically from north to south. In the second design, they are arranged alphabetically. Which sequence better serves the

About Amtrack Cascades	About Amtrack Cascades
Equipment	Equipment
Accessibility	Accessibility
Route Map	Route Map
Destinations Served	**Destinations Served**
Vancouver, BC	Albany
Bellingham	Bellingham
Mount Vernon	Centralia
Everett	Edmonds
Edmonds	Eugene
Seattle	Everett
Tacoma	Kelso
Olympia	Mount Vernon
Centralia	Olympia
Kelso	Portland
Vancouver, USA	Salem
Portland	Seattle
Salem	Tacoma
Albany	Vancouver, BC
Eugene	Vancouver, USA

Figure 7.14. Links to tourist information listed geographically and alphabetically.

information-seeking task most users will be engaged in? Most users have the name of a particular destination in mind, and so the alphabetical sequence is better than the geographical sequence. Viewing the relative locations of the destinations is apt to be a secondary concern—and the route map link (near the top of the navigation column) provides this view of the information.

Devising the Best Possible "Shape": Breadth and Depth

The breadth and depth of a website hierarchy are significant factors in effective user navigation. Depth refers to the number of levels a branch extends to. Breadth refers to the number of nodes across a single level. In Figure 7.15, all three branches reach three levels of depth, while the breadth at the second level is 3 and the breadth at the third level is 12.

Many decisions affect breadth and depth—the "shape" of your hierarchy. For example, if you add new pages, you will increase either breadth or depth. You also alter the shape of a hierarchy when you consolidate several pages into one

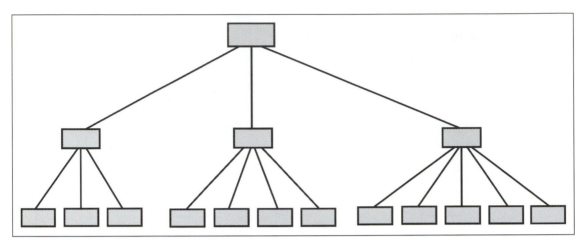

Figure 7.15. Measuring breadth and depth in a very small hierarchy.

page or split a page into several pages. Your first priority is always to create categories that are meaningful and useful. But it is also true that you should try to shape your hierarchy by favoring breadth over depth. Why? When users need to descend more than three or four levels, they are more apt to lose track of where they are in the hierarchy and more apt to give up on their goal. So, for example, users will be more successful navigating a wide 1 x 16 x 16 x 16 hierarchy than a narrow 1 x 5 x 5 x 5 x 5 x 5 hierarchy—even though the wide hierarchy is considerably larger than the narrow one (4369 nodes vs. 3806 nodes). The wide hierarchy is easier to navigate because it consists of four levels rather than six.

The potential problem with considerable breadth is that you will have a lot of links on some of your Web pages. If your 6 second-level pages are linked to 270 third-level pages, you will need to place, on average, 45 links on these second-level pages. That is a lot of visual clutter, and users must do a lot of scanning to find the link they want. This hierarchy would have a much better shape if there were, say, 10 second-level pages. Although many factors affect the navigability of a hierarchy, a study by Larson and Czerwinski (1998) suggests that with good design 32 links on a page is acceptable. Keep in mind, however, that in addition to your primary links, your pages will include utility links and are apt to include secondary links and external links.

Here are two examples of adjusting breadth and depth to improve the shape of a hierarchy. The City of Centerville's website had a second-level New Initiatives page that included four links, one entitled Pending Grants. The Pending Grants page (level 3) discussed pending grants in general terms and provided links to five short pages (level 4), each describing one of five pending grants. Because these descriptions were brief, the designers decided to "promote" them to the Pending Grants page, eliminating a level of depth.

In addition, the Centerville website had a third-level page with 50 links, each connecting to information about a particular kind of permit issued by the city. To reduce this excessive breadth (who wants to scan 50 links?), the designer created a shorter list of eight links, each representing a category of permit (building permits, public events permits, etc.). Now users scan for the pertinent category, click the link, and then click again from a relatively short list of links for information on the particular permit they are interested in.

Accommodating the Page Design—But Not Too Much

Another factor that often affects the grouping of links is page design. A typical situation is that the graphic designer is hoping for a simple, uncluttered design and doesn't want to fit numerous links on the home page and interior pages. One reason why the Tully's home page is attractive is that relatively few links appear on the home page.

The need for an effective hierarchy should take precedence over the page design, and a good graphic designer should be able to design around the links that are required on the pages. On the other hand, it is often possible to adjust the hierarchy to accommodate the page design.

Summary

This chapter focuses on the structure of hierarchies and the various types of links.

1. The hierarchy is by far the most prevalent information structure on the Web. This is because human beings naturally organize the world by establishing hierarchies. Furthermore, hierarchies are the ideal combination of freedom and orderliness, and they allow for much diversity in design.
2. There are three kinds of hierarchies: (1) the strict hierarchy, (2) the hierarchy with secondary links, and (3) the hierarchy with converging primary links. A website can—and a great many do—belong to both the second and third categories. But the strict hierarchy excludes the other two categories.
3. The strict hierarchy is defined by its reliance on standard primary links. It is very orderly, but it is also rigid and unrevealing. Extra navigational freedom is provided by the hierarchy with secondary links.
4. Associative secondary links are built when a designer sees a relevant association or connection between two nodes, very often nodes on different main branches of the hierarchy. Associative secondary links should be visually distinct from the primary links.
5. Systematic secondary links connect a group of nodes, very often a group of sibling nodes, in some kind of systematic pattern. Very often systematic secondary links are implemented as a navigation bar that extends across the top of the page or as a navigation column that extends down the left (or right) side of the page.
6. The third kind of hierarchy is the hierarchy with converging primary links. Two (or more) primary links converge on a single child node. Converging primary links can be used when the subject of a Web page seems to fit more than one logical category. In online stores and other sites this technique is

used on a large scale to give users multiple views of and pathways to the same content.

7. The child node of two (or more) converging primary links must be written so that it makes sense in the context of either branch. Furthermore, it is highly desirable that the interface of the child page accord with the route the user takes to reach it.

8. Upward links include the links that allow users to return from any page directly to the home page. Usually these links take the form of the organization's logo. Upward links also include links to the parent of the current page and to other pages located above the current page.

9. Utility links are those we build from almost every page of a website to such special pages (or clusters of pages) as the help system, site map, Search feature, and the checkout area of an e-commerce site. Utility links often appear together at the top right of the page or on a special utility bar located just below the banner or nav bar.

10. Spotlighting is the attempt to entice users to a page the designer considers important without relying on the user to follow a link on the nav bar or another standard interface element. We spotlight merchandise on sale, news bulletins, and so forth. Spotlighting normally takes the form of shortcut and duplicate links.

11. Shortcut links are downward links that skip one or more levels. Designers will place a conspicuous shortcut link on the home page to invite the user to jump directly to a third-level page. Tully's uses a spotlight shortcut link to take users directly to their employment page.

12. Often two links share the same origin and destination. Usually one is a spotlight link that duplicates the more fundamental link on the website's home page. Tully's uses a duplicate spotlight link to take users to their Giving Back to the Community page. Duplicate links are not limited to the home page; they may take the form of a conspicuous, enticing associative secondary link.

13. No part of the design process is more important than organizing content into an effective hierarchy. The four main tasks are these:

    1. Devising meaningful groups
    2. Sequencing pages within groups
    3. Shaping the hierarchy for breadth and depth
    4. Accommodating the page design

14. The fundamental activity in organizing a hierarchy is creating groups. At each level in the hierarchy the groups become more specific. The user makes a succession of choices, choosing one group after another. For the user to succeed, to make the correct choices, the groups must correspond to the user's mental model of the subject matter.

15. The designer must also sequence the pages (nodes) in each group according to the principle that best suits the user's needs. A very widely used sequencing principle is order of importance. Very often designers devise a "holistic" sequence that embodies various principles.

16. In organizing a hierarchy your first priority is always to create categories that are meaningful and useful. But you should also shape your hierarchy, favoring increased breadth over depth. With good design, 32 links on a page is acceptable.

17. Another factor that often affects the grouping of links is page design. A good graphic designer should be able to design around the links that are required on the pages. On the other hand, it is often possible to adjust the hierarchy to accommodate the page design.

References

Larson, Kevin, and Mary Czerwinski. 1998. Web page design: Implications of memory, structure and scent for information retrieval. *Proceedings of ACM CHI '98 Human Factors in Computing Systems* (Los Angeles, CA), 25–32.

Rosenfeld, Louis, and Peter Morville. 1998. *Information Architecture for the World Wide Web.* Sebastopol, CA: O'Reilly & Associates.

Discussion and Application

Items for Discussion

1. It is often useful to think about Web navigation in terms of kinship relationships. Look at the associative secondary link in Figure 7.2. This link connects two third-level nodes on different branches. Characterize these two nodes in terms of kinship relationships. Also, choose one of these two nodes and identify its parent, aunts, and grandparent.

2. The figure below shows nodes arranged in a hierarchical configuration, but without any links. Sketch in the lines representing various kinds of hierarchical links following the instructions given on the following page.

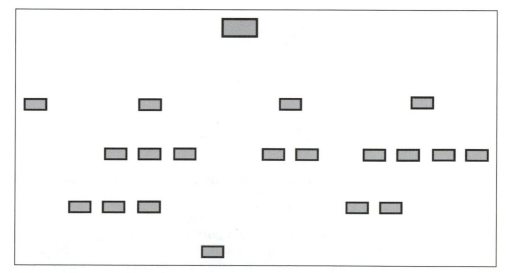

Figure 7.16. Nodes arranged in a hierarchical configuration, but without any links.

1. Draw all the standard primary links (using straight lines).
2. Using a curved dotted line, create an associative secondary link between any third-level node on the second branch of the hierarchy and any third-level node on the third branch of the hierarchy.
3. Create a systematic secondary link across all the second-level siblings using a straight dotted line.
4. Using straight lines to represent converging primary links, make the single fourth-level node the child of any two third-level nodes.
5. Draw an external link originating from the home page.
6. Using a curved dotted line, create a shortcut spotlight link. Identify this link with a label.
7. Using a curved dotted line, create a duplicate spotlight link. Identify this link with a label.
8. Select any third-level node and draw a line to the top node to represent an upward link to the home page. Recall that because all or most of the pages in a website link to the home page, these lines would not be used in an actual node-link diagram.

3. The figure below shows six nodes comprising a web-like information structure. Notice that every node is linked to every other node (all-to-all). Choose any one of the nodes and both blacken it and enlarge it, so that it represents the top node in a hierarchy. Then, heavily darken the links from this node to each of the others so that these links become primary links. From the perspective of hypertext theory describe the structure you have created as precisely as possible.

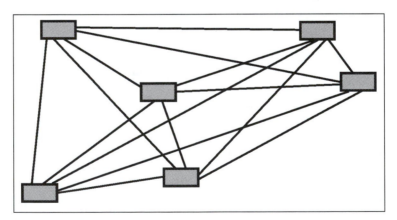

Figure 7.17. A web-like structure consisting of six nodes linked all-to-all.

4. On the following page is a portion of a municipal website home page. It consists of a heading and four links. Do you see something illogical about this group of links? How might this problem affect users? Can you think of a heading that might replace Emergency Services?

   Emergency Services
   Police Department
   Fire Department
   Earthquake Preparedness
   High Water Areas Assessment

5. In the list of links shown above, the phrase "high water areas assessment" means that the city will check your property for potential flooding. How well does this link communicate its meaning? How would you re-phrase the link?

   Furthermore, the designers of this municipal website have not provided a link to ambulance service because residents get ambulance service from the county rather than the city. What do you think of this decision?

6. Find a website that contains a variety of links and link groups. How many of the nine kinds of links explained in this chapter can you find in this website?

7. The figure below shows the main links on the Asthma Horizons home page and an alternative version discarded by the design team. Compare the two versions and explain what might be the reason or reasons for the changes.

Final Sequence:	**Discarded Sequence:**
Causes and Symptoms	Medications and Treatments
Dealing with an Episode	Dealing with an Episode
Medications and Treatments	Causes and Symptoms
Controlling Your Environment	Controlling Your Environment
Children and Teens	Special Populations
Special Populations	Public Policy
Public Policy	Research
Research	Children and Teens
Northwest Focus	Northwest Focus
About Us	About Us

Figure 7.18. An effective and ineffective sequence of the main links on the Asthma Horizons home page.

Application to Your Project

1. Examine your website, prototype, or node-link diagram (or other representation). Which kind of hierarchy are you creating: (1) a strict hierarchy, (2) a hierarchy with secondary links, (3) a hierarchy with converging primary links, or (4) a hierarchy with both secondary links and converging primary links? Why is this so?

2. If your website employs systematic secondary links, have you considered how these links will appear on the interface? In other words, will you employ navigation bars, navigation columns, or something else?
3. Are you planning on spotlighting certain pages? If so, how?
4. Is your hierarchy organized into meaningful groups with appropriate sequencing of the pages in each group? Can you improve the shape of the hierarchy?

8

The Navigational Interface

Introduction

In this chapter we switch from a website's underlying structure to the user interface. Because the vast majority of websites are primarily information environments, we focus on the navigational interface. That is, we are primarily interested in how users find and work with content rather than with online computing functions such as a spreadsheet, a calendar/datebook, or the checkout portion of an online store.

You will learn how to use the most important kinds of link groups that make up the navigational interface. These are navigation bars, tabs, navigation columns, links in the main content area (MCA links), and drop-down list boxes. We will begin at the home page and consider the different roles that these elements play at successively deeper levels of the hierarchy. Then we turn to the design of online computer functions and offer a set of human-computer interface guidelines. Finally, we briefly consider help information for websites.

There is no limit to the ways you can design a website's navigational interface, but this chapter will explain the design ideas that are central to vast numbers of professional websites and that embody the most enduring principles. Even if you plan to create the most innovative or unusual websites, this chapter is a good foundation for your work. In the next chapter, "Linking," we will consider the navigational interface from a different perspective: how individual links are designed to facilitate efficient navigation.

Revealing Structure at the Home Page

The home page, the top of the hierarchy, is usually the first page of the website the user sees. The home page, therefore, introduces the site, attempts to engage the user, and offers links into the interior of the site. Thereafter, it serves the user as a major landmark and base of operations.

173

To properly introduce the website, the home page must prominently feature "identity" information. Minimally, this is the name of the site, but further information, such as the purpose and owner of the site, is apt to be present. When this information appears together, as it usually does, it is often referred to as the identity element. Often the identity element appears in a banner-like area across the top of the page. The identity element of the Zompco Corporation consists of the company name and the slogan: "World leader in rotary brushes."

Nav Bars on the Home Page

Nav bars are staples of the Web. Basic home page nav bars, such as the one shown in Figure 8.1, contain standard primary links that establish the main branches of the hierarchy and take the user down to the second level. Their location near the top of the page confers two benefits: (1) In conjunction with the identity element, the links on the nav bar help users better understand what the website offers; and (2) the nav bar leaves the main content area fully available for content.

One drawback of nav bars is that they must fit the width of the Web page. Consequently, designers must at times format nav bars in two rows and format individual links as two-line "run-over" entries.

Very often the nav bar and other link groups are mirrored at the bottom of the page in the form of small text links, as shown in Figure 8.1. Visually handicapped people can read these links using text-only browsers when the other

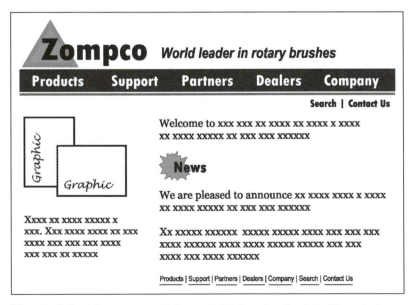

Figure 8.1. A home page with a standard navigation bar. These links are mirrored (along with the utility links) by text links at the bottom of the page.

links on the page are implemented as graphics. Also, when pages scroll, these bottom-of-the-page links save users from having to scroll to the top of the page to click a link.

Basic Tabs on the Home Page

Sets of tabs appear very often on the Web with many design variations. Tabs are especially prevalent in e-commerce websites. Web tabs are based on the metaphor of the tabs on file folders that fill drawers in a traditional office.

A basic set of Web tabs is shown in Figure 8.2. As in most tab designs, the home page opens with the Welcome tab selected. This little trick makes the operation of the tabs more intuitive, though it is slightly illogical because it suggests that the home page is one of the second-level pages.

When the user clicks any of the other tabs, that tab moves to the front and the second-level page associated with that tab is displayed. Tabs, therefore, inherently provide something like the highlighting or marking that designers often choose to provide with nav bars and columns. Unlike nav bars, two-row tab sets are truly hard to use and, hence, inadvisable. The problem is that when the user clicks a back-row tab, the user's eye has to track it to its new front-row position.

Nav Columns on the Home Page

Navigation columns, shown in Figure 8.3 and seen everywhere on the Web, are similar in function to nav bars and tabs, but offer designers several advantages.

First, people can more easily scan and read vertically than horizontally. This is a minor factor in the case of a short, easy-to-grasp group of links such as Products,

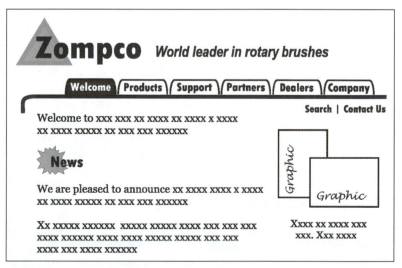

Figure 8.2. A typical set of one-row tabs.

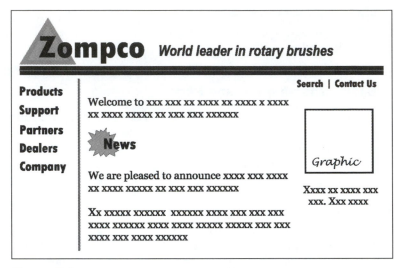

Figure 8.3. A home page with a standard navigation column.

Support, Partners, Dealers, and Company. But with more numerous links and links that are lengthier and more semantically challenging, vertical formatting becomes important. This is one reason why the Asthma Horizons design team chose to use a nav column rather than a nav bar (shown in Figure 8.10).

Nav columns also offer great flexibility. Assuming that the designer is willing to allow the page to scroll, there is no set limit to the number of links. Also, there are fewer problems trying to fit multi-word links into tight spaces. Within limits, a nav column can be made wider to accommodate links. Finally, adding links or re-sequencing links is less likely to require a major redesign effort than with nav bars or tabs.

Using Nav Bars, Tabs, and Nav Columns in Combination

There are various ways to combine these link groups. In particular, we often see a nav bar or set of tabs used with a nav column. This arrangement shown in Figure 8.4 is regularly referred to as the "inverted L." Note that the links to the four market-specific pages (Auto industry, etc.) comprise a distinct group of second-level nodes.

When websites are large and heavily linked, there may be multiple link groups on the home page and interior pages. This kind of complexity, unless handled skillfully, is apt to cause trouble for users.

Pages with MCA Links

A very different but also prevalent design for the home page is to place the primary links and, if desired, spotlight links in the main content area, as shown in Figure 8.5. Now there is ample screen real estate for many links, short or long, and links can be fully explained with supplemental text.

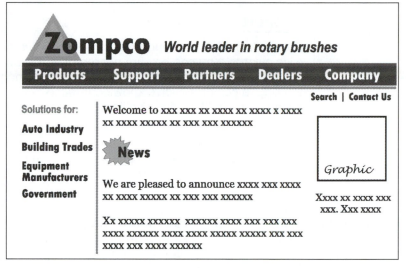

Figure 8.4. A home page that employs both a navigation bar and column and that divides the nine main home page links into two logical groups.

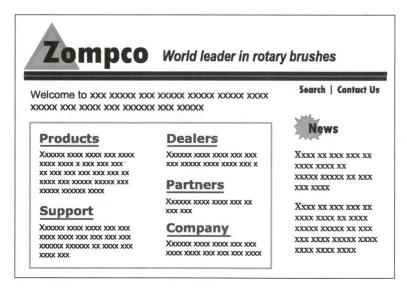

Figure 8.5. A home page with primary links in the main content area and the spotlight link News. The links are fully explained with supplemental text.

The trade-off, of course, is that the home page is not left entirely free for content. Content and linking must be effectively integrated. For example, Figure 8.6 shows an MCA link annotated with supplemental text that both explains the

---

Support

Zompco's customer support regularly wins industry-wide awards. You can be sure of prompt and expert responses. We offer Web-based order and payment tracking, a comprehensive knowledge-base, email support, and a 24/7 phone hotline.

Figure 8.6. An MCA link annotated with a nugget of useful information. Linking is effectively integrated with content.

destination of the link and provides a brief nugget of information intended to benefit someone who does not choose to follow the link. MCA links, of course, are used on interior pages as well, generally as primary links directing users downward in the hierarchy. You will find that strict hierarchies often employ MCA links.

Displaying Both Second- and Third-Level Choices on the Home Page

There are more complex designs in which nav columns and tabs provide access to both the second and third levels of the hierarchy. When these designs are successful, they offer users more navigational freedom, and they enable users to make better decisions about navigation because more of the choices are visible at once. As we explain below, the second level of the hierarchy may consist of actual Web pages or it may be "virtual," both real and not real at the same time.

Nav Columns That Link to Second- and Third-Level Pages

A home page nav column that displays links to Web pages at both the second and third level is shown in Figure 8.7. For example, if the user clicks the Products link, the user displays the product overview page (second level) that briefly introduces Zompco's five products and offers links to the five product description pages (third level). Alternatively, the user can jump directly to any of the five product description pages. (These are shortcut links that do not serve a spotlighting function.) Although adding links to the third level makes the nav column longer, this is very often an excellent design strategy.

A design that is different in appearance but similar in function is shown in Figure 8.8. Here, the user can click Products, Support, and other links and reach the second-level pages. But when the user pauses the mouse pointer over each of these links, a pop-up display area appears with links to the third-level pages. This design eliminates the problem of a lengthy nav column. It is even possible

Products
Product 1
Product 2
Product 3
Product 4
Product 5

Support
Consult Knowledge-Base
Check on Orders
Review Payments
Report a Problem
Phone Customer Support

Partners
Amalgamated Widgets
Rock Island Wire
General Gear Corporation

Dealers
Dealer Information

Company
President's Message
History of Zompco
Careers at Zompco
Community Outreach
Investor Relations

Figure 8.7. A two-level nav column with links to the second and third levels.

to code pop-up links to the fourth level of the hierarchy (e.g., the features of each product).

Nav Columns with a Virtual Second Level

But what if the designer doesn't want to provide overview pages? What if the designer prefers for the user to navigate directly to the third level—for example, to one of the five product description pages? No problem. Now the phrases Product, Support, and so forth are implemented as headings rather than links. The headings delineate only a virtual, or logical, second level of the hierarchy.

Tabs with a Virtual Second Level

Similarly, there are tab designs with a logical but not a physical second level. In other words, when the user clicks a tab on the home page, the tab moves to the front and a subtab appears with links to the third level of that branch. Such a design is shown in Figure 8.9.

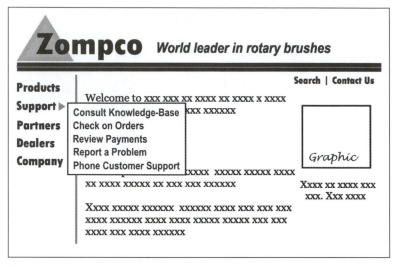

Figure 8.8. A nav column that links to the second level and employs a pop-up display area with links to the third level.

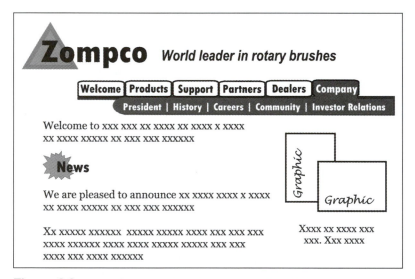

Figure 8.9. A tab design with a virtual second level. The user has clicked the Company tab but has not left the home page. Instead, the user will choose from a subtab of third-level links.

Revealing Structure at the Second Level

We certainly hope and expect that users will follow a link from the home page to the interior pages of our website. In this section we assume that the user has navigated to the second level. Like the home page, second-level pages and, indeed, all interior pages must provide identity information to orient the user. This identity information consists, at least, of the website name (possibly in the form of a logo) and the name of the current page.

The interior identity elements should signal both transition and continuity—transition to the new page and continuity with the previous page and the entire website. Properly designed, these identity elements lend coherence to the user's experience. For example, as shown in Figure 8.10, the name of the website is often made smaller and in other ways less visually dominant than it was on the home

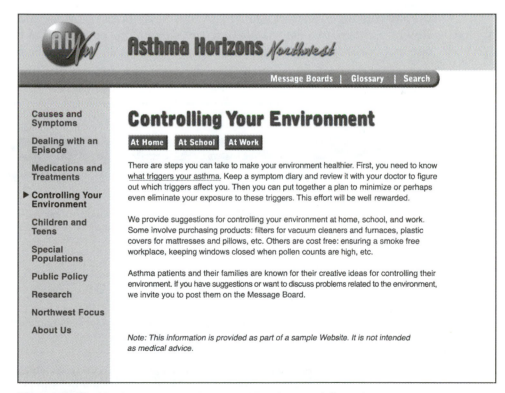

Figure 8.10. The home page and a second-level page of the Asthma Horizons website. To help draw the user's attention to the name of the second-level page, Controlling Your Environment, the name is both large and bright red.

page. This change provides a visual cue that the user has moved into the interior of the website. Similarly, on interior pages, the page name (the new, important information) rather than the website name (the old information) must draw the user's attention.

Nav Bars, Nav Columns, and MCA Links at the Second Level

The roles of link groups change at the second level because navigation has become more complex. In addition to lower-level pages, there are now sibling pages and the home page to consider. As shown in Figure 8.11, the nav bar that provided the standard primary links on the home page very often re-appears in modified form on the second level. Its function, however, is new. The same links that pointed downward and served as primary links now serve as systematic secondary links connecting the sibling pages at the second level. Downward linking will now be provided by another kind of link group. In Figure 8.11, primary links to the third level appear in the nav column. The page also includes two associative secondary links that appear in the main content area embedded in the text. The Zompco logo is the upward link to the home page.

It is much the same with second-level nav columns. In Figure 8.12, the original nav column is retained while MCA links take the user deeper into the hierarchy. In addition, two associative links are shown, one embedded in the text and one in a boxed area on the far right. There are certainly many other possibilities.

Figure 8.11. A second-level page with a nav bar providing systematic secondary links to sibling nodes, a nav column with primary links to child nodes, and two associative secondary links in the main content area.

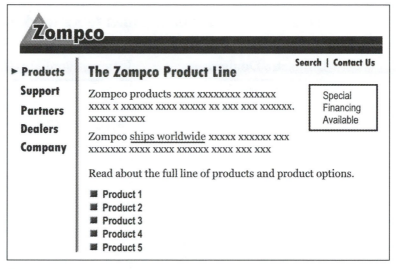

Figure 8.12. A second-level page with systematic secondary links in a nav column, primary links to third-level pages in the main content area, and associative secondary links also in the main content area.

Drop-Down List Boxes

The drop-down list box, shown in Figure 8.13, is a very handy interface element. A drop-down list box can appear anywhere on a website, but the second level is very typical. A drop-down list box initially occupies no more space than a few words of text but when clicked, expands instantly to display a list of links. Because the items in the drop-down list can scroll, the list can be long without making the page itself scroll. Users succeed best with drop-down list boxes when the links are familiar items that belong to a tightly defined logical category—for example, states or nations.

Drop-down list boxes are often used for an entirely different purpose—to solicit information from users on a form as part of an online computing function. For example, users in the checkout portion of an online store are often asked to choose from a drop-down list box to indicate the nation they live in. In this case the user is not navigating anywhere, but is just providing information.

Revealing Structure at the Third Level and Below

As websites grow deeper, navigation becomes still more complex for the designer as well as for users. In particular, there are more choices regarding systematic secondary links. The designer may wish to connect the sibling pages, the parent and aunt pages, and the pages of other possible ancestor generations.

With this kind of complexity, users rely as much on their semantic knowledge, both general and subject specific, as on the visual design of the interface. For

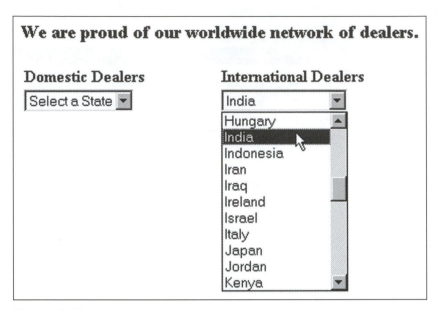

Figure 8.13. A portion of the Zompco Dealers page showing a closed and
an open drop-down list box.

example, most people know that the features of any product are specific attributes
of that product (a kind of subdividing of the product), that the products are logical siblings, and that corporations often provide a general overview of their product line. When the semantic distinctions are not as clear and crisp as these or
when the user is relatively unfamiliar with the subject matter, the likelihood of
unsuccessful navigation increases.

The Third Level

At the third level, a key decision is whether to retain the nav bar or nav column
that appeared on the home page and on the second-level pages. If retained, it will
provide systematic secondary links to the parent and aunts of this page. The basic
principle is simple: When a nav bar or nav column appears on the home page, it
establishes the main branches of the hierarchy and points downward. At the second level, this interface element links laterally to siblings. At the third or deeper
levels, it links upward to ancestors. Another key decision at the third level is
whether to provide another interface element (probably a nav column) to provide
systematic secondary links to the siblings of this page. Both these choices have
been made in the third-level product description page shown in Figure 8.14. In
some cases the same kind of linking is provided with two nav columns, as shown
in the Figure 8.15.

Designers should not automatically provide this kind of extensive linking.
The accelerated navigation provided by the systematic secondary links may not
justify the extra complexity and the consumption of valuable screen real estate.

Let's imagine, for example, that Zompco sells its products to disparate markets and that customers who care about Product 3 rarely care about the other Zompco products. If so, why complicate the interface with links that let users move directly among the products? Users who do want to consider more than one

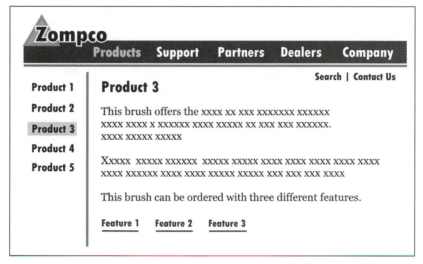

Figure 8.14. A third-level Zompco page that explains Product 3. The nav bar provides links to the parent and aunt pages. The nav column provides systematic secondary links to the siblings.

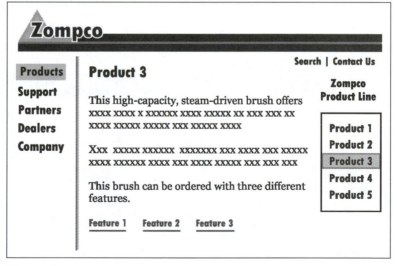

Figure 8.15. A third-level Zompco page with two nav columns. One nav column provides links to the parent and aunt pages. The second (right hand) nav column provides systematic secondary links to the siblings.

product need only ascend one level to the product overview page and then descend a level.

The Fourth Level

Let's consider a fourth-level page, shown in Figure 8.16, that explains one of the special features of Product 3. With three ancestor generations, the designer of this page has given up on providing systematic secondary links to the five Zompco products. This makes sense, because the user who visits this page is definitely focusing carefully on Product 3 and will definitely want to jump across the hierarchy to learn about all the features. There is, however, an upward link to the Product 3 page, the parent of this feature page. This upward link allows the user to revisit the general information about Product 3 and, if desired, investigate the other products.

In a more complex website than our Zompco example, the Product 3 page (and the other product description pages) might have groups of child nodes other than those explaining features. For example, the Product 3 page might have links to pages explaining the international standards Product 3 meets or special Zompco technologies incorporated in Product 3. This opens up further linking possibilities.

Below the Fourth Level

There is much to be said for not going below the fourth level—though certainly many large websites do so. At the fifth level and deeper, disciplined decisions must be made as to how much linking to provide.

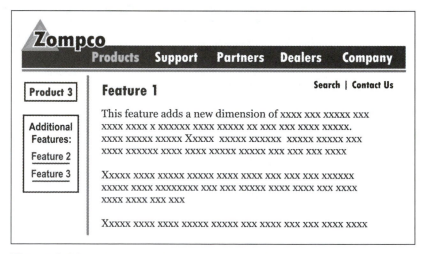

Figure 8.16. A fourth-level Zompco page explaining one of the special features of Product 3. Systematic secondary links connect all the special feature pages for Product 3.

When a hierarchy becomes very deep, the best plan may be to break off a piece of this hierarchy and create a separate website, which many people call a "subsite." For example, if Zompco has a research division with its own hierarchy of labs, projects, and researchers, and if the top node of the research division is already at the third level in Zompco's Company branch, it might be better to create a separate Research.Zompco.com subsite with appropriate links extending in both directions between this site and the main Zompco site.

Special Techniques for the Navigational Interface

Having examined the most fundamental ways to design a website's navigational interface, we now consider three somewhat specialized techniques:

1. Omitting a logical top node
2. Defaulting to the eldest sibling
3. Dividing one physical page into multiple nodes

Omitting a Logical Top Node

On almost every hierarchical website, the home page is the top node in the hierarchy. On occasion, however, websites are designed so that the logical top node is omitted, as shown in Figure 8.17. There is a physical home page, of course, but it is made to look and function like a second-level page. As we explain below, this strategy of omitting the top node is often a means for solving a problem of conflicting needs within an organization.

Let's assume that Bigtime University consists of four units: the Downtown Campus, the South End Campus, the North End Campus, and the Distance Learning Division. The Downtown Campus is by far the largest and best known. What should happen when users point their browsers to www.bigtime.edu? One possibility is a standard home page divided into four sectors, one for each unit of the university. This design, however, displeases officials from the Downtown Campus, who point out that 90% of the website's visitors are looking for the Downtown Campus. These officials would prefer the home page design shown in

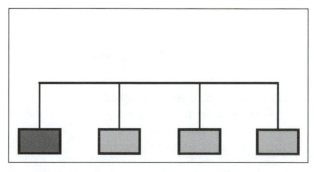

Figure 8.17. A hierarchy in which the home page (at left) functions as a second-level page.

Figure 8.18. A standard home page design for Bigtime University. The lesser units appear to be children (divisions) of the Downtown Campus.

Figure 8.18. Here the Downtown Campus is pre-eminent; in fact, the other three units appear as children (or, administratively speaking, divisions) of the Downtown Campus. Unsurprisingly, officials of the other units reject this design and are threatening to establish entirely separate websites with URLs such as www.bigtime-north.edu.

Figure 8.19 represents a compromise. When users point their browsers to www.bigtime.edu, they arrive at a website that does indeed feature the Downtown Campus and indicates its pre-eminence. The page, however, also represents the Downtown Campus as the eldest sibling, the first among equals, rather than the parent. Logically, there is no top node to this hierarchy.

Defaulting to the Eldest Sibling at the Third Level

Designers can omit the logical second-level node and take the user directly to the eldest sibling at the third level. They often do so when they see no need for a page of overview information. For example, consider the design shown in Figure 8.20 and illustrated diagrammatically in Figure 8.21.

Because there is no (second-level) product overview page, users who choose the Products branch on the home page are taken to the first of the five product description pages and, in addition, see links to the other product description pages. On the Products branch, the second-level is virtual.

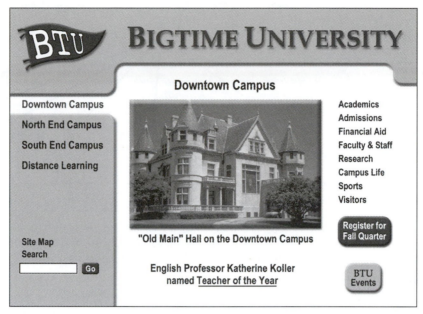

Figure 8.19. A compromise design in which the lesser units of Bigtime University appear as siblings of the Downtown Campus, though the Downtown Campus is the pre-eminent ("eldest") sibling.

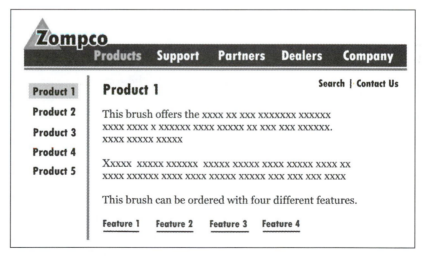

Figure 8.20. Omitting the second level and defaulting to the eldest sibling.

Dividing One Physical Page into Multiple Nodes

Long scrolling Web pages can be divided into separate sections, each introduced with its own heading and each containing its own chunk of text and, perhaps,

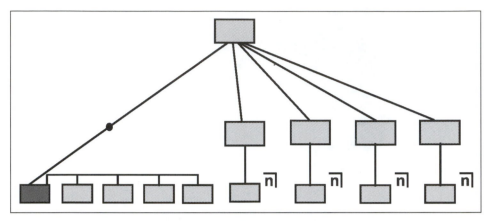

Figure 8.21. A node-link diagram of a website that omits the second level and defaults to the eldest third-level page. The black dot on the first branch indicates that the second level is only a virtual level.

accompanying graphics. From the perspective of hypertext theory these sections are separate nodes—even though they share the same physical Web page. Furthermore, links are coded so that when any section of the page is the target of a link, that section automatically scrolls to the top of the browser window, further reinforcing the status of each section as an independent node.

Figure 8.22 shows one use for this technique. The top of a long scrolling page contains the Zompco product overview node. The product overview includes five links, one for each of the five product description nodes that appear further down on the same long page. The user can choose one of the links to jump to the chosen product description or can scroll among and easily compare the product descriptions. If the product descriptions are lengthy, the designer may build a link at the end of each product description back to the top of the page. Finally, because the product overview and the five product descriptions reside on one physical page, the user can conveniently print all this information at once rather than opening and printing six separate pages.

The Browser Interface and Multiple Windows

The interface of a website includes the browser that the website runs in. For the most part, Web designers design for the capabilities and interface features of the major browsers—though in some respects browser behavior can be customized for a website.

Individual users, however, exercise considerable control over their own browser. They can and do customize their browser settings; for example, they can select the toolbars they will use, the default fonts, and the colors of visited and unvisited text links. They also decide which plug-ins to install in their browser and whether or not to accept cookies. And, of course, users can resize a browser window at any time. In contrast to all these complexities, consider print, a medium in

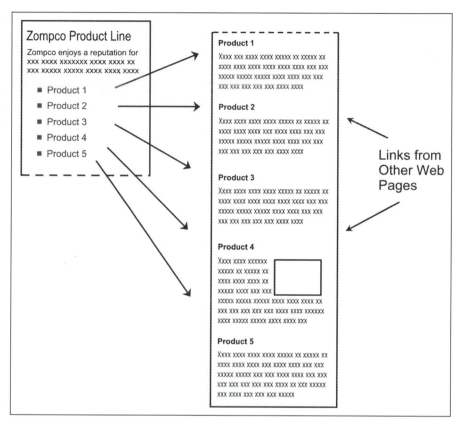

Figure 8.22. A long scrolling Web page consisting of the Zompco product overview (the parent node) and the five Zompco product descriptions (the five child nodes).

which the designer fully controls page dimensions, fonts, colors, and all other aspects of the design.

The Back Button

Perhaps the most important browser feature from the designer's perspective is the Back button and its counterpart, the Forward button. Designers don't control these buttons, but they are a significant aspect of user behavior and so affect design.

Users, of course, use the Back button (along with the History feature) to retrace their steps. The Back button, however, creates problems. First, the behavior of Back is hard for users to predict when they are criss-crossing a group of pages they have visited multiple times. Second, Back does not deal successfully with framesets. Finally, the Back button draws the user's eye away from your Web pages to the browser's interface.

Designers need to carefully consider how much their users should have to rely on the Back button. It is desirable to build sufficiently complete navigation on the pages of a website that the user does not need to rely heavily on Back.

Multiple Windows

Links can be coded to display a Web page in a new window (a new instance of the browser). Windowing, therefore, is one aspect of browser behavior that designers do control. There are many reasons why designers may want users to keep two pages of a website open at the same time. In an online tutorial, it may be very helpful if a key table or graph remains on the screen, usually in a smaller window, while the user navigates through lessons in the main window. A food manufacturer's website may spawn a supplementary window with a recipe and links that will display still more recipes in this same window. Sometimes a website displays its site map in a supplementary window, leaving the main window free for content. Note that clicking in the site map controls what appears in the main window. To save screen real estate, supplementary windows are often configured to appear without toolbars.

Designers often code external links so that the new website opens in a separate window. For example, if Asthma Horizons contains a page with links to various asthma research centers, users will want this page to stay open as they peruse the various research centers. From a different perspective, site owners may want to enrich their site with external links without encouraging users to abandon their own site. If the original site remains visible, the user is more apt to return to it.

Coding your website to spawn multiple windows (which the user must close one by one) is, at least in some instances, an imposition on the user. Therefore, use this technique with discretion. Far more offensive, except under very special circumstances, is to trap the user by forcing the new website to appear in a frame within the original website.

Websites as Online Computing Environments

Although most websites are primarily information environments, online computing is also a significant aspect of the Web. For example, the Nutrition Calculator in Dietwatch.com combines spreadsheet and database capabilities for planning diets and resembles the behavior of software user interfaces much more than it fits the navigation paradigm.

Buttons and drop-down list boxes are employed in online computing functions as well as in the navigational interface. But online computing environments employ command menus, dialog boxes, and other interface elements that are not normally part of the navigational interface. For example, as shown in Figure 8.23, online stores often employ a "spin box" so that users can specify the quantity of an item they are purchasing.

Where do Web designers go to learn how to design online computing functions? Currently, we rely primarily on a large, well-established body of knowl-

Figure 8.23. Indicating the number of apples being purchased with a spin box.

edge about user interface design. Good resources include Ben Shneiderman (1997), Theo Mandel (1997), and Craig Marion's Software Design Smorgasbord website (www.chesco.com/~cmarion). Because much of our knowledge of interface design has evolved through the study of software, many user interface design resources emphasize software interfaces.

Unfortunately, there are some significant differences between the design of software user interfaces and the user interfaces for computing functions on the Web. For example, the Back button on Web browsers was conceived as a means to return to a previous location in information space. When Back is used in online computing, its behavior often confuses users, especially because the behavior is often inconsistent from one website to the next. If I decide during checkout not to make the purchase, does Back cancel my purchase (like Undo) or just return me to the previous page in checkout? We are only now beginning to focus on the Web as an environment for online computing. Useful resources include Vanessa Donnelly (2001), Jared Spool et al. (1998), Keith Instone's website Usable Web (www.usableweb.com), and Jakob Nielsen's website Alertbox (www.useit.com/alertbox).

Below we list and explain eight user interface design guidelines adapted from the literature on user interface design. These guidelines are sufficiently general that they pertain to alarm clocks, microwave ovens, and indeed almost any kind of human-crafted interactive system; however, we will illustrate these guidelines with examples from computing, the Web, and especially the Web's online computing interface. Systems should

1. Be flexible and give users ample control.
2. Handle errors gracefully and allow for changed intentions.
3. Be responsive and reveal the system status.
4. Be familiar, natural, self-disclosing, and memorable.
5. Be uncluttered and consistent.
6. Be efficient.
7. Account for individual differences.
8. Be enjoyable to use.

1. Systems Should Be Flexible and Give Users Ample Control.

Systems should empower people rather than restrict what they can do. It is better if users can choose which part of an extended audio sequence they wish to listen to rather than having to play the entire sequence from beginning to end. It is better if users can store not only their own mailing address in the checkout portion of an online store but also the addresses of people to whom they regularly send gifts.

On the other hand, too much user control presents the risk that systems will become too complex for users to understand and remember.

Systems should be allowed to act on the user's behalf, but only when the designer has strong evidence that the system is truly capable of making choices that will match the user's needs. In general, the user should be able to override choices the system makes on the user's behalf.

2. Systems Should Handle Errors Gracefully and Allow for Changed Intentions.

There will always be various kinds of user errors and miscommunications between the user and the system. Systems should be able to handle these gracefully. In the case of minor errors, systems should usually be able to infer the user's intentions and transparently correct the error. For example, if a Web user enters a credit card number during checkout and, ignoring the specified format, types hyphens between groups of numbers, the website should accept the number with the hyphens rather than treating the entry as an error. In the case of more serious problems, systems should point out the user's problem and allow the user to fix the problem easily. So, for example, if a Web user forgets a required field when filling out an online form, the website should point out what the user forgot to do and should not require the user to start the entire process from the beginning.

Apart from errors, users should simply be able to change their minds. For example, in a well-designed check-out system, the user should be able to cancel the checkout at any moment up to the final confirmation of the order.

3. Systems Should Be Responsive and Reveal the System Status.

Systems should carry out commands quickly; users do not like to wait. An obvious implication of this guideline is that Web pages should display in just a few seconds and Web transactions and downloads should not require an unreasonable amount of time. Users also demand immediate feedback. So, for example, if a website cannot immediately download a file, the user should at least know at once that the command has been accepted and that the download has been initiated. Finally, users should understand the system's current status. For example, users should get regular updates as to the progress of their download and when shopping, should always be able to look at the contents of their shopping cart.

4. Systems Should Be Familiar, Natural, Self-Disclosing, and Memorable.

These criteria are hard to separate, but the general idea is clear enough. Our goal is for users to encounter an interface for the first time and use it successfully and without undue effort. Familiarity is a big plus. Most Web users understand the controls on the players that start, pause, and stop dynamic content because the controls resemble those on VCRs, CD players, and many other devices.

Some interfaces are natural in the way that an automobile's steering wheel is natural: There is an easy-to-grasp correspondence between the interface element and what it does. For example, spin boxes are natural insofar as people will instinctively perceive a correspondence (or "mapping") between the up and down arrows and a greater and lesser quantity of items. As an example of unnatural interface design, consider an earlier era of computing when users resized windows by typing values into a text box rather than by simply dragging the edges of the window. Underlining as an indicator of hot text is not natural, but it has become familiar.

Even when they are not familiar or natural, interface elements can at least be self-disclosing. Clear labels may well make a control self-disclosing. The user doesn't need to guess or consult a manual or expert. Finally, interfaces should be memorable, especially because they may be used infrequently. The best way to make an interface memorable is to make it familiar or natural.

5. Systems Should Be Uncluttered and Consistent.

Human beings are limited in the amount of information they can pay attention to and make sense of. Too many options and too much clutter in general increase the effort that is required and reduce the user's overall effectiveness in understanding and working with an interface. Simplicity is a key principle in interface design.

Another key principle is consistency. Controls with similar functions should look and behave similarly. For example, a command button that is used to submit similar kinds of user information on three different pages of a website should have the same label rather than Submit, Send, and Done. Conversely, when controls have different functions, the differences should be reflected in their appearance and behavior.

Consistency means more than consistency within your own website. If your website is one of a group of related sites, you may well want to seek consistency with the existing sites. Finally, consistency means following accepted and emerging standards and conventions. As standards and conventions evolve, interfaces become easier to design because we can increasingly count on users coming to our websites with relevant expectations and knowledge from their prior Web use.

6. Systems Should Be Efficient.

Systems should let people achieve their goals without expending excessive time or effort. Transactions should not require too many steps, although securing a mortgage loan will and should require more steps than buying a book.

There is often a trade-off between systems that are self-disclosing and systems that are efficient. A wizard-like interface that slowly guides the user through a task, devoting a new page to each option, can be made fully self-disclosing. But a command-line interface, which requires users to know strings of commands and parameters, is very efficient once the user has mastered the system.

7. Systems Should Account for Individual Differences.

People differ greatly in their knowledge and skills regarding computer and Web use. If your website requires users to download a plug-in program such as Flash to function fully, you may well find that some users resist what for them is an intimidating task or do not succeed in downloading and installing the plug-in. It is best to provide alternative functionality.

Two other important dimensions of individual difference are human disabilities and people who are using less capable technology. As we have noted, it is both a practical strategy and an ethical obligation to create websites that exclude as few people as possible.

8. Systems Should Be Enjoyable to Use.

When interfaces are well designed, they tend to be enjoyable to use. They give people pleasure in the same way that many people take pleasure in a handsomely designed, well-crafted tool or a fine automobile.

Website Help

The navigational interface of a website does not normally require a help system or even a help page. Why should this be so? Navigating among hundreds or thousands of Web pages can be a challenging task, but navigation as an activity doesn't normally need to be explained. In a sense, the site map is the help system for the navigational interface because the site map, more than any other part of the website, reveals the site's node-link structure.

A website's online computer functions do, however, require carefully designed help information. Not only is the user apt to have more difficulty with online computer functions but, as in the case of checkout or a download, the consequences of failed actions are apt to be more severe than problems with navigation.

What kind of help should we provide? Although it is possible to incorporate all of the required help information into a single help system, as is generally done in desktop software, this may not be necessary or even desirable on the Web. Rather, a link to a page of help information for, say, checkout can be placed on the checkout pages. Likewise, the Search feature will have its own help page or set of tips. In other words, a good design option is to place information on the page where people will need it. In some situations, it may be necessary to supplement help with a tech support technician or other expert who will communicate with users via email, message boards, or real-time dialogs.

Summary

1. Because most websites are primarily information environments, the Web interface is primarily a navigational interface. Although there is no limit to the number of possible designs, there are fundamental designs, explained here, that embody the most important and enduring design principles. These principles are a good foundation for even the most innovative and unusual design work.
2. The home page must prominently feature identity information, consisting minimally of the site name but very often including the site's purpose and owner. The identity information usually takes the form of an identity element located near the top of the page.
3. Nav bars, sets of tabs, and nav columns very often appear on home pages and contain the standard primary links to the second level. Nav columns offer de-

signers more flexibility because they do not take up limited horizontal screen space. Also, people can more easily scan and read vertically than horizontally.

4. There are various ways to combine these links groups. In particular, we often see a nav bar or set of tabs used with a nav column—the "inverted L."

5. When primary links are placed in the main content area (MCA links), there is ample screen real estate for many links, regardless of their length. The trade-off is that the home page is not left entirely free for content. Often MCA links are annotated with supplemental text that both explains the destination of the link and provides information that will benefit someone who does not choose to follow the link.

6. There are very effective designs in which nav columns provide access to both the second and third levels of the hierarchy. Sometimes nav columns display a virtual second level with links to the third level. Some tab systems do so as well.

7. Identity information appears on interior pages as well as on the home page. This identity information should signal both transition and continuity—transition to the new page and continuity with the previous page and the entire website. For example, the name of the website is often made smaller and otherwise less visually dominant than it was on the home page.

8. At the second, third, and deeper levels, nav bars and columns often provide systematic secondary links to connect siblings or ancestor levels. Nav columns also provide primary links to the next level down, as do MCA links. At the third and deeper levels, designers must limit their use of systematic secondary links. Often designers complicate Web pages by providing more extensive linking than users really need.

9. Drop-down list boxes are a handy, space-saving interface element. Because the items in the drop-down list can scroll, the list can be long without making the page itself scroll. Users succeed best when the links are familiar items that belong to a tightly defined logical category—for example, states or nations.

10. It is desirable for a hierarchy not to extend below the fourth level—though many large websites do so. At the fifth level and deeper, disciplined decisions must be made as to how much linking to provide. In fact, it may be best to create entirely separate websites (subsites).

11. Websites sometimes omit the logical home page; the physical home page is made to look and function like a second-level page. This strategy is often a means for solving a problem of conflicting needs within an organization.

12. Designers can omit the logical second-level node and take the user directly to the eldest sibling at the third level. They often do so when they see no need for a (second-level) page of overview information.

13. Long scrolling Web pages can be divided into separate sections that should be regarded as separate nodes. Users navigate very conveniently among these nodes by scrolling among them, and they can print all the nodes at once rather than printing individual Web pages.

14. From the designer's perspective perhaps the most important browser feature is the Back button (and the Forward button). Because the Back button causes problems, designers need to carefully consider how much their users should have to rely on the Back button. It is desirable to build sufficiently complete

navigation on the pages of a website that the user does not need to rely heavily on Back.

15. Links can be coded to display a Web page in a new window (a new instance of the browser). There are various reasons why users may want to display two pages of one website. Also, designers often code external links to open in a new window so that their own site is not replaced. Users, however, are inconvenienced when they need to deal with and close numerous windows.

16. Online computing entails interactivity that does not fit the navigation paradigm but rather is much closer to the behavior of software user interfaces. We are just beginning to understand how to design user interfaces for online computing functions. In large measure we now draw upon our knowledge of interface design, including well-established interface design guidelines.

17. A site map often serves as the help system for a website's navigational interface. A website's online computer functions, however, require help information. A good design option is to place the information on the pages where people will need it.

References

Donnelly, Vanessa. 2001. *Designing Easy-to-Use Websites.* Harlow, England: Pearson.

Instone, Keith. Usable Web. www.usableweb.com

Mandel, Theo. 1997. *The Elements of User Interface Design.* New York: John Wiley & Sons.

Marion, Craig. Software Design Smorgasbord website. www.chesco.com/~cmarion

Nielsen, Jakob. Alertbox. www.useit.com/alertbox

Shneiderman, Ben. 1997. *Designing the User Interface: Strategies for Effective Human-Computer Interaction.* 3d ed. Reading, MA: Addison Wesley Longman.

Spool, Jared M., Will Schroeder, Tara Scanlon, Carolyn Snyder, and Terri DeAngelo. 1998. *Web Site Usability: A Designer's Guide.* San Francisco: Morgan Kaufmann Publishers.

Discussion and Application

Items for Discussion

1. Describe the Web page shown in Figure 8.24 using the concepts and terms you've learned in this book. What kinds of links and link groups are employed? Draw a partial-node link diagram that shows the location of this page in the website's hierarchy.

2. Compare the identity information on a sampling of Web pages on two different websites. What are the differences? Which design ideas are effective or ineffective in introducing the website and lending coherence to the user's experience as the user navigates the site?

3. An online electronics store is planning a big year-end sale of discontinued items. Their design calls for creating a drop-down list box on the home

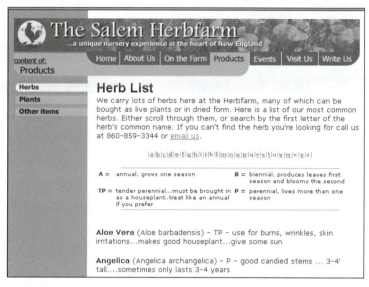

Figure 8.24. A page of the Salem Herbfarm website.
(www.salemherbfarm.com)

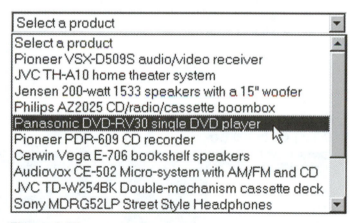

Figure 8.25. A drop-down list box with links to items that
are on sale.

page with links to the full description of each item. A section of the drop-down list box is shown in Figure 8.25. You've been called in to consult on this design. What will you say about this drop-down list box? One problem (at least) should come to mind.

4. Some websites display the primary links in a nav bar, even though there are more primary links than fit across the page. One way to do this to add a right-pointing arrow at the right end of the nav bar, as shown in Figure 8.26. When the user clicks the arrow, the current links are replaced by a new set.

Figure 8.26. A navigation bar with more links than can be displayed on the page at one time. Clicking the More arrow replaces these links with five new ones. Clicking again restores the original links.

The user can click the arrow again to restore the original set of links. Evaluate this design.

5. Describe the Web page shown in Figure 8.27 using the concepts and terms you've learned in this book. What kinds of links and link groups are employed?

6. Find two websites that provide help information for online computing functions. What do you like and dislike about the design of the help information on the two websites?

7. Our examination of the Bigtime University home page included a design in which the Downtown Campus is pre-eminent and the other three units appear as children (or divisions) of the Downtown Campus. We also saw a compromise design in which the Downtown Campus is first among equals, the eldest sibling. What if a different administrative decision had been made? What if it had been decided to give each unit equal status (or as equal as possible)? Create a design for Bigtime University that achieves this goal.

8. As you know, designers often depart from standard principles of Web design when fun or artistic expression are major goals of the website. Often

Figure 8.27. The home page of the Port of Seattle website. (www.portofseattle.org)

these sites are not easy to navigate. Find two whimsical websites that create navigational problems for users. Evaluate these sites.

9. Choose a relatively simple non-computerized device such as an alarm clock or a parking meter (that counts down the remaining legal parking time). Evaluate the device from the point of view of the eight user interface guidelines presented in this chapter. For example, if you were evaluating an alarm clock, one question you would ask is how well the alarm clock reveals the system status. Is it easy for the user to know whether the alarm clock is set to go off?

Application to Your Project

1. Review the reasoning behind your use of the various link groups in your website. Explain why each kind of link group is present and why you've designed it as you have.

2. Consider the directionality of your links. Where will you provide reciprocal links? Where will the user need to use the Back button? Do you think that users will be able to move efficiently through your website?

3. Decide if one or more of these strategies might be useful in your website:

   • Omitting a logical top node
   • Defaulting to the eldest sibling
   • Dividing one physical page into multiple nodes

4. If your website entails online computing functions, evaluate the online computing interface using the eight user interface design guidelines presented in this chapter.

9

Designing Effective Links

Introduction

Linking is the heart of the Web and hypermedia. From the user's perspective, clicking links more than anything else differentiates the Web and hypermedia from television, print, and all other media. Linking is also the characteristic of the Web that most governs Web design. The navigational interface is largely about linking.

The term "link" is used in two different ways. In its broader use, it refers to the complete pathway between nodes. In its more restricted meaning, the term refers to a hot area (or "link origin") on the screen. We have been using the term link in both senses. In this chapter, however, our emphasis is on the narrower definition: We will look at how links appear on the page, how we recognize and read them, and how they direct users to a destination.

We have organized this chapter around these four design principles:

1. Make clear "what's hot and what's not."
2. Design Web pages so that users will encounter and notice links.
3. Ensure that links are easy to scan and read.
4. Ensure that all links clearly indicate their destinations.

The chapter concludes by explaining how to perform user tests on your links and your website's navigational interface.

Make Clear "What's Hot and What's Not"

It is crucial to provide clear cues as to which elements on a Web page are actually links. In other words, the user must know "what's hot and what's not." Otherwise, several serious problems arise. First, the user may fail to recognize a link and never find out about a page with valuable information. Second is a "false hit." That is, something on the screen looks hot and entices the user to move the mouse to that spot and perhaps even to click. Just a few false hits will test a user's patience. When users are wondering what's hot and what's not, they often slowly slide the mouse pointer around the screen watching to see if the pointer will turn from an arrow to a hand. Except in websites created for fun or artistic expression, this behavior is proof of faulty design.

Here are the five cues that users most rely on to determine that page elements are hot:

1. Underlining, buttons, and tabs
2. Semantics
3. Location and grouping
4. A raised, 3-D appearance
5. Icons

Underlining, Buttons, and Tabs

Like other communications media, the Web is built upon conventions, shared understandings between designers and users. Among the most important and best established Web conventions is the use of underlined text, buttons, and tabs to indicate a link.

Underlining has been used to indicate text links in numerous hypertext systems, including the online help systems known to many millions of computer users before the Web was conceived. In the case of the Web, underlining appears automatically, with blue as the default link color, when a text link is coded.

One drawback of underlining in comparison to plain text is the extra visual complexity, but this does not prevent underlining from being a very useful and prevalent technique. Because users associate underlining with links, designers should never use underlining for any other purpose. Because underlining is a reliable cue, there is usually no need for such phrases as "click here" or "click the text below" to indicate the presence of a link:

Not:

Asthma sufferers should understand how dust mites trigger asthma attacks. To learn more about this, <u>click here.</u>

But:

Asthma sufferers should understand <u>how dust mites trigger asthma attacks.</u>

By default, text links change color (typically to purple) once they've been clicked, and the user will see this new color upon returning to the page for a period of time specified by the user in the browser settings. This change of color is useful, for it reminds users when they have already followed a particular link. This cue, unfortunately, is lost when designers create text links as graphics in order to fully control the font and other attributes of the link.

A Web button is a small demarcated area with text or a graphic that indicates a link. As you know, most buttons are small rectangles or rounded rectangles, and many have a raised, 3-D appearance produced with a drop shadow. But much variation is possible. For example, the buttons that make up nav bars may be demarcated by short vertical lines that suggest but do not fully bound the button area. Users readily understand that Web tabs are hot and that the selected tab is frontmost.

Semantics

Often, you do not need to use any sort of visual cue to indicate a text link: The semantics of the link (the meaning of the words) is sufficient. For example, in most contexts words and phrases such as "Products" or "Job Opportunities" or "Temperature by City" will be interpreted reliably as links. Designers like semantically cued links because they eliminate the extra visual complexity of underlining. But you must be sure that users will recognize that these words are links. Some users, for example, would interpret these words entirely as content (good advice to follow) rather than as a link:

> Learn how inhaled steroids can help manage asthma

Also, there is potential confusion about what is a heading introducing a group of links and what is a semantically cued link.

Location and Grouping

There are conventional locations for individual links and groups of links. In fact, nav bars and columns are recognized as much by location as by anything else. Likewise, links in the main content area are laid out in familiar ways, especially in various kinds of vertical lists and table-like arrays. In Figure 9.1, where the cues are based on location alone, we have a pretty good idea which text elements are links.

The 3-D Appearance

Human beings instinctively take note of the 3-D appearance produced by a drop shadow and related techniques on both the printed page and the screen. In hypermedia, the 3-D appearance strongly suggests a link. As shown in Figure 9.2a, the 3-D appearance suggests a physical button ready to be pressed. Designers make good use of this cue. Conversely, they are wary about giving a 3-D appearance to anything that's not hot. For example, if 3-D bullets are used with items in a list, the items may draw a useless click. Earlier in the history of the World Wide Web, buttons were often represented with a very noticeable 3-D appearance. Now slightly shadowed or entirely flat buttons are more prevalent.

Sometimes designers choose to reinforce semantically cued text links with small, blank raised buttons, as shown in Figure 9.2b. These buttons are often called "chiclets," due to their resemblance to chiclet chewing gum. This technique is effective, and is visually more attractive than building very wide buttons to en-

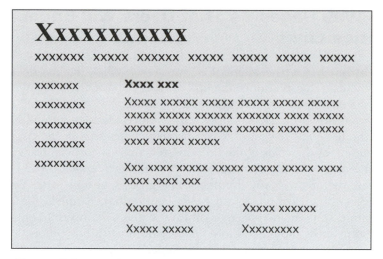

Figure 9.1. A Web page with the text shown only as Xs. Even so, location and grouping suggest that the horizontal text elements along the top of the page, the list at the left, and the phrases arranged in the table-like array at the bottom of the page are probably links.

(a)   (b)

Figure 9.2. A single raised button with button text and two blank ("chiclet") buttons with accompanying text.

compass lengthy phrases. When using these chiclet buttons, make the text hot too, in case the user clicks the text.

Icons

An icon is a graphic intended to convey a single specific message. For example, a question mark is widely used to represent a link to help information. Most icons are clearly identifiable as icons: They are usually small and are drawn very simply, with few details.

Icons appear often in the physical world; for example, a cigarette with a diagonal bar through it and a surrounding circle announces "No smoking." On the Web, almost every icon we see is a link. The design challenge, therefore, is not signaling users that icons are hot but rather making clear the meaning of the icon, the destination of the link.

Design Web Pages So That Users Will Encounter and Notice Links

Even when a page element is unmistakably hot, the link doesn't benefit the user if the user doesn't notice the link or doesn't pass his or her eyes over that portion of the page (i.e., doesn't encounter the link).

Very often users simply fail to notice a link or a small group of links because the links are relegated to an inconspicuous area of the page, the font size is too small, or the color of the link doesn't contrast sufficiently with the background of the page. All the more so, when the link is overshadowed by large graphics, GIF animations, visually dominant link groups, and so forth. Because they are small, drop-down list boxes can easily be overlooked unless the designer places them amid some blank space or otherwise gives them visual emphasis. Clearly, while some links should be more visually dominant than others, any link worth including at all should be made noticeable. This problem speaks once again to the importance of simplicity in design.

Links may not even be encountered if they are located below the scroll line and the user fails to scroll the page. Even experienced users may sometimes fail to notice the presence of a scroll bar, and all users often choose not to scroll a page. To ensure that users encounter all your links, you can avoid creating pages that will scroll. Most designers, however, consider this too great a restriction. A reasonable strategy, therefore, is to place your most important links above the scroll line—though the exact location of the scroll line varies with the user's computer equipment and how the user configures the browser. Perhaps the best strategy is to provide high-quality content that motivates your users to scroll.

Ensure That Links Are Easy to Scan and Read

Each of your Web pages and your website as a whole will be easier to use if individual links and link groups are properly phrased and formatted. Below we provide guidelines for vertical lists of links, nav bars, tabs, and embedded links.

Parallel Phrasing of Links

Parallel phrasing is a well-known principle of effective writing. It refers to using the same or similar syntax for all the items in a list or series in order to make the items easier to scan and read. The standard for parallelism for Web links appears to be significantly more relaxed than for many kinds of print writing. For example, the very typical nav column for a corporate website shown in Figure 9.3a includes noun phrases, a prepositional phrase, a command (imperative) sentence, and a normal (indicative) sentence.

This relaxed parallelism is acceptable partly because the phrases are short and familiar. In contrast, the violations of parallelism on the student's personal website shown in Figure 9.3b are jarring. Parallelism problems arise less often

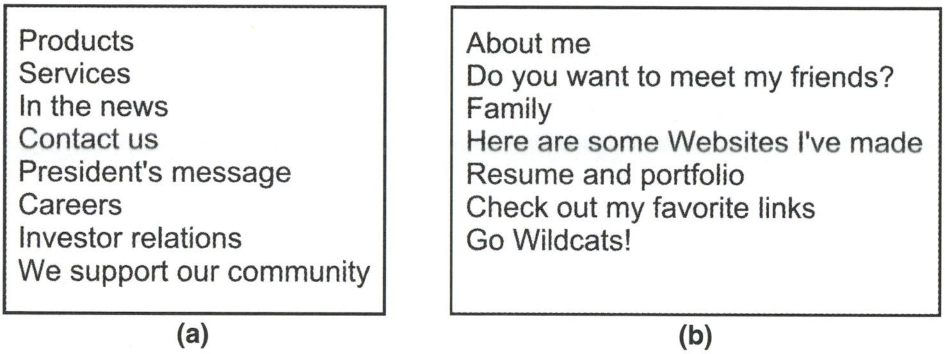

Products Services In the news Contact us President's message Careers Investor relations We support our community

(a)

About me Do you want to meet my friends? Family Here are some Websites I've made Resume and portfolio Check out my favorite links Go Wildcats!

(b)

Figure 9.3. Relaxed but acceptable parallelism on a corporate website and jarring variations in syntax on a student's personal website.

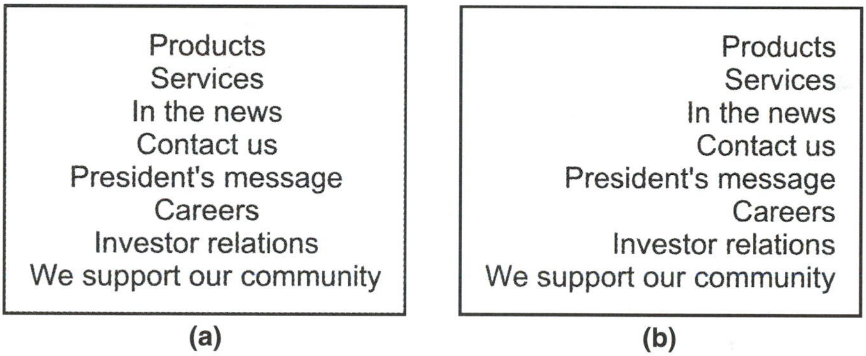

Products Services In the news Contact us President's message Careers Investor relations We support our community

(a)

Products Services In the news Contact us President's message Careers Investor relations We support our community

(b)

Figure 9.4. A list of centered links and a list of right aligned ("flush right") links.

with nav bars and tabs than with nav columns or MCA links because single words and very short phrases allow for fewer variations in syntax.

Left Aligning Vertical Lists of Links

Vertical lists of links aligned at the left margin ("flush left") are more readable than lists that are centered or right aligned, as you can see by comparing Figure 9.3a with Figure 9.4a and b. Left alignment is more readable because the user's eye more quickly and easily finds the beginning of each new line. Occasionally graphic designers choose to arrange a set of links in a free-form pattern in the main content area. While such a design may at times be desirable, the links will be especially difficult to scan and read.

Run-Over Items in Vertical Lists

When a list of links is placed in a nav column or in the main content area, it is often necessary to format the longest links as run-over lines. Be sure to provide adequate visual cues to differentiate a run-over link from two separate links. For example, Figure 9.5a uses initial upper-case letters ("sentence style" capitalization), bullets, and line spacing to clearly differentiate new entries from run-over lines. On the other hand, because initial upper-case letters are the only cue employed in Figure 9.5b, it is not immediately apparent that the list consists of three rather than five links.

Nav Bars and Tabs

Link text should be centered within nav bars and tabs. In the case of two-row nav bars, align the buttons when the text on the buttons is similar in length, as shown in Figure 9.6a. Otherwise, it is necessary to offset the buttons in some visually attractive manner (Figure 9.6b).

Finally, recall that numerous embedded links make a paragraph difficult to read. This is because (1) these links are read horizontally rather than as a vertical

Dinner Options

- Deluxe table service with champagne

- Full dinner buffet

- Café Organique specialty boxed vegetarian dinners

(a)

Dinner Options

Deluxe table service with champagne

Full dinner buffet

Café Organique specialty boxed vegetarian dinners

(b)

Figure 9.5. Differentiating run-over lines effectively with initial upper-case letters, bullets, and line spacing and less effectively using only initial upper-case letters.

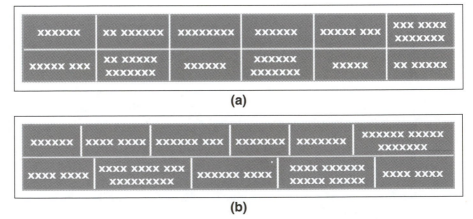

(a)

(b)

Figure 9.6. A nav bar with aligned buttons and with offset buttons.

list, (2) there is visual distraction caused by the underlining and color change, and (3) the phrasing may be compromised to fit the meaning and syntax of the paragraph rather than clearly signaling the destination of the link. Therefore, use embedded links sparingly.

Ensure That All Links Clearly Indicate Their Destinations

Links must make clear their destinations—the page that the link will display. Even in well-designed websites, users will periodically follow a link to an unwanted page. Designers, however, should work very hard to minimize these frustrating occurrences. Below we discuss a variety of issues related to this principle. We also take note of a closely related point: As they indicate their destinations, links must also express appropriate meanings.

Thinking About Audience and Purpose

To design links that will communicate their destination clearly, you need to think about your audience and their information needs. Let's look at the list of links on the home pages, shown in Figure 9.7, for two "bed and breakfast" establishments. These are small, family-run hotels that offer a more personal experience for vacationers than the typical hotel or motel.

The proprietors of the Magnolia Inn have a clear picture of their potential guests and how the website will be used. This is reflected in the choice, phrasing, and sequencing of the links. The link About the Magnolia Inn provides general information, with photographs, regarding the appearance and features of this beautiful and historic structure. Because the bedrooms in most bed and breakfasts are furnished uniquely and with special care, guests often take great interest in the room they will choose. The Magnolia Inn website, therefore, offers a link that specifically invites Web users to learn about each of the bedrooms. Naturally, the lavish, home-made breakfast and suggestions for daily activities also warrant

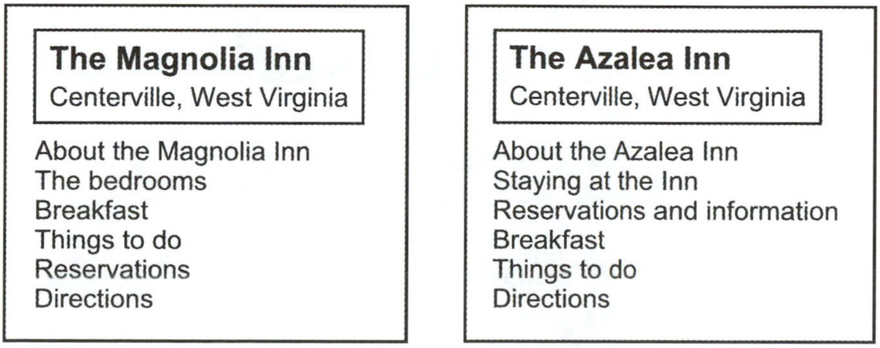

The Magnolia Inn Centerville, West Virginia	**The Azalea Inn** Centerville, West Virginia
About the Magnolia Inn The bedrooms Breakfast Things to do Reservations Directions	About the Azalea Inn Staying at the Inn Reservations and information Breakfast Things to do Directions

Figure 9.7. The home page links for two bed and breakfasts.

links. Finally, there are two business-oriented links that enable Web users to reserve a room and set their minds at rest about finding the inn once they get to Centerville. Because of the thoughtful, user-centered linking, potential guests immediately find a link that corresponds to each of their information needs. Furthermore, much like the better of the two Amtrak designs (discussed in Chapter 7, "Hierarchies") corresponds to a traveler's information needs, the sequencing of the Magnolia Inn links corresponds to the likely steps in planning a stay at a bed and breakfast.

In contrast, the Azalea Inn presents potential guests with fuzzy and less useful categories. In particular, the link Staying at the Inn is too vague. Is this where you can learn about the bedrooms? Also, the link Reservations and Information should be shortened to Reservations to give it a more specific focus. In the current design, the first three links all seem to promise some kind of general information. Furthermore, the sequencing of Reservations and Information seems haphazard. Don't users think about making a reservation *after* they've learned about the breakfasts and the available activities? It is interesting that a few different words have given the Magnolia Inn a distinct competitive advantage over the Azalea Inn.

Length and Clarity of Phrasing in Links

Length is a key issue in phrasing links. Length is an opportunity, a chance to clearly and specifically explain the destination. But you do not have many words to work with or your links will become too lengthy. Therefore, even more than with core content each word must count.

At times just a word or brief phrase is sufficient to indicate the link destination, as shown in Figure 9.8. Notice that the heading conveys much of the meaning.

On the other hand, when links represent technical or highly specialized concepts, lengthy phrases may be necessary to fully explain the link:

The limited success of school systems in identifying children with asthma

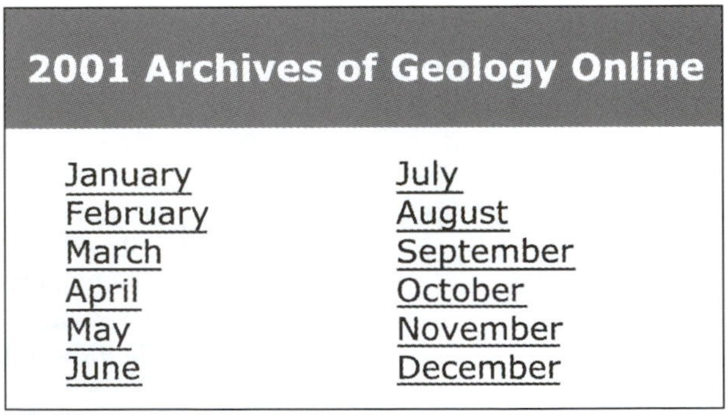

2001 Archives of Geology Online

January	July
February	August
March	September
April	October
May	November
June	December

Figure 9.8. One-word links that are clear and precise.

Mayor's Message

Mayor Compeau explains plans
to protect City wetlands.

Figure 9.9. A link with
supplemental
text.

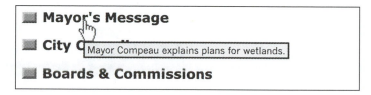

Figure 9.10. A link in which the supplemental text is a pop-up
message that appears when the user mouses over
the link.

Designers are sometimes tempted to overly abbreviate or compress link text to fit
space. Although you can often succeed with clever phrasing, you also run the risk
of removing essential meaning from the link:

School system success in asthma identification

The lesson here is not to impair the clarity of links (or to make the phrasing awk-
ward) because you like a particular page design. Instead, modify the design. For
example, to get more space for lengthy links, use the main content area rather
than a nav bar or column.

As shown in Figures 9.9 and 9.10, links can be explained with supplemental
text. The first design does not save space, but users can instantly choose between
reading or ignoring the supplemental information. The space-saving alternative is
to create a "mouse rollover" pop-up message (perhaps using the ALT tag). The
drawback here is that the user needs to move the mouse over the link to get the
more detailed layer of information.

The Problematic Nature of Icons

Icons offer some significant advantages over text links:

- A familiar icon is processed more quickly and easily than a text link.
- Many icons communicate across languages and cultures.
- Because icons are a graphical element, they can be made visually interesting
  and attractive and can be incorporated into a website's overall visual design.
- Icons often save space.

On the other hand, icons often fail to indicate the destination of the link. Many
concepts are surprisingly difficult to communicate reliably with an image. Anyone who has played the board game Pictionary knows it is much easier to win
when you are sketching an object such as "chair" rather than an abstraction such
as "disappointment." Try to guess the meanings of the two icons that appear in
Figure 9.11. The intended meaning of the icon on the left is "features of the system" (based on the idea of a feature film). Many users, however, will conclude
that this icon stands for "video" or "multimedia." The intended meaning of the
icon on the right is "system services" (based on a serving person holding a tray).
At least some users, however, will be puzzled.

Figure 9.11. Icons that are subject to misinterpretation.

One way to ensure that icons will communicate is to supplement them with some kind of text explanation. As users gradually learn the meaning of the icon, they will begin to ignore the label. Mouse rollovers are a reasonable option for labels.

Designing Icons

Icon design is a complex topic and is beyond the scope of this book. But we offer some basic principles here:

1. If an icon represents an actual object, users must immediately recognize what this object is. In other words, before users can begin to figure out that the scoreboard on a sports website represents game scores, they must know they are looking at a scoreboard.

2. There should be a straightforward relationship between the icon and the message the icon is meant to convey. If the relationship is based on a pun or an obscure connection (as we saw above with the cinema and waiter-and-tray icons), the icon is apt to fail.

3. Simple designs (relatively free of detail) work best. First, because icons are small, anything but a simple design is apt to be overly cluttered and hard to make out. Second, simple designs suggest a category or concept rather than a particular instance, which is usually necessary for an icon to function properly. For example, the icon of a blouse in an online clothing store should not contain excessive detail or it will appear to represent a particular blouse rather than a category of merchandise.

4. Labeled icons should still be memorable so that users will quickly learn the meaning of the icon and stop relying on the label.

5. Test all but the most familiar icons with users. Designers tend to be far too optimistic in assuming that their icons will communicate clearly. Be prepared to label your icons.

Link Typing and the Meanings Inherent in Linking

Nodes can be usefully categorized according to an attribute of the node such as content type or subject matter. For example, Figure 9.12 shows a website devoted to the jazz luminary Louis Armstrong; icons are used to signal that the destination of a link is audio or video content.

With Fats Waller (1.68 MB)

 From the 1962 Pasadena Concert (7.83 MB)

Figure 9.12. The use of a speaker icon to indicate an audio node and a video camera icon to indicate a video node. File sizes are given so that the user can estimate downloading time.

Likewise, in an online encyclopedia, a flower icon might appear beside all botany links and an animal icon beside zoology links, or these links might consistently appear under headings such as Botany and Zoology. Categorizing links in this manner is usually termed "link typing." The term may seem strange because the attributes belong to the nodes. But it is through the links that the categories are being presented to users.

Link typing also includes distinguishing between internal and external links. Often internal and external links are organized under headings. Also, external links can be signaled with an icon such as a spider web (to show that the destination of this link is "out on the Web").

Link typing can entail more than revealing information to users. In some hypermedia systems, such as Xerox NoteCards, link types are recorded in a database built into the system. This means, for example, that the system can display only links belonging to a certain type (or combination of types). Consider, for example, the usefulness of a hypermedia encyclopedia that enables the user to view master lists of links filtered by subject area (e.g., just the botany links).

There is another dimension, subtle but important, to link typing. While content type and subject area are relatively straightforward ways of classifying nodes, link typing can convey complex and rich information. For example, the All Music Guide website (www.allmusic.com) consists primarily of thousands of musicians' biographies, each concluding with numerous links to other biographies grouped under such headings as Roots and Influences, Followers, and Worked With. The headings type the links and in so doing convey information that often cannot be found in the biographies themselves. In other words, you can learn a great deal about a particular musician by examining these links—even if you never click them. For a sophisticated discussion of the meanings inherent in linking, see Nicholas Burbules (1998).

Because meaning resides in links, designers need to guard against the possibility of expressing unintended meanings. For example, an environmental organization maintains a website dealing with regional issues. One Web page contains a lengthy news article, "Proposed General Entropy Lead Mine Threatens Tecumseh Valley." At the end of the news article, there is a heading, Related Links, with these links listed below it:

Earth Justice League files suit in District Court

Tecumseh Valley Environmental Council plans fundraising events

City of Tecumseh refuses to issue permit

Zompco Corporation issues statement regarding proposed lead mine.

Notice that the appearance of the Zompco link among the three pro-environment links suggests that Zompco is an ally in this fight—whereas, in fact, Zompco issued a statement supporting the lead mine.

The designers should have phrased the Zompco link to more fully convey its meaning. Another approach is to type the links with such headings as Working for the Valley and Our Opponents on the Move. Note also that the environmental organization's website does not indicate which links are internal and which external.

As a designer, you should carefully consider the value of typing links, the intended and unintended meanings expressed by all your links, and the ethical implications of these meanings. Apart from link typing, the prominence of links within a website conveys meaning. If the sole link to a particular page appears deep in the hierarchy, users (if they find this link at all) perceive the content differently than if the link is more prominently placed.

Customized and Adaptive Linking

On most websites a particular page displays the same links for every user. Some websites, however, notably Web portals such as Yahoo, allow users to create personal pages with their own customized links. It is also possible for systems to take the initiative and adaptively display a different set of links under different circumstances (Brusilovsky, Kobsa, and Vassileva 1998). For example, a news website might display a different set of links to each user based on a user profile that is itself based on the user's previous visits. A Web or CD/DVD tutorial can develop a user profile by scoring correct and incorrect answers and can adaptively lead users to remedial content and remove links to more advanced topics. A closely related technique is to adaptively change the content without changing the links. For example, the tutorial might give two different learners two different variations on the same explanation.

Although there is great potential in adaptive linking, it is not easy for adaptive systems to draw correct inferences about human behavior and information needs. For example, someone with no real interest in hockey might visit a few hockey websites and then purchase a ticket to a Maple Leafs game to fill an evening during a business trip to Toronto. A highly adaptive Web portal might show this person unwanted hockey links long afterward. Finally, citizens must be vigilant about allowing governments, corporations, and other organizations to manage and filter the information we get over the Web.

User Testing of Links and Navigation

In Chapter 3, "Designing and Building," we pointed out that a key part of any Web development effort is to seek useful evaluations of the design and that user testing is the most reliable form of evaluation. We also provided general guidelines on performing user tests. Here we focus on ways to test your links and the navigational interface.

- Ask subjects to pick out the hot areas on your Web pages. Presumably, they will correctly identify what's hot and what's not. Pay special attention to semantically cued links.
- Ask subjects to predict the destinations of both text and icon links. If you are choosing between two ways of phrasing certain links or two designs for certain icons, you can test the competing versions on two groups of subjects to determine which version is more successful. Afterward, you can ask both groups of subjects to review and comment on the competing designs.
- In the case of icon links, ask subjects to identify the object being represented and to explain what they think the icon means. Even if you plan to label an icon, you should test the icon without the label to see how well the icon itself communicates. You can return to these icons in a subsequent test session to see how well subjects remember their meanings.
- Ask subjects to navigate through your hierarchy to find particular information. Not only may you discover links that mislead users, you may also discover situations in which users make choices too quickly and fail to scroll farther down on the page where they will encounter the appropriate links.
- Test the overall meaningfulness of your hierarchy and how fully subjects can attain situation awareness. One way to do this is to ask subjects to draw a node-link diagram of your website after they have examined it. In the case of a small website with straightforward semantic meanings, subjects may well be able to create a reasonably accurate and complete node-link diagram. In the case of large and complex websites, they may only be able to approximate the structure or represent portions of it.

In describing these tests, our general assumption has been that you are testing a clickable prototype of your website. In many cases, however, you can perform these tests on design sketches or sample pages. Some of these tests can be performed still earlier in the development process using an outline, node-link diagram, or set of note cards. For example, you can ask subjects to predict the destinations of links when the links are only penciled in on 3 x 5 cards. In other words, you would ask "What cards do you expect to find under the card "Controlling Your Environment?" Remember that you must test early enough in the development process to make whatever design changes your tests call for.

Summary

1. Clicking links more than anything else differentiates the Web and hypermedia from television, print, and all other media. Also linking more than anything else governs Web design.
2. The term "link" refers to the complete pathway between nodes and more narrowly to a hot area (or "link origin") on the screen.
3. **Principle 1: Make clear "what's hot and what's not."**

   - There are five cues that users rely on most to determine that page elements are hot: (1) underlining, buttons, and tabs, (2) semantics, (3) location and grouping, (4) a 3-D appearance, and (5) icons.

- Never use underlining for any other purpose than to indicate a link.
- There is usually no need for such phrases as "click here" to indicate the presence of a link.
- Semantically cued links eliminate the extra visual complexity of underlining. Be sure, however, that users will recognize that these words are links.
- There are conventional locations for individual links and groups of links. Location and grouping help users understand what's hot and what's not.
- The 3-D appearance strongly suggests a link. Be wary about giving the 3-D appearance to anything that's not hot. Sometimes designers choose to reinforce semantically cued text links with small, blank "chiclet" buttons.
- An icon is a graphic intended to convey a single specific message. On the Web, almost every icon we see is a link. The design challenge is making clear the meaning of the icon, the destination of the link.

4. **Principle 2: Design Web pages so that users will encounter and notice links.**

- Often links are overlooked among more dominant page elements. Avoid inconspicuous links.
- Users don't always scroll Web pages. Therefore, it is wise to place your most important links above the scroll line. Also, provide high-quality content that motivates your users to scroll.

5. **Principle 3: Ensure that links are easy to scan and read.**

- Observe parallelism in phrasing Web links. The standard for parallelism, however, appears to be significantly more relaxed on the Web than it is in print.
- Left align vertical lists of links. Be sure to provide adequate visual cues to differentiate a run-over link from two separate links.
- Center link text within nav bars and tabs. In the case of two-row nav bars, align the buttons when they are similar in length. Avoid two-row sets of tabs.
- Numerous embedded links make a paragraph difficult to read. Use embedded links sparingly.

6. **Principle 4: Ensure that all links clearly indicate their destinations.**

- To design links that will communicate their destination clearly, you need to think about your audience and their information needs.
- Phrase links carefully. Resist the temptation to overly abbreviate or compress link text. Sometimes the best solution is to annotate links with more detailed information, possibly using a mouse rollover.
- Icon links, when familiar, are processed more quickly and easily than text links. Also, many icons communicate across languages and cultures. Icons, however, often fail to indicate the destination of the link, unless the icon is very familiar or is labeled. Follow the established principles for designing and evaluating icons.
- Nodes can be usefully categorized according to an attribute of the node such as content type or subject matter. This technique is usually termed "link typing." Some hypermedia systems filter links on the basis of link

typing. Link typing can convey complex and rich information. Designers need to guard against the possibility of expressing unintended meanings.

- Some websites, notably Web portals such as Yahoo, allow users to create personal pages with their own customized links. Other websites adaptively display a different set of links under different circumstances. Adaptivity is difficult to do well and presents societal risks, but offers great potential.

7. There are many ways to perform user tests on links and the navigational interface. For example, you can ask subjects to pick out all the hot areas on your Web pages or predict the destinations of individual links. You can perform these tests using a clickable prototype, sample pages, or design sketches. Some tests can be performed still earlier in the development process.

References

Brusilovsky, Peter, Alfred Kobsa, and Julita Vassileva, eds. 1998. *Adaptive Hypertext and Hypermedia.* Dordrecht, The Netherlands, and Boston: Kluwer Academic Publishers.

Burbules, Nicholas, C. 1998. Rhetorics of the Web: Hyperreading and critical literacy. In *Page to Screen: Taking Literacy into the Electronic Era.* Ilana Snyder, ed. London and New York: Routledge, 102–22.

Discussion and Application

Items for Discussion

1. On the Web page shown below, is it clear what's hot and what's not? Explain.

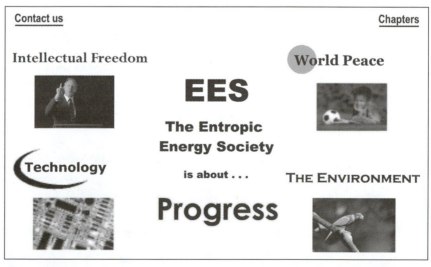

Figure 9.13. A Web page for a professional society with poorly designed links.

2. Examine the way in which embedded linking is handled in the following paragraph. Identify the problem or problems you see here and try to explain the reasons.

> Negative reports regarding <u>Zompco</u> have been issued during the last two weeks by several securities analysts. They are <u>demanding</u> that Zompco prove that its business model is viable. Perhaps in response to this criticism Zompco hiked some prices last week. Unfortunately, a server glitch <u>halted</u> shopping for two days.

Figure 9.14. A paragraph with poorly designed embedded links.

3. A government agency was designing an intranet for agency employees. The home page included the links listed below. When the agency performed user tests on the prototype, they discovered that many users seemed confused by three of these links. Which links do you think were the problem? Explain the problem and suggest how one or more of the links might be re-phrased.

<u>Governor's Message</u>

<u>Featured Program</u>

<u>What's New</u>

<u>What's Happening</u>

<u>Coming Soon</u>

<u>Media Releases</u>

4. A physician contributed some reviews of recent research to the Research part of the Asthma Horizons website. The physician also suggested links to these pages. However, the graphic designer is concerned that these lengthy links will interfere with the page design he is working on. Also, the editor is wondering whether users may be intimidated by these lengthy links. Together they write shorter versions, which appear below the physician's links.

How successful are the shorter links? Do they communicate adequately to users of Asthma Horizons? Hint: You must read the revised versions from the perspective of someone who has not read the more complete physician's versions.

<u>Formoterol provides rapid and long-lasting protection against exercised-induced asthma</u>

<u>Formoterol protects against exercised-induced asthma</u>

<u>The influence of household smoking on the development of asthma in children</u>

<u>Smoking influence on childhood asthma</u>

<u>Long-term treatment with inhaled steroids shown not to affect adult height in children with asthma</u>

<u>Inhaled steroids and growth in children with asthma</u>

<u>Care for asthmatic children shown to improve when caregivers keep diaries</u>

<u>Effectiveness of asthma caregiver diaries for children</u>

5. Below are two icons, used in two different websites, to take the user to a page where the user can type some identifying information and gain access to a portion of the website. Assess these two icons. Would you advise using either of them?

Figure 9.15. Two icons for logging on to a website.

6. As you have seen in Figure 9.12, a speaker icon can be used to indicate an audio node and a video-camera icon to indicate a video node. Think of some possible alternatives and assess these.

Application to Your Project

1. Assess all the links on your website according to these criteria:

   - Is it clear "what's hot and what's not"?
   - Are you confident users will encounter and notice your links?
   - Are your links easy to scan and read?
   - Do all your links clearly indicate their destinations?

2. What kind of user testing would be most useful to you in improving your website's navigational interface?

10

Writing for the Web

Introduction

Writing for the Web is similar in many ways to writing for print. Just as with print, you always begin by analyzing your audience and purpose. Just as with print, you need a strong command of grammar and usage, a good vocabulary, and the ability to control style and point of view so that you can reach a common ground with your audience and achieve your own communication goals.

How we write for the Web resembles writing for print in another important respect: What we do depends very largely on genre. There is no one way to write for the Web, just as there is no one way to write for print. Indeed, writing for a website very often resembles writing for the analogous print genre. The features and news stories for a website about country-and-western music will be written much like features and news stories in country-and-western music magazines. Research reports in online academic journals bear many similarities to those written for print journals.

Amid these commonalities, however, there are differences between writing for print and the Web. The most significant are these:

1. The Web medium encourages casual, restless reading behavior.
2. Web writing is not necessarily text. Sometimes we write for oral delivery.
3. The Web is a strongly non-linear information environment. This is the most significant difference and the one we will explore in greatest detail.

Writing for a "Non-Sticky" Medium

Patterns of behavior develop around each communications medium. One characteristic we see in Web use is the willingness to quickly abandon a website as soon as the user experiences just a bit of boredom, disappointment, or frustration. The phrase "surfing the Web" captures this behavior. Website owners are keenly aware of the casual, restless character of much Web use, and they often talk about "stickiness," the much-desired ability to hold users for a reasonable amount of time.

In contrast, restlessness is not an inherent characteristic of print. Even if people are not immediately engaged by a book, they will usually stay with it for a while before abandoning it. People will settle down with a newspaper or magazine, even though they jump around among the articles. Nor is restless behavior characteristic of cinema. After paying their admission at a movie theater or renting a VCR or DVD movie, people are inclined to sit through the movie, even if it starts slowly or is only modestly satisfying. Television is less sticky than cinema, especially in the era of remote control devices and dozens of channels.

Causes of Restless Behavior

One factor that contributes to the lack of stickiness is limited legibility and other problems that arise in reading from the computer screen. Another factor is that almost all websites are cost free and easily and quickly accessed. With very little investment to get in, there is little reluctance to get out. Along similar lines, users can almost always find a website that is comparable to the one they are looking at. Websites with unique or unusual content hold special value. Finally, these patterns of behavior, once they start, become habitual and are carried to each new website. They become part of the cultural context of the medium though, like other aspects of culture, they are subject to change.

Note that hypermedia delivered on CD/DVD is stickier than the Web, even though a website and a CD/DVD title may be quite similar in regard to content and interactivity. This difference stems from the effort entailed in acquiring and loading a CD or DVD and the fact that there is a physical medium to be owned and looked after. Also, because CD/DVD titles are often more video intensive and provide a more cinematic experience, they share some of the cultural habits that people bring to cinema.

Web Writing Guidelines and the Rhetorical Perspective

Web experts have offered advice for writing for the Web. These recommendations generally reflect the Web's lack of stickiness and emphasize writing for people who are inclined to scan and skip. Here is a good set of general guidelines adapted from Jakob Nielsen (2000, 1997).

1. Keep your writing concise and direct.
2. Make sure each sentence conveys useful content.
3. Provide ample blank space. Don't crowd the page with text.
4. Don't expect people to read more than short amounts of text on the Web. Avoid long scrolling pages. Provide links that let users access more detailed information if they want it (layering).
5. Write for scannability. Use short paragraphs, subheadings, and bulleted lists.

6. Build paragraphs around topic sentences so that readers can quickly and readily grasp the central idea of each paragraph.
7. Create an overall structure in which the key points are explained early on. Don't save important information for the conclusion. Write so that the reader can leave off at any point and still come away with your most important content.

These guidelines are sensible and useful. On the other hand, these guidelines (and indeed any set of guidelines) can't possibly be the complete answer to writing for the Web. How we write depends on the particular rhetorical situation. For example, brevity and scannability are not the main concerns for someone reading about a promising treatment for a serious medical condition he suffers from or about the prospects of a company he has invested in. If readers are strongly interested in the content, they will most certainly read extended text, and they will not hesitate to scroll for more information. Likewise, genre affects people's reading habits and expectations. Scientists will not be surprised by or highly resistant to extended text in an online research journal. Similarly, people who read memoirs or other forms of personal writing on the Web will not expect short paragraphs and bulleted lists.

Regard these (and similar) guidelines as a good default strategy that helps us address the Web's lack of stickiness. They are especially relevant to home pages, for here we want inviting, easy-to-scan writing that establishes its value quickly and draws the user further into the website. On the interior pages the content can become more detailed, and in other ways make greater demands on the reader. The real answer is writing (and other content) that responds to people's needs and interests and is trustworthy, current, clearly and smoothly written, and handsomely and functionally formatted.

Writing Audio Discourse

Many websites incorporate video and animation sequences, and these often include audio discourse. Furthermore, many websites incorporate audio-only sequences without video or animation. For example, a city website might include audio narration that the user can play while viewing pictures of city landmarks.

When you write for a narrator, whether off screen or on screen, your writing must fit the narrator and the rhetorical situation. Stated differently, you need to create the kind of narrator that fits the audience, purpose, and theme of the website.

Furthermore, you may want to influence the narrator's oral delivery of your text. You can prepare a narrator's script that employs boldface to show emphasis, ellipses to show pauses, and so forth. You might even produce your own demo audio version of the narration.

Often you need to coordinate your writing with shifts in the "camera eye." For example, let's imagine that Asthma Horizons includes an animated lesson on the function of the lungs explained by an off-screen narrator. At some point the animation switches from an external view of the lungs to a microscopic view of the individual alveoli (air sacs). The narration should reflect this shift with transitional phrases and sentences—for example: "Now as we explore the interior of the lungs. . . ."

The principles and techniques of writing for narrators and actors belong to the fields of public speaking, broadcasting, and cinema and are beyond the scope of this book. Good resources include Bruce Gronbeck, Douglas Ehninger, and Alan Monroe (1999) and J. Michael Straczynski (1996).

Writing for a Non-Linear Environment

As you know, the Web is predominantly a non-linear environment, an environment in which users have a lot of choice in what they view next. In the case of hierarchies, users are generally invited to explore any branch of the hierarchy or to follow the secondary links. The other information structures, except for the linear structure, also offer significant navigation options. For writers, the most important difference between print and the Web is non-linearity.

It is definitely a mistake to equate the print medium with linearity. Even though the sequence of bound pages encourages linear reading, print documents range all the way from the strict linearity of the novel to the complete non-linearity of the encyclopedia. Print, however, is and will remain a much more linear medium than the Web.

There are important benefits (or at least potential benefits) in non-linear information environments: Readers are more able to find and read exactly what they care about. Furthermore, they are more fully empowered to follow their unique interests and make their own connections among ideas. This was an important theme in Vannevar Bush's "As We May Think," and it remains important today, especially in the writings of postmodern Web and hypermedia theorists.

From the writer's perspective, links can function as enticing "hooks" to draw readers who may not have a strong initial interest in the topic. For example, in Figure 10.1, we see a writer who is working very hard at creating enticing links to draw users into an online essay on evolutionary biology that the writer thinks the audience might not otherwise take an interest in.

If these benefits were not important, Web designers would simplify their task and build sites consisting of one very long page. Instead, we accept the challenge of designing non-linear information environments.

The drawbacks of non-linear writing—as you will see—are significant. Risks include excessive redundancy, dull writing, irritating loose ends, confusion, and missing information. In the remaining sections of this chapter, you will learn how to avoid these pitfalls and succeed with non-linear writing.

Caution Referring to Other Pages

Both online and in print, writers use phrases such as these to refer to other parts of a document:

As noted previously, . . .
You will recall that . . .

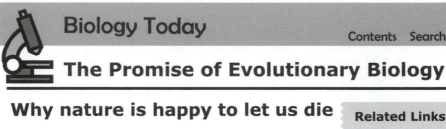

Figure 10.1. An non-linear essay on evolutionary biology that draws the user into the subject matter.

As you will learn, . . .

We demonstrate this later.

On the Web we use such phrases within a single lengthy Web page and perhaps within a linear sequence of Web pages. But we must be very careful about referring users to other pages in a website. In a non-linear environment, we usually do not know where users have been or where they will go next. These phrases, then, are apt to prove false (the user *does not* recall X and *will not* encounter Y) and so become irritating or confusing loose ends. The standard way, of course, to refer to other parts of a website is by building a link. Links, however, are invitations; they don't embody assumptions about the routes taken by individual users.

Managing Pre-Requisite Relationships

Pre-requisite content refers to something the user should read before going on to something else. Many kinds of printed books exhibit a complete chain of pre-requisite relationships in which each chapter depends upon the previous one. At least from the writer's point of view, there is one pathway through the material. The reader is certainly free to leave this pathway (just like hikers can choose to leave a trail) but the writer is no longer responsible for the quality of the reader's experience.

Even in a non-linear environment there are usually many pre-requisite relationships, also referred to as "dependencies." Managing these dependencies is very complex and also very important. This is how you keep users from entering a danger zone where they (1) will be confused and frustrated by the incompleteness of the information they are receiving or (2) will not receive information the author considers important or even essential.

Note that being unaware of missing information can be much worse than confusion. A badly designed website may allow a user to read about a new medical treatment without encountering the pre-requisite node that explains who shouldn't undergo this treatment.

Designers should think carefully about dependencies when the initial structure of the website is first worked out. Also, a writer or editor should check for dependency problems later in the development process. Athough your goal is to prevent users from navigating into danger zones, the designer's responsibility is not absolute. Users who bounce through a website mostly following associative secondary links are apt to encounter pages they won't fully understand. Furthermore, even when you design so that users must encounter pre-requisite information, there is no way (short of extreme measures) to force users to actually read the pre-requisite information you present them with.

Modularity

Modularity refers to content that has no pre-requisites. It can stand alone and still provide a satisfying experience for the reader—or, at least, this is the author's intention. Encyclopedia articles are modular because each article is written without regard to what other articles the reader might previously have looked at. The encyclopedia assumes a certain general level of literacy and a certain degree of knowledge about the world, but beyond this baseline level of education, no assumptions are made about the reader's prior knowledge regarding any article. Similarly, the articles in newspapers and general-interest magazines are usually modular.

On the Web, every home page has to be modular, and often many other pages are as well. A certain number of websites are fully modular, in the manner of an encyclopedia. For example, The Electronic Labyrinth by Christopher Keep, Tim McLaughlin, and Robin Parmar is a valuable website devoted to hypertext history and theory. Each page is skillfully written to make good sense to readers with a strong humanities background, and each contains links to draw users to other articles. An article from the Electronic Labyrinth appears as Figure 10.2.

The All Music Guide, (www.allmusic.com) is another modular website. Essentially a digital encyclopedia of musicians, it invites users to jump freely from one biography to another following their interests and making their own intellectual connections.

The encyclopedic approach works well when the user's focus is on individual articles (what we often think of as using a book as a "reference"), but becomes problematical when the user is trying to obtain a systematic and broad understanding of a complete body of knowledge. This is because the articles are short, because each addresses one topic, and—most of all—because the author is not guiding the reader by providing any sort of sequence or overall organizing principle.

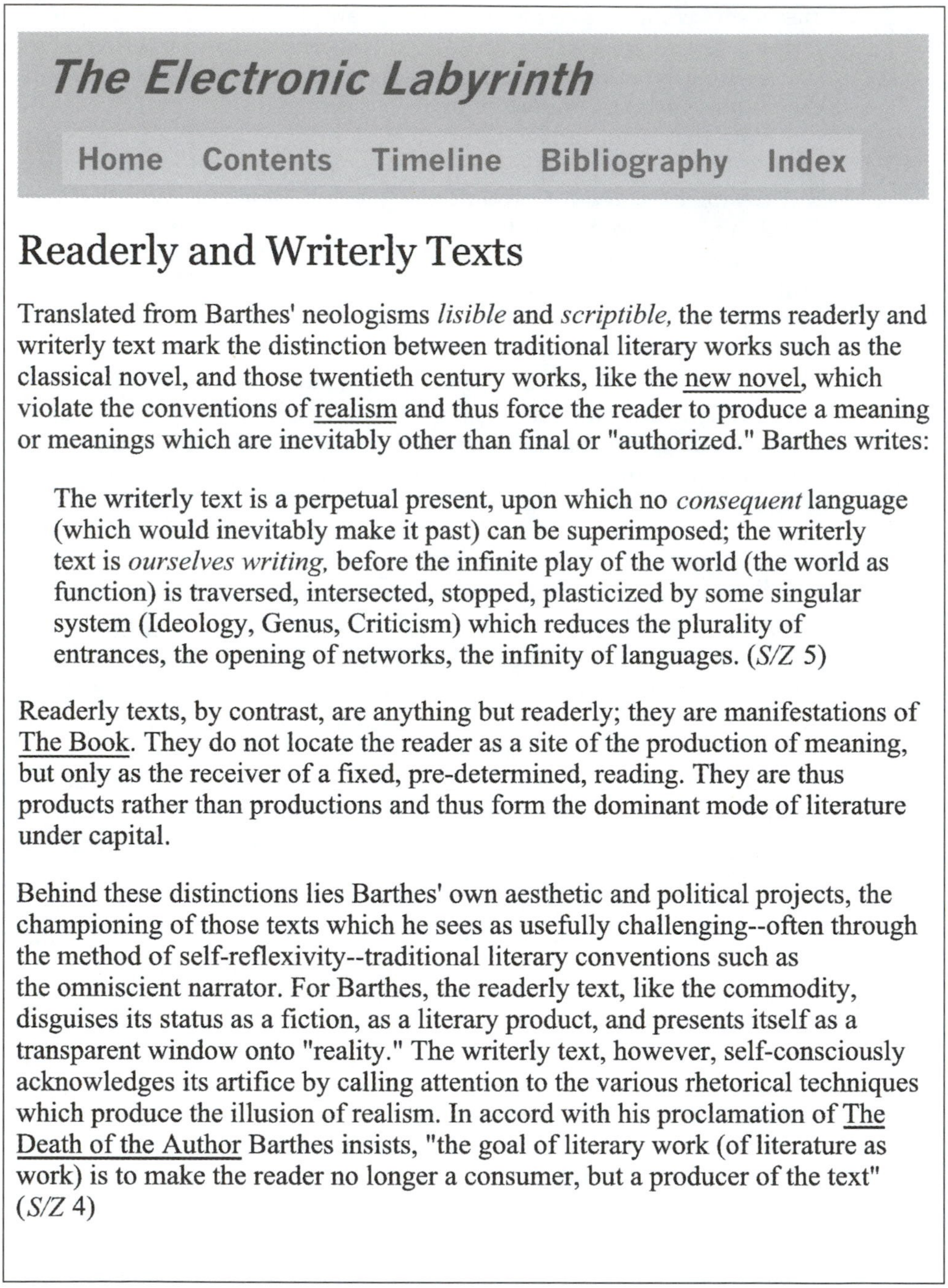

The Electronic Labyrinth

Home   Contents   Timeline   Bibliography   Index

Readerly and Writerly Texts

Translated from Barthes' neologisms *lisible* and *scriptible,* the terms readerly and writerly text mark the distinction between traditional literary works such as the classical novel, and those twentieth century works, like the <u>new novel</u>, which violate the conventions of <u>realism</u> and thus force the reader to produce a meaning or meanings which are inevitably other than final or "authorized." Barthes writes:

> The writerly text is a perpetual present, upon which no *consequent* language (which would inevitably make it past) can be superimposed; the writerly text is *ourselves writing,* before the infinite play of the world (the world as function) is traversed, intersected, stopped, plasticized by some singular system (Ideology, Genus, Criticism) which reduces the plurality of entrances, the opening of networks, the infinity of languages. (*S/Z* 5)

Readerly texts, by contrast, are anything but readerly; they are manifestations of <u>The Book</u>. They do not locate the reader as a site of the production of meaning, but only as the receiver of a fixed, pre-determined, reading. They are thus products rather than productions and thus form the dominant mode of literature under capital.

Behind these distinctions lies Barthes' own aesthetic and political projects, the championing of those texts which he sees as usefully challenging--often through the method of self-reflexivity--traditional literary conventions such as the omniscient narrator. For Barthes, the readerly text, like the commodity, disguises its status as a fiction, as a literary product, and presents itself as a transparent window onto "reality." The writerly text, however, self-consciously acknowledges its artifice by calling attention to the various rhetorical techniques which produce the illusion of realism. In accord with his proclamation of <u>The Death of the Author</u> Barthes insists, "the goal of literary work (of literature as work) is to make the reader no longer a consumer, but a producer of the text" (*S/Z* 4)

Figure 10.2. The Electronic Labyrinth, an example of the encyclopedia model. (www.eserver.org/elab)

The Electronic Labyrinth is especially interesting because it reflects and expresses a postmodern philosophical perspective. The authors definitely want readers to make their own connections. This intention is implicit in the word "labyrinth," meaning a maze. But will all visitors possess the intellectual ability and commitment to create his or her own synthesis of this complex intellectual territory? At least some people will prefer a traditional linear treatment of the same general subject area, such as Ilana Snyder's *Hypertext: The Electronic Labyrinth* (1996).

It is possible to back off from an uncompromising encyclopedic structure and provide readers with some authorial guidance. For example, the Electronic Labyrinth provides a kind of electronic table of contents in which the articles appear grouped into general categories. This strategy adds a limited hierarchical dimension to what is primarily a web-like structure.

Open-Endedness

Open-endedness is the user's perception that relevant information is missing, that something pertinent has been left unsaid. A limited degree of open-endedness is acceptable; indeed, in the hands of a skillful writer, open-endedness can create interest and suspense. On the other hand, clumsy and excessive open-endedness results in annoyance and confusion. Open-endedness, therefore, is an important aspect of writing for the Web, whether nodes are modular or whether they have pre-requisites.

Consider, for example, the website of a professional basketball team that includes a linear sequence of pages recounting the team's history. On a page entitled Years of Struggle (Figure 10.3), interest and suspense are generated by skillfully withholding information and only hinting at Elena's career as the Cougars' star player:

After four exciting but losing seasons, Coach Ito was desperate to build the team that would finally bring success to Cleveland. In a flurry of trades, she acquired Vivian Sinnick from Atlanta and Mary Villa from Los Angeles. She persuaded the Cougar owners to pay the hefty sum necessary to pick up veteran center Estelle Winchell, who was available as a free agent. And then, almost as an afterthought, she signed the unknown Croatian guard who had not yet played basketball in the United States.

NEXT: Elena!

Figure 10.3. A skillful instance of open-endedness. In this linear sequence, the writer builds suspense by withholding the identity of the player who will be featured on the next page.

In contrast, consider a bank whose website includes pages with tips on money management. One page tells the story of an unfortunate individual whose entire checking account was wiped out by a thief who stole the individual's debit card. Users, however, will wonder how the thief got the PIN number. Was this a special kind of debit card that allows ATM withdrawals without entering a PIN number? Did the thief use some sophisticated computer trick to figure out the PIN number? Did the individual foolishly tape the PIN number to the front of the debit card? Without this item of missing information, the open-endedness reaches the level of puzzlement and irritation. In fact, even if the answer is available via a link, the user is not likely to perceive anything positive in the strategy of temporarily withholding this information.

Audience and Purpose Determine What Is Pre-Requisite Information

The concepts of pre-requisite information and modularity depend on audience and purpose. What is pre-requisite information for one person may not be for another. Let's say a mathematics professor is examining an online or print textbook on statistics to see if it's suitable for her course. For this audience, each chapter is modular; for a student trying to learn statistics the chapters will be highly dependent.

In regard to the purpose, consider a middle school student who needs to find out the date of the beginning of the Normandy Invasion. The student goes to a library and stumbles upon a long and complex book on World War II, a book that most readers choose to read straight through. The student, however, goes to the index and finds the page that gives the single fact he is after. For this student's very limited purpose, a non-linear (random access) experience with this complex linear book has been entirely successful. If this had been a historical website about World War II, the student might have met his or her limited needs by typing "Normandy Invasion" and "date" into the site's Search feature.

Linear and Multipath Writing

There is no reason, of course, why Web content needs to be non-linear. With a highly dependent subject area such as mathematics, a complex argument or explanation, or a narrative with foreshadowing and flashbacks, the best or only option may be a linear presentation. This may consist of a sequence of Web pages linked with Next and Previous buttons or a "paper like" screen document created with Adobe Acrobat (PDF file).

If your subject matter tends somewhat toward a linear presentation but you need to give users a limited degree of navigational freedom, consider the multipath information structure. For example, Figure 10.4 represents part of an online statistics tutorial in which the learner can choose between examples drawn from the social sciences or the natural sciences. Whichever choice the user makes in regard to learning multivariate regression, the user will be prepared to learn simultaneous regression. A major theme in Chapter 13, "Non-Hierarchical Information Structures," is how to write for the other information structures.

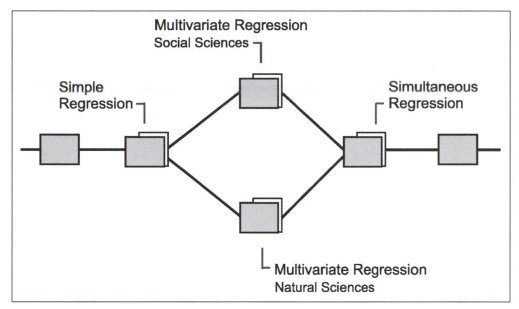

Figure 10.4. A multipath tutorial in which either alternative pathway provides the necessary pre-requisite information.

Another option is to allow users complete navigational freedom but to implicitly suggest a linear sequence, as shown in Figure 10.5. This strategy accommodates readers with different backgrounds: Knowledgeable readers might well choose to skip the more basic information presented in Sections 1 and 2, while newcomers to this topic would probably read all the sections in sequence.

Strategies for Dealing with Complex Dependencies

Writers will discover that non-linear writing is sometimes so easy as to appear automatic. It is worthwhile to understand why. The Company branch of the Zompco hierarchy consists of these third-level pages: President's Message, Careers at Zompco, Investor Relations, Outreach to the Community, and Zompco's History. There is considerable semantic distance among these pages. In other words, they cover fairly separate topics, and so writers face few problems stemming from the user's freedom to visit these pages in any order. Typically, dependencies become more complex at the lower levels of a hierarchy, where the semantic distance is less. For example, if the Investor Relations page has several child pages, these pages will be more closely tied to one another, and challenges may well arise writing them as independent modules.

There are many ways to design Web pages so as to manage dependencies. Here we examine three fundamental strategies. We do so by considering the Products branch of the Zompco hierarchy. A second-level product overview page provides links to each of five third-level product description pages. In explaining each of these technologically sophisticated products, the designer does

Energy Technology Reports

Tech Center   Current Reports   Archives

Using Bacteria To Remove Pyrite from Power-Plant Stockpiles

by R. Losch, West Virginia University

This report discusses a promising new technology for removing sulfur from the coal that is stored at power plants. Bacteria can decompose pyritic sulfur into water-soluble compounds that can be easily removed.

1 Sulfur pollution from coal—A major problem

2 The need to remove pyrite from power-plant stockpiles

3 Bacteria can decompose pyritic sulfur in coal

4 The Bureau of Mines study

5 Alternative technologies for removing pyrite

Figure 10.5. An online technical report with a suggested linear sequence.

not want to leave a product inadequately explained, but neither does the designer want to tediously explain the same technology several times. The three strategies are (1) the gateway strategy, (2) the proximity strategy, and (3) the glossary strategy. Figure 10.6 illustrates a simple instance of each strategy and shows that the distinction among them is the location of the pre-requisite information in relation

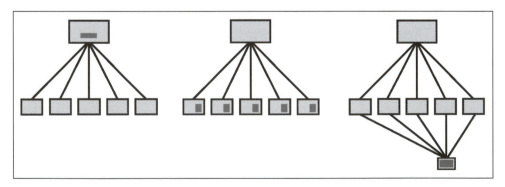

Figure 10.6. The placement of pre-requisite information (above, with, and below) in the gateway, proximity, and glossary strategies.

to the content that is explained by the pre-requisite information. The pre-requisite information can be placed (1) above, (2) with, or (3) below (respectively). For a sophisticated discussion of hypertext dependencies, see Scott Fisher (1994).

The Gateway Strategy

Let's say that Zompco incorporates state-of-the-art Strato-Arc technology in all of its products. An explanation of Strato-Arc technology is pre-requisite information because the company does not want potential customers to make a purchasing decision without knowing about this important advance. It is very easy and effective to include an explanation of Strato-Arc technology on the product overview page, the parent of the product description pages. The product overview page is now serving a gateway function: It is unlikely that users will bypass this explanation.

Let's assume that Zompco starts selling two groups of products, one based on Strato-Arc technology and the other based on Mega-Warp technology. The product overview page can be readily adapted to this situation, as shown in Figure 10.7.

The gateway strategy, however, is harder to employ and often clumsy when different nodes require different pre-requisite information. For example, one or more Zompco products might incorporate both technologies or certain products might incorporate various combinations of three advanced technologies. At this point, the other strategies, possibly in conjunction with the gateway strategy, become attractive alternatives.

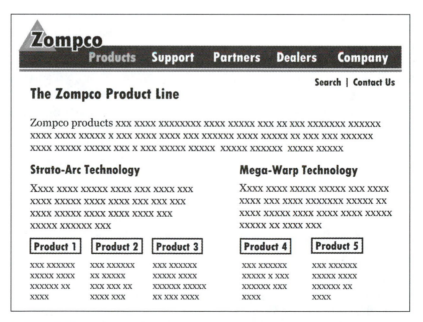

Figure 10.7. A portion of the Zompco product overview page that invites the user to examine the Strato-Arc and Mega-Warp product groups.

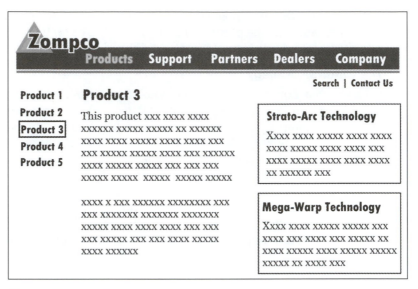

Figure 10.8. A Zompco product description page with sidebars, each explaining an advanced technology used in this product.

The Proximity Strategy

The proximity strategy entails placing the pre-requisite information on the same page as (that is, in close proximity to) the content that the pre-requisite information explains. In effect, the designer is modularizing these pages. This strategy handles dependencies flexibly: A Web page, as shown in Figure 10.8, may contain one or several different items of pre-requisite information. Furthermore, pre-requisite information can be customized. For example, Mega-Warp technology can be explained differently from one product to the next.

One problem with the proximity strategy is that a potential customer who is examining the full Zompco product line will encounter considerable repetition as the different Zompco technologies are explained on each product description page. A means of alleviating this problem, shown in Figure 10.8, is to format the pre-requisite information so that users can easily skip it.

The Glossary Strategy

A third strategy, represented in Figure 10.9, is to provide links (converging primary links) to one or more "glossary" nodes that provide the pre-requisite information. The idea here is similar to adding a glossary of technical terms at the back of a book so that users can refer to the glossary entries when they encounter an unfamiliar term. Using the glossary strategy, the Zompco Web designer provides links from each product description to one or more glossary nodes explaining a particular advanced technology used in that product.

Like the proximity strategy, the glossary strategy handles complex dependencies flexibly. Whatever technology or technologies a product incorporates,

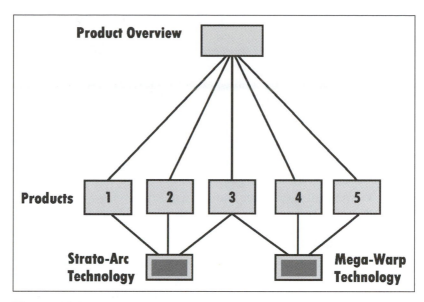

Figure 10.9. Two glossary nodes that explain the Zompco technologies employed in Zompco products. Note that Product 3 incorporates both technologies.

there will be links from that product's product description page to one or more glossary pages. In contrast to the proximity strategy, the product description pages are kept short and there is no repetition. If the user is on the Product 1 page and follows the glossary link to the page explaining Strato-Arc technology, the user can ignore that link when she sees it on the other product pages. In fact, the browser's visited link feature will conveniently remind the user that she has read this information.

One drawback to this strategy is that the user must be proactive in accessing the pre-requisite information. If the pre-requisite information is of great importance, for example, information about the appropriateness of a medical treatment, either the gateway or proximity strategy should be used, and the user might even be required to click a checkbox confirming that she has read the pre-requisite information.

Adaptive Behavior Can Enhance Web Writing

In the previous chapter, "Effective Links," we looked at the prospect of websites that adaptively display a different set of links and possibly different content at the destinations of links in order to meet the needs of individual users. This kind of adaptive behavior could certainly be employed to handle the problem of complex dependencies. For example, the Zompco website might adaptively provide all the pre-requisite information the user needs when clicking a particular product description page. If that user then clicks another product description page, any pre-requisite information the user has already viewed (e.g., the explanation of Strato-Arc technology) would be removed from this page. Adaptive behavior, however, must be employed cautiously. Perhaps the user chose not to read the explanation on the first product description page. Perhaps the user wishes to read it again. There is an inevitable gap between what systems can infer about users and the variety in human motivations and behavior.

Summary

1. Writing for the Web is similar in many ways to writing for print. Furthermore, there is no one way to write for the Web, just as there is no one way to write for print. There are, however, differences in how we write for each communications medium.

2. The Web is a "non-sticky" medium. Habits of casual, restless reading behavior arise from limited screen legibility and rapid, cost-free access to unlimited information. Consequently, it makes sense to write with the expectation that users are apt to scan and skip. On the other hand, how we write depends on the particular rhetorical situation.

3. People will read extended text if the writing responds to their needs and interests and is trustworthy, current, clearly and smoothly written, and handsomely and functionally formatted. A good strategy is for the home page to be especially inviting and easy-to-scan so as to draw users to more detailed, more demanding content on the interior pages.

4. The Web, in contrast to print, often includes audio discourse. When you write for a narrator, whether off screen or on screen, your writing must fit the narrator and the communication situation. You may want to prepare a narrator's script. Often you need to coordinate your writing with shifts in the "camera eye."

5. In contrast to most print genres, the Web is a strongly non-linear information environment. Users are continually invited to choose what to view next.

6. Non-linearity empowers readers to find and read exactly what they care about, to follow their unique interests, and to make their own connections among ideas. Non-linearity allows writers to create links that function as enticing "hooks" to draw readers who may not have a strong initial interest in the topic.

7. On the Web we must be very careful about phrases such as "As noted previously" and "As you will learn" except when they point within a single lengthy Web page and perhaps within a linear sequence of Web pages. In a non-linear environment, these phrases are apt to prove false because we usually do not know where users have been or where they will go next.

8. In non-linear writing a complex challenge is managing pre-requisite relationships, also referred to as "dependencies." The risk is that users will navigate into a danger zone where they (1) will be confused and frustrated by the incompleteness of the information they are receiving and (2) will not receive information the author considers important or even essential.

9. Modularity refers to content that has no pre-requisites. It can stand alone and still provide a satisfying experience for the reader. Encyclopedia articles are modular. On the Web, every home page is modular, and often many other pages are as well. Novels and other linear documents are absolutely dependent; each chapter is built on the preceding chapters.

10. Modularity does not rule out a limited degree of open-endedness, the perception on the part of the reader that some information has been left out.

11. The concepts of pre-requisite information and modularity ultimately depend on the audience and the audience's purpose. What is pre-requisite information for a novice may not be so for an expert. Content may be modular because the user has a very limited or specialized purpose in reading the material.

12. There is no reason why a website must be non-linear. When there are complex dependencies, a linear or multipath structure may be better. Another option is to allow users complete navigational freedom but to implicitly suggest a linear sequence.

13. At times modularity arises almost automatically because there is considerable semantic distance among the nodes. That is, they cover fairly separate topics. This situation often occurs at the second level of a website's hierarchy. Semantic distance tends to decrease at deeper levels, making dependency problems more complex.

14. Three important strategies for managing complex dependencies are (1) the gateway strategy, (2) the proximity strategy, and (3) the glossary strategy. The distinction among them is that pre-requisite information appears (1) above, (2) with, and (3) below the content it explains.

15. Although very valuable, these strategies are not without drawbacks: The gateway strategy may be hard to employ and clumsy when different nodes require different combinations of pre-requisite information. The proximity strategy risks tedious repetition because the same pre-requisite information appears on multiple nodes. The glossary strategy requires users to be proactive in accessing the pre-requisite information.

16. Although there are inevitable limitations, adaptive systems can potentially address the problem of complex dependencies.

References

Fisher, Scott. 1994. *Multimedia Authoring*. Boston: AP Professional.

Gronbeck, Bruce E., Douglas Ehninger, and Alan Monroe. 1999. *Principles and Types of Speech Communication*. 14th ed. New York: Addison Wesley Longman.

Keep, Christopher, Tim McLaughlin, and Robin Parmar. 1995. The Electronic Labyrinth. www.eserver.org/elab

Nielsen, Jakob. 2000. *The Practice of Simplicity*. Indianapolis, IN: New Riders Publishing.

Nielsen, Jakob. 1997. Be succinct! (Writing for the Web). *Alertbox* (March 15). www.useit.com/alertbox/9703b.html

Snyder, Ilana. 1996. *Hypertext: The Electronic Labyrinth*. Carlton South, Victoria: Melbourne University Press.

Straczynski, J. Michael. 1996. *The Complete Book of Scriptwriting*. Cincinnati, Ohio: Writers Digest Books.

Discussion and Application

Items for Discussion

1. The Centerville School District conducts an annual science fair. Figure 10.10 shows the letter they mail to community members who have volunteered to serve as judges. Plans are now underway to build a website for the science fair, and the designers are planning to include the letter on the website. How would you change the letter to take full advantage of the online medium?

2. A print book, *The Male Executive's Guide to Dressing for Success*, is being adapted for the Web. The book consists of an introductory chapter, followed by nine more chapters on selecting these items of dress: slacks, shirts, sport jackets, neckties, shoes, socks, hats, outerwear, and formal attire. The book was written as a fully linear document. For example, the chapter on neckties is written with the assumption that the reader has read all the previous chapters.

   The designer intends for the Web version to be non-linear: The user should be able to read the introductory node and then proceed directly to any of the subsequent chapters. Explain how the print version will need to be re-written for the Web version.

3. Find a movie review that you consider well-written. Choose an "essay-type" review rather than any kind of capsule or summary review. (It's best if you've seen the movie.) Create a non-linear version of the review with modules such as these:

   - Plot and genre (mystery, comedy, etc.)
   - Setting
   - Acting and directing
   - Theme and significance
   - Overall evaluation and recommendation

   What is gained and lost in the revised version?

4. Find a travel guide for Europe (or for several nations within Europe) with a chapter on each nation. Almost certainly this travel guide is not designed to require linear reading. Can you identify information design techniques that enable the travel guide to function well as a non-linear document? For example, can you find instances of the gateway, proximity, and glossary strategies?

5. Find a relatively brief article from a print encyclopedia that is informative but not especially interesting or enticing. Re-write the article in a livelier,

Thank you for volunteering to be a judge at the 2002 Centerville Schools Science Fair, sponsored by the Centerville Consolidated School District and FOSEC (Friends of Science Education in Centerville). This letter tells you everything you need to know to serve as a judge.

Arrangements

The judging will be held on Friday, May 8, from 6:00–9:30 pm at the Centerville Town Hall. When you arrive, sandwiches (including veggie sandwiches) and beverages will be ready. While you eat, there will be a 10-minute briefing and a chance for you to ask questions. Our goal is for the judges to get started between 6:15 and 6:30. (There will be a second briefing for those who get delayed.) If you have further questions, please send an email to Gila Delgado, Science Fair Coordinator, at giladelgado@trapazoid.net.

The judging process

During the briefing, you will be teamed up with a judging partner, and your team will be assigned a particular group of entries. For example, you and your partner might judge two rows of 7th grade entries. The job consists of these steps:

1. Find the entries that your team will be judging. (We will have folks to help you with this.)
2. Examine each entry from the point of view of the Guidelines (see below) and discuss your impressions with your partner.
3. Work with your partner to write brief, helpful, encouraging comments on the Judging Form.
4. Decide which are the best of the entries you have judged. Give these entries an Honorable Mention award, a red ribbon. All this should be done by 8:15.
5. Meet with the other teams judging the same category that you're judging. For example, you might meet with the two other teams that judged 7th grade entries. Collectively, pick the very best entries in the entire category and give these entries an Outstanding award. Finally, look for an entry that might be considered for Best of Show.

Limiting the number of Outstanding awards. Winners of the Outstanding award receive a blue ribbon and a savings bond. Outstanding awards can only be given on a limited basis. On the night of the judging, we will know how many awards we can give for each category (a likely number will be three).

If you don't find many Outstanding entries. It is possible that there will be fewer Outstanding entries in a particular category than the number we have budgeted for. If your group of judges decides to give out, say, only one Outstanding award, please let us know so we can allocate more awards to other categories.

Team entries. Some entries are the work of more than one student. In order to win an award, a team entry should be significantly better than the individual entries it is competing against. Also, please note that if a team entry wins the Outstanding award, all members of the team receive a savings bond.

(Continued)

Writing your comments

The judges' comments are the single most important part of the competition. The students take the comments very seriously. Comments need not be long: a paragraph will be sufficient. The comments should be helpful and encouraging and should be written at the grade level of the entry and at the level of sophistication shown by the entrant. So, for example, do not use the phrase "statistically significant" in comments for a 7th grader, unless this is a very sophisticated 7th grader whose entry reveals a familiarity with statistics.

Here is a sample comment that might be appropriate for a 7th grade entry:

This is a good investigation. It is certainly interesting and important to determine how different amounts of detergent affect the growth of algae in pond water. You should have made one more sample to show how much algae grows when there is no detergent at all in the water. This sample would have made for a useful comparison with the other samples (a "control" for your experimental variables). Your display is attractive, and the explanations are clear and well written. Tables, however, are easier to read if the numbers line up. We hope you continue your interest in studying the environment.

Guidelines for judges

1. Was the problem clearly stated? Was a hypothesis stated?
2. Were variables adequately controlled? Was the experiment repeated several times to establish validity and/or was the sample size sufficient?
3. Were conclusions justified and properly drawn from the experimental process?
4. Were written materials effectively and correctly written? Were graphs, illustrations, and all other visual aspects of the display presented effectively?
5. How original is the topic?
6. How ingenious was the method of finding a solution?
7. How difficult was the experiment?

Figure 10.10. The letter to judges for the Centerville Science Fair.

more intriguing manner. Very often encyclopedia articles provide references (very much like hypertext links) to other articles in the encyclopedia and to external sources. Can you make this encyclopedia article more interesting by adding or changing references?

6. Comment on this assertion:

Many people say that one advantage of the Web (and other forms of hypermedia) over traditional print books is that the Web provides users with more navigational freedom. But how can this be? I can open any book to any page at any time. Nothing can be faster or easier. On the Web, I can only follow links that the designer has created, unless I use the Search feature—which takes time and does not always lead to success. As I see it, printed books offer greater navigational freedom than the Web.

7. A small university has built a subsite on its main site for the athletics department. You are designing a section of this subsite specifically devoted to recruiting student athletes. The basic hierarchy will consist of an introductory page and a second-level page for each of these six sports: volleyball, baseball, basketball, soccer, golf, and swimming.

   Your plan is for the introductory page of the recruiting section to include information about general academic and sports policies that are common to all six sports. Now you've been asked to strengthen the recruitment effort by adding this information: Members of the golf team, volleyball team, and swimming team are given free access to the golf course, volleyball courts, and swimming pool belonging to a local country club. What are the effective and ineffective ways to add this information?

8. A physician is planning to write a textbook on human physiology. The general plan is to write a chapter for each of the major systems of the human body: the nervous system, digestive system, circulatory system, respiratory system, and so forth.

   The physician's original idea was to make each chapter fully modular in order to give instructors unlimited choice as to which systems of the human body to teach and the sequence in which they will be taught. It soon became clear, however, that there would be too much redundancy among the chapters. What ideas can you suggest for designing this book?

9. The brochure copy shown in Figure 10.11 announces a presentation by digital communication expert William Horton. The presentation, "Beyond

---

Beyond the F1 Key

The revolution in communication technologies has smashed the barrier of effective human-to-human communication. The Web, multimedia, digital video, intranets, and a thousand acronyms promise to remake our lives for the better. For the promise to be fulfilled though, we need a corresponding revolution in technique. We cannot create twenty-first century media with eighteenth century skills.

"Beyond the F1 Key" is a truly interactive presentation, in which the audience selects the topics from ones such as these:

- Are you dot.COMpetitive?
- Are you new-media literate?
- What are some new careers and new missions?
- How can you get vaccinated against chaos?
- What are some simple things that work?
- Do you write world-class Help?

Along with a bit of fun, the presentation offers advice on how we can keep our sanity, our jobs, and our sense of humor amid the most important change in the way our species communicates since the invention of the alphabet.

Figure 10.11. A description of an "interactive" presentation.

the F1 Key," was the keynote address at a conference. Characterize this presentation, drawing upon the ideas presented in this chapter and the book as a whole. What benefits and potential problems do you see in Horton's "interactive" presentation?

Application to Your Project

1. If your website will contain extended text, have you thought about this text from the standpoint of stickiness? In other words, do you feel confident that this text is important enough to your users that they will be motivated to read it? Are there text elements that should be re-written and reformatted for brevity and scannability?

2. Analyze your design from the point of view of pre-requisite information, modularity, and open-endedness. Do you see problems? Can your users enter danger zones in your website? What strategies might you use to address these problems?

Graphic Design

Introduction

Graphic design for the Web encompasses a very wide range of decisions about the visual dimension of a website. On one hand, graphic design is broad and integrative. We see this especially in page layout, an important aspect of graphic design. On the other hand, graphic design entails many highly specific decisions. So, for example, various people on a design team may contribute to the idea of a fictitious "Mama Ragú" welcoming visitors to the website that promotes Ragú Italian food products. But it is very likely the graphic designer who chooses the photograph and, if necessary, alters it to fit the design. (For a quick advance peek at Mama Ragú, see Figure 11.7.)

These are the main goals of graphic design for the Web:

- Adding aesthetic appeal
- Helping to express the theme of the website
- Helping to show the logical relationships among all elements that appear on the page, both core content elements and elements of the interface

Well-funded Web development projects include a professional graphic designer. Ideally, the graphic designer is involved from the earliest stages when concept sketches are being drawn. On large projects, the graphic designer may be working full-time; on smaller projects, the graphic designer may be brought in at strategic intervals. When there is no professional graphic designer, someone must step into this role, though it is a challenge for a non-specialist to achieve really good results.

Professional graphic designers cross many boundaries in their work. They are often skilled at interface design, information design, and creating core visual content, especially illustrations. Many small Web design firms are staffed entirely by graphic designers or consist of a single graphic designer.

This chapter will provide you with a quick education in graphic design, especially as it pertains to the Web. Here is what we cover:

- Aesthetic appeal on the Web
- Uses of line, shape, and color
- Designing screen text
- Expressing theme with style and mood
- Principles of composition
- Strategies for page layout

Although this chapter can point you toward success in graphic design, it cannot do the whole job. You should develop the habit of carefully considering the visual design of the websites you visit, and you should take note of magazine advertisements, posters, commercial signage, and roadside billboards. It is very valuable to read books, take courses, and work closely on a project with a trained graphic designer. The readings suggested in this chapter can contribute greatly to your sophistication in graphic design and related areas.

You should strive for sophistication in graphic design even if you don't plan to practice graphic design. You should be able to communicate clearly with a graphic designer in order to explain what you want. You should be able to recognize when a website's visual design is unsuccessful and to articulate the reasons for your judgment.

To achieve good results in your own designs, follow well-established design principles. Also, be patient: What a professional designer can do quickly, you may need to achieve by successive approximation—and by soliciting lots of feedback. When you finally get it right, it's not so important that you had to discard numerous bad versions of your design.

Aesthetic Appeal on the Web

The word "aesthetic" refers to the human response we associate with beauty. Aesthetic appeal is a key goal of graphic design on the Web because it engages users. Aesthetics is especially important on the home page, where users make a split-second decision whether to stay or leave. Furthermore, an aesthetic design lends prestige and credibility to the organization that owns the website, subtly asserting, "These people know what they're doing."

Aesthetic design does not mean that the pages of a website should be regarded as objects of fine art and evoke the response, "How beautiful!" You don't need flowers or sunsets on your website. Done well, even a bus schedule will be perceived as visually attractive. If a website communicates about starvation and disease, the graphic design may be stark and grim. But users can still recognize the aesthetic quality of the design, just as they recognize the ugliness in a thoughtless or misguided design.

Uses of Line, Shape, and Color

Line, shape, and color are always present. You can think of them as resources, or "raw materials," of graphic design.

Line

Lines connect two or more points and are the essential element of graphic design. Lines can be given a variety of stylistic attributes. For example, there are hard-edged lines and soft-edged lines that fade into their backgrounds. All these attributes can be created easily with illustration software applications. The main stylistic attributes are listed below:

- Straight lines
- Curved or swirly lines
- Jagged lines
- Irregular or hand-drawn lines
- Dotted and dashed lines
- Lines with high or low contrast against their backgrounds
- Lines with hard or soft edges
- Lines that are thin or thick
- Lines whose orientation is vertical, horizontal, or diagonal

These line types, of course, can be used in combination: There are jagged dotted lines, and a line can change from jagged to straight. In many cases our response to a line is influenced by our notion of how someone might draw that kind of line. So, for example, jagged lines suggest energy and informality and, possibly, damage and violence. Swirly lines also suggest energy and informality but at the same time suggest freedom of movement and joy. Dotted lines suggest thoughtfulness, someone with a message to communicate.

Shape

Shapes are formed by lines. Shapes can also be implied by lines that do not fully complete a shape. When lines are sufficiently thick, we perceive them as shapes. Shapes are a fundamental component of almost any possible Web page. Shapes define objects and suggest planes. As we show later, shapes are the basis of page layout.

Shapes as Objects in a Design

Shapes and lines make up the objects that appear as core content elements. Extremely complex, often irregular shapes, combinations of shapes, and lines (with or without color) make up drawings of people, buildings, products, and so forth. When the artist is skillful, we don't even think of these representations as shapes: We don't notice that the shoulders and chest of Napoleon Bonaparte approximate a blue trapezoid (wider at the shoulders, narrower at the waist) and that the head is a complex oval. In addition, regular geometric shapes—circles, octagons, stars, diamonds, and so forth—serve many roles in our designs. Recall that Zompco employs a triangle as its corporate logo.

Shapes as Planes

Perspective drawing, shadowing, and other techniques have been used for centuries to create the illusion of 3-D space. But simple juxtapositions and modifications of shapes can subtly suggest multiple planes and give extra interest to an image. One prevalent technique is to allow shapes to overlap so that one seems to be sitting on top of another. Another prevalent technique is a "reverse-out": The designer visually cuts out pieces of a shape to suggest an underlying plane showing through. Both techniques are shown in Figure 11.1.

Color

Color affects us strongly and in complex ways. It is a major aspect of almost any website design. Color and in particular color for the Web make for a complex subject encompassing the properties of light, differences among operating systems and Web browsers, and the physiology and psychology of human perception. Here we offer just the briefest introduction to Web color. We approach the topic from the perspective of a designer working with the color-selection features of a software application. A good resource for color theory and design is Jill Morton (1998). For a comprehensive book that explains how to implement graphics on the Web, see Lynda Weinman (1999).

The Make-Up of Color

Capable computers give us a choice of 255 different hues, ranging through the full color spectrum (red, orange, yellow, green, blue, indigo, violet). Each hue corre-

Figure 11.1. The use of overlapping and a reverse-out to suggest multiple planes. Users will perceive three planes in this graphic, shown in gray, white, and black.

sponds to a particular wavelength of light. Black, white, and gray are not hues: Black is the absence of light; white comes from mixing red, green and blue light; gray is a mixture of white and black.

A hue in its pure form is said to be "fully saturated." Most often, however, we do not use hues in their fully saturated form. We can modify a hue by changing its "value" (or "luminance"), its lightness or darkness. This is the equivalent of adding white or black to the hue. The computer's color-selection feature offers 128 gradations of white and 128 gradations of black. Lighter values of a color are often called "tints"; darker values "shades." We can, for example, lighten the hue of red to various tints of pink or darken it to various shades of scarlet. We get shades of brown by darkening yellow.

Very often designers also want to "dull" or "mute" a color. This is the equivalent of adding different quantities of gray, at any given value of a hue. Computers allow us to de-saturate a hue with gray in 255 gradations (or "tones"). So, for example, having tinted the fully saturated red hue to a light pink, you can mute the light pink to a dull light pink and even further to a pinkish light gray.

You may have noticed that all the combinations of hue, value, and de-saturation with gray amount to approximately 16 million colors. Clearly, then, it is no small feat for computers to faithfully reproduce the colors intended by the designer. Even with capable computers, there are a variety of minor problems in displaying color. Furthermore, to avoid significant display problems for people using computers with 8-bit color capability, you must restrict yourself to the 216 guaranteed ("browser-safe") colors. You must therefore decide whether to take advantage of 16 million colors or restrict yourself to this subset, depending on the computer capabilities of the audience you intend to serve.

How We Respond to Color

Colors are perceived as warm or cool. The warm colors are red, orange, and yellow. The cool colors are green and blue. People respond strongly to the warmness or coolness of colors, and so this "warm-cool color contrast" must be an important consideration in your design.

Colors also have various associations. For example, green is associated with vegetation and fertility, with envy, and with the visual signal "Go." There is also the ugly "puke" green. Some color associations operate across many cultures (green as vegetation and fertility) while others do not (green as envy). Furthermore, the context greatly affects how people respond to any color. Red appearing as flowing blood is very different from a sumptuous red carpet.

A significant number of people, mostly males, have some kind of difficulty in interpreting colors ("color blindness"). Therefore, avoid color coding as the sole cue for important information; for example, don't use color coding as the only means to distinguish among easy, moderate, and difficult hiking trails.

Color Combinations and Color Harmony

When designing Web pages, think in terms of color schemes and color harmony rather than individual colors.

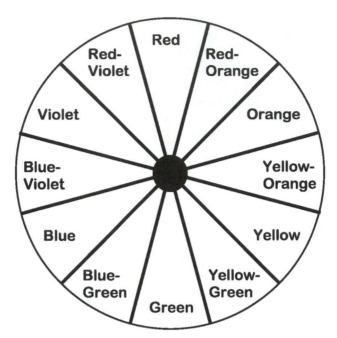

Figure 11.2. The standard (Itten) 12-hue color wheel.

The five most important kinds of color harmony are described below using the standard (Itten) color wheel shown in Figure 11.2. These harmonies, broadly speaking, pertain to hues in their various values and levels of de-saturation with gray.

- *Monochromatic.* Monochromatic is the simplest kind of color harmony. It consists of only a single hue with variations in value and saturation.
- *Complementary.* Complementary color harmony consists of any two colors that are opposite or nearly opposite on the color wheel. Complementary harmony provides very strong contrasts. Therefore, if a design makes extensive use of a particular color, you may want to employ the complementary color over a much smaller area as an accent color.
- *Analogous.* Analogous harmony employs three to five colors that are neighbors on the color wheel. The differences among these hues are not extreme; they form a pleasing progression of related colors. Often the most important, or "key" color, is the middle color in this progression.
- *Triadic.* Triadic harmony employs any three colors spaced fairly evenly on the color wheel. Usually the key color is saturated while the others appear in darker values.
- *Split complementary.* Split complementary color harmony consists of a key color, the complementary (opposite) color on the color wheel, often used as an accent, and the two neighbors of the key color or the complementary color.

In the world of print, color is expensive; each color you add to a publication increases the printing costs significantly. On the Web, color is free. On one hand, this is a great bonus for designers. On the other, it is very easy to misuse color. A key guideline, therefore, regarding color and color combinations on the Web is restraint.

Enhancement of Graphic Files

Image editing software applications, such as Photoshop and Paint Shop Pro, give designers many ways to enhance a graphic. For example, it is possible to soften the focus of a photograph or add a rippled look or texture to a drawn graphic. Many enhancements entail modifying color. Two of the most important color enhancements are brightening an image and colorizing an image.

Brightening refers to increasing luminance, tinting the colors toward white. We can improve an under-exposed photograph by moving the brightness into a normal range. At times, however, we brighten an image beyond a normal level in order to eliminate detail, lessen the image's impact, or generalize its meaning. For example, in an alternative design for the Asthma Horizons home page shown in Figure 11.3, the brightening of the photographs helps to suggest the general idea of an active lifestyle. Otherwise, the photographs might suggest that this website is about sports. Plus, the light tint serves as a good background for text.

Another technique is colorizing, converting an image to a uniform hue and saturation while retaining the original values of the colors. A designer, for example, can give an antique look to a conventional black and white photograph by colorizing it a light, sepia brown.

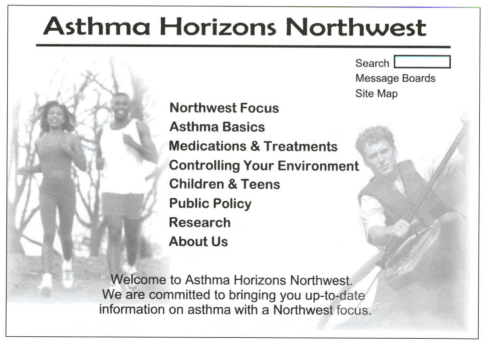

Figure 11.3. A version of the Asthma Horizons home page in which images are de-emphasized by increasing the brightness.

Colorizing can also give a group of images greater unity. For example, a designer scans and digitizes three graphics to make a collage. She then brightens and softens the focus of the border areas so the graphics blend better. Even so, the result is not attractive because the original graphics represent very different styles and use very different colors. There is a black-and-white newspaper photograph from the 1920s, a painted poster for a 1950s Hollywood movie with pastel tints, and a contemporary color photograph with a sharp focus and fully saturated colors. By colorizing the entire collage in values of medium green, the designer adds a strong element of visual unity. Note that the colorized image exhibits monochromatic color harmony.

Designing Screen Text

Many decisions about the appearance of words on the screen are considered an aspect of graphic design. Below we discuss choice of fonts, the contrast between text and background, and related issues. See Thomas Williams (2000) for guidelines and citations from the research literature regarding legibility and other aspects of information display.

Fonts

In print, we distinguish between body fonts and display fonts. Body fonts are those well suited for extended ("body") text. Display fonts are suited for headings, titles, and other brief but prominent text elements, referred to as "display" text. This distinction also pertains to the Web. Most link text can be considered a special kind of display text.

Body Fonts

For body text, designers must choose fonts with good screen legibility. Some fonts have been designed specifically for screen use, including Verdana and Georgia from Microsoft and Myriad and Minion from Adobe. Various established print fonts, such as Palatino and Helvetica, also display well on screen. Fonts are highly legible when they are composed of strong, clear strokes that are not distorted by the relatively poor resolution of most computer monitors.

Many fonts (among them Georgia, Minion, and Palatino) include serifs. These are the small horizontal "feet" at the base of vertical strokes and other small cross strokes that finish off such letters as E and s. Many good print fonts are unsuitable as body fonts on the screen because of their small, delicate serifs.

Another consideration is font size. Make sure your fonts are large enough for easy reading. A generally reliable choice is 12 point (HTML font size 3). The optimum size, however, depends on the particular font you are using and other factors. Align body text on the left; use boldface, italics, and all upper-case characters sparingly; and avoid underlining entirely except to indicate a link.

An important consideration is line length. Most computer monitors are significantly wider than they are deep—just the opposite of most books and many other paper documents. This creates the possibility of lines of body text that stretch all the way across the screen and consist of more than 100 characters. These lines are both unattractive and hard to read. Users do best with a moderate line length, approximately 40–60 characters. One way to avoid overly long lines is to employ a single column of text with wide margins. Or, use multiple columns, but guard against lines of text that are too short.

Display Fonts

Because display elements are brief and often larger in size, you can take greater liberties in regard to legibility. There are a great many highly expressive fonts used primarily for display purposes. Just a few are shown in Figure 11.4.

Even if your body and display fonts are well chosen, too many fonts and even too many sizes of the same font will give your pages an overly busy, unattractive appearance. Many print documents employ a single body font (traditionally a serif font) for body text and a second font (traditionally a sans serif font), possibly in more than one font size, for the headings. Typically there is more font variation on the Web than in print, particularly because designers often employ one or more additional fonts for nav bars, nav columns, and other aspects of the navigational interface. Even so, be sure that you are adding extra variation only with good reason and that the fonts you choose work well together.

What the User Sees

There can be differences between the fonts you specify and what individual users actually view. If you specify a font that is not installed on the user's machine, the system will display a substitute font. This situation can be partially alleviated by

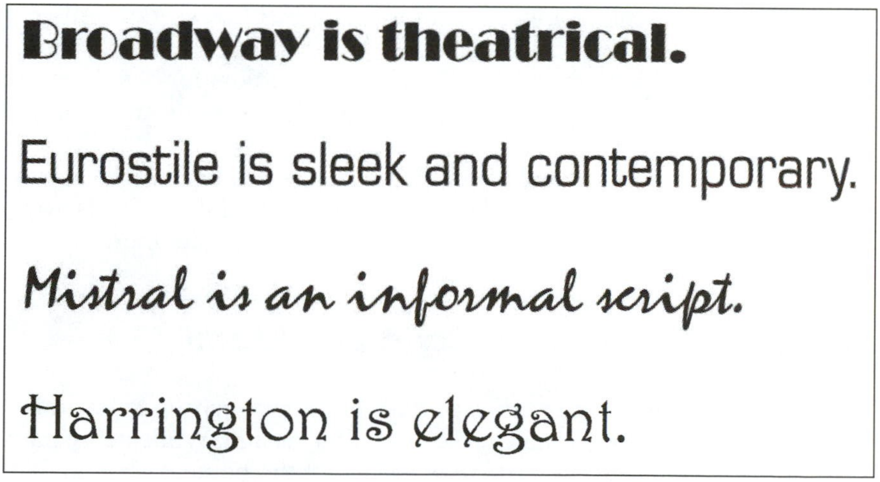

Figure 11.4. A small sampling of highly expressive display fonts. Of these fonts, only Eurostile might be used as a body font.

specifying a second, third, and even fourth choice for any text element. For example, you can specify Verdana with two fairly similar sans serif alternatives, Helvetica (typically installed on Macs) and Arial (typically installed on PCs), and a final alternative of using the system's default sans serif font. If you are intent on incorporating a particular display font in your design and it is not a highly prevalent font, you will need to create the display element as a graphic. Keep in mind, however, that text elements created as graphics load more slowly than regular text and require more effort when you update the website. Font problems should gradually lessen with increased use of downloadable fonts.

A good general guide to fonts and typography is Robert Bringhurst (2000). At Eyewire (www.eyewire.com) you can find many useful tips and, in their Type Viewer, you can preview font samples from Adobe and other major makers of fonts. Valuable information on font technology plus links to many additional sources can be found on the Microsoft Typography website (www.microsoft.com/typography). Also, consult the World Wide Web Consortium website (www.w3.org) for the latest standards on specifying fonts and formatting text.

Text and Background

An important factor in text legibility is ample contrast between text and background. You will recall that increasing this contrast was one of the reasons for brightening the kayaking and jogging graphics on the Asthma Horizons home page shown in Figure 11.3. It is surprising how many websites employ dark text over a dark background color, text over an overwhelmingly complex pattern, and other nearly illegible combinations of text and background. The guidelines presented below lead to good legibility.

Nothing is more legible than black text on a plain white or near white background, although various dark text colors do provide ample contrast against light background colors. Light blue, for example, often works well as the background for black text. A sound strategy is to strongly favor black text on a light background for body text and to reserve strong colors for headings and other display elements and, more generally, for drawing the user's attention to some aspect of the design.

White or other light fonts against black and other dark backgrounds may also be legible, but you should carefully judge legibility on a case-by-case basis. One font and font size may be significantly better than another.

Expressing Theme with Style and Mood

The theme is the core message that connects a website to its audience. Helping to express the theme is a key role of graphic design. While every page contributes to the theme, this is, in particular, the job of the home page. You have already seen several designs for the Asthma Horizons home page in which warm colors, a sunburst motif, and carefully selected photographs of active individuals helped to convey the theme and evoke the appropriate mood. Below we consider several

Table 11.1	Some Moods Produced by Graphic Design		
Playful, cheerful	Cool, hip	Energetic, dynamic	Staid, stolid, settled
Happy, joyful	Dramatic	Sleek and modern	Dignified
Warm, welcoming	Mysterious, spooky	Business-like, direct	Somber, grave

other instances in which graphic design decisions help express the theme. Before doing so, we look more closely at mood.

Mood in Web Design

The term "mood" describes emotions, attitudes, or associations that users experience when they view and read the pages of a website. The appropriate mood helps to establish the theme. Because moods are general responses rather than specific messages or statements, we use single words or phrases to describe moods. The prevailing moods of the Asthma Horizons website are cheerfulness, optimism, and energy. Human beings have a very complex emotional life, and so there are many moods and many ways to describe moods in words. A sampling is shown in Table 11.1.

It is important to recognize just how subtle and complex moods are. For example, in featuring a photograph of kayakers against beautiful snow-capped mountains, the Points West website projects joy—but joy in a serene, meditative form. On the other hand, the website for a rafting company that encourages customers to bump the rafts and splash one another will attempt a rambunctious, playful kind of joy. Although Annie and Peter rejected Hank's idea to put an animated kayaker on their home page, an animation could certainly contribute playfulness to the overall mood.

It is also important to recognize that moods are highly individual. Designers can only *attempt* to evoke a particular mood. Whether they succeed depends to a large degree on how well their design is attuned to the audience. But even when a designer understands an audience well, individuals will always respond somewhat differently.

The Theme of the Steinway & Sons Website

We do not need to infer the theme for the website of Steinway & Sons, the world-famous, highly prestigious manufacturer of pianos (Figure 11.5). Their theme appears as the welcoming statement on the home page:

> Welcome to Steinway & Sons. For over 140 years, Steinway has been dedicated to the ideal of making the finest pianos in the world. Whether you are a professional artist, a student, or enthused listener, we hope you enjoy exploring the rich tradition of these beautiful instruments.

The visual design of the home page helps to express this theme. The spare, uncrowded page layout and the black background (suggesting a concert piano) elicit a mood of calm and dignity. So does the Classical Greek lyre shown at the

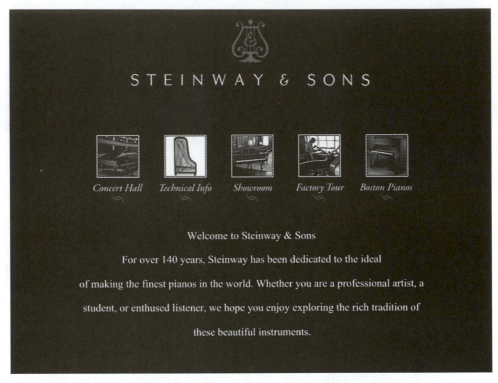

Figure 11.5. The home page of Steinway & Sons. (www.steinway.com)

top of the page (the Steinway logo). The images on the five graphical buttons suggest Steinway craftsmanship, and the images make extensive use of golden brown wood colors—which also suggest the precious metal.[1]

Graphic designers know that widely spaced upper-case letters have a formal, dignified quality, and that technique is employed here. The welcome message is displayed in the default font specified in the user's browser.

The Theme of the Mi Zong Luohan Gongfu Club Splash Page

Some websites employ a preliminary "splash" page that is initially displayed when the user types the website's URL. The role of the splash page (or splash animation) is to make a strong first impression—to establish the theme of the website in a very focused and compelling manner. One reason splash pages can succeed is that users are not asked to make choices regarding links. There is usually just a single link (sometimes labeled "Enter") to the true home page. On the other hand, there is a definite risk to this design concept: Given the non-sticky nature of the

---

[1]This page actually scrolls to display a site map. The design, however, does not encourage users to scroll the page.

Figure 11.6. The splash page, produced as a student project, for the Mi Zong Luohan Gongfu Club of Seattle, Washington.

Web, some users may object to the extra click and leave before reaching the true home page.

Seattle's Mi Zong Luohan Gongfu Club employs an effective splash page, shown in Figure 11.6. The antique book projects a mood of intensity and mystery and conveys the idea that Gongfu is not just a means of self-defense or a form of exercise but rather a centuries-old discipline with a strong spiritual dimension. To pursue Gongfu is to undertake a life-changing journey into another culture and another world.

The book is depicted with soft lines and the rich brown colors of weathered leather and the tarnished metal plates. Although the colors resemble the Steinway colors, there is a great difference in the textures. Whereas the Steinway page suggests the smooth, polished surface of a piano, the Gongfu Club splash page suggests more complex textures of leather and hammered metal. Also, while both have black backgrounds, the Gongfu design, but not the Steinway design, employs a light source to suggest 3-D space.

Finally, the Gongfu Club designer has playfully violated the fundamental rule that users should always know "what's hot and what's not." The only hotspot on the page is the clasp on the book, and so the user's effort to find this hotspot and "unlock" the book suggests the idea that committing to the study of Gongfu is more than an easy, casual act.

The Theme of the Ragú Website

Mama Ragú lives in the old neighborhood, follows family traditions, and of course serves delicious, home-cooked Italian meals. As the main figure in the Ragú website (Figure 11.7), she conveys the themes that Ragú food products are prepared in the old-fashioned way (to serve Ragú is almost home cooking) and that meals are the center of family life.

The banner-like identity element is bright tomato-sauce red, Mama's 1950s brick house is a muted pink, and Mama herself is a black-and-white image, suggesting an era when most people took black-and-white photographs. The user will find many clever "retro" touches when exploring the rooms of her house. The rounded, thick-stroked display font on the right nav column is one of several playful fonts used throughout the site.

Various text elements suggest Mama's old-fashioned, Italian-flavored speech and attitudes. At the same time, a strong strain of wit and whimsy runs through Ragu.com because site visitors are fully aware that Ragú is part of a large corporation.

Ragu.com offers Italian recipes, of course. But it also gives people reasons unrelated to food for visiting the site, many centered on romance ("How to stay romantic after you have kids"). Ragu.com also solicits and publishes narratives

Figure 11.7. Mama Ragú and the Ragú website. (www.ragu.com)

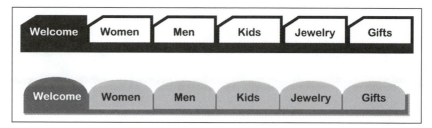

Figure 11.8. A set of tabs for an online store with inappropriately angular shapes and hard-edged, high-contrast lines and an improved set of tabs that elicits a warmer, friendlier mood.

("Tell Mama your most romantic moments"). Ragu.com is an early corporate website and a pioneer in projecting wit and charm, in offering substantive reasons to return regularly, and in creating among site visitors a sense of shared values and community.

Expressing Theme with a Set of Tabs

One aspect of Web graphic design is contributing to the styling of interface elements. Buttons, nav columns, tabs, and other interface elements, no less than core content elements, possess such stylistic attributes as line, shape, color, and font choice. As we see below (in regard to Bigtime University), graphic design decisions can address problems in the navigational interface. Here we see the decisions through which a set of tabs better expresses the theme of a website.

The two sets of tabs shown in Figure 11.8 are equally functional, but the top set with its angular shapes and hard-edged, high-contrast lines is inappropriate for an online store selling clothing and related merchandise. Someone skilled in graphic design would almost certainly employ rounded tabs that elicit a more relaxed, friendlier mood, as shown in the bottom set of tabs. Similarly, the Welcome tab on the top set of tabs is a fully saturated "pure" blue that contrasts strongly with the pure white on the rest of the tabs. In the improved version, the tab colors harmonize: The Welcome tab has been muted with gray and the other tabs are a tint of the Welcome tab.

Seven Principles of Composition

Principles of composition are fundamental to graphic design. They focus the designer's attention on important aspects of the design, enable the designer to spot problems, and point toward solutions. Below we explain and illustrate seven valuable principles of composition:

- Emphasis
- Grouping

- Subordination
- Simplicity
- Proportion and scale
- Balance
- Unity

You should know that principles like these have been formulated by various experts in graphic design and that there are significant differences among the many sets of principles. This set, we think, is especially helpful to Web designers not trained in graphic design. They apply both to highly artistic home pages and to straightforward interior pages that present bus schedules, municipal budgets, and technical reports. Also realize that the success of any Web page design is a very complex matter and that a page may certainly be successful even if it seems to violate one or even more of these principles.

Below are three excellent books that present principles of composition in far more detail and in a much broader (though non-Web) context than we do here. For an all-around introduction see David Lauer and Steven Pentak (2000), for a more advanced discussion see Wucius Wong (1993), and for guidance in applying graphic design principles to the design of software user interfaces, see Kevin Mullett and Darrell Sano (1995). In addition, if you wish to understand the physiological and psychological basis of human perception, see Vicki Bruce, Patricia Green, and Mark Georgeson (1996).

Before turning to these principles, we introduce a very useful technique for analyzing a design: the squint test. The idea is to blur your vision to eliminate semantic meaning and obscure minor visual features. In this way you can better assess the relationships among the main visual elements in the design. You don't even need to really squint. You can, for example, reduce the size of an image on your computer screen.

Emphasis

In contrast to text, where our eyes follow the sequence of words set down by the author, there is no fixed route through a graphic. Designers, however, seek to emphasize certain parts of the graphic and thereby exert some control over the user's gaze. Usually, they intend one element or area of the screen to be the user's initial focus and then either plan a specific visual pathway for the user's gaze to follow or else plan for some elements to be secondary in emphasis and still others to be tertiary. Here are some of the means for drawing and guiding the user's attention:

1. *Location.* Certain locations on the page are more prominent than others. Placing an element near the top of the page is a powerful means of emphasis. On the other hand, placing an element very low on the page, especially below the scroll line, guarantees that it will not be seen quickly. For users whose language is read left-to-right, a position on the left side of the page is more conspicuous than on the right.

2. *Size.* Larger objects are more prominent than smaller ones. We often create visual hierarchies of greater to lesser emphasis based on decreasing size.

3. *Contrast and surrounding blank space.* An object stands out against a contrasting background but may be easily overlooked when the background is similar in hue or color value. Also, blank space enhances contrast whereas an object can be readily overwhelmed by an overly busy background. Notice that the Steinway lyre, medium gray against a black background, still stands out adequately as an element of secondary emphasis. The lyre, however, would be lost if the background were speckled or mottled or if the lyre were located near dominant design elements.

4. *Distinctiveness.* An object that differs in shape, color, or some other respect from those around it stands out. The photograph of Mama Ragú is especially dominant because it is essentially the only black and white element on the page.

5. *Depth.* A 3-D appearance stands out amid flat surroundings. So, for example, the 3-D appearance produced by a drop shadow will result in extra prominence. This technique, however, should be used sparingly or it becomes an ineffective gimmick. Also, recall that the 3-D appearance suggests a link and may prompt useless clicks.

6. *Movement.* Human beings respond to movement, including on-and-off flashing; however, we immediately reject design elements whose movement is simply a gimmick devoid of any real value.

7. *Interesting content.* The preceding techniques are "pre-attentive"; they operate instantly and automatically. It takes a moment longer for users to decide whether a screen element is meaningful to them, but quality content can hold the user's attention. Consider that Web advertising banners use every pre-attentive trick in the book but ultimately fail to interest people because the content is not compelling.

Grouping

Grouping is essential for establishing logical relationships among elements on the page. Grouping is employed everywhere on the Web. For example, nav columns group a set of related links, and related products are often grouped in a Web page's main content area.

Grouping is achieved through proximity and similarity. For example, the 16 squares shown in Figure 11.9 are perceived as four groups due to proximity. The grouping would be further enhanced through similarity had each of the four groups been given a distinctive color.

Grouping by similarity can be seen in the evolution of the Bigtime University website (discussed in Chapter 8, "The Navigational Interface"). An early design, shown in Figure 11.10, was unsuccessful because users did not consistently recognize that the links in the right navigation column pertained specifically to the Downtown Campus and not to the university as a whole. Some users, for example, would futilely click the Faculty and Staff link trying to learn about a faculty

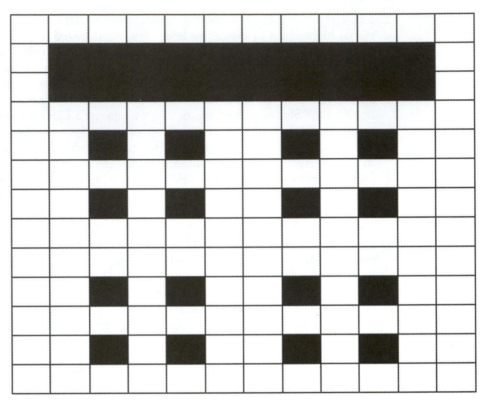

Figure 11.9. Sixteen squares perceived as four groups because they are clustered together (proximity). The four groups are subordinated to the rectangle because the rectangle is larger and closer to the top of the image.

member at the South End Campus. The navigational interface is much improved in the revised design (Figure 11.11). Now the light color strongly groups the right nav column, the information in the main content area, and the link (currently selected) to the Downtown Campus on the left navigation column. Users, for example, now recognize that they need to click the South End Campus link to display information about a faculty member in that unit of the university.

Subordination

Subordination is closely associated with grouping and emphasis. Collectively, they play a major role in revealing the logical relationships among the elements on each Web page.

Very often a set of grouped elements is visually subordinated to another element through emphasis. This is shown in Figure 11.9, where the 16 squares are subordinated to the rectangle that is larger in size and positioned higher on the image. Indentation will also subordinate a group of elements.

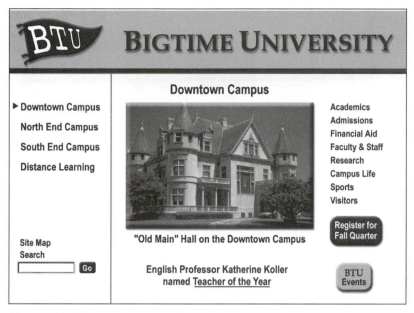

Figure 11.10. An unsuccessful design in which some users did not realize that the links in the right nav column pertain to the Downtown Campus.

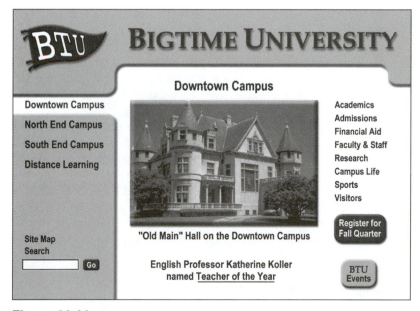

Figure 11.11. Improving the navigational interface through grouping by similarity. The light color visually ties the right nav column and main content area to the Downtown Campus link on the left nav column.

This visual subordination should correspond to the text semantics. In the case of online stores, two or more product descriptions are often grouped and subordinated by means of a heading expressing the product category. Similarly, a designer will group two related news stories under a single "spanner" headline to make clear that both stories deal with the same news event.

Note that subordination is not identical to emphasis. In a drawing of a bouquet of roses, one rose might be shown catching the direct rays of the sun. This rose has been given visual emphasis over the rest of the roses, but the other roses are not logically subordinate to this rose.

Simplicity

Simplicity means restricting the amount of visual data that the user's eyes must process. This is how to achieve simplicity:

1. Use relatively few visual elements.
2. Establish strong visual resemblances among these elements (similarities in size, color, shape, etc.).
3. Arrange these elements in a visually consistent pattern.

There are many benefits to simplicity. First, simplicity is one of the most reliable means of achieving aesthetic appeal. Second, your efforts at emphasizing an element, grouping elements, and subordinating elements will be more likely to succeed when the overall design is simple. Simplicity, in other words, concentrates the effects of your design. Do fewer things, and each thing you do will count more.

Several other important design guidelines are variations on the principle of simplicity: (1) avoid clutter, (2) restrict the number of fonts you employ, and (3) align page elements on the same horizontal and vertical grid lines rather than scattering them on the page. (The use of grid systems in design was explained in Chapter 3, "Designing and Building.")

Simplicity certainly contributes to the visual appeal and to the calm, dignified mood of the Steinway home page (Figure 11.5). There is visual complexity *within* the five graphical buttons, but the buttons have the same dimensions and are fully aligned.

Often it is necessary to place many visual elements on a page. When simplicity is impossible, strive for a closely related principle: economy. Economy means reducing the number of lines, shapes, alignments, and everything else that the user's eyes will need to process, retaining only those that serve a purpose.

Proportion and Scale

Proportion refers to pleasing relationships of dimension and size. For example, certain ratios of the line lengths making up rectangles and other shapes are thought to result in inherently pleasing proportions. Other ratios may be unat-

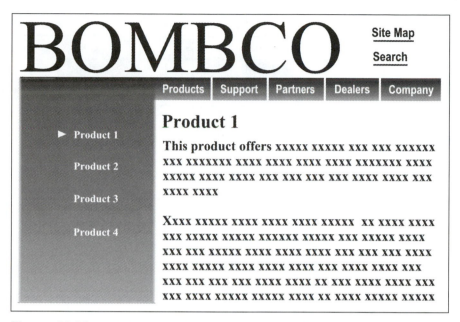

Figure 11.12. A Web page with an unattractively wide navigation column.

tractive. Closely related to proportion is scale. Scale pertains specifically to relationships of size. When something seems too big or too small for its role in a design, we say it is out of scale. Often scale is based on expectations we draw from the physical world. If you are designing the website for a company that rents bicycles in the downtown district of a city, you should have a good reason for scaling a bicycle larger than a building. The nav column shown in Figure 11.12 violates proportion and scale because it is both unusually wide and out of scale with the nav bar.

Balance

Balance is a design principle through which we create interesting and aesthetically pleasing compositions. Much as we judge the weight of objects in the physical world, elements in a composition are perceived as having "visual weight." Each page, furthermore, has a balance point (like the fulcrum of a seesaw) in relation to which the visual elements on one side are balanced against the visual elements on the other. Larger objects are weightier as are objects that are darker or more visually complex. Furthermore, an object far from the balance point has more visual weight than an object closer to the balance point. (This is akin to the extra "weight" a person exerts sitting at the far end of a seesaw.)

Some compositions are balanced symmetrically; the two halves of the page are mirror images (or nearly so). Symmetrical balance is a traditional design idea;

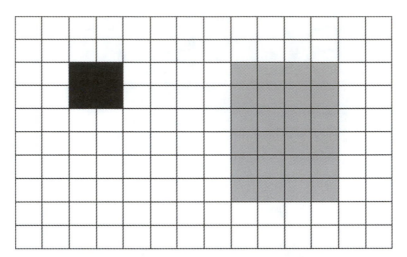

Figure 11.13. Asymmetrical balance achieved because the smaller shape is darker and is located farther from the balance point.

it tends to evoke a mood of formality, stability, and repose, as we can see in the highly symmetrical Steinway home page.

More often designers try to achieve an approximate visual balance without symmetry. These more complex forms of balance add informality and energy to a design. Figure 11.13 illustrates "asymmetrical balance by value and position." In other words, the shape on the left side of the page balances the much larger shape on the right side because the left shape is darker and is farther from the balance point.

Sometimes designers try to achieve a visually effective imbalance among the elements on a page. On the other hand, visual imbalance is often a result of unskillful design, as shown in Figure 11.14.

Judgments regarding balance, other than symmetrical balance, are complex and involve the interplay of numerous factors. You may well find these kinds of judgments to be difficult, and you will likely find differing opinions when you solicit evaluations of your design.

Unity

Unity is the perception that all the visual elements of a composition fit together into a unified whole. The Steinway, Gongfu Club, and Ragú pages all exhibit unity. Unity is threatened by too much variety in shape, color, line attributes, fonts, and other aspects of a design. There is considerable disunity in the frog training home page (Figure 11.14), stemming from too many fonts, a juxtaposition of the smooth lines on the frog drawings with the irregular lines of the frog photograph, and other flaws as well. There are many ways to add unity to a design. Recall how a designer can colorize three disparate graphics to achieve unity among them.

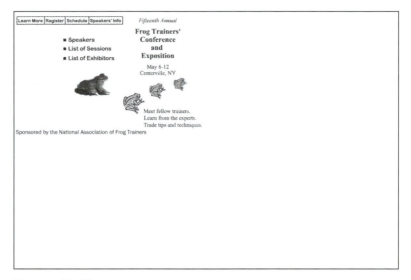

Figure 11.14. A home page with dysfunctional visual imbalance.

Unity also implies that all aspects of the design contribute to the theme. The Steinway home page would exhibit disunity (as well as poor legibility) if the background were changed to lime green with orange speckles. Finally, unity pertains to unity among all the pages of a website taken as a whole. We've referred to this as continuity.

Page Layout

Page layout refers to placing core content elements on the pages of a website. Web pages always have some kind of layout, good or bad. We've been looking at various page layouts throughout this chapter and throughout this book; now page layout becomes our focus. First we consider the ways in which shape forms the basis of page layout. Then, we consider how page layout changes between the home page and deeper levels of the website hierarchy.

Page Layout and Shape

When page layouts divide pages into regions, they create shapes. From the opposite perspective, we can say that various kinds of shapes underlie page layout. Broadly speaking, the universe of shapes gives us three kinds of layout: rectilinear (grid-like) layouts, geometric layouts (other than those that are rectilinear), and free-form layouts.

Rectilinear layouts are by far the most prevalent. For a wide range of purposes, designers choose to divide Web pages into vertically and horizontally oriented rectangles and into squares, a special form of rectangle. This is also true of newspapers, magazines, and many other kinds of print documents. The prevalence of

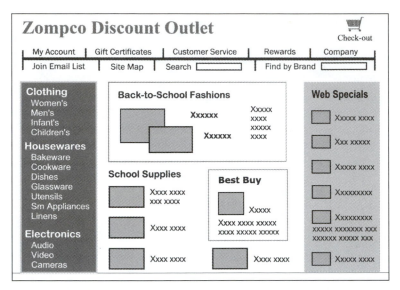

Figure 11.15. A highly complex page layout.

rectilinear designs is reflected in the examples we have used in this book; for example, the Asthma Horizons home page (other than the initial concept sketch) and all the Zompco designs are rectilinear.

The rectilinear designs we have shown exhibit only a moderate degree of complexity. But websites such as portals, news websites, and many online stores often employ the kind of highly complex layout shown in Figure 11.15.

Why should rectilinear page layouts be so prevalent? First, columns of text and very often graphics as well are best framed within vertical and horizontal lines. At the very least, we benefit from a consistent left margin when reading text. Also, rectangles make for an orderly and economical way to divide a page into separate regions and to show subordination among them. Finally, rectangles, especially when the horizontal dimensions are greater than the vertical, are thought to be inherently pleasing because in the physical world such shapes are stable (e.g., a brick lying on its side won't tip easily) and provide a good foundation for the placement of other objects.

Certainly designers should not overlook alternatives to rectilinear design, such as those shown in Figure 11.16a–c. The triangle-based geometric design shown in Figure 11.16a has the energy of diagonal lines and divides the page in an interesting and pleasing manner. It is often difficult to show logical relationships with triangles and other geometric shapes, but in this case it is clear that the large triangle is super-ordinate to the two smaller ones below it. Geometric designs include those based on circles, as shown in Figure 11.16b. Here the page is divided by two bold semicircles of about equal size and status.

The category of free-form layout covers a large territory, but we can say that free-form layouts don't exhibit any obvious division into regular shapes. The design shown in Figure 11.16c features three large irregular areas defined by sweeping curves and a rhythmic repetition of soft lines (the raked gravel of the Japanese rock garden).

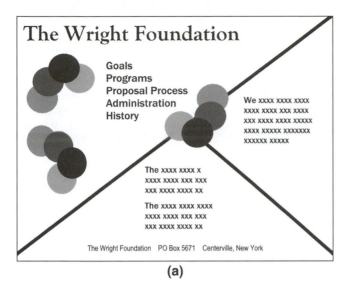

(a)

(b)

(c)

Figure 11.16. A geometric layout based on triangles, a geometric layout based on circles, and a free-form layout.

Figure 11.16c is interesting for another reason. Usually photographs and other core content elements are integrated into the page layout. But because the Haiku Garden home page is designed around a single photograph, this image is both a core content element and the means by which the home page is spatially divided. Although written for print designers, Leonard Koren and R. Wippo Meckler's *Graphic Design Cookbook* (1989) is a rich source of ideas for using all kinds of shapes in the page layout of websites.

From the Home Page to Deeper Levels

When there's a home page that is attractive and professional in appearance, a theme that strikes a responsive chord, and content that promises to be worthwhile, the user is motivated to enter a website. Now the designer especially wants a page layout that exhibits a logical, orderly visual structure and makes text elements easy to read. For this reason interior pages are especially apt to adhere to a rectilinear layout, even when the home page is geometric or free-form.

Furthermore, at the third level and below relatively simple page designs are, with good reason, especially prevalent. Why? Because at successively deeper levels of the hierarchy, the user is often choosing a more specific topic. Layouts, such as those shown in Figures 11.17 and 11.18, correspond to this narrowing focus.

Figure 11.17 shows a single column of text. The user's attention is brought to bear on a single topic. The column is set off by two wide decorative margins that provide a pleasing contrast with the text and, in addition, serve to limit the line length, a potential problem with single-column designs. Note that in the world of print, designs like this might well be regarded as an unacceptable waste of paper. Online, this issue disappears.

Figure 11.17. A page layout with a single column of text
and wide margins.

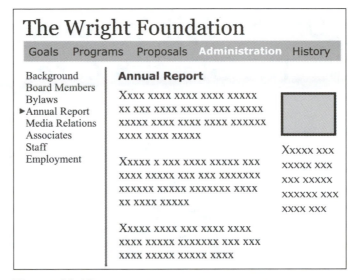

Figure 11.18. A page layout with a right column containing supplementary elements.

Another prevalent and effective design, shown in Figure 11.18, is a left nav column, a wide column for the main content, and a narrower right column containing supplementary graphics, text, and links. Even with the supplementary elements, the page has a single primary focus. Although simple and designed for functionality, these page layouts still leave plenty of opportunity for attractive and creative design.

Profile: The Starfish Café

The owners of Homer's Starfish Café have decided that it's time to get a website, and they are talking to Hank, who knows the place well. The weathered, ramshackle Starfish is a major venue in Homer for blues, folk, and other kinds of "roots" music.

The owners hope that more tourists will show up if they learn about the Starfish when they plan their trip. Also, they want to give locals and tourists alike an easy way to find out who is playing and who is scheduled to play. They tell Hank that they want to convey this theme: "The funky, famous Starfish is the home of roots music in Homer, Alaska." They give Hank a rough idea of the main branches of the hierarchy.

Hank produces three design sketches. Before meeting with the Starfish owners, he pays a call on Peter and Annie to get their opinions, and he lays the sketches out on Annie's kitchen table.

"One of them really sucks!" says Annie.

"I'd have to agree," says Peter. "But the other two have possibilities."

Question

What is your judgment about Hank's design sketches (Figures 11.19–11.21)? Analyze and evaluate them using everything you've learned in this chapter and in the book.

Figure 11.19. Version A.

Figure 11.20. Version B.

Figure 11.21. Version C.

Summary

1. Graphic design for the Web encompasses a very wide range of decisions about the visual dimension of a website. Graphic design is broad and integrative but also entails highly specific design decisions.
2. These are the main goals of graphic design for the Web: (1) adding aesthetic appeal, (2) helping to express the theme of the website, and (3) helping to show the logical relationships among all elements that appear on the page, both core content elements and elements of the interface.
3. Skill in graphic design does not come quickly or easily. Non-professionals should follow well-established design principles and exercise patience as they work. Even if you do not wish to practice graphic design, you should be able to communicate with a graphic designer and evaluate designs.
4. Aesthetic appeal need not evoke the response, "How beautiful!" Done well, even a bus schedule will be perceived as visually attractive. Also, grim or somber content can most certainly be aesthetic.
5. Line, shape, and color are resources, or "raw materials," for graphic design. Lines connect two or more points. Designers utilize these attributes of line: straightness, curvedness, jaggedness, a hand-drawn appearance, dots and dashes, low or high contrast, hard and soft edges, degrees of thickness, and orientation.

6. Shapes are formed (and implied) by lines. Shapes and lines make up the objects that appear as core content elements. We can overlap shapes and use reverse-outs to suggest multiple planes.

7. Colors are defined in terms of hue, value (luminance), and saturation with gray. Although the computer's combinations of hues, values, and saturation give us 16 million colors, designers often limit themselves to the 216 browser-safe colors.

8. Colors are perceived as warm and cool. Colors have numerous other associations, many of which are culturally dependent. A significant number of people, mostly males, have some kind of difficulty in interpreting colors ("color blindness").

9. There are five important kinds of color harmony: monochromatic, complementary, analogous, triadic, and split complementary.

10. Use image editing software applications such as Photoshop and Paint Shop Pro to enhance graphics. You can, for instance, brighten or colorize an image.

11. Graphic design includes specifying the visual appearance of text. Body fonts, serif or sans serif, must have good screen legibility; you can take greater liberties with display fonts. Avoid excessive line length, too many fonts, and backgrounds that provide inadequate contrast. Recognize that users may not be able to display the font you've specified on their machines.

12. The term "mood" describes emotions, attitudes, or associations that users experience when they view and read the pages of a website. The appropriate mood helps to establish the theme. Because moods are general responses rather than specific messages or statements, we use single words or phrases to describe moods—for example, joyful, dignified, and somber. Moods are highly individual. Designers can only *attempt* to evoke a particular mood in their users.

13. Splash pages and splash animations precede the home page and provide an opportunity to convey the theme and mood in a compelling manner. Users, however, may object to the extra click that is required.

14. The squint test is a useful technique for assessing the relationships among the main visual elements in a design. Blur your vision to eliminate semantic meaning and obscure minor visual features.

15. Here are seven fundamental principles of composition that apply both to highly artistic home pages and to straightforward interior pages:

- *Emphasis.* Use stylistic attributes such as size and location to emphasize certain parts of the image and thereby exert some control over the user's gaze.
- *Grouping.* Use proximity and similarity to establish logical relationships among elements on the page.
- *Subordination.* Very often a set of grouped elements is also subordinated to a more dominant element to establish a hierarchical relationship among them.
- *Simplicity.* There are numerous benefits to restricting the amount of visual data that the user's eyes must process. Achieve simplicity by employing a relatively small number of similar visual elements arranged in a consistent pattern.
- *Proportion and scale.* Certain relationships of dimension and size result in pleasing proportions. Scale refers to appropriate or inappropriate relationships of size.

- *Balance.* Because elements in a composition are perceived as having "visual weight," they are usually positioned in some kind of balanced arrangement. Designers may balance a composition symmetrically, achieve approximate balance without symmetry, or achieve an effective imbalance.
- *Unity.* Unity is the perception that all the visual elements of a composition fit together into a unified whole. Unity also implies that all aspects of the design contribute to the theme. Finally, unity, or "continuity," pertains to unity among all the pages of a website taken as a whole.

16. Page layout refers to placing core content elements on the pages of a website. Rectilinear layouts are by far the most prevalent. The major reasons are that columns of text and very often graphics are best framed within vertical and horizontal lines and because rectangles make for an orderly and economical way to divide a page into separate regions and to show subordination among them. Do not, however, overlook possibilities for geometric layouts (that are not rectilinear) and free-form layouts.

17. Interior pages are especially apt to adhere to a rectilinear layout. At deeper levels in the hierarchy, designers often favor a single content column with wide margins. Also prevalent is a left nav column, a wide column for the main content, and a narrower right column containing supplementary graphics, text, and links.

References

Bringhurst, Robert. 2000. *The Elements of Typographic Style.* DIANE Publishing Company.

Bruce, Vicki, Patricia R. Green, and Mark A. Georgeson. 1996. *Visual Perception: Physiology, Psychology, and Ecology.* 3d ed. East Sussex, UK: Psychology Press.

Eyewire. www.eyewire.com

Koren, Leonard, and R. Wippo Meckler. 1989. *Graphic Design Cookbook: Mix and Match Recipes for Faster, Better Layouts.* San Francisco: Chronicle Books.

Lauer, David A., and Steven Pentak. 2000. *Design Basics.* 5th ed. Fort Worth: Harcourt.

Microsoft Typography Group. www.microsoft.com/typography

Morton, Jill. 1998. *Color Logic for Website Design (Color Voodoo #5),* a digital book available in Adobe Acrobat (PDF) format at www.colorvoodoo.com

Mullet, Kevin, and Darrell Sano. 1995. *Designing Visual Interfaces.* Englewood Cliffs, NJ: Sunsoft Press/Prentice Hall.

Weinman, Lynda. 1999. *Designing Web Graphics 3: How to Prepare Images and Media for the Web.* Indianapolis, IN: New Riders Publishing.

Williams, Thomas R. 2000. Guidelines for designing and evaluating the display of information on the Web. *Technical Communication* 47.3: 383–396.

Wong, Wucius. 1993. *Principles of Form and Design.* New York: Van Nostrum.

World Wide Web Consortium. www.w3.org

Discussion and Application

Items for Discussion

1. Visit www.websitesthatsuck.com or another website that calls attention to bad design on the Web. Examine some of the featured websites and, when available, the criticism that is offered. Do you agree with the criticism? To what degree do the shortcomings of these websites pertain to graphic design? What other kinds of shortcomings are present?

2. Visit www.cwd.dk, www.worldbestwebsites.com, or another website that showcases good design. Examine some of the featured websites and, when available, the commentary that is offered. Do you agree with the commentary? To what degree are these websites being praised for their graphic design?

3. Examine the display fonts in Figure 11.4 and try to imagine each font as a major part of the opening title sequence for a movie or movie genre (e.g., romantic comedy). What movie or genre might work well with each font? If you know of other expressive fonts, associate these with a particular title sequence.

4. What legibility problems can you identify in Figure 11.22?

5. Go Ask Alice! (www.goaskalice.columbia.edu) is a website that provides information about health and well-being especially for young adults. Originally intended for Columbia University students, it is now widely visited by young people throughout the world.

   The layout of the Alice home page, shown in Figure 11.23, bears some resemblance to the Steinway home page, but the theme and style are entirely different. Formulate what seems to be the theme of this website and explain how the style expresses the theme. Also, how does the name of this website contribute to the theme?

   Note: The page has a white background, the identity element and the eight square buttons are predominantly red (transitioning into dark blue), and the three rounded buttons are dark blue.

6. Although there is a great deal of diversity among the websites of North American colleges and universities, certain themes are very prevalent. The following might be called standard themes:

   a. Come to Lockwood. Students here enjoy a warm, supportive environment with small classes and close ties with faculty.

   b. Come to Lockwood. Learn amid our magnificent campus setting and spectacular scenic location.

   c. Come to Lockwood. We offer the best combination of education, personal growth, and campus fun. Take part in campus activities. Root for our championship sports teams.

   d. Come to Lockwood. We are a major research institution with the best and newest facilities. Our faculty are leaders in their fields. You can take part in cutting-edge research.

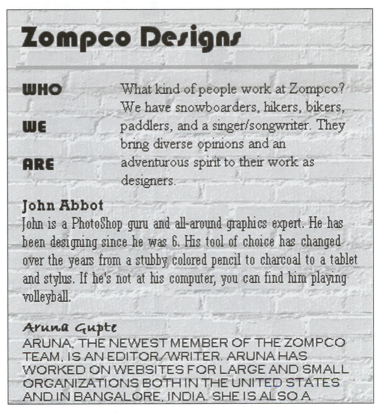

Figure 11.22. A Web page that presents legibility problems.

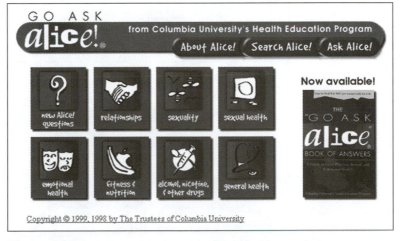

Figure 11.23. The home page of the Go Ask Alice! website. (www.goaskalice.columbia.edu)

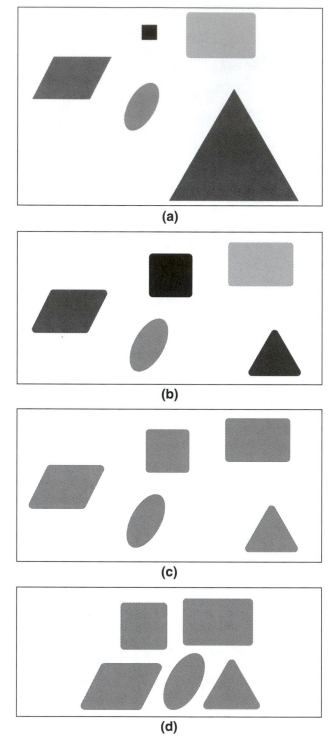

Figure 11.24. A series of images showing increased unity.

e. Come to Lockwood. We represent tradition and prestige. Lockwood dates back to the Colonial era. Lockwood graduates have been leaders in business and government for many generations.

These themes may be expressed strongly and explicitly or just subtly. There are often combinations of these standard themes. Visit the websites of six different North American colleges or universities, identify the themes, and analyze how these themes are expressed. Try to get a representative sampling of schools. For example, look at a large state university, a small regional state university or college, a small private university (possibly an "elite" school), and a community college.

7. The images shown in Figure 11.24a–d represent a progression from disunity to strong unity. Trace the succession of images noting the changes and how these changes contribute to greater unity.

8. Expand upon the analysis of the Ragú home page presented in this chapter. Be sure to visit the website so that your analysis can include interior pages.

9. Comment on this intriguing statement about design: Innovate, but only as a last resort.

Application to Your Project

1. Review the theme you initially developed for your website. Is this theme still appropriate for your website? How well is the theme expressed? Are there stylistic elements that don't seem to fit? Does the design evoke appropriate moods?

2. Can you give a reason for each design decision you have made on your home page and on the interior pages? If certain pages depart from your grid system, can you give reasons why this is so?

3. Have you checked to see that your text, colors, layout, and core content elements display properly on a wide range of computers? This includes different platforms (Macintosh, Windows, Sun), different operating systems, different browsers, and different versions of a browser.

12

Site Maps, Search, and Indexes

Introduction

Throughout this book our focus has been navigation from page to page via links. There are, however, important alternatives to standard navigation: the site map, the Search feature, and the index.

Site maps offer users a global view of a website's structure and allow them to directly access a destination page by clicking its name. The Search feature, or just "Search," treats the contents of a website as information in a database. After the user types a search query, the search engine examines the website and displays a list of links to the pages that match, as closely as possible, the user's information need. A site map and Search are valuable additions to all but very small websites. Indeed, for some websites, Search is intended as the user's main form of navigation or, at least, a first step that jumps the user into the neighborhood of his or her final destination.

The index is the Web equivalent of the traditional back-of-book index. Indexes are much less prevalent than site maps or Search, but should be considered as a supplement to the site map and Search feature when the content is relatively stable. In this chapter we will investigate the site map, Search feature, and index. You will learn how they work, how people use them, and how to design them effectively.

Most Web portals offer a Web-wide search engine. We close this chapter by explaining the steps you can take so that your website will be found by users of portals.

Site Maps

Typical site maps are shown in Figures 12.1 and 12.2 and are discussed below. Users can benefit considerably from this kind of global view of a website's structure.

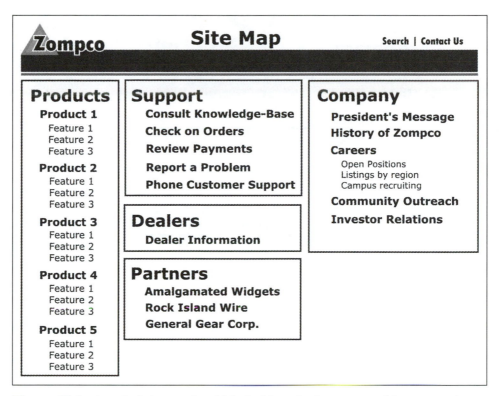

Figure 12.1. A typical site map in which the hierarchy is represented by means of boxes and indented lists.

Consider, for example, the difference between navigation by means of street signs in an unfamiliar city and navigation using the global view provided by a street map. Street signs primarily show you the street you are on and nearby streets, and you must infer from limited information where these go and how they intersect. In contrast, a street map (or a view from an observation tower) shows the complete terrain. Recall that designers, as well as users, benefit from a global view of website structure, and for this reason employ outlines, arrangements of note cards, and node-link diagrams.

Site maps are especially beneficial for websites that employ the web-like information structure and for complex multipath structures. Why? With these less orderly structures users have extra difficulty inferring the overall structure of the site from the standard links offered on individual pages. In much the same way, a street map is more valuable for a city full of winding, maze-like streets than a city that follows a regular plan.

Problems with Site Maps

Site maps are only beginning to reach their full potential. Currently, site maps present problems in regard to maintenance, scope, and inconvenience of use.

Figure 12.2. A typical site map in which the hierarchy is represented by indented lists and horizontal columns.

Maintenance

The content and structure of most websites changes frequently, and site maps must be updated to reflect these changes. Site map maintenance, however, is not a task to which website owners want to allocate significant resources. To ease the maintenance problem, website owners often call for basic site maps, such as those shown above, that consist of easily updateable text links. Some site maps are simply indented lists of links. Highly graphical site maps are harder to update and are impractical unless the website will remain stable for a long time. A different kind of solution, the semi-automatic generation of site maps, is discussed below.

Scope

A major limitation of today's site maps is their scope, the number of pages that can be represented. Because of the relatively small viewing area provided by computer monitors, designers often can represent only several dozen pages while their website might consist of several hundred or more pages. Indeed, site maps usually go no deeper than the fourth level (as is the case in Figures 12.1 and 12.2), and often go no deeper than the third level.

Designers strive to maximize scope without making the site map page too lengthy or cluttered. They use various means of grouping and subordination to fit as many links as possible into the limited amount of screen space. They also abbreviate the names of pages. The site map shown in Figure 12.1 employs boxes and large, visually dominant links to represent the second-level of the hierarchy, a smaller font size to represent the third level, and indentation along with the transition from boldface to a normal font style to show the entire fourth level on the Products branch and part of the fourth level on the Company branch. The site map shown in Figure 12.2 represents exactly the same pages but in a different, more complex format that employs a combination of indented lists and horizontal columns. This page will scroll slightly. Designers must experiment to determine what techniques will work best for the kind of website they are representing and the scope they are trying to achieve.

Inconvenience

Designers usually provide a utility link to the site map on every page. Even so, site maps are inconvenient to use. In particular, they require users to switch their attention from the current content page to the site map and back to a new content page. For this reason, users often ignore site maps, even when the site map would serve their needs well. In much the same way, visitors to an unfamiliar city are not always willing to pull a street map from their pocket, even when using the map makes good sense. The need to switch attention is also a significant problem for the Search feature and index.

Designers can increase scope by designing site maps that scroll extensively or by creating multi-page site maps that let users click to view deeper levels of the hierarchy. These techniques, however, exacerbate the convenience problem. At times, a good technique is to code the site map to open in a supplementary window that does not significantly overlap the content window. Each click on a site map link displays a new page in the main window. This technique allows users to more easily switch their attention between site map and content, and it encourages users to use the site map repeatedly to navigate the website.

The Sarnoff Corporation website, shown in Figure 12.3, illustrates another way to address the convenience problem. Because the hierarchy is narrow, just four main branches, the designers provide a multi-level nav bar, a kind of "mini site map," on many pages of the website. Users then can view the hierarchy down to the third level without leaving their current page. The same benefit accrues from the two-level navigation column shown in Figures 8.7 and 8.8 in Chapter 8, "The Navigational Interface."

The Promise of Better Site Maps

Sophisticated Web technologies are beginning to surmount the limitations of standard site maps. Inxight Software's Star Tree Studio enables developers to create a site map that can be updated semi-automatically. Furthermore, these site

Figure 12.3. A two-level nav bar that functions as a site map. (www.sarnoff.com)

maps, called Star Trees™, address the scope problem as well. As shown in Figures 12.4 and 12.5, the Star Tree site map is formatted as a 3-D radial hierarchy with a "fish-eye" (hyperbolic) perspective. By presenting users with this fish-eye view, the site map can display more levels than are normally feasible. Furthermore, because the site map appears in a supplementary window and because users manipulate the site map by dragging with the mouse pointer, the interaction is relatively convenient. (Star Trees are implemented as Java applets and run in Java-enabled browsers.)

In the initial view, shown in Figure 12.4, the first two levels of the hierarchy and much of the third level are fully visible. This view provides a rich context for the user to decide which branch of the hierarchy to explore. As shown in Figure 12.5, the user has chosen News and Events. By dragging the News and Events link to the middle of the diagram, the user moves the third-level links on this branch (Customer Showcase, News, Press Releases, etc.) from the extreme periphery of the screen into full view. By continuing to drag, the user can bring the fourth and deeper levels into full view. The user double clicks any link to display the corresponding page in the website's main content window.

We noted that design teams encode pertinent information in their node-link diagrams by means of attributes such as the thickness of lines. Users can also benefit when information is encoded into site maps. Star Tree Studio, for example, gives

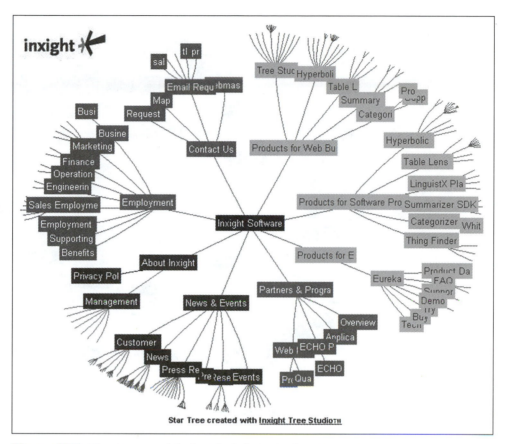

Figure 12.4. The site map of the Inxight Software website (www.inxight.com) generated as a Star Tree. The user is about to drag the News & Events link (lower center of the figure) toward the upper right to reveal deeper levels on that branch.

Web developers significant control over the visual attributes of their site maps. So, for example, links can be color coded by subject matter and variations in line thickness can indicate the most important branches of the hierarchy.

Star Trees support a special kind of Search feature. When the user types a word or phrase into the search text box (not shown in the figures), a highlight appears on any link on the site map containing this word or phrase. So, for instance, if the user types "Murax," the name of an Inxight product, the user will know where on the site map to look for information about this product, even though no links pertaining to Murax were visible in the initial view. This capability resembles link typing and filtering by subject area, discussed in Chapter 9, "Effective Links."

Ideally, site maps would also automatically display a "You are here" marker to show users their current location in the website hierarchy. This capability, in fact, was present in various pre-Web hypermedia products.

If you can imagine a site map that represents every page and all significant links among pages, encodes rich information on the site map (enabling the user to

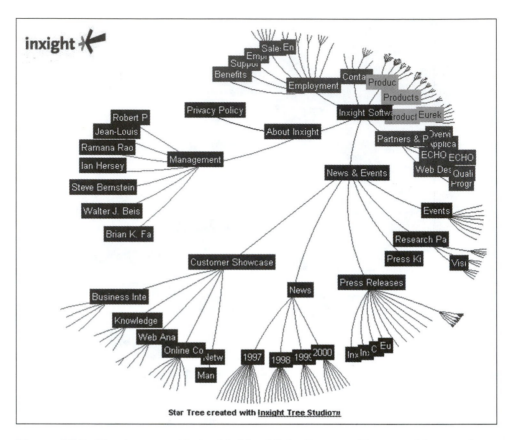

Figure 12.5. The site map with the third-level links Customer Showcase, News, and Press Releases in full view. The user can continue dragging the News & Events link to bring the children of these third-level links into full view.

reliably choose which page to visit), automatically shows the user's current location, is uncluttered and easy to use, and barely draws the user's eyes from the content, you have envisioned the ideal means of Web navigation. In a theoretical sense, all of our nav bars, nav columns, and other links are just an attempt to approximate this perfect site map.

The Search Feature

From a general, non-technical perspective we can say that the Search feature consists of three components: (1) the query form, (2) the search engine—which is unseen by the user—and (3) the results list. The query form is where the user types a search query consisting of one or more words—the "search terms"—that are intended to retrieve links to pages with the desired information. The search engine processes the user's query, trying to match it with the content of the website, and generates the results list. The results list consists of individual entries, each containing a link to a Web page the engine has found along with descriptive information to help the user choose among the entries.

To understand Search, you must understand users' search behavior, the operation of the search engine, and the most important design options for the query form and the results list. These are covered below.

Here are some important resources for learning more about Search. Louis Rosenfeld and Peter Morville (1998) offer chapters that provide a good general perspective on information access and Search. For more specific information, see Wes Sonnenreich and Tim MacInta (1998). Avi Rappoport's website Searchtools.com provides very extensive information on Search, including technical information and reviews of many search engines. Also valuable are Usableweb.com and Webmonkey.com. Because Search is part of the broad area of information science, you can obtain a great deal of relevant background knowledge from Robert Korfhage (1997) or another good information science textbook.

Users' Search Behavior

When users follow links or scan a site map, they often have an information need, but they may also be opportunistically browsing, looking for something that interests them and readily switching their focus of attention from one topic to another. On the other hand, when people use the Search feature, they are almost always trying to fulfill an information need. It is unusual for someone to type a word or phrase into a query form unless they are trying to answer a question or find specific content.

This information need can be specific and clear-cut. For example, Parent A, who is thinking about moving to Centerville, Oregon, wants to know the following: Is there a chess team in the Centerville elementary schools? In contrast, Parent B, who is also thinking about moving to Centerville, has an information need that is more general and much harder to satisfy: Does Centerville provide good elementary school education? Both parents are going to explore the website of the Centerville School District, www.centervilleschools.org, and will use the Search feature.

Users seek to formulate a query that represents their information need as closely as possible. When we ask a knowledgeable human being for information, we can usually articulate our need fully, and the person will understand us and try to give us a good answer. When we type a word or phrase into a text box, the query is likely to be much cruder, much less pertinent to our information need.

Parent A has a relatively easy job. It should be possible to formulate the query "elementary" and "chess" or else "elementary school and chess" and quickly find a Web page that will provide a satisfactory answer.

Parent B has a much harder job. There are no simple measures for quality education. A query such as "elementary" and "quality education" may retrieve little more than a general statement that Centerville is committed to quality education in its elementary schools. Or, this query may retrieve press releases relating to bond issues or grant applications and mission statements from each of the elementary schools in the district. While pertinent, these pages are only useful clues about educational quality. They will not fully satisfy Parent B's information need.

Recognizing the complexity of her information need, a determined parent might well undertake a much broader query: Seeking information about educational programs, funding, assessment, student achievement, national test scores, and so forth, Parent B may be inclined to view a great many pages about elementary education in Centerville and about the entire Centerville school system.

Perhaps Parent B would be better off giving up on Search and navigating the Centerville School District website page to page. This depends on the size and complexity of the website, and how it is organized. Possibly, a great amount of material demonstrating the quality of elementary school education is concentrated on one branch of the website. In this case, why not navigate directly to that branch? On the other hand, this material may be scattered widely throughout the website and may not be well linked by associative secondary links. In this case, Search is the best strategy.

Parent B, of course, can employ a combination of strategies, navigating the hierarchy and searching with several different queries. Parent B should also search entirely different websites, such as the website of the Oregon State Department of Education.

There are also search engines with natural language query forms that invite queries phrased in the user's everyday manner of speaking: "Does Centerville provide good elementary school education?" At this stage in their development, natural language querying is often disappointing: The user may *think* that the natural language search engine is searching with a very pertinent query but in reality the engine throws out some of the words and searches with a query not so different (and perhaps worse) than the query the user would have formulated in a conventional search engine.

Precision and Recall

The concepts "precision" and "recall" are central to information science, to search engines, and to users' search behavior. Precision is the proportion of results that are relevant to the query (roughly speaking, the accuracy of the search). Recall is the proportion of relevant results to the total number of relevant results that are in the website (roughly speaking, the thoroughness of the search). Note that precision and recall do not pertain directly to the user's information need, but rather to its representation in the query.

Users always want high precision: Who wants to look at irrelevant items in a results list? Almost always, however, there is a trade-off between recall and precision, and so Parent B will need to tolerate a significant number of irrelevant results in her attempt to retrieve as much relevant information as possible. On the other hand, users often don't care very much about high recall. If Parent A finds a page that spells out the key facts about the elementary school chess team, she may not care about more pages with additional information on the subject.

Ranking

Because search results are not equally relevant to a query, a key capability of a search engine is to rank entries and place the most relevant entries high on the results list. In an ideal case, the first page or two of entries will be highly relevant and the user's eyes will never reach the middle and bottom of the results list where the less relevant and irrelevant items are concentrated. As you will see, however, effective ranking is not easy to achieve.

The Operation of the Search Feature

The term "search engine" designates a group of software programs that collectively underlie the Search feature and make it work. The query form and results list are the user interface through which users interact with the search engine. To understand Search and how to design a Search feature, you must know a little about search engines. There are many search engines and considerable differences among them, but the most basic principles are explained below.

The "crawler" (or "spider"), one component of the search engine, periodically examines all the pages on the website and, with related software components, builds a data file known as an index. The index stores information about the content of each page. The more often your Web content changes, the more often the crawler should re-examine the website and update the index.

Search engines use significantly different rules for deciding relevancy and ranking results, but let's consider how a typical search engine might evaluate the page Computers in the Classroom on the Centerville School site. The engine will assume that the name of the page (appearing in the HTML title tag) is a very strong indicator of the subject matter of the page. The engine will also tally up the occurrences of words (other than extremely prevalent words such as "the" and "of") and assume that words or phrases recurring on the page are closely related to the subject matter. Indeed, these words appear multiple times on this page:

education	teach	student	instruction	technology
skills	computer	software	network	World Wide Web

If the page has headings, the engine will give words in the headings (if they are not implemented as graphics) greater weight than words in body text.

The engine also evaluates keywords that the designer has placed in the page's keyword metatag. Designers should supply keywords that aptly describe the content of the Web page, and include synonyms, variants, and other relevant words that do not appear as text on the page. Adding keywords to a Web page is akin to compiling a back-of-the-book index. In both cases, you ask, "What words might users be using to look up the information they want?" So, for example, although the word "Internet" happens not to appear on the Computers in the Classroom page, it is provided as a keyword.

When the user types a query, the search engine consults the current index file and using its rules will retrieve certain pages and assign them relevancy scores. We can see that queries such as "teaching with computer," "education and computer technology," and "students Internet" should all rank an entry for the Computer in the Classroom page high in the results list.

As part of interpreting the user's query, many search engines simplify the query. Verb tenses are stripped away, plural nouns are made singular, and so forth. Therefore "instructor" is likely to succeed in a query (matching "instruction"), even if "instructor" doesn't appear on the page or as a keyword. Web-wide search engines operate much like the site-specific search engines under discussion here, though on a much larger scale.

Most site-specific search engines give the designer considerable control over the Search feature. You can exclude portions of the site from Search. Often you can supply synonyms. So, for example, if the school district consistently uses the word "wellness" rather than "health," the designer might configure the search engine to automatically add "wellness" as a search term whenever a user types "health." An important option, discussed below, is to augment a basic query form with a variety of options that encourage users to formulate more sophisticated queries. With a capable search engine and good design, you can make the search experience more convenient, less demanding, and more successful for your users.

Query Form Options: The Basic Query Form

There are many ways to design query forms. A fundamental choice is whether to provide only a basic, bare bones query form or whether to provide an extended query form with a variety of options. First we will consider the basic query form.

A basic query form, shown in Figure 12.6, consists of a text box into which users type a word or phrase and a button to initiate the search. (The computer's Enter key will also initiate the search.) Notice that there is a link, labeled More Search, that displays an extended query form.

When offered a basic query form, most users will control their search in large measure through the specificity or generality of their search terms. For example, someone will type "computers and education" if they want a great deal of information about computing throughout the school district, or they will restrict their search with a query such as "elementary school Internet."

Query Form Options: Pattern Matching

Although most users content themselves with the basic query form and basic queries, extended query forms, often referred to as "advanced search," employ drop-down list boxes, option buttons, and other elements of software user interfaces and invite users to formulate more sophisticated queries. A typical extended query form is shown in Figure 12.7. Extended query forms are highly desirable for larger websites, for subject areas in which more complex searches are likely,

Centerville School District   Site Map | Help

Centerville, Oregon

Search for: [＿＿＿＿＿] GO More Search

Figure 12.6. A basic query form.

and for sites whose users are more apt to take the time to learn and use the query options. The query option we explain first is pattern matching, followed by search zones, and finally customizing the results list.

Pattern matching enables users to easily specify logical relationships among their search terms. In so doing, users can create more sophisticated queries that more closely fit their information need and that are more apt to achieve higher precision and recall. The query form shown in Figure 12.7 permits these patterns:

- Any of the words
- All of the words
- The exact words
- Exclude these words

These patterns, as we shall see, are based on Boolean logic. Boolean logic entails making logical statements by stringing together the user's search terms with these conjunctions: And, Or, Not. These conjunctions are referred to as Boolean operators.

Any of the Words

The "any of the words" match casts a very broad net throughout the website. It will retrieve pages in which any of the query terms appear. For example, Parent B

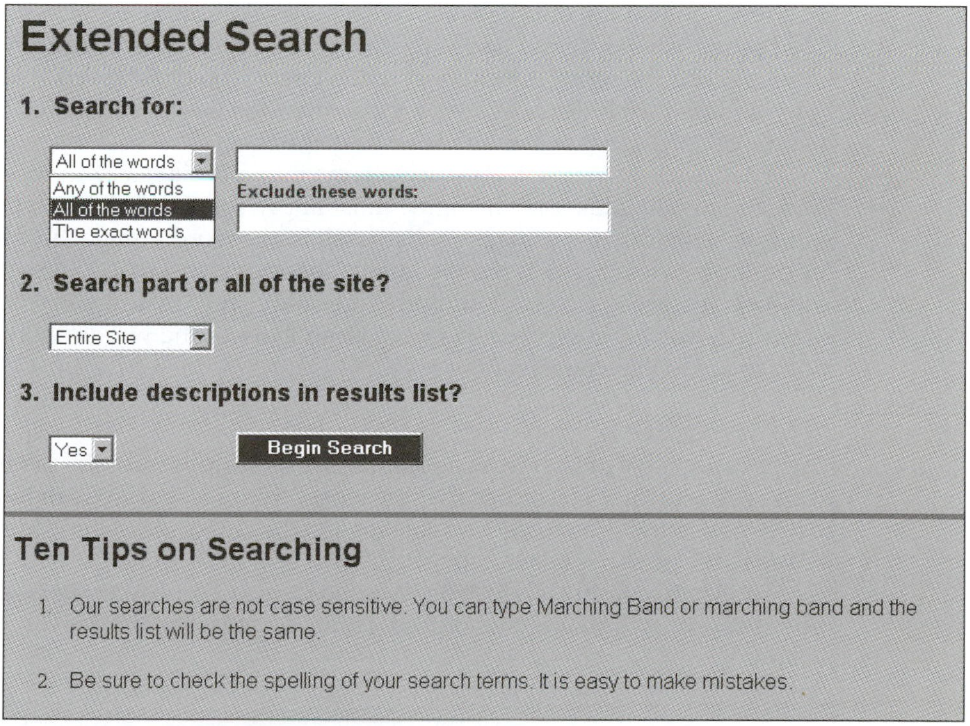

Figure 12.7. An extended query form with drop-down list boxes that offer typical advanced features.

might choose the "any of the words" match, type "quality improve plan achievement," and feel confident that she is getting most of the information on the Centerville School District website regarding quality education. On the other hand, this match might easily retrieve such irrelevant results as this: "Superintendent Ed Kirsch has plans for a month-long cruise throughout the Caribbean after he retires in June. Bon Voyage, Ed!"

From the point of view of Boolean logic, the "any of the words" is equivalent to placing "or" between the terms in the query. The user is saying "I want pages containing the words "quality" or "improve" or "plan" or "achievement." Note this is the "inclusive or," not an "or" that insists on a choice among alternatives.

All of the Words

The "all of the words" match is much more restrictive. The search will retrieve only pages in which all of the specified search terms appear. So, for example, Parent B might specify "elementary" and "quality" to get information about the quality of Centerville elementary schools.

From the point of view of Boolean logic, this match is equivalent to "and." The user is saying, "Unless a page contains 'elementary' and 'quality,' I don't want it." Parent B's query should retrieve many, though certainly not all, relevant pages with few irrelevant pages (moderate recall with very good precision). One major shortcoming of this query is that it will exclude broad discussions of quality education that are not specific to elementary education. Note that unsophisticated search strategies can easily result in a worthless and misleading search: If Parent B adds the term "education," to the query, she doesn't broaden the search but pointlessly excludes relevant pages because the word "education" doesn't appear on all pages that deal with elementary schools.

When a user types several search terms into a basic query form without any Boolean operators, the search engine must apply rules in order to interpret these words as a logical query. In general, the "all of the words" match is operative. So, for example, when a user types the query "Internet instruction," the search engine will look for pages that contain both "Internet" and "instruction." Some search engines, however, interpret this query as an "any of the words" match and will look for pages that contain either term.

The Exact Words

The "exact words" match requires all the words to appear on the page and in the exact sequence, and it requires that the tenses, plurals, and so forth be exact. This match will retrieve very few irrelevant results (high precision), but there is a strong risk of missing relevant pages (low recall). Even someone who has lived in Centerville all their life might type "Margie Denver Elementary School" and miss relevant results because the official name is "Margie S. Denver Elementary School."

Exclude

The "exclude" match is used with one of the other matches to eliminate a category of information. For example, a user might type "school computing" and then type "administrative" in the Exclude text box to eliminate anything having to with administrative computing.

From the point of view of Boolean logic, the "exclude" match is equivalent to placing "not" before one of the terms in the query. Similarly, the "exact phrase" match is equivalent to saying "Margie Denver Elementary School" and nothing else.

Complex Queries and the Limitations of "Advanced Search"

There is no limit to the number of search terms and logical connectives that can comprise a query. For example, Parent B could formulate this detailed and precise query regarding the quality of elementary education in Centerville:

> school OR education OR student OR teacher OR instruct
>
> AND
>
> quality OR success OR assess OR plans OR initiative OR progress OR evaluate OR budget OR fund OR levy OR tax

The first group of terms (preceding the AND) should find every page pertaining to schools and education (including non-elementary education) while the second group targets pages that provide clues about educational quality. Notice, however, that while the extended query form shown in Figure 12.7 makes Boolean searching easier, it also limits the complexity of queries to the exclude match plus one of the other three types of pattern matching. In other words, this form and certain others exclude the kind of complex query shown above.

Ironically, though few people do so, it is usually possible to formulate complex queries in a basic query form. Each search engine understands specific syntactic rules for interpreting Boolean operators. So, for example, a plus sign often denotes the "all the words match," a minus sign often denotes the "exclude match," and quotation marks often denote the "exact phrase" match. We see, then, that it is actually misleading to refer to an extended query form as "advanced search" in cases when it is the basic form that permits the most advanced searching.

Query Form Options: Search Zones

Another option that is useful with medium and large websites is search zones. This feature, shown in the extended query form (Figure 12.7), consists of a drop-down list box through which the user can restrict the Search to a single category they are interested in, thereby avoiding a great many irrelevant results. Because the designers of the Centerville School District website know that many users want information about just one particular school, they have created search zones for the individual Centerville schools plus a zone for the entire site. Search zones, in other words, greatly increase precision with only a small drop in recall.

On small websites, the benefit of zones is not great. Also, search zones should never be implemented when the subject matter of the website does not allow for clear, crisp categories. For example, it might be unproductive to categorize the Community Composting website into zones.

Similar to search zones are search "limits"; search limits provide a means to restrict the search within a range of values, typically two dates. This feature is especially useful for searching large archives and online research libraries.

Our discussion of search zones and limits is just one instance of a broad theme running through this chapter: The design of the Search feature, site map, and index should depend on the nature of the website (especially size and subject matter) and on the anticipated information needs and information-seeking behavior of the users.

Query Form Options: Customizing the Results List

The final query form option we consider, which is also shown in Figure 12.7, is specifying certain characteristics of the results list. Most important, the user may want to choose between viewing just the page name or including the description of the page.

The Placement of Query Forms and Help on Search

Users should be able to access Search from every (or nearly every) page in the website. The first approach, shown in Figure 12.6, is to place a basic query form on every page with a link to a dedicated search page with an extended form. Users enjoy the convenience of this layered approach: Those who are content with the basic form don't have to click to access Search or look at the more complex interface. The drawback is that even a basic query form takes up significant screen real estate. Even so, on websites in which you expect a lot of searching, be sure that your page design leaves room for a basic query form. The alternative, a means to conserve screen real estate, is to simply provide a link from each page to a dedicated search page.

Every Search feature requires help information. Novice users should be offered tips and some sample queries. Sophisticated users may want to understand how the search engine ranks queries and the syntax for using Boolean operators. Ideally a link to help information would appear alongside a basic query form on each Web page. Designers, however, rarely find room for such a link, and so users usually need to go to the dedicated search page to find help on Search.

The Results List

The results list provides users with a moment of heightened interest as they see the outcome of their search. But the results list also presents the user with a whole new set of decisions and actions and must therefore be designed to support the user through this second stage of information seeking. Figure 12.8 shows the first page of a 13-page results list for the query "computers and elementary" on the Centerville School District website. We will consider both the make-up of the results list page and the make-up of an individual results list entry.

The Results List Page

The top of each results list page should display a number indicating the total number of results that the search retrieved and which entries out of this total are currently being displayed (e.g., 1–10 out of a total of 127 results for "computers

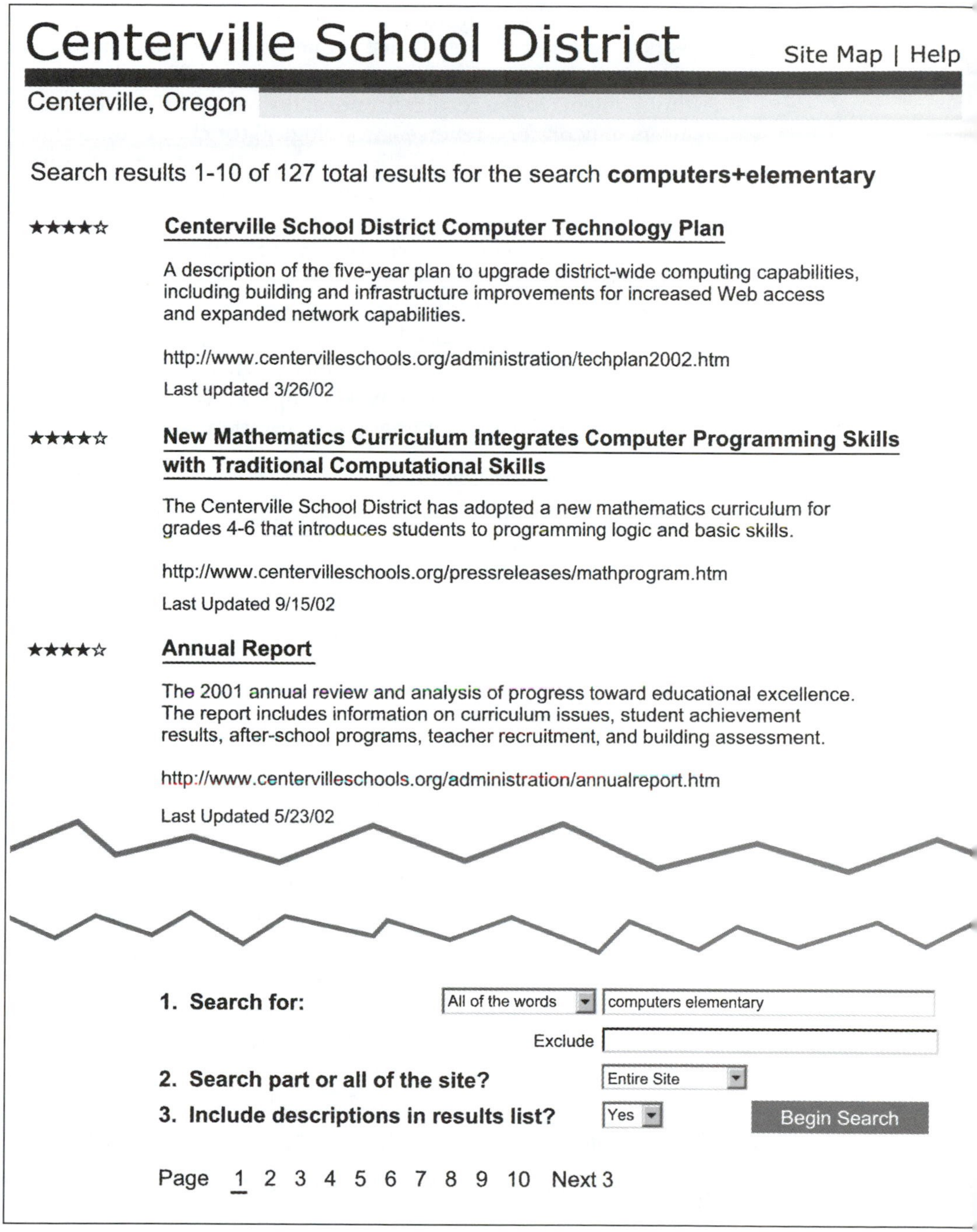

Centerville School District

Centerville, Oregon

Search results 1-10 of 127 total results for the search **computers+elementary**

★★★★☆ **Centerville School District Computer Technology Plan**

A description of the five-year plan to upgrade district-wide computing capabilities, including building and infrastructure improvements for increased Web access and expanded network capabilities.

http://www.centervilleschools.org/administration/techplan2002.htm

Last updated 3/26/02

★★★★☆ **New Mathematics Curriculum Integrates Computer Programming Skills with Traditional Computational Skills**

The Centerville School District has adopted a new mathematics curriculum for grades 4-6 that introduces students to programming logic and basic skills.

http://www.centervilleschools.org/pressreleases/mathprogram.htm

Last Updated 9/15/02

★★★★☆ **Annual Report**

The 2001 annual review and analysis of progress toward educational excellence. The report includes information on curriculum issues, student achievement results, after-school programs, teacher recruitment, and building assessment.

http://www.centervilleschools.org/administration/annualreport.htm

Last Updated 5/23/02

1. **Search for:** [All of the words ▼] [computers elementary]

Exclude [   ]

2. **Search part or all of the site?** [Entire Site ▼]

3. **Include descriptions in results list?** [Yes ▼] [Begin Search]

Page 1 2 3 4 5 6 7 8 9 10 Next 3

Figure 12.8. The results list for the query "computers and elementary" on the Centerville School District website.

and elementary.") The total number of results is especially important, for users need to know whether the results list contains a manageable number of entries or thousands of entries.

Although items in the results list normally appear in decreasing order of relevance, users may prefer a reverse chronological (or chronological) listing for back issues of journals, minutes of meetings, and similar content. If your website contains a significant amount of such content, try to offer this option.

It is necessary to provide a query form on the results list page so that the user can immediately begin a new search. This might well occur if the original search retrieved too few or insufficiently useful results or if the number of results was so large that the user wants to perform a new, more narrowly focused search. The query form should retain the user's search terms and options so that the user has a starting point for modifying the original search. Finally, when a query retrieves no results at all, the page that displays should offer some tips on searching, such as a reminder to check the spelling of the query, rather than the curt message: "No results found."

The Make-Up of Results List Entries

Individual results list entries must provide sufficient information about the Web pages they represent so that users can scan and compare the entries and choose one or more pages to visit. Essential elements of any entry are the page name, the page description, and the URL. The page name is taken from the HTML title tag. The page description usually comes from the description metatag. Alternatively, the description may take the form of a line or two of text from the page itself ("keyword in context"). Listing the URL provides a hint as to where the page is located within the website.

Very often the relevancy of each result is shown using either a percentage or a ranking system, such as a set of stars. Also, users benefit greatly from knowing the date the page was last updated (taken from the last-modified metatag).

Monitoring User Queries (Reviewing Search Logs)

Most search engines (including remote search services) can compile a "search log" of your users' search activity. This includes the number of searches conducted each week, the terms used in search queries, and the queries that did not produce any results. Clearly, this information can be put to very good use. It can tell you whether you need to add new keywords and whether you are providing the information your users are looking for.

Adding an Effective Search Capability to Your Website

Here we consider how you can implement Search on your website and choose the Search capabilities that you need.

Implementing a Search Engine

You have a great many choices in providing a Search feature for your website. In regard to implementation, there are three basic avenues you can follow:

- Programming your own search engine using development tools and existing code libraries
- Obtaining a search engine product and installing it on your website's server
- Using a remote search service

About the only reason to create your own search engine is to satisfy special needs that somehow cannot be accommodated by any other solution.

Search engine products, some of which are free, give you complete control of the search engine, within the parameters of its capabilities. If you choose a product that must be purchased, you are not committed to an annual fee, as you are with various remote search services. Search engine products, however, require technical knowledge and access to your website's server.

Remote search services offer significant benefits: You don't need technical expertise or access to your server. There are no processing demands on your server due to Search. There is often no charge for a basic level of service, particularly for small websites.

On the other hand, some remotes services will insist on placing advertising banners on your website in lieu of payment, and paying customers generally get a higher level of service with many more search options.

If you choose a remote service, you give up at least some control of your Search feature. For example, the remote service's crawler examines your pages on their schedule rather than yours, and if the remote service experiences slowdowns due to heavy use, the performance of your Search feature will also deteriorate. Finally, you are giving the service very extensive access to the internal workings of your website and the search behavior of your users. You need to be confident, therefore, that your service is responsible and ethical.

Somewhat akin to remote search services is using the search engine offered by your own Internet Service Provider. Here, too, you offload most of the responsibility for setting up and operating the Search feature.

Choosing Search Capabilities

However you implement Search, you need to pay close attention to the particular capabilities the search engine provides—many of which have now been discussed: You need to be sure the search engine provides all the query form options you need and that it interprets queries and ranks retrieved pages in a way that fits your content and users. You may need a frequent schedule for updating the index. You may consider search logs to be a high priority.

Other considerations, not yet discussed, include file formats. Can the search engine read Flash files, Adobe Acrobat (PDF) files, PostScript, and Microsoft PowerPoint files? A few search engines can search video files. Another consideration is language support. Can the search engine interpret and match queries in all the languages represented on the pages of the website? We have not nearly exhausted the number of options and issues for adding Search to your website. Searchtools.com and the other resources on Search listed on page 283 can get you off to a good start.

Optimizing Your Website for Web-Wide Search and Directories

Not only do we want to help people find their way around on our websites, we want to help them find our websites in the first place. Intranets are an important exception; here measures are taken to tell crawlers *not* to pick up the site.

One of the best ways to bring visitors to your website is through Web portals, such as Google, Northern Light, Yahoo, Excite, MSN, and AOL. Most, though not all, Web portals rely on Web-wide search engines to take users to their destinations.

In order for a Web-wide search engine to bring users to your website, it must index your website and assign your website a sufficiently high relevancy ranking for queries appropriate to your site. There are various measures designers and site owners take to get their websites "noticed" by Web-wide search engines. The job, however, is difficult. Because Web-wide search engines differ significantly in their technologies and policies, what works with one search engine does not necessarily work with another.

Let's consider the results that are retrieved when users interested in Centerville, Oregon, schools type "Centerville School District" into the query form of the search engine on the (fictitious) portal SuperDoodle:

> Centerville Florida School District Curriculum Resources
> Welcome to the Centerville School District Website, Centerville, Oregon.
> Partnership for Learning, Centerville School System, Centerville, West Virginia
> Arthur Luddinsky's Critique of the Expensive and Wasteful Centerville Schools
>   Technology Plan. No higher taxes!!!!!! No higher taxes!!!!!!

The Oregon Centerville School District is listed second, which is quite acceptable. Furthermore, if a user includes "Oregon" in the query, the appropriate Centerville School District will come up first.

The situation is far worse for Community Composting, which competes directly with many other composting websites and with the websites of companies selling composting equipment and supplies. With the query "composting," Community Composting appears as item 83 on SuperDoodle. Unless Community Composting is doing better with other search engines, the site owners need to optimize their site to get better results.

Submitting a Website

An important step a website owner can take is to "submit" the website to various Web-wide search engines. This entails completing an online form with information about the site. Although search engines will probably index an unsubmitted site, there may well be a delay of several months before the crawler finds its way to the website.

Because few people want to take the trouble to submit their website to the dozens of major portals, there are services, such as website-submission.com and Submitit.com, that will submit your website to many search engines for a fee. Avoid services that make outlandish claims about the placement they will achieve for your site or suggest that they will use unscrupulous strategies. In some instances you will succeed better with a portal if you personally complete the portal's submission form rather than relying on a service.

Seeding a Website for the Crawler

Another step a website owner can take is to "seed" the website for Web-wide search engines. That is, you can add keywords and make other modifications to improve your rankings. For example, the designers of the Centerville School District website added these keywords to their home page: Centerville, Oregon, school system, high school, middle school, elementary school, K–12, instruction, education. Note that these keywords do not contribute in any way to site-specific searching.

Web-wide search engines, like site-specific search engines, give special weighting to words that appear in the HTML title tag and in headings. Some Web-wide search engines rank words higher if they appear near the top of the page and give extra weight if two or more words in a user's query appear in proximity to each other on the page. Websites with numerous graphics do worse than sites consisting mainly of text, though crawlers do evaluate the ALT tags that describe graphics. Websites with pages generated dynamically from a database have trouble getting noticed by search engines, although there are ways to address this problem. Frames also cause special problems for search engines. The techniques for preparing a website for both Web-wide and site-specific searching will change significantly as XML becomes a standard.

To achieve higher rankings, some webmasters try a wide range of tricks, such as repeating the same keyword many times on one page or using the names of competing companies as keywords. Portals, however, are very shrewd about uncovering and defeating such tricks, and some will drop a website from their index for engaging in unscrupulous practices.

Some Web-wide search engines rank websites by calculating the number of incoming links to that website. The premise is that if numerous sites have built links to yours, you have worthwhile content. Some engines go still further and calculate the traffic on these incoming links.

Your website will be more valuable to your users if you provide external links to relevant websites. Furthermore, if you can arrange for reciprocal linking between these websites and yours, you may well boost your ranking with some important search engines.

Web Directories

Some Web portals take the form of a directory rather than a search engine. Increasingly, portals are both. You should certainly submit your site to directories as well as to search engine portals. Directories are created by human editors who evaluate a great many individual websites, decide which to include in the directory, and catalog the chosen websites according to the directory's hierarchy of subject areas. Well-known directories include Lycos, Yahoo, About.com, Looksmart.com, and Open Directory, which uses volunteer editors to review and catalog the sites.

Instead of typing a query, users click their way down the branches of the directory's wide and deep hierarchy to find websites that seem to meet their needs. For example, a user looking for websites about composting might start on the Home and Garden branch, drill down to Garden, then to Gardening Techniques, and finally to Composting.

Purchasing Priority

Ideally, portals would not accept payment from website owners for improved placement in results lists and directory lists and for other kinds of priority treatment. The reality, however, is far different. Because crawlers can take many weeks or months to find a new website (and may miss it altogether), search engine portals often charge for a fast-track submission service. Increasingly, they "rent" the top results-list placement for various search terms. A low-budget website such as Community Composting will definitely be at a disadvantage against the Amalgamated Composting Equipment and Supply Corporation and other companies that will pay for high placement whenever users type "compost" as a search term. Similarly directories often charge for inclusion or for priority listing as "featured sites."

Portals whose placements are biased by payment not only pose a major problem for site owners, but degrade the Web experience for users. This is especially true when a portal does not clearly reveal its biases. Users should pay attention to how Web portals operate and avoid portals with objectionable policies.

Good information on optimizing for search engines and directories is available from Search Engine Watch (searchenginewatch.com) and Searchengines.com. You can also learn a great deal by checking the submission guidelines of various portals.

Indexes on the Web

Along with site maps and Search, the website index is the user's third alternative to page-to-page navigation. Web indexes look and function somewhat like traditional back-of-book indexes: Both consist of an alphabetical list of index terms. But while print index entries employ page numbers to direct users to relevant pages, each Web index entry is a link, a standard HTML link, to the page most relevant to the term. (More complex Web indexes with index entries that link to multiple pages are possible but rarely seen.) A typical Web index is shown in Figure 12.9.

In contrast to Search, indexes are usually created by skilled human indexers who study the website, think of appropriate index entries, and decide which page is most relevant to each index entry. Showing users the most relevant page is, in fact, the main strength of Web indexes. For example, on the World Bank website a search with the query "mining" retrieves 300 results; however, the index entry "mining" takes the user to the home page of the World Bank's mining department subsite. This is almost certainly the single most generally useful page on mining. If the user wants to know about the World Bank's involvement in copper mining in Brazil, a search query is ideal. If the user wants a good general starting point about mining, the index is very effective.

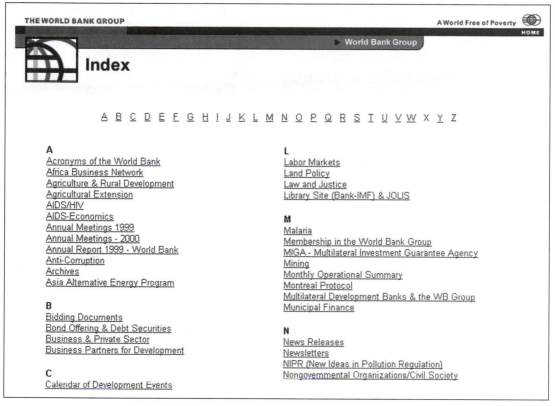

Figure 12.9. A typical Web index. Each index entry links to the Web page most relevant to that entry. (www.worldbank.com)

> **Dogs, movies about**
>   Dog of Flanders, A
>   Lady and the Tramp
>   Lassie
>   My Dog Skip
>   Top Dog

Figure 12.10. A two-level index entry from a movie review website.

Web indexes can also contain two levels of specificity. For example, a movie review website might include an index that lists movies by title, director, starring actors, and subject matter. Therefore, as shown in Figure 12.10, you might see a main subject heading for dogs with subentries for each movie that the indexer, reading all the reviews, judged to be about dogs.

This index will prove more effective than Search for people who think they might like to watch a movie about dogs. The query "dog" in a search engine should retrieve all the movies about dogs but will likely retrieve movies such as *Wag the Dog* and *Dog Day Afternoon,* which have nothing to do with dogs. On the other hand, a scholar studying movies about dogs might use Search to pick up incidental comments about dogs appearing in any of the movie reviews.

The Feasibility of a Web Index

Web indexes are not highly prevalent. This is largely because a good index is an intellectually demanding, time-consuming task and especially because maintaining an index is a real headache if the content of the website changes often. In contrast, a back-of-book index remains up-to-date for the life of the book.

Furthermore, Web indexes do not serve an irreplaceable function. What an index uncovers for the user, the user can also get, though often less conveniently, with the Search feature. Finally, Web indexes work best when the subject matter is semantically dispersed. In other words, an index is apt to be more useful on the World Bank site, which deals with many diverse projects taking place throughout the world, or a site encompassing thousands of movies than for a website like Zompco's where much of the information is tightly interwoven around the company's products and doesn't span a broad range of topics. Still, a good index prepared for the right kind of website will be greatly appreciated by users.

Creating a Good Index

Users of a Web index, somewhat like users of Search, begin with an information need. They don't formulate a query, but they do need to identify a word or phrase that is pertinent to their information need. The index, however, will do nothing for the user unless this word or phrase (or a variant form) appears as an index entry.

A good Web index, therefore, includes synonyms, alternative phrasings, and related terms. For example, the World Bank index includes the index entry "Agriculture & Rural Development." But it also includes an alternative phrasing (called an "inversion") "Rural Development & Agriculture." By inverting the two parts of the index entry, the indexer has doubled the likelihood that a user looking for a Web page on this topic will find it. Another inversion is "Development, Rural Areas." A good synonym is "Farming."

Providing these extra index terms is called "rich indexing." Rich indexing adds greatly to the effort involved in creating an index, but it also adds enormous value. Without rich indexing, the indexer is in effect saying to the user, "Make the right guess, or you're out of luck." The exception is the occasional user who is determined or desperate enough to scan the entire index looking for an entry to match his or her information need.

How do indexers know what words users will think of? They don't—at least not with any certainty. But they work hard to understand the information needs and vocabulary of users. They also review search logs and participate in user testing.

Preparing a Web index consists of these steps:

1. Examine the website looking carefully for the main topics. Decide which page is most relevant for each of these topics. (For example, which is the most important mining page.) Then think of appropriate index entries for this page, such as "mining" and "extraction industries." These are your "content-derived" index entries.

2. Think about your users and their information needs. Try to imagine them using your website. What questions would they be asking themselves? What words would they use when consulting the index? Work directly with users to get this information. Then determine which Web page is the most relevant for each of these words.

3. Carefully merge the two groups of index entries, avoiding entries that are too similar to be useful (e.g., farms and farming). Edit the entries, format the index pages in an attractive and functional manner, and build the links.

To compile a good Web index, you should understand back-of-book indexing. For a good book on back-of-book indexing, see Larry Bonura (1994).

Summary

1. The site map and Search feature are important alternatives to standard page-to-page navigation via links. Less prevalent but often very helpful to users is the index, the Web equivalent of the traditional back-of-book index.

2. Site maps offer users a global view of a website's structure and allow them to directly access a destination page by clicking a link labeled with the name of that page.

3. Site maps are especially beneficial for websites that employ the web-like information structure and for complex multipath structures. With these less orderly structures users have extra difficulty inferring the overall structure of the site from the links offered on individual pages.

4. Today's site maps present some significant problems: maintenance, scope, and inconvenience to the user. To ease the maintenance problem, website owners favor basic site map designs that consist of easily updateable lists of text links.

5. The problem of scope refers to the limited number of pages that can be represented on the site map due to the relatively small viewing area provided by computer monitors. To maximize the scope of a site map, designers abbreviate page names and use various means of grouping and subordination to fit as many links as possible into the limited amount of screen space.

6. Site maps are inconvenient to use. In particular, they require users to switch their attention from the current content page to the site map and back to a new content page. Likewise with the Search feature and index. Scrolling and multi-page site maps can improve scope but are especially inconvenient. Displaying a site map in a supplementary window improves convenience. Another technique is to provide a "mini site map" on each page of a website.

7. Promising new site-map technologies are addressing the problems of maintenance, scope, and convenience. There are tools to produce site maps that can be updated semi-automatically. Inxight's Star Tree site map provides a "fish-eye" (hyperbolic) view and can display more levels than are normally feasible. Manipulating the site map with the mouse pointer provides relatively convenient interaction.

8. The perfect site map is the ideal means of Web navigation. In a theoretical sense, all of our nav bars, nav columns, and other links are just an attempt to approximate this perfect site map.

9. The Search feature, or just "Search," treats the contents of the website as information in a database. The search engine's crawler builds a data file known as the index. When the user types search terms in the query form, the search engine interprets and simplifies the query, consults the current index file, and generates a results list consisting of brief descriptions and a link to each retrieved page.

10. Users try to formulate queries that closely reflect their information need (highly pertinent queries). They hope for a minimum of irrelevant results in the results list (high precision), and, depending on the situation, they may require a thorough search (high level of recall). In general, a higher recall requires lower precision. It is important for search results to be ranked by relevance in the results list. Users are unlikely to scan through a long results list.

11. A great many users stick to typing basic queries in a basic query form. Extended query forms allow for more sophisticated options. These include pattern matching with Boolean logic, designating search zones, and customizing the results list. Most basic query forms will actually accept sophisticated queries if users learn the search engine's query syntax.

12. Users should be able to access Search from every (or nearly every) page. A desirable approach, a layering strategy, is to place the basic query form on every page with a link to a dedicated search page with an extended form.

13. Most search engines can compile a "search log" of your users' search activity: the number of searches conducted, the terms used, and the queries that did not produce a match. This data can tell you whether you need to add new keywords and whether you are providing the information your users are looking for.

14. Make sure your search engine provides the capabilities you need. You can program your own search engine, obtain a search engine product and install it on your website's server, or use a remote search service (including services available from your ISP). Very possibly you can implement the Search feature without cost.

15. One of the best ways to bring visitors to your website is through Web portals. You should submit your website to portals and take other steps so that your site will appear high in their results lists. Many portals charge for priority treatment. Website owners should "seed" their sites for search engines by adding special keywords and through other means. Search engine portals are skillful at defeating the unscrupulous seeding tricks that some website owners employ.

16. Web indexes consist of an alphabetical list of index terms. Each Web index entry is a standard HTML link to the page most relevant to the term. Quickly showing users the most relevant page is the main strength of Web indexes. For example, the index entry "mining" will link to the most central of, say, 300 pages pertaining to mining.

17. Indexes are not prevalent because indexes are difficult to create and maintain, because they do not serve an irreplaceable function, and because they work best when the subject matter is semantically dispersed. Even so, a good index prepared for the right kind of website will be greatly appreciated by users.

18. Web indexes are created by skilled human indexers. A major indexing challenge is "rich indexing," providing synonyms, alternative phrasings, and related terms to increase the chance that there will be an index entry corresponding to the word the user has in mind when consulting the index.

References

Bonura, Larry S. 1994. *The Art of Indexing.* New York: Wiley.

Korfhage, Robert. 1997. *Information Storage and Retrieval.* New York: Wiley.

Rosenfeld, Louis, and Peter Morville. 1998. *Information Architecture for the World Wide Web.* Sebastopol, CA: O'Reilly & Associates.

Search Engine Watch. Danny Sullivan, ed. www.searchenginewatch.com

Search section. www.webmonkey.com

Searchengines.com. www.searchengines.com

Searching section. www.usableweb.com

Searchtools.com. Avi Rappoport. www.searchtools.com

Sonnenreich, Wes, and Tim McInta. 1998. *Web Developer.com Guide to Search Engines.* New York: Wiley.

Discussion and Application

Items for Discussion

1. Find three site maps that exhibit significant differences and answer these questions:

   - How are the site maps formatted? What techniques are used to show grouping and subordination?
   - What is the scope? Approximately how many nodes are represented on each of the site maps?
   - Assuming the site maps represent hierarchical websites, what is the deepest level of the hierarchy shown on the site map?
   - Are any special technologies used to make the site maps more effective?
   - Are there differences in the convenience of use?
   - Overall, which of the site maps is most successful and what design ideas contribute to that success?

2. Below are (1) the descriptions of the information needs of two parents who may move to Centerville and (2) the query each parent typed into the Search feature of the Centerville School District website. How effective do you think each query will be in satisfying the parent's information need?

Parent X has a child with a minor hearing loss and wants to know if the Centerville school system has an audiologist on staff. Parent X types this query:

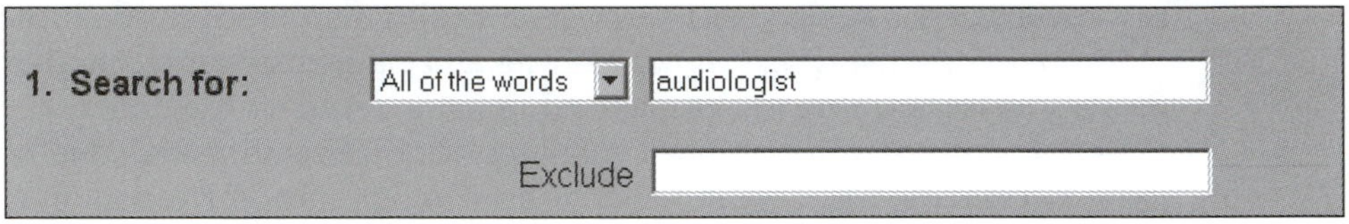

1. Search for: All of the words ▼ audiologist

Exclude

Figure 12.11. Querying the Centerville School District website regarding services for a child with a minor hearing loss.

Parent Y wants to find out how often graduates from Centerville high schools receive college and university scholarships because of their participation in the school's music program. Parent Y types this query:

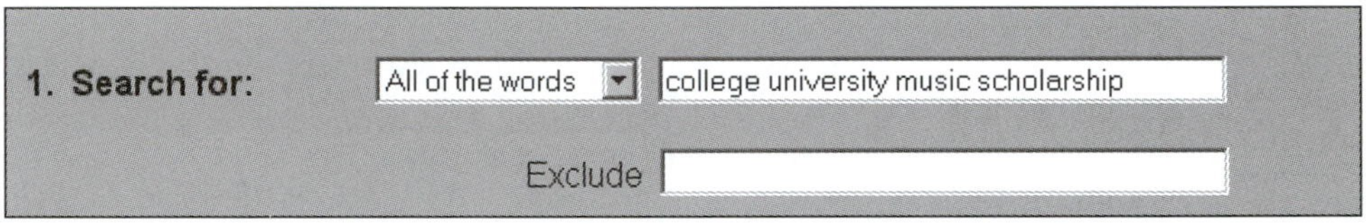

1. Search for: All of the words ▼ college university music scholarship

Exclude

Figure 12.12. Querying the Centerville School District website regarding music scholarships.

3. Assume you want to arrange for a remote service to provide the Search feature for your small business website. Explore the website of two companies that offer this service, and find out everything you need to know in order to decide which company you prefer. Key questions are these:

- Exactly what steps will I need to take to implement Search on the website?
- Will there be a charge?
- How often will the crawler update the website?
- What file formats does the service index?
- Do I receive server logs?
- Are there different levels of service and, if so, what are the benefits of the higher levels of service?
- What options are there for customizing the search query form?
- Does the service protect the privacy rights of clients (those who use the search service) and the rights of visitors to sites that use the service?

Websites to look at include Atomz (www.atomz.com), MondoSearch (www.mondosoft.com), and PicoSearch (www.picosearch.com).

4. Analyze the way you typically use a website's Search feature. Answer these questions:

   - Do you use the extended search query form or the basic query form?
   - Do you use Boolean logic when you think about and type your queries?
   - Is there a typical number of results list entries that you are willing to scan?
   - What is your general level of satisfaction with site-specific searching?

5. Figure 12.13 shows an extended query form that differs significantly from the form shown in Figure 12.7. Analyze this form and explain the similarities and differences. Indicate if there are equivalents to these matches: (1) Any of the words, (2) All of the words, (3) Exact words, (4) Exclude. Is this an effective query form?

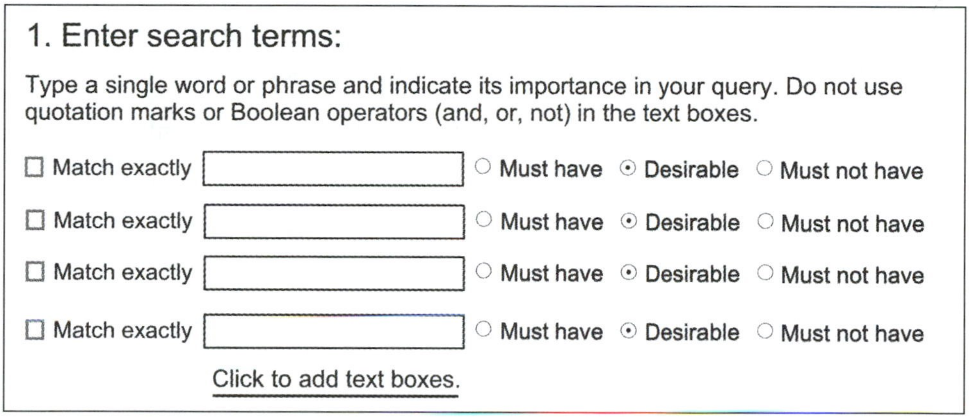

1. Enter search terms:

Type a single word or phrase and indicate its importance in your query. Do not use quotation marks or Boolean operators (and, or, not) in the text boxes.

☐ Match exactly [   ]   ○ Must have ⊙ Desirable ○ Must not have

☐ Match exactly [   ]   ○ Must have ⊙ Desirable ○ Must not have

☐ Match exactly [   ]   ○ Must have ⊙ Desirable ○ Must not have

☐ Match exactly [   ]   ○ Must have ⊙ Desirable ○ Must not have

Click to add text boxes.

Figure 12.13. An extended query form with non-standard pattern matching.

6. Examine three or four websites with results lists that exhibit significant differences. How are the lists formatted? Which do you consider most useful? What design ideas do you like?

7. Think of an information need you have (other than a potential purchase) and a website that will enable you to answer that information need. The website must have a site map and a Search feature. Formulate an effective query for that information need, perform the search, and use the results list to obtain a satisfactory answer. How efficient was the process?

   Examine the site map from the perspective of another individual trying to satisfy the same information need. How effective would the site map be in comparison with the search you performed? Will the user find the same information more quickly or less quickly using the site map?

8. Discuss Web indexes from the perspective of precision and recall.

9. Examine the World Bank index and at least one other Web index. How do they differ? How much rich indexing do you see? How well do you think

they serve the needs of their intended audiences? The World Bank index can be found under the heading Other Resources on the World Bank Search page (www.worldbank.org/search.htm). Two interesting Web indexes you can examine are these:

- The index to Leicester University, in the City of Leicester in Great Britain. The index is accessible from the Leicester University home page: www.le.ac.uk
- The Patron Saints Index. This is an indexed encyclopedia of Saints of the Roman Catholic Church. www.catholic-forum.com/saints/indexsnt.htm

Application to Your Project

1. Consider whether your site would benefit from a site map, a Search feature, and an index. With a clear focus on your website and your audience, investigate how to best design and implement whichever forms of information access you decide to incorporate.
2. Develop a plan for building traffic to your website. The plan should include optimizing your website for Web-wide search engines and directories. In certain instances, such as a website intended for family and friends, there may be no reason to try to draw other people to the site.

13

Non-Hierarchical Information Structures

Introduction

Although the hierarchy, in its various forms, is by far the most prevalent hypermedia information structure, other structures have been identified (Parunak 1991; Horton 1994). These are the most important non-hierarchical structures:

- Linear
- Multipath
- Matrix
- Web-like

These structures have been discussed in various contexts throughout the book. Now they are our focus.

You will definitely encounter situations in which one of the non-hierarchical information structures is the best way to organize your website or a part of your website. If you understand which structure is most appropriate and how to use it, you can better express the most significant relationships in the content you are presenting, provide the most efficient navigation, and create the most satisfying user experience.

We introduce each structure by describing its defining characteristics. Then we consider the following:

- The main uses of the structure
- How to design the interface for the structure
- The writing issues associated with the structure

The Linear Structure

In the linear structure, nodes are connected in one long chain. Linear structures are designed with the general expectation that users will navigate mostly forward, though possibly with some backward navigation, along this chain of nodes. The linear structure, then, is very orderly but highly restrictive.

Uses

Use the linear structure to encourage or require users to view information in a particular sequence. Very often we see this structure in tutorials, demos, and other kinds of instructional content where the designer wants to control how users will encounter the subject matter. Similarly, the linear structure is used for complex arguments and explanations where a particular sequence is important and also for historical or other chronologically structured material. For example, a portion of the elaborate Bacardi & Company website (www.bacardi.com) presents the company's 140-year history as a chain of nodes, each on a separate physical Web page, each with a title and a clear-cut organizing principle (many are organized by decade, such as "1920s").

Although linearity is the norm in many print genres, notably fiction, and is the rule in cinema, television, and music, the Web is very much a non-linear medium. Therefore, when extended content is presented linearly, users are apt to become restless unless your content truly corresponds to their needs and interests.

Interface Issues

Nothing more than Next and Previous buttons are needed to provide a basic interface for the linear information structure. Often, however, designers provide a more complete interface by increasing context and navigational freedom.

Increasing Context and Navigational Freedom

At times users are content to "fly blind," trusting that each successive page in a linear sequence will be relevant and worth looking at. On the other hand, users often like to know where they are going and can benefit from a reminder of where they've been. You can increase the context simply by labeling the Next and Previous buttons with the names of the two adjacent pages.

You can provide greater freedom with accelerator links, such as accelerator links that take the user to the first and last page of the sequence. Figure 13.1a illustrates both of these design options.

Still greater navigational freedom can be provided with all-to-all accelerator links, shown in Figure 13.1b. These accelerator links can be classified as systematic secondary links.

Figure 13.1c shows six links with all-to-all linking and all links labeled. Notice that this page has a familiar look: The nav column is what we typically use to link the sibling nodes in a hierarchy. Here, however, the subject matter of the six nodes calls

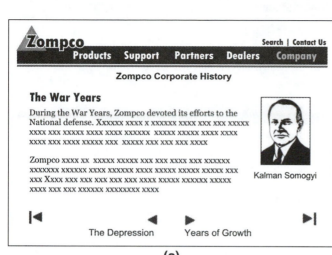

(a)

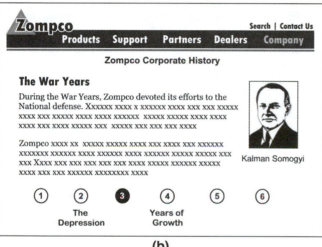

(b)

(c)

Figure 13.1. A linear structure with first and last accelerator links (represented by "arrow plus wall" icons); with all-to-all accelerator links; and with a nav column providing fully labeled, all-to-all linking.

for a linear sequence, and so the designer, to encourage users to regard these nodes as a linear sequence and to visit them linearly, has numbered the links.

The Ring

We can also increase navigational freedom by letting users cycle back and forth between the first and last node. In other words, we can turn a linear sequence into a ring. Rings promote a casual, even aimless kind of browsing. Users are discouraged from thinking, "OK, I've reached the end. I'm done." Instead they may continue to browse unhurriedly through pages they've already visited. An online collection of haiku, an online art gallery, or an online jewelry store might benefit from a ring structure.

Writing Issues

In the linear structure, the writing and the other content elements appearing on each node do not need to be modular. Writers can employ suspense, foreshadowing, flashbacks, and other narrative techniques; they can interweave ideas, just as in a traditional narrative and exposition.

On the other hand, you can fully modularize each page in a linear structure. Although modular writing (as we saw in the case of the Electronic Labyrinth) can be intellectually sophisticated, modularity can also be used as a strategy for making material less complex and so easier to read and learn. For example, if a website explaining dinosaurs to children included a linear sequence of eight pages, each explaining one of the eight ages of the dinosaurs (Triassic, Jurassic, etc.), the writer might avoid references to previous and upcoming pages and other forms of interweaving.

When the nodes of your linear sequence are not modular, consider carefully whether to provide all-to-all accelerator links to these nodes. This extra navigational freedom is beneficial for those who are familiar with the material or have a high tolerance for open-endedness, but users may also jump into a zone of confusion. As always, greater navigational freedom is not inherently better; it depends on the nature of the content and how the website will be used.

The Multipath Structure

The multipath structure, like the linear structure, carries the user from a starting node to an end node. The multipath structure, however, is not a chain. Segments are linear but the structure is characterized by branching.

Due to this branching, the multipath structure provides significantly more navigational freedom than the linear structure, but is less orderly, sometimes much less so. Multipath structures are rarely modular; there are strong and often complex dependency relationships. Stated differently, to productively read a Web page that appears toward the end of the structure, you must have read the appropriate pages earlier in the structure.

Uses

Like the linear structure, the multipath structure is very often used for teaching, guiding users through a procedure, and narratives. The multipath structure, however, because it branches, fulfills these roles differently. The branching takes two basic forms: (1) spur nodes and (2) split-join nodes. Each expresses a different logical relationship. Spur nodes offer a voluntary digression, an opportunity to view supplemental content. Split-joins represent a choice between two (or more) treatments of comparable material. Recalling the theoretical perspective of the Web as a dialog (Chapter 6, "Hypertext Theory"), the spur is akin to the lecturer who pauses at times to ask if you would like a point explained in greater depth and the split-join to the lecturer who asks which of two ways you would like a point explained.

Spur Nodes for Supplementary Content

With spur (or "satellite") nodes you invite the user to take a voluntary detour from the pathway of required core nodes to visit optional nodes before rejoining the pathway of core nodes. You can think of core and spur nodes as the linear structure with layering.

As shown in Figure 13.2a–d, there are various configurations of core and spur nodes. Figure 13.2a shows that a spur node can consist of a small or large amount of content. Figure 13.2b shows that a core node may have more than one spur node and that two core nodes may share a spur node. Figure 13.2c shows that a spur can take the form of a digression with multiple nodes, probably covering a related but different topic. We also see that spurs may originate their own spurs or link off in further directions—though there is a danger that the user will wander off and never return to the core nodes. Figure 13.2d shows that the designer can encourage (or even require) the user to proceed from a spur node to the next core node in the sequence.

The tutorial shown in Figure 13.3 employs the spur node form of the multipath structure. The eight core nodes provide the essential information about the MondoSearch remote search service. Each of the core node pages, however, contains links to one or more spur nodes offering supplementary information. These links appear as both Read More text links and hot graphics.

Spur nodes are very prevalent on the Web. The website 2020 Green (http://2020green.com), sponsored by the Aetna Corporation, consists of numerous brief lessons that instruct young people on various aspects of money management. Each core node originates several spurs that invite the student to explore a topic in more depth.

The Endurance website (www.kodak.com/US/en/corp/features/endurance/home/index.shtml) is a multipath documentary narrative recounting Sir Ernest Shackleton's Antarctica expedition of 1915. Each core node provides links to spur nodes consisting of photographs taken by Frank Hurley during the expedition. The photographs appear in small supplementary windows that the user dismisses to return to a core node and proceed with the story of the expedition. The Endurance and 2020 Green are among many multipath designs produced

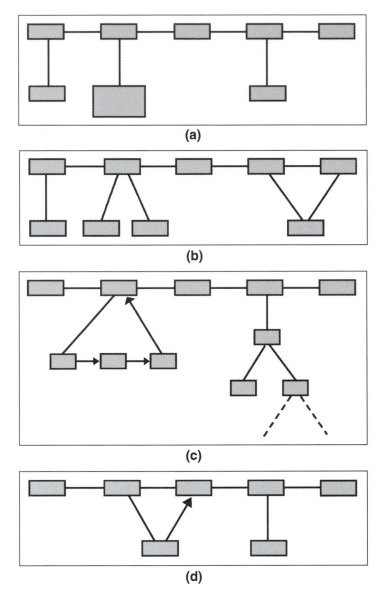

Figure 13.2. Node-link diagrams showing possible implementations of the spur node form of the multipath structure.

by the outstanding design firm Second Story (www.secondstory.com). Their website includes a portfolio section with commentary on these and other Second Story projects.

Split-Joins for Alternative Content

Split-joins present alternative pathways offering parallel information. Several possible implementations of the split-join are shown in Figure 13.4a–c.

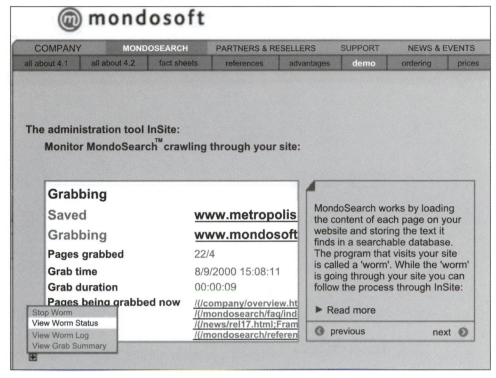

Figure 13.3. A multipath tutorial with spur nodes. The plus (+) icon at the lower left signals a hot graphic. A Read More link is at the bottom of the text column. (www.mondosoft.com)

Figure 13.4a shows a brief split-join, consisting of just two alternative nodes. Figure 13.4b shows an extended split-join, a sequence of parallel nodes. Figure 13.4c shows that complex configurations are possible. In all cases, however, the split-join offers alternatives: If the user takes one route, there is no need to take the other. Because significant branching is inherent to the multipath structure, there is little reason to think about secondary links.

Recall the example of a split-join presented in Chapter 10, "Writing," Figure 10.4. Users of an online textbook on statistics can choose between learning multivariate regression with a social sciences emphasis or with a natural sciences emphasis. These two alternatives converge in a single treatment of simultaneous regression.

Split-joins also occur in lengthy instructions, for example, the instructions that are often found on home improvement websites. The instructions for building a back yard deck might split when different conditions require different steps. That is, the section of the instructions explaining how to build footings might split so that the user can choose between a page dealing with level ground and a page dealing with sloping ground.

Checkout

One major use of the multipath structure is checkout and similar transactions in e-commerce websites. Transactions, however, are a special case of the multipath

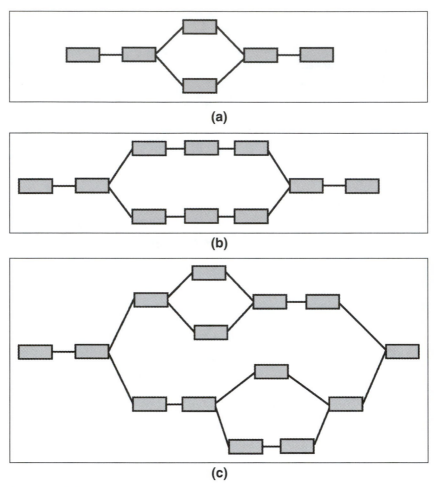

Figure 13.4. Node-link diagrams showing possible implementations of the split-join form of the multipath structure.

structure. This is because the branching logic is not reflected closely in the pages the user sees, the nodes that are visited.

Consider the flow diagram of a checkout procedure shown in Figure 13.5. If the user chooses the gift option on the Billing page, the website displays a spur node, an actual page pertaining to gifts. On the other hand, when the user chooses the method of payment, a split-join, the two payment options (credit card or credit certificate) are both handled on the same page. Here the split is only logical. In other words, because transactions are online computing functions, branching is reflected in the underlying system state but not necessarily in the user navigation.

Interface Issues

Just as with the linear structure, the two key dimensions of multipath interface design are context and navigational freedom. As we saw in the Mondosoft tutor-

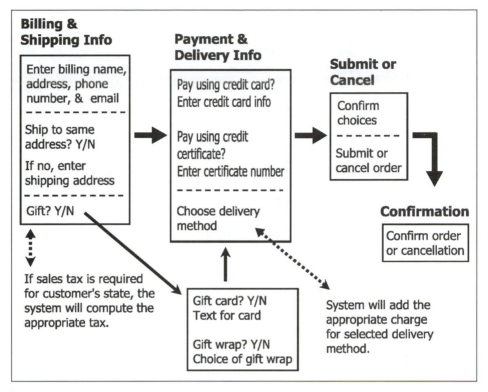

Figure 13.5. The logical branching of a checkout procedure. The branching does not correspond to the actual page-to-page navigation.

ial (Figure 13.3), Next, Previous, and Read More links often suffice for short, simple structures. On the other hand, as shown in Figure 13.6, designers may want to provide greater context and navigational freedom. Here the six core nodes are linked all-to-all with accelerator links, and the two nodes adjacent to the current node are labeled. Furthermore, the spur node is identified with the specific label "Women in the War Years." The most complete possible multipath interface, shown in Figure 13.7, is, in effect, a site map; it provides total context and direct access to every node in the sequence.

Some multipath websites manage the branching in the user's behalf. For example, educational websites that employ adaptive learning strategies quiz the learner or gauge learning in other ways and then guide the learner through the content. The system will decide that Student A needs the extra explanation available on a spur node but that Student B should take the fast track through a particular lesson. The system might even jump Student A back to an early part of the lesson.

Writing Issues

It is not easy to write and create other types of content for multipath structures. These structures almost always entail complex dependency relationships. In the case

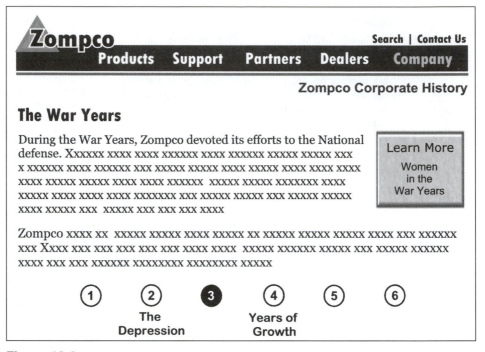

Figure 13.6. A multipath design with significant context and navigational freedom.

of spurs, the author must be careful that all of the information presented in spur nodes is truly supplemental. Nothing in a core node can build upon what's been presented in a spur node, or the author has violated his implicit contract with the user.

Similarly, in the case of a split-join, both alternatives must prepare the user for whatever follows when the split pathways converge. Nothing in the explanation of simultaneous regression can be based upon information that appeared in the social science treatment of multivariate regression but not in the natural science treatment and visa versa.

You can see that for even a moderately long multipath structure, the dependency relationships will be difficult to keep track of. In the same way, if the author of a textbook declares in the preface that Chapters 4, 7, and 8, are optional chapters, this author must remember to honor this commitment and not present material in Chapter 12 that builds upon one of these optional chapters. Designers often shy away from lengthy and complex multipath structures because of the difficulty of managing the dependencies.

The Matrix Structure

The matrix information structure, shown in Figure 13.8, is the hypertext equivalent of a traditional print table. Readers scan a print table's columns and rows to find the table cell with the desired information. On the Web, users navigate to the

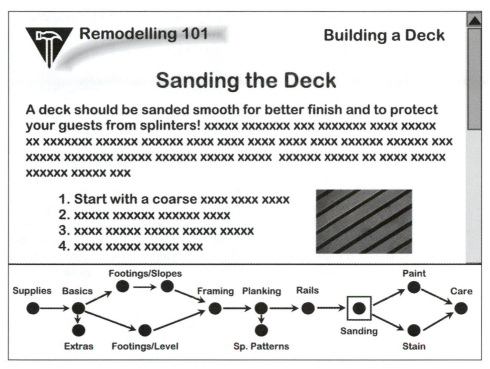

Figure 13.7. A page in a multipath structure with all links shown and labeled. This is the equivalent of a site map. Notice that framesets are used to allow the "site map" links to remain visible at all times; otherwise, the links would fall well below the scroll line.

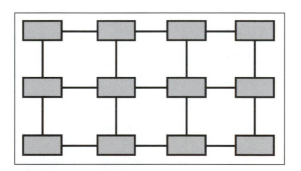

Figure 13.8. The matrix information structure.

desired table cell in a similar manner. However, whereas the cells in a print table are very limited in size, each individual cell of a Web matrix, when displayed by the user, fills the page's main content area.

Clearly the matrix is a very orderly structure. It also provides a considerable degree of navigational freedom. Excluding the exterior (the outer edges) of the matrix, the user can always navigate in four directions: left, right, up, and down.

Furthermore, as you will see, the user does not navigate one cell at a time. Rather, accelerated linking is integral to almost all matrix interfaces; the user can reach any cell in the matrix with two clicks.

Uses

The matrix structure is not very prevalent because it requires highly orderly subject matter that can be plotted along two axes and is useful to people as they navigate along either axis. Matrix websites are mostly used for what we can very broadly term "reference" purposes and, more specifically, the making of comparisons.

As shown in Figure 13.9, the online publisher and bookseller Fatbrain.com employs the matrix information structure to let users shop for books. Users can choose a subject area (e.g., Business, Engineering & Science, and so forth), and for each subject area they can choose a book category: New Titles, Bestsellers, Monthly Promotions, and Bookstore (featured books). The figure shows the page displaying the category New Titles in the subject area Business. But the matrix encourages us to peruse other business books in, say, the Bestsellers category as well as New Titles in other subject areas.

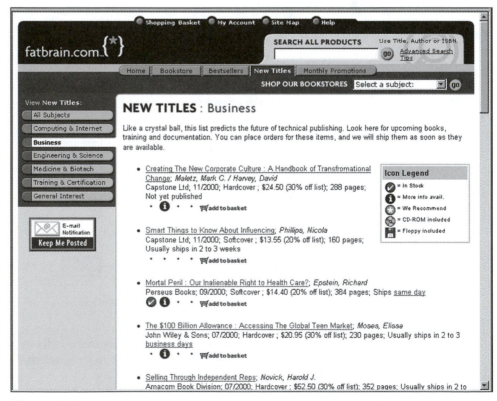

Figure 13.9. A Web page that is a node in the matrix information structure. (www.fatbrain.com)

Notice that while Fatbrain employs the "inverted L" combination of a nav bar and nav column, these interface elements serve a different role than they do in a hierarchy. In a matrix, there are no hierarchical levels and there is no navigating from general to specific. Rather, in this highly orderly structure the nav bar and nav column are the axes, or coordinates, of the matrix.

Fatbrain, however, is not exclusively a matrix structure. First the user needs to navigate into the matrix from the Fatbrain home page. Furthermore, each node in the matrix includes spur links to pages that describe a book in detail. Links to five of these spur nodes (for example, Creating the New Corporate Culture) can be seen in the figure.

For another use of the matrix structure, consider a medical reference dealing with respiratory conditions. One axis consists of the conditions; the other consists of categories of information: Definition, Causes, Prevalence, Pathology, Therapy, etc. A physician might want to know all the categories of information regarding a particular condition. Or, a physician might want to peruse one category of information, such as Diagnosis or Therapy, for several conditions—especially so because this medical reference deals with related conditions.

It is possible to organize historical material into a matrix structure. For example, if a small group of political leaders played key roles in a week-long historical event, a matrix structure might provide a narrative of each leader's activities on each of the seven days. So, for example, the user could examine the activities of all the individuals on the third day, examine the role of a particular individual for all seven days, or simply criss-cross the matrix in a casual manner.

Interface Issues

The key interface issue in regard to the matrix hierarchy is size. How do we design the interface when the matrix is large? In the case of Fatbrain, only 28 nodes make up the matrix: seven choices on the vertical axis and four on the horizontal axis (not counting the Home link at the far left of the nav bar). The Fatbrain interface, therefore, is very straightforward and intuitive, in large part because it strongly recalls the appearance of a print table with its column labels arrayed across the top and row labels running down the left side. But what about larger matrixes, when at least one of the axes consists of more links than will fit along the top or left side?

One solution, shown in Figure 13.10, can be seen in the student-produced Lurker's Guide to Babylon 5, a website for fans of the successful science fiction television series. The design problem here is that there are more than 100 episodes of Babylon 5. The solution is to let the user choose an episode from the drop-down list box (labeled "List") or to click through each episode in the series using the Next and Previous (right and left) arrows. So, for example, the user can view the synopsis of the 100th episode by choosing that episode from the drop-down list box and then view the synopsis of the 99th or 101st episode by clicking on the arrows. (A minor flaw in the interface is that the horizontal orientation of the arrows suggests that the arrows operate on the horizontal axis—for example, that clicking the right arrow would display the credits for "Comes the Inquisitor.")

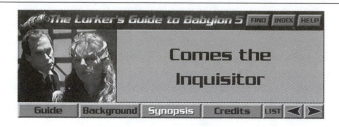

Synopsis by Matthew Murray (mmurray@wsu.edu)

In the Zocalo, G'Kar tries to convince the patrons that the Narn were only the first victims at the hands of the Centauri, and that more will follow. The patrons, however, become little more than annoyed, claiming that the Centauri are only the Narn's problem. G'Kar tries to warn them otherwise, but they refuse to listen to him. Eventually, another Narn convinces G'Kar to stop his speech. Vir, standing on a walkway above, has heard it all.

Delenn walks to the end of a darkened corridor where she sees Kosh partially hidden in the shadows. "Lennier said you were

Figure 13.10. A matrix interface that can accommodate a large number of items on one axis of the matrix. (The Lurker's Guide is no longer on the Web.)

When matrixes get really large, for example, if there are dozens or more choices on both the vertical and horizontal axes, the interface will likely rely on drop-down list boxes on both axes and the Search feature. Now the website takes on the character of a database that the user queries rather than an information space of nodes and links that the user navigates.

Symmetrical Hierarchies

It is important not to confuse the matrix structure with a near relative, the symmetrical hierarchy. There is certainly nothing wrong with symmetrical hierarchies—but troubles will arise for the designer who cannot clearly distinguish between them.

Let's say the Zompco Corporation publishes a print service manual explaining routine maintenance for five of their products. The service manual is organized as shown in Figure 13.11. You can see that the exact same section headings appear under each chapter. This is why it's called a symmetrical hierarchy. Might such a manual be converted to a matrix website? No way—even though the highly regular character of the symmetrical hierarchy suggests that a matrix might be possible. First, each chapter may have been written as a linear sequence (e.g., you can't adequately understand the section about testing Product 3 unless you've read the preceding sections of that chapter). Second, even if each section in the manual were completely modular, few people would have any reason to read, say, the Parts, Materials, and Tools sections for multiple products. In other words, one reason this manual would fail as a matrix is because there isn't a good reason to use it as a matrix.

The Internet Movie Database (IMDb) is partly an online database but is also an effectively designed symmetrical hierarchy. In its most typical mode of

Product 1
Determining When Maintenance is Required
Parts, Materials, and Tools
Maintenance Procedures
Testing and Re-installation

Product 2
Determining When Maintenance is Required
Parts, Materials, and Tools
Maintenance Procedures
Testing and Re-installation

Product 3
Determining When Maintenance is Required
Parts, Materials, and Tools
Maintenance Procedures
Testing and Re-installation

Product 4
Determining When Maintenance is Required
Parts, Materials, and Tools
Maintenance Procedures
Testing and Re-installation

Product 5
Determining When Maintenance is Required
Parts, Materials, and Tools
Maintenance Procedures
Testing and Re-installation

Figure 13.11. The table of contents of a print service manual that is organized as a symmetrical hierarchy.

use, the user types a movie title into the text box of the Search feature and displays a page with key facts (the "main details") about the movie, as shown in Figure 13.12. The links along the left allow the user to display 40 categories of information about the movie. Note that the Main Details link is highlighted in white and its selection circle is marked. Note also that selection circles are grayed when there is no information available for particular categories.

The information in each category is modular; the user can click any category in any order. But this website is not a matrix. Although this website is very richly linked, you cannot directly navigate "across" the rows, displaying, for example,

Figure 13.12. An implementation of a symmetrical hierarchy.
(www.imdb.com)

the main details for the entire collection of movies. To design a true matrix interface for this website would be difficult indeed; moreover, because IMDb is a collection of diverse movies rather than a highly focused collection (such as
respiratory diseases or episodes of a TV series), there is much less reason to employ the true matrix structure.

Writing Issues

The writing issues for the matrix are largely implicit from the previous discussion. When you write for a matrix, each node must be modular. Furthermore,
keep in mind that users are criss-crossing the matrix along two axes. Therefore,
you want to write text and develop other content so that it will be as useful as
possible however the user is accessing the page. For example, the writer of the
Emphysema Diagnosis page of the medical reference should describe the symp-

toms both for the person carefully studying emphysema and for the person who is comparing the symptoms of numerous respiratory conditions.

The Web-Like Structure

The web-like information structure is not defined by any set of rules. Anything can be linked to anything. Therefore, the web-like structure is very apt to be unsystematic, even when each link is thought out with great care. Like the matrix, but unlike the other structures, there is no inherent "directional flow," no tendency for the links to carry the user to an end node, down to the bottom of a hierarchy, or anywhere else. The entry point is arbitrary, which is also true of the matrix.

The web-like structure always provides ample navigational freedom. Just how much depends entirely on how densely the web is linked. Two examples of the web-like information structure, one sparsely and one densely linked, are shown in Figure 13.13.

The most extreme possibility is all-to-all linking. This results in a vast number of links (as expressed by the formula $X = (N^2 - N)/2$, where N is the number of nodes). All-to-all linking is almost always a mistake. Not only will the user become overwhelmed by the number of links (except in the very smallest of structures), but the author is not offering any sort of guidance to the user. Instead, authors provide a moderate number of very carefully considered links.

Although this information structure is almost always referred to as a web or as web-like, it is actually misleading to use the term "web" to denote a lack of

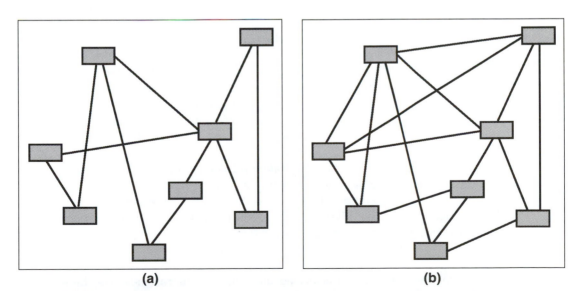

(a)   (b)

Figure 13.13. Two examples of the web-like structure—one with sparse linking and one with dense linking.

structure. Most webs in the physical world are produced by orb spiders and are, in fact, surprisingly systematic. Indeed, these spider webs are somewhat matrix-like and somewhat like radial hierarchies, where the branches emanate (spoke-like) from a central point. It is only a much smaller group of spiders, the cob spiders, that produce disorderly webs. Unstructured websites, then, are web-like only in that they resemble cobwebs. So, too, the World Wide Web, a vast and utterly unstructured set of individual websites, is nothing like the spider webs we usually encounter.

The unsystematic nature of the web-like information structure complicates navigation. The user's prospects for understanding the overall node-link structure are greatly reduced. When the user sees a link to any particular node, the user may or may not be able to guess the subject matter of the nodes that lie beyond that node. There is no broad principle governing linking, such as the principle of general to specific that characterizes the hierarchy. Though we refer to these links as primary links, they are associative in character, individual invitations to pages the designer thinks you might want to visit next.

Uses

The web-like structure will not serve the needs of a busy purchasing manager who needs 200 rotary brushes and wants to know about the features of the various Zompco products. It would be a strange online bookstore in which the book description pages were linked according to no other principle than the owner's interests and tastes. Although attempts have been made, the web-like structure has not proven to be a good way to teach chemistry, art history, or other organized bodies of knowledge.

But there are good uses for the web-like structure. Recall the Electronic Labyrinth website and the All Music Guide discussed in Chapter 10, "Writing." Both follow the encyclopedic model; they consist of individual articles that are enriched by extensive linking.

Mark Bernstein's Hypertext Gardens, shown in Figure 13.14, does not follow the encyclopedic model but rather is a carefully crafted essay that cogently presents the virtues of unsystematic information structures. Bernstein celebrates gardens and parks as a model for hypertext because they are more regular and navigable than an unplanned wilderness but more engaging than a highly regular structure.

Often, web-like websites partly take on the character of other structures. Although the Electronic Labyrinth encourages people to use the web-like aspect of its interface, it also provides a table of contents and a time-line, and so is in part hierarchical and linear. Hypertext Gardens is in part multipath, especially because there is a concluding page.

Relaxed Hierarchies

Some websites can be characterized as "relaxed" hierarchies. The hierarchical structure of the website is de-emphasized on the interface, creating a web-like experience for the user. Often we see relaxed hierarchies when corporations seek to portray themselves as fun and hip.

HYPERTEXT GARDENS
A New Path

In learning to hold the reader's attention, we may seek guidance from the literary arts, from narrative theory and criticism. Like creators in any new field, however, hypertext authors should look to many disciplines for forms, techniques, and insights. Lessons from literature are found in "Patterns of Hypertext" and "Chasing our Tales"; here, I explore how architecture and landscape design might guide us in crafting hypertexts.

Beyond Navigation   The Limits of Structure

Gardens and Parks

The Virtue of Irregularity

HYPERTEXT GARDENS
Rigid design

Rigid hypertext is streetscape and corporate office: simple, orderly, unsurprising. We may find the scale impressive, we admire the richness of materials, but we soon tire of the repetitive view. We enter to get something we need: once our task is done we are unlikely to linger. We know what to expect, and we rarely receive anything more.

Figure 13.14. Two pages from Hypertext Gardens.
(www.eastgate.com/garden)

Figure 13.15. A relaxed hierarchy. Although there is a hierarchical structure, the main branches are inconspicuous. The website is web-like in spirit. (www.conelrad.com)

A notable instance of the relaxed hierarchy is Conelrad.com, shown in Figure 13.15. Conelrad (the name comes from an emergency civil defense radio network) takes a nostalgic but harsh look at the nuclear culture of the Cold War era of the 1950s and '60s. This website's complex theme might be stated as such: We may laugh now at the U.S. government's blandly bureaucratic and often willfully blind response to the prospect of a nuclear holocaust and the strange and sometimes perverse reflections of the Cold War in film and television. Enjoy these artifacts of Cold War culture, but don't forget what they tell us about our society's potential for irresponsible behavior.

Conelrad is visually overwhelming (the color scheme is bright red and black on a mustard yellow background) and, in a light-hearted way, unsettling. There are many spotlight links that encourage opportunistic navigation. The only links that systematically reveal the main branches of the hierarchy are inconspicuous text links at the bottom of the home page and interior pages. Throughout the site an informal approach to structure prevails; it is web-like in spirit.

If Conelrad were a scholarly archive, a much more sedate and orderly visual style and a more explicit hierarchy would be in order. Instead, the theme of Conelrad is cleverly embodied in its appearance and structure.

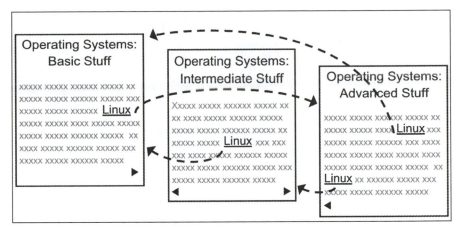

Figure 13.16. A dysfunctional network of associative secondary links in a group of Web pages.

Web-Like Linking Among Several Pages

Finally, we point out the "evil twin" of the web-like structure. Unskilled designers sometimes build a web-like network of associative secondary links among the words and phrases that recur in a group of Web pages.

For example, the four occurrences of the word "Linux" that appear in Figure 13.16 are linked in a dysfunctional manner. The first instance of the word invites the user to jump to the advanced material and therefore deep into the zone of confusion. The subsequent instances pointlessly take the user back to less advanced material.

Futhermore, the sentences in which these embedded links appear often fail to indicate the destinations of the links and why the user might choose to follow them. This kind of dysfunctional linking also results when print documents are moved online and linked through an unintelligent automated process.

Interface Issues

The navigational interface of web-like websites takes various forms. Very often links are embedded into paragraphs of text or else grouped at the bottom of the page. Be cautious about employing a nav column or nav bar; you don't want to mislead users by suggesting a hierarchy or another systematic information structure.

Better site maps may greatly change our experience navigating web-like structures. The user could easily switch from casually browsing the Web pages to a view that provides complete situation awareness.

Writing Issues

By and large the web-like structure demands modularity. Because the designer cannot predict which pages the user has already visited and the background

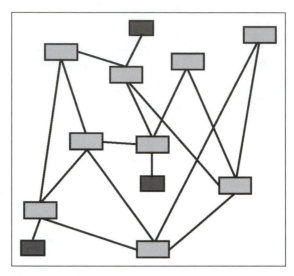

Figure 13.17. A web-like structure that contains three isolated nodes.

knowledge the user has acquired, dependency relationships are avoided. Like encyclopedia articles, each page must make sense to the intended audience.

There are, however, important exceptions to the general requirement of modularity in web-like structures. Consider, for example, the web-like structure shown in Figure 13.17. Here we have three isolated nodes—akin to spur nodes—that (excluding the Search feature, site map, and index) can be reached from only one other node in the structure. The designer, therefore, can make these isolated nodes dependent on information the user will obtain en route to the isolated node (from the "parent" of the isolated node).

Conclusion: Finding the Right Information Structure

As you have seen, there is much diversity in how websites are structured. In addition to the hierarchy, which has three forms, we have four other structures, which also have various forms. Furthermore, there are many hybrids. For example, linear and multipath structures are often included in a hierarchy. There are more complex hybrids as well. The following paragraph from the portfolio section of the Second Story website describes a website that incorporates multipath, matrix, and web-like elements:

> To capture the spirit of the multi-faceted Bill Bowerman, this Web documentary simultaneously explores three story lines: Bowerman as athlete, designer, and teacher. While users watch one story, two others can be accessed in parallel, capturing the

complexity of Bowerman's passion and the depth of his influence. By combining random accessibility with self-running modes, users can actively explore how the different threads of Bowerman's life intertwined, or sit back and watch the narrative unfold. The site utilizes Flash to combine animation, photographs and music not only as storytelling devices, but also as clues to the user's progression along the story line.

Amid these many possibilities, designers need to find the structure that best suits their project. To do so, it is necessary to understand the subject matter and the audience's information needs. Bad structure is certainly possible. It is possible to string content together with Next and Previous buttons, even though users will want more flexible navigation. Conversely, many websites clutter the interface with numerous links that no user will ever care about. If you don't know what you're doing, you can build a matrix website for content that doesn't fit the matrix structure at all.

The designers at Mondosoft thought carefully and decided that users would do best with a multipath structure with spur nodes. Peter and Annie, sitting around a kitchen table, sketched out a hierarchy because they could offer branches corresponding to the information needs of their site visitors. Similar decisions regarding much larger websites are made by design teams at major corporations. Despite the vast differences among projects, the thinking that leads to effective structure is much the same.

Summary

1. The linear, multipath, matrix, and web-like information structures are important alternatives to the hierarchy. In the tables below we review the defining characteristics, uses, interface issues, and writing issues for each of these structures.

The Linear Structure

Defining characteristics	Users navigate along a chain of nodes, moving toward an end node. The structure is very orderly but highly restrictive.
Uses	For instructional purposes, chronological material, complex arguments, and whenever a designer wants to control how users will encounter the subject matter.
Interface issues	Although the interface need not employ anything other than Next and Previous buttons, designers often increase navigational freedom with accelerator links and label these links to provide greater context for navigation.
	Rings let users cycle smoothly from the last node to the first node (or backwards from the first node to the last node).
Writing issues	Nodes in the linear structure need not be modular. Designers can employ suspense, foreshadowing, flashbacks, and other narrative techniques.

The Multipath Structure

Defining characteristics	Users navigate toward an end node by following a branching structure. The structure offers significantly more navigational freedom than the linear structure but is usually less orderly.
Uses	For teaching and explaining, guiding users through procedures, and narratives. Spur (or satellite) nodes invite the user to take a voluntary digression to supplementary content. Split-join nodes present alternative pathways offering parallel information.
Interface issues	Nothing more than Next, Previous, and Read More links often suffices. Designers, however, may want to provide greater navigational freedom and context through more extensive linking and the labeling of links.
Writing issues	The multipath structure almost always entails complex dependency relationships and therefore presents significant challenges for writers.

The Matrix Structure

Defining characteristics	In this very orderly structure, users navigate left, right, up, and down the hypertext equivalent of a traditional print table.
Uses	Broadly speaking, for reference purposes. The matrix structure requires subject matter that can be plotted along two axes and will be useful to people as they navigate along either axis.
Interface issues	It is easy to design the interface for a small matrix. This is because the links arrayed at the top and left recall the appearance of a print table. Larger matrixes may well require drop-down list boxes and the Search feature and begin to take on the character of databases. Don't confuse the matrix with the symmetrical hierarchy. Symmetrical hierarchies cannot be usefully navigated across both axes.
Writing issues	Each node must be entirely modular. Try to write nodes to be as useful as possible when read along either axis.

The Web-Like Structure

Defining characteristics	Users navigate a structure that is not defined by any rules and that is usually highly unsystematic. There is no "directional flow." Navigational freedom is always ample and can become overwhelming. The web-like information structure presents the user with significant navigation challenges.
Uses	For encyclopedia-type websites and for web-like essays. The "relaxed" hierarchy is web-like in spirit; the hierarchy is de-emphasized on the interface. Unskilled designers may thoughtlessly build a web-like network of associative links among the words and phrases that recur in a group of Web pages.
Interface issues	Very often links are embedded into paragraphs of text or else grouped at the bottom of the page. The interface should not suggest order and regularity. Better site maps could greatly change our experience navigating web-like structures by enabling users to gain situation awareness when they wish to.

Writing issues	The web-like structure generally demands modularity. Dependency relationships, however, may be employed. Isolated nodes can be made dependent on information that the user will obtain en route to the isolated node.

2. There is significant diversity in how websites are structured. Designers must find the most suitable structure. To do so, they must understand the subject matter and the audience's information needs.

References

Horton, William K. 1994. *Designing and Writing Online Documentation: Hypermedia for Self-Supporting Products.* 2d ed. New York: Wiley.

Parunak, H. Van Dyke. 1991. Ordering the information graph. In *Hypertext/Hypermedia Handbook.* E. Berk and J. Devlin, eds. New York: McGraw-Hill, 299–325.

Portfolio Section, Second Story. www.secondstory.com

Discussion and Application

Items for Discussion

1. Find a linear document, print or online, that can be re-designed as a multipath document. In other words, the document should have multipath logical relationships: These are (1) optional examples and more detailed explanations and (2) alternative treatments of the same topic. (The latter are more difficult to find than the former.)

   Either diagram the revised document or build it. How successful is the new design? What's gained? What's lost?

2. Investigate two hypermedia courses. They can be Web-based courses or CD/DVD multimedia titles. How is the content presented? What content types are employed? What kinds of user feedback are possible? Are there active social spaces? What special technological capabilities are employed? How effective do you think the course is? How does it compare to face-to-face instruction?

   If you cannot find or gain access to a hypermedia course, you can often examine demos of courses offered on the websites of online universities and training companies. See, for example, demos at Cardean.com (www.cardean.com), America's Learning Exchange (www.alx.org), and Online Learning (www.online-learning.com).

3. Examine several of the websites available for perusal on the Second Story website (www.secondstory.com) or a comparable Web design company. Diagram the node-link structure of one of these websites. The diagram does not need to be complete; it just needs to suggest the overall information structure. Briefly evaluate this website.

4. A website that provides bus schedules has been structured as a hierarchy. The user chooses a particular route number from a list (e.g., Bus 372—Woodinville

to Lake City), then chooses a particular bus stop (e.g., Kenmore Park and Ride), and views the times when Bus 372 stops at the Kenmore Park and Ride. Assess this design.

5. Examine this chapter of *Principles of Web Design* from the perspective of information structures. (To do so, you need to look closely at the headings and subheadings.) What observations can you make?

6. Read Mark Bernstein's Hypertext Gardens (www.eastgate.com/garden). It should take no more than 45–60 minutes to explore and read. Assess the argument.

7. *Spoon River Anthology,* by Edgar Lee Masters, is a book-length collection of poems consisting of monologues spoken by deceased townspeople of the (fictitious) Illinois town Spoon River. The speakers tell us about their lives, many of which are marked by struggle and disappointment. Each monologue is fully modular, and yet—as you can see in Figure 13.18—they are interconnected. After reading about Minerva Jones, you are apt to take an interest in Butch Weldy and Doctor Meyers. Gradually, you may become deeply involved in the lives of all the speakers.

Masters does not explicitly link the monologues in any way: There is no index, no cross referencing. Still, it is easy to turn *Spoon River Anthology* into hypertext by treating each monologue as a node and building links wherever a speaker refers to another person. Hypertext versions of *Spoon River Anthology* (which is no longer covered by copyright) are available on the Web. See for example, the Antelope Publishing version at www.antelope-ebooks.com/Spoon/spoon.html

Describe how you might create an enhanced version of *Spoon River Anthology* that does more than provide a link when one speaker refers to another. What content types other than text might you employ? What might the interface of your enhanced version of *Spoon River Anthology* consist of?

Minerva Jones

I am Minerva, the village poetess,
Hooted at, jeered at by the Yahoos of the street
For my heavy body, cock-eye, and rolling walk,
And all the more when "Butch" Weldy
Captured me after a brutal hunt.
He left me to my fate with Doctor Meyers;
And I sank into death, growing numb from the feet up,
Like one stepping deeper and deeper into a stream of ice.
Will someone go to the village newspaper
And gather into a book the verses I wrote?—
I thirsted so for love!
I hungered so for life!

(Continued)

Doctor Meyers

No other man, unless it was Doc Hill,
Did more for the people in this town than I.
And all the weak, the halt, the improvident
And those who could not pay flocked to me.
I was good-hearted, easy Doctor Meyers.
I was healthy, happy, in comfortable fortune,
Blest with a congenial mate, my children raised,
All wedded, doing well in the world.
And then one night, Minerva, the poetess,
Came to me in her trouble, crying.
I tried to help her out—she died—
They indicted me, the newspapers disgraced me,
My wife perished of a broken heart,
And pneumonia finished me.

Figure 13.18. Two related monologues from *Spoon River Anthology.*

8. A design team is planning a website for people interested in the famous gardens of Great Britain. The design combines several information structures in interesting ways. A sample "garden page" is shown in Figure 13.19.

The website will feature 12 major gardens in Great Britain. The home page will include hot thumbnail photographs of each garden. When clicked, each thumbnail graphic displays a garden page consisting of a larger photograph of that particular garden, with links to a text description of the garden and links to supplementary photographs of the garden. There are also labeled Next and Previous buttons on each of the 12 garden pages so that the user can view the 12 gardens in sequence. The designers have chosen to sequence the gardens geographically, from the north to the south of Great Britain. There is also an All Gardens link so the user can navigate to any garden page at any time.

Finally, there is an especially interesting and useful set of links. Each garden has special features: a noteworthy tree, shrub, pond, bench, statue, and so forth. The designers have determined that many users will want to look at every instance of a particular feature that may be visible in the 12 garden page photographs. The photographs, therefore, are image maps, and the user can pause the mouse pointer over a feature and pick from a list of pop-up links to jump directly to any of the other photographs in which that same feature appears. So, for example, in the figure, the user has paused the mouse pointer over a trellis and will now choose one of the three other garden page photographs in which there is a trellis.

1. Analyze the design and draw a node-link diagram. Hint: To keep the node-link diagram from becoming too complex, diagram only six rather than the full twelve garden pages.
2. Describe ways in which the design could be improved or augmented. Might more content be added? Do you have ideas regarding the interface?

Figure 13.19. One of the 12 garden pages in the British Gardens website. The user has clicked the trellis to display the pop-up menu.

Application to Your Project

Review the node-link structure of your website. Is there a portion of it that should be converted into a different information structure? For example, is there a linear sequence that might better be structured as a multipath?

APPENDIX A:
Twenty-Five Guidelines for Getting Started

Here are 25 guidelines you will find very helpful if you are starting to design and build a website before you have completely read this book. The guidelines serve as a "quick start." They cover only the most essential issues, and don't explain these issues in full. But they will get you going in the right direction.

1. Define your purpose.

Begin by thinking about your purpose for creating the website. What do you want to achieve? Here is a purpose statement for a website that promotes composting:

> Our goal is to introduce composting and promote composting. We want people to understand how easy it is to compost, how much it benefits the environment, and how they can benefit from composting. We want to show a range of composting methods, pointing out that composting can work for every lifestyle, even for apartment dwellers. As a secondary goal, we want this website to be a resource for those who already compost.
>
> We need to make clear that this is a non-profit website developed as a community service. We will mention vendors of composting products (and provide links) but avoid promoting any particular vendor. Also, we will emphasize the feasibility of building, rather than purchasing, a compost bin.

If your current purpose is to improve your skills or fulfill a school assignment, simulate a realistic project with a realistic purpose.

2. Define and analyze your audience.

You need to think about your audience—the people you hope to bring to the website. Who are they? What are they looking for? Your website will only succeed if it meets the audience's interests and needs.

Defining and analyzing your audience is a complex task. It is useful to consider such demographic categories as age, gender, education, ethnicity, and income. Let's say, for example, that you are designing a website that provides information about bus service in your community. Recognizing that your audience includes a significant number of elderly people may remind you that many elderly people need to know which bus stops have benches.

More directly useful than demographic information is subject-specific information. This consists of your audience's background, beliefs, attitudes, and preferences in regard to the subject matter of your website. For example, if you are designing a website for a guide service that takes visitors to Homer, Alaska, on day-long kayak excursions, it is essential to know the kind of outdoor experience most of these people are seeking and their concerns about kayaking.

It is often very valuable to conduct research about your audience through interviews, surveys, and other means. It may be wise to divide your audience into different segments and, possibly, to focus more attention on certain of these segments.

Keep in mind that different audiences have different computer technologies available to them. Many international audiences especially may have slow Internet connections and older computers. Don't design websites that your audience will have difficulty using. Follow accessibility guidelines so that visually handicapped people can use your website.

3. Define your theme. Let purpose, audience, and theme guide your design decisions.

The theme is the core message that connects your website to your audience. Here is the theme of the composting website:

> Composting is easy to do, it benefits the environment, and you will have a supply of rich soil enhancer or mulch for your garden and lawn.

You may or may not actually state the theme in your website, but your understanding of your purpose, audience, and theme will guide you in making a great many design decisions. It will help you decide what information to include and what to leave out. It will guide you in choosing words for your sentences and colors for your page design.

It is a very good idea to write out your purpose, a statement about your audience, and your theme. Doing so is essential in a group project.

4. Review other websites looking for useful ideas about design and implementation. Do not, however, copy design ideas blindly and do not violate copyright law.

Although you don't want to slavishly copy other websites, you should look for ideas you can borrow or adapt. When reviewing other websites, think in terms of evolving Web genres. Think about what your users may be expecting and how you can fulfill these expectations and, at times, depart from them.

Most text, images, and other content created after 1922 are protected by copyright and cannot be legally used or even adapted without permission of the copyright holder. There is no special right to use copyrighted material because it is on the Web. For further information, see Appendix B, "Copyright."

5. If you are working in a team, value the team and contribute effectively. Maintain good ties with other people who are important to the project.

Well-staffed, well-run teams achieve the best results. On the other hand, getting a team organized and keeping it running requires a commitment on the part of each team member. Accept the "overhead" of some wasted time and effort. Accept the fact that the outcome won't be exactly as you would have done it working solo. The results and the team experience are well worth what you give up.

It is important to communicate and work with people who are not on the team but who are nevertheless important to the project. These include people who must authorize and approve the project, who can help with technical problems, who have content that you can use, and who can serve as evaluators and reviewers.

6. Plan carefully so you don't miss your schedule or wind up with an unfinished website.

Many Web development projects are seriously delayed. Some projects, especially student projects, don't get finished at all. The reason is usually insufficient time. To ensure a successful project, limit the scope and plan and schedule carefully. Be sure to allocate time for unexpected problems such as technical glitches, delays in getting authorizations for continuing the project, and delays in receiving content elements you have been promised. You may want to develop your website in stages. Get the first stage up and running and then begin on the next.

In addition to limited time, you will face constraints such as your budget, limitations in your skills or the skills of your team members, and the policies and requirements of the organization for which you are producing the website. Your design decisions, then, should be guided by purpose, audience, and theme—but also by the constraints you are working under.

7. Choose the most appropriate content types: text, graphics, animation, video, and audio.

Decide which content types will be most effective in each part of your website. In particular, don't employ animation, video, or audio (dynamic content types) just for novelty or to produce a snazzy special effect. Also, keep in mind that dynamic content, especially video and extended animation sequences, are difficult or expensive to create or obtain and may make considerable demands on your users' computer technologies.

Text and graphics are an excellent combination and predominate on the Web. Photographs show actual appearances; drawn graphics, such as diagrams and line drawings, allow for more control of what is represented. Similarly, video captures actual appearances better than animation, but animation can both exclude unwanted detail and represent what can't actually be captured with video. Brief animations such as flashing arrows can be used to draw the user's eye, but do so only for a good reason. Sound can be a core content element, for example in a documentary about a jazz musician, but background sound is apt to annoy users who are trying to get their work done.

8. Envision your website as a hierarchy.

When we build a website, we connect our Web pages with links. A website, therefore, can be usefully envisioned as an arrangement of Web pages and links. In

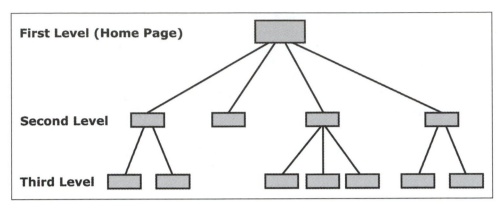

Figure A.1. The hierarchical information structure.

other words, Web pages are "nodes" in an information structure consisting of nodes and links.

The hierarchical information structure, shown in Figure A.1, is by far the most prevalent. We will assume for now that your website will be organized as a hierarchy or is in large part hierarchical. Non-hierarchical structures are covered in Guideline 23.

You are already very familiar with all kinds of hierarchies. For example, we divide the planet Earth into continents, nations, provinces and states, and still smaller divisions. Most books are structured as hierarchies: chapters, sections, subsections. A table of contents is a map of a book's hierarchical structure.

We navigate books and websites differently, however. Most books are designed to be read from beginning to end—linearly. We experience the hierarchical structure as we pass through the sections and subsections, but we are not encouraged to navigate freely among the sections.

In contrast, Web users, starting at the home page, are encouraged to choose which branch of the hierarchy to descend. At the second level and subsequent levels, they are offered similar choices. The links that define the basic hierarchical structure of a website are called "standard primary links."

9. Employ different kinds of links to give your users navigational freedom.

The basic (or "strict") hierarchy shown in Figure A.1 is often too restrictive and unrevealing. Therefore, as shown in Figure A.2, the standard primary links that define the basic hierarchy are usually supplemented by other kinds of links.

Systematic secondary links let the user navigate directly across the branches of the hierarchy. Without these links, the user must move upward in the hierarchy in order to switch branches. Associative secondary links enable users to find relevant information they might otherwise miss. For example, a visitor to the West Virginia tourism website selects the Northern West Virginia branch and de-

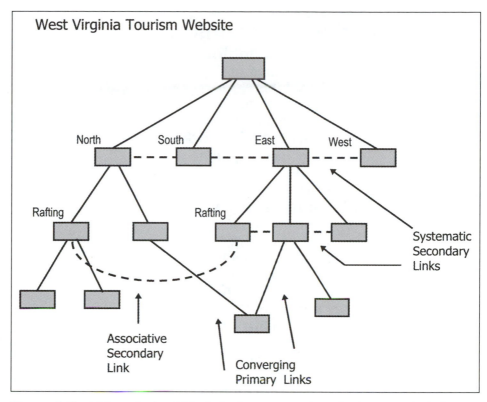

Figure A.2. A hierarchy in which the basic structure of standard primary links has been augmented with systematic secondary links, an associative secondary link, and a converging primary link.

scends to a third-level page listing whitewater rafting opportunities. A well-placed associative secondary link will reveal that there are also whitewater rafting opportunities in Eastern West Virginia.

Converging primary links provide two (or more) major routes to one Web page when that page contains information that belongs to two (or more) logical categories. For example, there might be links from two (or more) branches of the website to the page describing the West Virginia State Fair.

10. Organize the content of your website.

A key task in designing a website is organizing your content elements into a meaningful structure that users can grasp and navigate effectively. Stated differently, you need to organize content into categories and subcategories that reflect how users are likely to look for information. Doing this is much like organizing your ideas when writing a report or other print document.

One very good procedure is to create an outline, especially using your word processor's outlining feature. Figure A.3 shows a portion of an outline, still in an

▭ **Asthma Horizons**
✣ **Causes and Symptoms**
     ▭ *What is asthma?*
     ▭ *Symptoms*
     ▭ *Asthma triggers*
     ▭ *Testing and diagnosis*
✣ **Dealing with an Episode**
     ▭ *Early warning signs*
     ✣ *Responding to an episode*
          ▫ Discuss mild, moderate, and severe episodes
✣ **Medications and Treatments**
     ✣ *Short-term relief*
          ▭ **Inhalers**
     ✣ *Long-term help*
          ▫ Check on long-term treatment with inhalers
     ▭ *List of medications*
     ▭ *Participating in drug studies*
✣ **Controlling Your Environment**
     ✣ *At home*
          ▫ Discuss dust mites, cleansers, second-hand smoke
     ✣ *At school*
          ▭ **Tips for dorm life**
     ▭ *At work*

Figure A.3. A partial outline of a website hierarchy produced using the outlining feature in Microsoft Word.

early stage of development, for a website that provides information about asthma.

One drawback of an outline is that it doesn't explicitly show any links. The standard primary links are implied by the subordination of the outline entries, but there is no indication of the secondary links (no link lines connecting the outline entries).

Another useful way to organize a hierarchy is to create a node-link diagram, as shown in Figure A.4. Node-link diagrams are more difficult to create and update than outlines, but all the linking can be shown explicitly. You can create either a complete or partial node-link diagram.

As you organize the content of your website, try to keep the hierarchy from getting too deep. Beyond three or four levels, navigation becomes more difficult, and users are less apt to remember the routes they took or the terrain of nodes and links. By dividing the content into a larger number of categories, especially on the home page, you reduce the depth. Also, more specific categories are often more meaningful to users and enable them to make better choices.

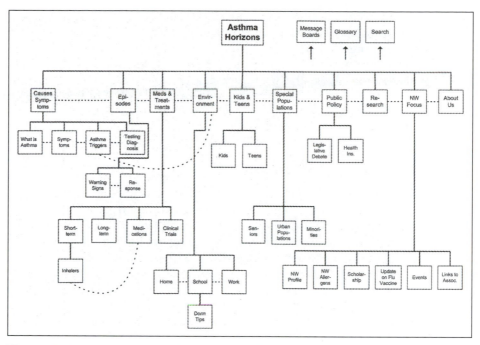

Figure A.4. A partial node-link diagram for the Asthma Horizons website. Notice that the secondary links appear as dotted lines.

11. Before building your website, create successively more complete versions of your design. Use them to evaluate your design.

The Web development process culminates in actually building the website. But your design should evolve in stages. Generate, record, and share your design ideas by creating concept sketches, design sketches, sample pages, and a prototype. In addition, these versions of your design are essential for obtaining evaluations at various stages of the project. Even at the earliest stages of the project, you can obtain useful feedback from potential users and seek out expert advice.

Designers are likely to create concept sketches, preliminary explorations of design ideas, in the earliest stages of the project. But only when the node-link structure has been worked out, at least partially and tentatively, can the designer progress from concept sketches to design sketches and sample HTML pages. This is because design sketches and sample pages show how the links will appear on the pages, and until you know the node-link structure of the website, you really don't know how many links must appear and what kinds of links they will be.

From the design sketches and sample pages, designers usually progress to a clickable prototype. This is a reasonably polished functioning test version of representative portions of the website. The prototype stage is a good time to thoroughly evaluate your design. One means of evaluation is for experts to review the proto-type. Another is to conduct user testing.

Arrange for people who approximate your eventual users to work with the prototype and carry out tasks that will reveal any problems in your design. If necessary, revise the prototype and perform further evaluations. When the evaluations and your own best judgment tell you that you have a high-quality, easy-to-use design, you can shift gears from the design phase to building the website.

12. Design the home page.

The home page is the top node of the hierarchy and is usually the first page the user sees. The home page, therefore, must orient the user by identifying the web-site clearly and indicating the purpose. Very often this function is served by a banner-like "identity element" extending across the top of the page. The home page must offer worthwhile content and promise still more so that users are moti-vated to follow a link into the interior of the website.

The home page generally includes one or more link groups: a navigation bar, set of tabs, navigation column, or group of links in the middle of the page (the main content area). These link groups establish the main branches of the hierar-chy and other pathways into the interior of the website. Figure A.5 shows a nav bar consisting of five standard primary links that establish the main branches of the Zompco website hierarchy. Finally, the home page also includes links to the Search feature and the site map.

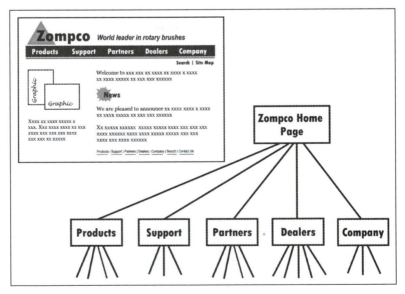

Figure A.5. The relationship between a home page and the website's underlying structure. The five buttons on the nav bar are five links that can take the user to any of the five second-level Web pages (nodes).

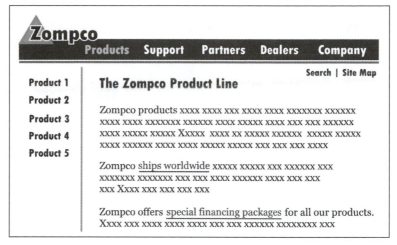

Figure A.6. A second-level Web page with a nav bar linking to sibling pages, a nav column linking to child pages (third level), and two associative secondary links in the main content area.

13. Design the interior pages.

On the second and deeper levels of the website, the key orientation information is the page name. The website name, logo, and other design elements seen on the home page are retained, but may be smaller and otherwise less visually dominant. The transition to something new plus continuity with previous pages create a coherent, satisfying experience for the user. The logo, furthermore, usually provides a direct link from each page back to the home page.

The interior pages should enable the user to understand, at least approximately, the underlying structure of nodes and links and the user's current location in the hierarchy. This requires skillful design, for at the second and lower levels of a hierarchical website there are links pointing upward, downward, and across the hierarchy. In designing the navigational interface, strive for simplicity; in particular, don't clutter the screen with links no user will want to follow.

The link groups on the home page often re-appear in modified form at lower levels of the hierarchy and serve a new function. For example, as shown in Figure A.6, the same nav bar that appeared on the home page appears again on the second level. Now, however, the links point laterally, providing systematic secondary links to sibling pages. It will be a new group of links, in this case links in the nav column, that point downward and take users to the third level of the hierarchy. If this same nav bar appears on the third-level page, it will serve a new role: It will point upward to the parent and aunts of the third-level page.

14. Apply user interface guidelines when designing the interface for online computing functions.

Many websites provide online computing functions such as the checkout on an online store or a spreadsheet on a financial planning website. The interface for these online computing functions may include command menus, dialog boxes, and other interface elements resembling those in standard software applications. These guidelines will serve as a good starting point for designing the interfaces for online computing functions. Systems should:

1. Be flexible and give users ample control.
2. Handle errors gracefully and allow for changed intentions.
3. Be responsive and reveal the system status.
4. Be familiar, natural, self-disclosing, and memorable.
5. Be uncluttered and consistent.
6. Be efficient.
7. Account for individual differences.
8. Be enjoyable to use.

15. Design your links carefully so they lead users reliably to their destinations.

Make sure users will notice your links. Don't let them be overshadowed by more dominant elements on the page. Also, be cautious about placing important links below the scroll line, where users may never encounter them.

Links must provide clear cues that they are indeed links. In other words, the user must know immediately "what's hot and what's not." Two very strong and familiar cues are buttons and underlining. Very often designers omit underlining to lessen the visual complexity of the page. This is a good practice as long as the location, grouping, or phrasing of the text clearly signals that it is a link.

Perhaps most important, links must clearly indicate their destinations. Users should not wonder where a link will take them or be fooled into following a link to an unwanted destination. Take great care with the phrasing of links. Beware of shortening link text to fit a button or some other limited screen space. It is easy to eliminate important meaning.

16. Be careful about using icons.

Very often icons serve as links on websites. Familiar icons, such as a question mark for a help system, work well. It is surprisingly difficult, however, to reliably communicate a specific meaning with an image. Unless your icon is familiar to your audience or you have strong evidence that the meaning will be clear, add a label to the icon. Although they require a physical action on the part of the user, mouse rollovers are often a good means of labeling icons.

17. Add relevant links to other websites.

Well-chosen external links add value to your website and keep users coming back. Make clear, however, which links are external. Users are disconcerted when they unintentionally eject themselves from a website. Also, when you provide external links, you must periodically check them to be sure the URLs are still current. Finally, to increase traffic to your website, ask appropriate websites to build links to your site.

18. Avoid excessive text, especially on the home page. Strive for high-quality writing that will motivate your audience to continue reading.

Web users tend to be restless and will quickly leave a website that doesn't engage them. These, then, are good general guidelines on writing for the Web:

- Avoid a long, unbroken "wall" of extended text.
- Write for scannability: Use short paragraphs, subheadings, and bulleted lists.
- Make key points early. Don't hold them back until the end.

On the other hand, websites serve many different purposes, and no set of guidelines will fit all kinds of Web writing, all rhetorical situations. A personal memoir presented online should not be broken into short paragraphs and bulleted lists.

The real answer, then, is writing (and other kinds of content) that responds to people's needs and interests and is trustworthy, current, clearly and smoothly written, and handsomely and functionally formatted. Users will read extended text on the Web and will scroll pages that matter to them.

A sound strategy is for home pages to feature inviting, easy-to-scan writing that establishes its value quickly and draws users further into the website. On the interior pages the content can become more detailed and can make greater demands on the reader.

19. Write for a non-linear environment.

When writing for the Web, you usually don't know what pathways your users will follow. For this reason, you cannot refer to other pages in your website using phrases such as "As noted previously" or "As you will learn." Such phrases rest on the assumption that the user has visited or will visit particular pages.

A related but more difficult problem is managing pre-requisite information, the background information that users should read before going on to something else. Depending on the circumstances, discourage or absolutely prevent users from bypassing pre-requisite information. For example, users should not be able to navigate to an invitation to enroll in a clinical trial for a serious medical condition unless they will first encounter an explanation of who is eligible for the clinical trial.

20. Pay attention to the visual aspects of text. Keep in mind that the screen is different from the page.

Writing for the screen is different from writing for the page. Here are the key techniques for putting text on the screen.

- Because computer screens are wider than they are deep, guard against overly long lines of text. Designers often format screen text with wide margins or multiple columns to avoid this problem.

- Choose fonts, whether serif or sans serif, that are recognized for their good screen legibility. Good choices include Verdana (a sans-serif font) and Georgia (a serif font). Make sure your text is large enough to be easily read; the right size, however, depends on the font you are using and other factors. Recognize that there can be a difference between the fonts you specify and what particular users are actually able to view on their computer.
- Align body text to the left. Avoid underlining except to indicate a link. Use italics and boldface sparingly. Beware of poor contrast between the text and background color. Avoid heavily patterned or textured backgrounds.

21. Enhance the appearance of your website through graphic design.

A wide range of important decisions about the appearance of a website fall into the category of graphic design. Effective graphic design adds aesthetic appeal, helps to express the theme of the website, and helps to show the logical relationships among all elements that appear on the page. It is relatively difficult for someone without training and extensive experience in graphic design to achieve superior results. Non-professionals are more likely to succeed when they follow well-established design principles.

Line, shape, and color are the "raw materials" of graphic design. Lines can be given a variety of stylistic attributes; lines can be straight, swirly, jagged, hand-drawn, dotted or dashed, etc. Most Web pages are laid out by means of a grid system of rectilinear shapes. Overlapping shapes can subtly suggest multiple planes and give extra interest to an image. Colors consist of hues that can be brightened, darkened, or dulled. Colors are perceived as warm or cool and have a variety of associations. When designing Web pages, think in terms of color schemes and color harmony rather than individual colors.

22. Employ the graphic design principles of composition on your Web pages.

The seven principles of composition listed below will focus your attention on important aspects of a design, enable you to spot problems, and point toward solutions. Ultimately, you should be guided by your overall judgment rather than what any particular principle seems to be dictating.

Emphasis

Use attributes such as greater size, strong contrast, a higher location on the page, and a unique appearance to emphasize certain elements. This enables you to approximately guide the user's eyes as they move across the page.

Grouping

Group elements, using proximity and similarity, to establish logical relationships among elements on the page. For example, if four links in the main content area pertain to Topic A, four to Topic B, four to Topic C, and four to Topic D, the 16 links should almost certainly be grouped into four clusters to visually show this logical relationship among the links.

Subordination

Subordination is closely associated with grouping and emphasis and also plays a major role in showing logical relationships. For example, two news stories might be grouped by proximity and similarity but also subordinated to a visually dominant heading which makes clear that both stories deal with the same event.

Simplicity

Simplicity adds aesthetic appeal and makes it easier to reveal the organization of the information on your pages. Achieve simplicity by using relatively few visual elements, by establishing strong resemblances among these elements (similarities in size, color, shape, etc.), and by arranging these elements in a visually consistent pattern.

Proportion

Certain relationships pertaining to the dimensions and size of page elements seem appropriate and pleasing. For example, a very wide button will seem out of proportion, especially in comparison with standard buttons. Objects on a page should normally be scaled as they exist in the physical world—e.g., normally, a bicycle should appear smaller than a building.

Balance

Balance refers to our perception of visual "weight" among elements on a page. A large, dark object has more "weight" than a smaller, lighter object. An object near the edge of the page has more visual weight than an object nearer the middle. (This is akin to the extra "weight" a person exerts sitting at the far end of a see-saw.) Graphic designers only occasionally design for symmetrical (mirror-image) balance. Rather, they usually try to achieve an overall visual balance among the elements on the left and right side of the page. At times, designers try to achieve a visually effective imbalance among elements.

Unity

Unity is the perception that all the visual elements of a composition fit together into a unified whole. Unity is threatened by too much variety in shape, color, line attributes, fonts, and other aspects of a design. Unity also implies a fit between style and theme. Disunity would result if wild skateboarding colors somehow took over a website that promotes traditional, stately dining room furniture.

The squint test

In analyzing a design use the squint test. By blurring your vision, you eliminate semantic meaning and obscure minor visual features. This will enable you to better assess the main visual elements in the design.

23. Consider a non-hierarchical structure for your website or a portion of the site.

There are times when your content and your user's information needs call for a non-hierarchical information structure. Also, non-hierarchical components are often included within fundamentally hierarchical websites.

In the orderly but highly restrictive linear structure, users navigate back and forth along a chain of nodes. The multipath structure is similar to the linear structure, but allows for a limited amount of branching. Both these structures are used for tutorials, demos, procedures, arguments, and narratives.

The matrix structure is like a table. It is highly systematic. The user navigates up and down the columns and back and forth across the rows. In a matrix medical reference, the rows might consist of medical conditions and the columns might consist of categories of information (Definition, Causes, Prevalence, etc.) about those conditions. Because a matrix requires highly structured subject matter, it is not prevalent.

In the web-like structure anything can be linked to anything. It is difficult, however, for the user to get a global view of the content. Print and online encyclopedias are essentially web-like in structure. The "relaxed" hierarchy is web-like in spirit; there is an underlying hierarchy, but it is de-emphasized on the interface.

24. Add a site map to your website.

A site map is a navigation device that reveals the overall structure of the website. It shows users what topics are available on the website and how the website is linked. It also provides instant access to any page represented on the site map. A site map is a valuable addition to all but very small websites.

Some site maps are highly graphical, but to simplify building and maintenance many site maps consist simply of text links with relatively simple formatting. The major challenge in designing site maps is representing the hundreds or more pages that comprise many websites. Often designers must limit the scope of the site map to the first three levels of the website hierarchy.

25. Add a Search feature to your website.

A Search feature is a valuable navigation device that enables users to access Web pages by typing search terms rather than by following links. Add a Search feature to all but small websites.

You can install a search engine or use a remote search service to provide the Search feature for your website. Carefully investigate the capabilities they offer and any requirements associated with their use. Many are cost free. Remote services do not require you to have technical expertise. When you employ a Search feature, you must code your Web pages so that the search engine can find the appropriate pages in response to user queries. Add metatag keywords and otherwise optimize your site for the particular search engine you have chosen.

The query form is where the user begins the search and types the search terms. The design of the query form depends on the capabilities of the search engine, the nature of the website, and the needs and search skills of the audience. Usually it's best to offer a simple search box for basic queries and an extended form with further search parameters for more advanced queries. Provide tips or help for advanced search features.

The results list is what the search engine displays in response to a user's query. The results list should indicate the total number of results that the search retrieved and which entries out of this total are currently being displayed. Individual results list entries should include the page name, the page description, the URL, and the relevancy ranking. Users also benefit from knowing when the page was last updated.

Web indexes consist of an alphabetical list of index terms, each linked to the most relevant page. Indexes are a useful supplement to the Search feature and site map. Indexes are not highly prevalent, however, largely because preparing an index is a time-consuming task that requires a skilled indexer. Still, consider adding an index if your website doesn't undergo frequent change.

Web portals consist of Web-wide search engines and directories of websites. To draw users to your website, take steps so that your website is listed prominently by Web portals. This includes submitting your website to portals and "seeding" your website with keywords to get a better ranking from Web-wide search engines.

APPENDIX B:
An Introduction to Copyright Law*

Copyright law is complex, has many "gray areas," and changes frequently. This appendix is a very basic introduction to copyright law with a focus on content being presented on the World Wide Web. It is not intended to serve as legal advice. Furthermore, although copyright issues pertaining to the Web almost always have international implications, this document is written from the perspective of the United States. Before making decisions about copyright and related legal issues, you should consult an intellectual property attorney or, at least, extend your knowledge well beyond what this brief introduction offers. The most authoritative source of copyright information in the United States is the Copyright Office of the U.S. Library of Congress, at www.loc.gov/copyright. There are, however, many other sources of valuable information, print and online, some of which are listed at the end of this appendix. Your particular needs should dictate which resources to use.

The Basic Idea: Most Content Is Someone's Intellectual Property

The basic idea is that most of the content you find around you, whether on the Web or not, is the intellectual property of the people who made or acquired it. This includes text, graphics, music, and cinema. Copyright law prohibits you from making use of this material without consent. Very often, the owners of copyrighted material expect to be paid.

In general, copyrighted material has a copyright notice on it, but material without a copyright notice (including, for example, email) is very likely still protected by copyright. Furthermore, altering the copyrighted content, for example scanning a graphic and re-working it, does not, in general, protect you, even if you alter it extensively. If the owner of the content can prove copying, you can be held liable for infringement.

In certain cases, even linking from your website to another website may be illegal, especially if you are linking in such a way as to make another person's content appear to be your content or if the owner of the copyrighted material loses revenue because of your linking.

---

*The authors wish to thank intellectual property attorney Karen Wetherell Davis, of the firm Elliot, Ostrander, & Preston, P.C., Seattle, Washington, and Portland, Oregon, for her assistance with this appendix.

Ideas That Can't Be Copyrighted

Certain ideas can only be expressed in one way, and so they cannot be copyrighted. No one, for example, can copyright a list of the presidents of the United States from George Washington to the present day. However, someone's ranked list of the presidents from the best to the worst could be covered by copyright.

Content in the Public Domain

There are categories of content that no one owns. In legal terms, this material is "in the public domain." For example, songs such as "Swing Low, Sweet Chariot" or "She'll Be Comin' 'Round the Mountain When She Comes" are called "traditional." No one knows exactly who wrote them, and they've never been copyrighted. You could use an audio track of your friend's guitar version of a traditional folk song if you obtain written permission from your friend, who owns the rights to her own performance. It would not be legal, however, to use your friend's version of a current hit song.

Some content, notably government documents, is explicitly placed in the public domain rather than copyrighted as soon as it is created. Furthermore, copyrights expire after a certain length of time. Unfortunately, numerous factors dictate whether a copyright has expired. Here are two reliable rules:

- You can use anything first copyrighted or published in the United States before 1923.
- For works created on or after January 1, 1978, copyright duration is the life of the author plus 70 years; for works created for hire and owned by corporations, copyright duration is 95 years.

Creating Your Own Content

One way to get around the copyright problem is to produce your own original content. This content does not need to be entirely dissimilar from a copyrighted work you would have liked to use. Copyright law protects the expression of ideas, not the ideas themselves. As long as your expression is original, you are not violating copyright. Ideas can be protected by patent law if they take the form of new inventions.

Let's consider in more detail the distinction between ideas and the expression of ideas. You cannot legally copy a movie review published in a newspaper. But if you write your own review and if you, like the newspaper reviewer, make the points that the plot was predictable, the dialogue was clichéd, and the acting was weak, you are not violating copyright as long as you don't say these things with the same or substantially similar expression. If there are strong parallels in the organization of the two movie reviews (you cover the same points in the same order), you are in a gray area. If the copyright owner were to challenge you, only a court case would provide a definite answer to the dispute.

Licensing and Purchasing Content

If you cannot meet your needs with content in the public domain or content that you create, the best solution is often to license the right to use copyrighted material. There are many vendors who license "stock" (or "clip") content—images, animation, video, and audio—for reasonable fees. You can also find stock content available for free on the Web. You must, however, pay close attention to the conditions under which you are allowed to use any stock content. It is often possible to license music or portions of a film owned by a major record label or studio; the fee, however, is likely to be high.

If you hire an artist or another kind of content creator, you will generally want to become the copyright holder of the content you purchase. This requires the content creator to sign a "work for hire" agreement.

Fair Use and Permissions

There are instances in which you may legally use copyrighted material, for example, a passage from a book or newspaper. Copyright law includes a provision for "fair use." Unfortunately, there is great uncertainty surrounding fair use, and the legal analysis of a fair use defense is very subjective. This explanation must be viewed only as a most general guideline, but the following criteria make a case for fair use. The more that apply, the stronger the case.

1. The use you are making is for purposes of comment, criticism, scholarship, education, or news reporting. Parody (but only genuine parody) falls under this category.
2. You are using a relatively small amount of the total work (the smaller the better) and not the "heart" of the work.
3. The work you are using has been published and is a commercial work.
4. Your use does not affect the potential market or value of the work—most significantly, no one would read or otherwise use your excerpt to avoid buying the copyrighted work.
5. You aren't making any money from using it, or your purpose is not primarily commercial.

So, for example, if you write movie reviews for your website, you could feel confident about the legality of beginning a review in this manner:

Carmen Reyes, writing in the *New York Times,* states, "The plot of *Nightmare on Elm Street 11* is unsatisfactory. The bad guy in a slasher movie should not come to grief by carelessly revealing his identity in an email message." In my opinion, Ms. Reyes misjudges how deeply email mistakes resonate with movie viewers.

You are clearly satisfying the first four criteria for fair use, and depending on the purpose of your website, you may be satisfying the fifth.

Often, your use of someone's copyrighted material actually enhances their reputation or promotes their business, and so they will grant you free permission to use their content, most likely with the requirement that you acknowledge the source. Don't expect a national magazine to grant you the right to reproduce a recent cover story, but your local newspaper may allow you to put their review of a recent rock concert on your website.

Copyright and Plagiarism

Don't confuse copyright with plagiarism; they are two entirely different issues. Plagiarism is primarily a breach of ethics and academic regulations. When your work incorporates the words of another person or your own expression of their ideas, you cite this person's work in order to acknowledge their intellectual contribution and to provide a means for readers to examine your sources. Acknowledging an author, however, doesn't give you the intellectual property right to use that author's words in your project—likewise with a photograph or an audio or video sequence.

Other Restrictions

Finally, there are other intellectual property rights and closely related rights that limit what you can create and publish. People have legal rights to their own name, likeness, and image—just because you draw an original image of a rock star, doesn't mean you can sell a T-shirt or mouse pad with this image. Even the likenesses of a few famous buildings, such as the Chrysler Building in New York City, have been registered as trademarks and cannot be freely reproduced. Also, people have privacy rights: If you videotape an individual in private life (as opposed to a public figure) playing with his or her child in a public park, you would want to obtain written permission before putting this video sequence on a website.

Sources for More Information

Websites

The Copyright Crash Course Online Tutorial
www.utsystem.edu/OGC/IntellectualProperty/faculty.htm

This is a brief, very readable introduction with some special attention to concerns of university faculty members.

The Copyright Website
www.benedict.com

This commercial website offers a great deal of information on all aspects of copyright, along with the site owner's strong opinions. Important copyright disputes are reviewed at length.

Ladera Press

www.laderapress.com

> This legal publisher offers a brief, well-written primer that explains copyright, patent, and trademark law from the perspective of the Web developer. Also look at the "Copyright Myths" section of the website.

Nolo

www.nolo.com

> A valuable source of well-written material on almost every area of the law. Browse the "Internet Law" and "Trademarks & Copyrights" law centers. Also includes a legal dictionary and encyclopedia.

The Stanford University Fair Use Website

http://fairuse.stanford.edu

> This website offers links to many statutes and judicial opinions.

World Intellectual Property Organization

www.wipo.int/index.html.en

> A valuable resource that provides a global perspective on intellectual property.

Books

Brinson, J. Dianne, and Mark F. Radcliffe. 2000. *Internet Law and Business Handbook: A Practical Guide* (with disk). Menlo Park, CA: Ladera Press.

> In addition to intellectual property, this book covers such areas of the law as contracts and employment.

Fisherman, Stephen. 1999. *The Copyright Handbook: How to Protect and Use Written Works.* 5th ed. Berkeley, CA: Nolo Press.

> A useful book with a "how to" focus. Provides step-by-step guidance and sample forms.

Stim, Richard. 1999. *Copyright Law.* Albany, NY: Delmar Publishers.

> A comprehensive, well-written book.

APPENDIX C:
Project Reports

Reporting is an important aspect of almost every Web development project. Preparing the appropriate kinds of reports is a complex matter. The key issues are these: (1) when they are written, (2) whom they are written for, (3) the purpose or purposes, and (4) their content. In this appendix, we explain Web project reporting.

Each kind of project requires somewhat different kinds of reports. Here we look at the reporting that took place during the development of the Asthma Horizons Northwest website. The kinds of reports prepared for this project are listed below. The project notebook, although not a report, is also discussed.

- Progress reports
- The comprehensive planning report
- Task reports
- The comprehensive design report
- The completion report

These kinds of reports and the project notebook are discussed in Chapters 2 and 3 ("Planning" and "Designing and Building") in the sections on reporting. This appendix includes two sample reports: the comprehensive planning report and one of the task reports.

Because reports can only be well understood in the context of the rhetorical situation they are part of, we briefly sketch out the administrative history of Asthma Horizons Northwest, with particular attention to project coordination and reporting. First, we describe Asthma Horizons from its inception to the end of the planning phase. Later, we continue this history from the design phase to the building phase and site launch.

The Inception and Planning of the Asthma Horizons Northwest Website

Dr. E. L. Bird, an allergist in Portland, Oregon, first recognized the need for an asthma information website with a Northwest regional focus. Dr. Bird recruited a group of health care professionals and community leaders. Together they formed Asthma Web Northwest (AWN), a non-profit organization chartered in the State of Oregon. The mission of AWN was to initiate and manage the website they planned to create. They chose the site name Asthma Horizons Northwest and registered the URL. Dr. Bird was elected the head of the AWN Board of Directors.

Dr. Bird and other AWN board members talked informally with charitable foundations. The Wright Foundation expressed interest in funding Asthma Horizons. In

August 2001, AWN submitted a proposal to the Wright Foundation; in September it was accepted, with a year of trial funding to begin on January 1, 2002.

AWN hired Julie Knoll, an experienced Web producer with a broad range of skills. AWN also hired Erin Mayovsky, a writer/reporter with experience in medical journalism. Mayovsky's duties include coordinating the volunteers who are expected to contribute content and otherwise participate in running the website. A graphic artist, Ron Eng, is contributing on a free-lance basis.

The Project Notebook

At the outset of the project, Knoll set up a project notebook, which is actually a collection of computer files available to everyone on the Asthma Horizons local area network. The notebook includes informal minutes of team meetings, the content list, preliminary versions of graphics, and many more items.

In these first weeks of the project Knoll, Mayovsky, and Eng have little trouble keeping the entire project plan in their heads, but Knoll recognizes that over time the project history will be harder for anyone to remember. Also, people will join the project and others will leave. Establishing a well-organized project notebook (not just a collection of disorganized files) will make it much easier to meet reporting requirements and to communicate effectively with the various people involved in the project.

Progress Reports

In mid-January the first progress report is prepared for AWN. The report briefly recounts the activities of the project team from January 2, the day they began work. The progress report also sets forth the tasks that are scheduled for the next several weeks. If any significant problems had arisen, they would have been noted in the progress report. A second progress report is scheduled for the design phase in mid-February and another for the building phase at the end of March. As long as the team is working on the Asthma Horizons website, they will prepare progress reports for AWN.

The Comprehensive Planning Report

The first big payoff from keeping the project notebook comes at the end of the planning phase when Knoll, with the assistance of Mayovsky, prepares the comprehensive planning report. The report appears below.

A crucial goal of the comprehensive planning report is to communicate with external audiences, first and foremost AWN. AWN board members will read the report and may return to it later, especially if questions arise as to whether the project is progressing as planned. In addition, this report will serve as the basis of the reports that AWN will submit to the Wright Foundation to request further funding for the project.

The report does not assume any familiarity with the project. It is not necessary, for example, to read the progress report or other documents to fully understand this report. Therefore, if a new member is added to the AWN board, this person can easily use the comprehensive planning report to "get up to speed."

This report, possibly with some modifications, may serve other external audiences—for example, other potential sources of funding. It might also be given to volunteers and job candidates to help them decide if they want to join the Asthma Horizons team.

The comprehensive planning report also serves a crucial role as an internal report. It is a "big picture" reminder of what the team has agreed upon, the status of the project at a key milestone, and where the project is headed. Therefore, it is a way to fight "drift," a way to ensure that the team maintains a common image of the project.

You may notice that the headings used in this planning report differ somewhat from the headings shown in the list of planning report sections in Chapter 2. This is to be expected. Every planning report must reflect its own unique circumstances and will consist of different sections with different headings. For example, because the business model of Asthma Horizons Northwest is very simple (foundation support), it is noted briefly in the purpose statement. In contrast, an e-commerce website would certainly have a lengthy section describing its business model.

Asthma Horizons Northwest
Planning Report

submitted to
Asthma Web Northwest

prepared by
Julie Knoll, Producer
Asthma Horizons Northwest
January 27, 2002

This report describes the Asthma Horizons Northwest website as it is currently envisioned and the status of the project at the close of our four-week planning phase.

Statement of Purpose

Asthma Horizons Northwest will be an important resource for asthma sufferers, their families, and friends. Focusing on the states of Alaska, Idaho, Oregon, and Washington, Asthma Horizons will provide background information about this medical condition, current information on treating and managing asthma, information about regional issues, and links to further resources. Although there will be references to the medical research literature, the site is not intended for physicians or other medical professionals. The site will include message boards that will provide a social space through which users can share their experiences and gain confidence and inspiration. Asthma Horizons will be an English-language website, but it will be designed to serve non-native as well as native speakers of English. The site will project professionalism and objectivity. It will be visually pleasing, and informal in style. There will be no advertising or other commercial activity on the site.

Audience Analysis

Audience analysis has been an important planning activity, as it will continue to be throughout the design and building phases. We divide our analysis into demographic characteristics and asthma-specific characteristics.

Asthma Demographics

There is relatively little statistical information available regarding asthma in the Northwest and in the United States generally. Data come primarily from the very limited National Health Interview Surveys (NHIS). Statistics do indicate, however, that Asthma affects over 5% of the national population, is more prevalent among children than adults, and is more prevalent in low-income populations. Asthma is both more prevalent and more severe among Blacks than the general population. Asthma and other respiratory problems are associated with poor air quality and with smoking. For reasons that are not well understood, asthma and asthma mortality have been increasing since the early 1980s across all ages and racial groups.

Asthma incidence in the Northwest United States broadly resembles the national profiles. Therefore, Asthma Horizons Northwest targets a very diverse population including Blacks, Asians, Hispanics, and Native Americans living in urban, suburban, and rural environments in both coastal and inland regions.

Because our audience consists of Web users, people with higher levels of education and income are represented more heavily than they are in the general population. In addition, many older people do not use the Web. We hope and expect to reach a broader audience as Web use becomes more widespread.

Subject-specific Information

We know that asthma sufferers have a strong interest in understanding and managing their condition. We will therefore seek to provide comprehensive health information.

Through our interaction with the intended audience and with physicians and other caregivers, we have some reliable information about the specific interests and concerns of many asthma sufferers and their families.

- A broad range of asthma sufferers, especially those just learning about the condition, would like easy-to-understand information regarding asthma triggers and how to avoid or mitigate them. Simple animations offer great promise in explaining technical concepts such as lung function and the use of inhalers.
- In most instances, parents of asthmatic children are highly motivated to find solutions. Parents will read more detailed information than other audience segments.
- Public policy issues are as important as purely medical issues. Asthma sufferers are concerned about reimbursement for medications by health plans. Parents of asthmatic children are especially concerned about the administration of medication at school. Much public policy information is regional in nature.
- We know that severely asthmatic children often experience social problems, particularly because they miss school frequently and may not participate in active play and sports. This points to the importance of creating message boards and real-time chat environments specifically for children and young adults.

Theme and Style

This is the theme of Asthma Horizons Northwest:

Asthma can almost always be effectively managed and asthmatics, especially when they take an informed role in managing their condition, can live active, happy lives.

The theme echoes the website name, for "horizons" suggests unlimited possibilities. This theme should guide both the appearance of the site and the information we provide. To convey this theme visually, we will favor warm colors, in particular sunshine yellows. We will also favor sky blue, especially because this color accords with the idea of the sky and horizons.

Comparison with Similar Websites

We have closely examined numerous health information websites, both asthma related and non-asthma related, both profit and non-profit. We have gathered a great many useful ideas regarding what kinds of content to provide.

Because Asthma Horizons will be the only Northwest-focused asthma website, there are no sites we regard as competitors. Indeed, we plan to establish reciprocal links between our site and other asthma information websites.

Website Content

We have made considerable progress in brainstorming a content list, a collection of likely content elements for our website. We are also making preliminary plans for obtaining or generating these content elements. Our immediate goal is for the content list to be complete enough to effectively guide us as we devise the structure of the website hierarchy in the design stage. Long term, our goal is content that will result in an informative, compelling website.

Plans for Content Acquisition

A major challenge for the project team will be to provide high-quality, up-to-date content despite our small staff and limited budget. Dr. Bird's original plan was that Asthma Horizons would rely heavily on volunteers from the medical community and elsewhere for content or, at least, for assistance in generating content. We are extremely encouraged by the many offers of assistance we have already received.

We are also making plans with other asthma information websites to share content elements. For example, we may trade an animation created here for one created elsewhere.

Early Design Reviews

Erin Mayovsky has been meeting with asthma patients and family members in order to gain first-hand knowledge of our target audience and to conduct early evaluations of certain aspects of our design. She has attended patient self-management meetings and has spoken to asthma patients in clinics and hospitals.

The feedback Erin has obtained confirms our general understanding of the audience and their information needs. Erin's description of the content we plan to provide elicited a very positive response.

On two occasions Erin was able to conduct vocabulary polls. She is now compiling a list of medical terms that must be either avoided or explained. This list will be given to anyone who writes for Asthma Horizons.

She also asked potential users for feedback regarding a concept sketch of the home page. A generally unenthusiastic response helped to convince the team to undertake a brand new design.

Requirements: Staffing, Equipment, Schedule, and Budget

The Asthma Horizons project team intends to operate in a highly efficient manner, making the best possible use of every dollar and every hour.

Staffing

The Wright Foundation grant provided funds for three full-time positions, and we recognize that the staff budget will not increase over the near term. We believe the best way to staff the project is to supplement the current full-time staff of Knoll and Mayovsky with two half-time positions: a graphic designer and an office manager/volunteer coordinator. Ron Eng is a very talented and enthusiastic contributor to the project and is willing to stay on permanently as a half-time employee (with benefits). A half-time office manager/volunteer coordinator would free up Knoll for more authoring and other activities and would also enable Mayovsky to work more productively. We request immediate authorization to fill these positions.

We will also spend operations money on consultants. We intend to bring in a consultant to assist us with the design of user tests. In addition, we may need a small amount of assistance with some difficult coding.

The project team is very willing to take over the task of publicizing the website from AWN. This task, however, will require an extra staff position, a significant increase in travel expenditures, and some other budget items.

Equipment

The three well-equipped, networked PCs (with printer and scanner) provided by the grant will take care of our hardware and software needs for the immediate future. We expect to need software upgrades in about two years.

Julie Knoll's former employer, the Zompco Corporation, has kindly donated three older PCs that are adequate for most purposes other than working with graphics. Julie and Erin will continue to use their personal laptops for work-related purposes.

Schedule

The project is currently on schedule. The schedule shown on the following page is aggressive but can be met with hard work and careful management.

Budget

Final budget figures will be available shortly. We will email a spreadsheet file to all recipients of this report. The budget items are these:

- Salaries and benefits
- Rented office space and utilities
- Operations, including consultants and general office expenses
- ISP charges for Internet access and website hosting
- Purchase of stock media (clip art, etc.)
- Travel

Tasks	January	February	March	April
Planning	**Jan 2 – Jan 31**			
Analyze aud/purpose/etc.	1/2–21			
Audience research	1/9–23; 1/27-31			
Evaluation activities	1/9–16; 1/20-31			
Prepare progress report	1/15			
Content planning/acquisition	1/16–31			
Prepare planning report	1/23–25			
Design		**Feb 1 – Mar 8**		
Develop content elements		2/1–3/8		
Work out site structure		2/7–3/1		
Create sketches/pages		2/9–23		
Prepare progress report		2/15		
Build prototype		2/20-26		
User testing		2/27–3/2		
Revise design			3/3-8	
Prepare design report			3/6-8	
Building			**Mar 9 – Apr 16**	
Set up work environment			3/9-10	
Develop content			3/11-26;	4/3-12
Code special features			3/11-26	
Content edit/review				3/26-4/2
Prepare progress report				3/30
Respond to reviews				4/3-12
QA testing				4/10-16
Prepare completion report				4/13-14
Launch and party				4/16

The Design Phase of Asthma Horizons Northwest

AWN approved the planning report and the project moves smoothly into the design phase. There are now four paid staff members, several volunteers, and two student interns working on the project. With more people involved, good communication is even more essential. Now the team begins to rely heavily on task reports.

Task Reports

During the design phase, the project team divides into numerous two-person task teams to tackle particular parts of the project. For example, Ron Eng is working with a physician on a GIF animation showing the function of the lung. Erin May-ovsky is working with a student intern on the profile features that will appear approximately every month.

The weekly project meetings play a crucial role in coordinating everyone's efforts, but members of the project team (especially volunteers and interns) occasionally miss meetings, and details of the discussion are sometimes forgotten. Task teams, therefore, distribute via email brief reports such as the one shown below.

```
Date:    March 1, 2002
To:      Project_Team <team@asthmahorizons.org>
From:    Mike Schultz <mikey@asthmahorizons.org>
Re:      Task Report for the Profile Feature
Attachments:

  1. Rigby.doc
  2. Rigby.jpg
  3. CampAerie.jpg

This report, prepared by Mike and Erin, summarizes the
current plans for the profile features.

PURPOSE
The profile features will provide fresh content for return
visitors, will add a personal quality to the website
(equivalent to feature stories in newspapers), and will
support and recognize individuals who have a special story
to tell or who have made significant contributions to the
asthma community.

THE DESIGN
Profile features will employ different formats. These
include question-and-answer interviews, biographical profile
in narrative form, and picture essays. Brief audio and video
sequences may be employed. Possible topics appear below:

  • An interview with Chad Brown, the Seattle Seahawks'
    football player who "tackles" asthma Sunday after
```

Sunday. We will look for other successful asthmatic
athletes.

- A narrative of Dr. Jeff Altman's many contributions to
  the asthma community in the Northwest.
- A photographic essay of the Carmelo family's 15-day
  kayak expedition in Iceland's Jokulfjords Sea. Two of
  the children suffer from moderately severe asthma.
- An interview with Virginia Kopald, Head Nurse at the
  emergency respiratory unit of Portland Hospital.
- An interview with an elderly person who can describe
  growing up with asthma in the 1920s and 1930s.

Ideally, a new feature will appear about every month (with
older features made available in an archive). We have
decided, however, not to use the name "Monthly Feature" so
that we will not be committed to changing features on a fixed
 schedule.

SAMPLE PROFILE

We wrote a sample profile (see attached files) to get a
"feel" for the style, tone, and level of detail the profile
should take. Also, we wanted to get user feedback regarding
profiles. Our sample profile is an interview with Ms.
Eleanor Rigby, founder of Camp Aerie.

We conducted a small focus group meeting at the Boise
Respiratory Clinic. Participants liked the idea of the profiles
and, in general, expressed interest in the topics that we
described. The sample profile was well received. Participants
said that the addition of a video sequence would add extra
interest.

The Comprehensive Design Report

At the end of the design phase, a comprehensive design report is written. Like the comprehensive planning report, this report is intended for both external audiences and the project team. This report updates and expands upon the comprehensive planning report.

The Building Phase

During the building phase a progress report and more task reports are written. At the end of the building phase, Asthma Horizons "goes live." This event is coordinated with the start of the publicity effort that will draw people to the website.

At this stage of the project, a completion report is prepared. In this case, the Asthma Horizons project team and AWN work together to prepare a completion report whose main audience is the Wright Foundation. The report formally announces that the website has been launched successfully and describes future plans for the website. A key goal of the report is to predispose the Wright Foundation to approve the next funding proposal.

APPENDIX D:
Implementation Resources

Our focus throughout this book has been the design of websites. This appendix will point you to useful resources in print and on the web that can help you with implementation—actually building your website.

Authoring, Programming, and Scripting

There are a great many good books devoted to HTML, Java, JavaScript, XML, DHTML, and other implementation topics. Keep in mind, however, that the Web offers good no-cost information on these topics.

Our brief list includes the books by Powell and Niederst because they are especially well done and broad in scope. We list Paciello because it is hard to find a book on accessibility. We list Donnelly because this is one of few books that truly focuses on development issues specific to large corporate websites.

Books

Donnelly, Vanessa. 2000. *Designing Easy-To-Use Websites: A Hands-on Approach to Structuring Successful Websites* (with CD-ROM). Harlow, England: Addison-Wesley.

Focuses on the processes and technologies necessary to create large corporate websites. Offers extensive coverage of content management. Also describes the roles of various members of the development team in a complex corporate environment.

Niederst, Jennifer. 1999. *Web Design in a Nutshell: A Desktop Quick Reference.* Sebastopol, CA: O'Reilly & Associates.

Provides detailed information on key topics for Web designers, including creating links, tables, frames, and forms; the use of cascading style sheets; graphics formats; animated GIFs, audio, and video; and a general introduction to JavaScript, DHTML, and XML.

Paciello, Michael G. 2000. *Web Accessibility for People with Disabilities.* San Francisco: CMP Books.

Covers the requirements of the disabled and techniques for making websites accessible. Provides an overview of the legal requirements as well.

Powell, Thomas A. 2000. *Web Design: The Complete Reference.* Berkeley: Osborne/ McGraw-Hill.

A comprehensive, well-executed resource on Web development. Also includes Web design.

Websites

CNET Builder.com

http://builder.cnet.com

Good information for Web developers. The How-To Library includes "Authoring and Site Design" and "Programming and Scripting." The Reference section includes a cascading style sheet reference table and a color code converter for translating RGB values into hexadecimal code.

JAVA™ Technology and XML

http://java.sun.com/xml/index.html

Provides a wide range of information on Java and XML, including tutorials for beginner XML coders.

Microsoft Developers' Network

http://msdn.microsoft.com/workshop/default.asp

Extensive information on Web design and development. Note in particular the sections entitled: "Design" and "DHTML, HTML, & CSS."

NCSA Beginner's Guide to HTML (National Center for Supercomputing Applications at the University of Illinois at Urbana-Champaign)

www.ncsa.uiuc.edu/General/Internet/WWW/HTMLPrimer.html

Although no longer being updated, this guide is still a good starting point for learning HTML.

W3C User Interface Domain: HyperText MarkUp Language Home Page

www.w3.org/MarkUp

Provides links to the current W3C guidelines, specifications, and recommendations on HTML and XHTML. In addition, it contains links to information on building accessible websites. Two useful tools are also available on this page: HTML Tidy for checking HTML code for mark-up errors and Bobby for testing your pages for accessibility.

WebDeveloper.com

www.webdeveloper.com

A comprehensive site for Web developers.

Webmonkey

www.webmonkey.com

A reference site for Web designers and developers. See the Authoring and Programming sections in the How-To Library. Note also the Quick Reference links, particularly the browser compatibility chart and the style sheet guide.

WebReference.com

www.webreference.com

Another comprehensive resource for Web designers and developers.

WebReview.com

www.webreview.com

A magazine-style website intended for Web designers and developers. Take a look at the "Web Authors," "Designers," and "Developers" tracks. See also the WebReview Guides on Style Sheets and Web Browser Compatibility.

XML.com: XML from the Inside Out

www.xml.com

A website devoted exclusively to XML information and services. Content is useful both for beginners and experienced XML coders.

Graphics

Especially valuable resources appear below. We list books on Adobe Photoshop and JASC Paint Shop Pro because they are industry standards.

Books

Rose, Carla. 2000. *Sams Teach Yourself Adobe Photoshop 6 in 24 Hours.* Indianapolis, IN: SAMS Computer Publishing.

A well-written, unintimidating introduction to Photoshop. Although graphics are in black and white, color versions are available on the book's website.

Shafran, Amy, and Lori Davis. 2000. *Paint Shop Pro Web Graphics,* 3d ed. Cincinnati, OH: Muska & Lipman Publishing.

A well-written, fully illustrated guide to the basic and intermediate-level features of Paint Shop Pro version 7.0. The focus is on graphics for the Web.

Weinman, Lynda. 1999. *Designing Web Graphics 3: How to Prepare Images and Media for the Web.* Indianapolis: New Riders Publishing.

A comprehensive guide to creating Web graphics.

Websites

CNET Builder.com

http://builder.cnet.com

> See the Graphics & Multimedia section in the How-To Library.

Web Page Design for Designers

www.wpdfd.com/wpdhome.htm

> Offers monthly editorials on design issues. The site also includes an overview of Web design, product reviews, and a comprehensive list of links for further resources.

Webmonkey

www.webmonkey.com

> See the Design section in the How-To Library for information on graphics and fonts.

WebReference.com

www.webreference.com

> See in particular Dimitry's Design Lab: http://webreference.com/dlab and Production Graphics with Wendy Peck: http://webreference.com/graphics

WebReview.com

www.webreview.com

> See in particular the Designers track.

Animation, Video, and Audio

Because Macromedia Flash is the industry standard for extended animation sequences, we cover books on this product.

Books

Beggs, Josh, and Dylan Thede. 2001. *Designing Web Audio.* Sebastopol, CA: O'Reilly & Associates.

> Step-by-step instructions for implementing audio. Includes case studies and interviews with audio and Web producers. Covers implementation techniques and the underlying theory.

Curtis, Hillman. 2000. *Flash Web Design: The Art of Motion Graphics.* Indianapolis: New Riders Publishing.

Covers design principles and deconstructs real-world Flash projects. Includes information on incorporating audio and video-like effects.

Franklin, Derek. 2000. *Flash 5! Creative Web Animation* (with CD-ROM). Berkeley, CA: PeachPit Press.

Provides a good introduction to Flash and its features.

Long, Ben, and Sonja Schenk. 2000. *The Digital Filmmaking Handbook* (with CD-ROM). Hingham, MA: Charles River Media.

A comprehensive source of information on digital filmmaking from concept through production.

Mohler, James L. 2001. *Flash 5.0. Graphics, Animation, and Interactivity.* Albany, NY: Delmar Publishers.

Explains Flash techniques in an easy-to-understand manner, provides complete coverage of vector animation, and explains how to incorporate sound with animation.

Rose, Jay. 1999. *Producing Great Sound for Digital Video* (with CD-ROM). San Francisco: Miller Freeman Books.

A comprehensive guide to producing digital soundtracks.

Websites

Digital Playroom

www.dplay.com

Tutorials and articles about audio.

Poison Dart Frog Media

www.dartfrogmedia.com

A good introduction to digital audio with an interactive demo.

Streaming Media World

www.streamingmediaworld.com

Covers audio, video, SMIL/SYMM, and related topics.

See also CNET Builder.com and Webmonkey (listed previously) for good information on dynamic content.

CREDITS

Figure 1.2 is used with permission of Ben Shneiderman, Copyright 1989 Addison Wesley.

Figure 4.2 is used with permission of the Oregon Tourism Commission, © 2000 Oregon Tourism Commission.

Figure 4.3 is used with permission of IPIX (Internet Pictures Corp.).

Figure 7.9 is used with permission of J. Welinske, WinWriters.

Figure 7.13 is used with permission of Tully's Coffee.

Figure 8.24 is used courtesy of The Salem Herbfarm, Salem, CT.

Figure 8.27 is used with permission of the Port of Seattle, December 1999.

Figure 10.2 is used with permission of Christopher Keep, Tim McLaughlin, and Robin Parmar. The Electronic Labyrinth, © 1993–2000 Christopher Keep, Tim McLaughlin, Robin Parmar.

Figure 10.11 is used with permission of William Horton. Abstract copyright © 2000 William Horton Consulting, Inc. (horton.com).

Figure 11.5 is used with permission of Steinway & Sons.

Figure 11.6 is used with permission of Matthew Jaquish.

Figure 11.7 is used with permission of Lipton.

Figure 11.23 is used with permission of Columbia University. Copyright © 2000 The Trustees of Columbia University in the City.

Figure 12.3 is used with permission of Sarnoff Corporation, Princeton, New Jersey.

Figures 12.4 and 12.5 are used with permission of Inxight Software, Inc. © 2000 Inxight Software, Inc. All rights reserved.

Figure 12.9 is used with permission of the World Bank, Washington, D.C.

Figure 13.3 is used with permission of MondoSoft, Denmark.

Figure 13.9 is used with permission of Fatbrain.com. Copyright © 1996–2000 Fatbrain.com, Inc.

Figure 13.10 is used with permission of Dan Wood and Steven Grimm. Design by Dan Wood and Steven Grimm.

Figure 13.12 is used courtesy of Internet Movie Database (www.imdb.com).

Figure 13.14 is used with permission of Mark Bernstein. "Hypertext Gardens" by Mark Bernstein. (www.eastgate.com/garden)

Figure 13.15 is used with permission of Ken Sitz. © 1999 conelrad.com.

INDEX